Charles P. Sohner

El Camino College

American Government and Politics Today

Second Edition

Scott, Foresman and Company · Glenview, Illinois
Dallas, Texas · Oakland, N.J. · Palo Alto, Cal. ·
Tucker, Ga. · Brighton, England

To Nancy Constance,
who proved that love persists
and
To Amy Liberty,
in whom it was born again

Credits for Part Opener Photographs

Part One, H. R. Haldeman: James H. Pickerell

Part Two, Student rally: STOCK, BOSTON, J. Berndt

Part Three, 1972 Democratic Convention: © Leonard Freed, Magnum

Part Four, President Ford and Cabinet: THE NEW YORK TIMES/George Tames

Part Five, Unemployment Office, NYC: Charles Gatewood

Library of Congress Cataloging in Publication Data

Sohner, Charles P
  American government and politics today.

  Includes bibliographies and index.
  1. United States—Politics and government—Handbooks,
manuals, etc. 2. Civil rights—United States.
3. Political participation—United States. I. Title.
JK274.S645   1976   320.4'73   75-29000
ISBN 0-673-07984-8

2 3 4 5 6 7 8-RRC-80 79 78 77 76

Preface

Like the original edition, this revision emphasizes those aspects of American government which personally involve the average citizen—civil rights and political participation. Again like its forerunner, it examines politics primarily from a power perspective, stressed even more than before.

However, there are differences as well. I have spent the greater part of my adult life emphasizing the faults of American government, pointing out the gaps between our lofty ideals and the often shameful realities of public life. Perhaps this was reflected in the first edition. The persistence of poverty, racism, and other evils indicates that I did not overstate the case, nor state it with any obvious effect. However, today there is a pervasive cynicism in our land which reveals that we have lost hope too soon. Textbook titles seem to exploit it,[1] and public opinion polls confirm it. Without minimizing the deficiencies of the American way of government, this edition is a modest attempt to restore some balance in its assessments. It looks at our record with enough legitimate pride to dilute some justifiable guilt. It urges what Thomas Wolfe called "hopeful fatalism."[2]

If hope is to be sustained, political corruption must be attacked. This topic was too often ignored before Watergate and too much exaggerated after it. Considerable space is devoted to it here, as well as to the related and knotty problems of political morality.

Other significant changes in the current edition include:

(1) A simplified vocabulary and sentence structure;
(2) A new concluding chapter on public policy which stresses "victimless" crime, labor relations, and the C.I.A., and a new chapter on constitutional development;
(3) New material on population shifts, pornography, abortion, church-state relations, campaign finance reforms, ethnic politics, affirmative action, the seniority system, domestic spyings, impeachment, and recent developments in other areas.

My indebtedness to others in the preparation of this manuscript includes those whose help was acknowledged in the preface to the first edition. The

---

[1] Note, for example, Alan Wolfe, *The Seamy Side of Democracy* (New York: David McKay Company, Inc., 1973); Michael Parenti, *Democracy for the Few* (New York: St. Martin's Press, 1974); Theodore L. Becker and Vernon G. Murray, eds., *Government Lawlessness in America* (New York: Oxford University Press, 1971); Jethro K. Lieberman, *How the Government Breaks the Law* (Baltimore: Penguin Books, Inc., 1972); and Gene L. Mason and Fred Vetter, eds., *The Politics of Exploitation* (New York: Random House, 1973). All these books have something to recommend them. I object only to the distorted inferences inevitably drawn from their cumulative impact.

[2] *You Can't Go Home Again* (Garden City, New York: The Sun Dial Press, 1942), pp. 734 ff.

names of Nadine Hata, Will Scoggins, Lance Widman, and Helen Puckett must be reiterated, however, and joined with those of El Camino's Joseph Georges and Wallace Good. Bruce Borland of Scott, Foresman provided necessary encouragement and wise advice. So too did William Hathaway of the University of Minnesota, David Lindsay of Central Missouri State University, Derwin D. Terry of St. Petersburg Junior College, Joyce Gelb of City University of New York, and Noreen Warwick of Richland College. Janice Adleman spent countless, often thankless hours editing the manuscript.

Naturally, I am indebted primarily to the one who, as always, has helped me the most—my wife Michelle. Any errors, unfortunately, are my responsibility.

Contents

PART ONE

AMERICAN POLITICS IN PERSPECTIVE

Families, and communities, and indeed free nations, rest not on law and not on force but on a certain indispensable faith and confidence, mixed with some affection and much charity, each person for his fellow man.

Walter Lippmann

Iron rusts in the rain; trees bend in the wind; nothing exists in a vacuum. That is why this book begins with a look at the broad arena in which American politics operates. Chapter 1 discusses the basic nature of politics and government primarily in terms of power. It also contrasts the United States government with other systems. Chapter 2 explores some of the factors that make our nation unique—the land, the people, and the ideals which comprise our political culture. Chapter 3 deals with our own peculiar historical experience: the Constitution which is the basic framework of our government and the underlying political principles which it embodies. In short, we begin with these chapters because politics in America requires some understanding of both the nature of politics and the nature of America.

1 THE NATURE OF POLITICS:
What's it all about?

People, crushed by law, have no hopes but power.*
                                    Edmund Burke

Aristotle, often called the father of political science, wrote that man is a political animal. One can argue about whether this was a compliment or an insult. As the United States (a political creation) approaches its two-hundredth birthday, most Americans seem to believe that politicians are a pretty bad lot. According to a 1973 Harris survey, 60 percent feel that "most elective officials are in politics for all they personally can get out of it for themselves." Fifty-five percent believe that our leaders really don't care what happens to the average person. In addition, 74 percent think that "special interests get more from the government than the people do."[1] Given these attitudes, it is not surprising that nearly two-thirds of the people, the highest percentage in 20 years, would not like to see their children go into politics.[2] If the survival of a free nation depends on faith and confidence, as Walter Lippmann said in the quotation on page 1, then America is in trouble. Only about a third of the people put much faith in those running the national government or sitting on the Supreme Court.[3]

---

*It may also be true, as indicated in Chapter 12, that people crushed by power have no hope but law.

Yet Americans have contradictory feelings about their political leaders. They reserve their greatest respect for Washington, Lincoln, and other famous presidents. Even among the living, a 1974 Gallup poll showed that eight out of the ten most admired men were politicians. A ninth, Secretary of State Henry Kissinger, was appointed by a politician.[4]

What is the truth of the matter? Is politics a "dirty game" or a "noble calling"? Probably the best answer is that it is neither. Like a stick of dynamite, politics can be used for good purposes or bad ones, to build tunnels or to kill people. Such an answer is not a cop-out. It recognizes that an accurate picture of politics is painted with few blacks and whites but with many shades of gray. It is a portrait full of shadows. To understand it one must develop what social scientists call a "tolerance of ambiguity," in other words, a willingness to live with complexity and contradictions. To accept these may be the mark of an educated human being.

With such acceptance, one can ask an even more important question: Can politics be made better? Can it be used more frequently for noble purposes? This book is written with the conviction that it can. Whether it will depends on all of us.

THE STUDY OF POLITICS

Politics refers to government action and the factors which affect it.[5] It includes a vast array of official decisions, ranging from building sidewalks to bombing cities. The study of these activities, called political science, is often hard to isolate from philosophy, economics, history, law, sociology, and even religion. But political science today focuses mainly on the state.

The Nation-State

The state here refers not to New York or California; rather, *the state is the largest area under common control* — currently an entire nation. The nation-state, as it is sometimes called, is defined as: (1) a fixed territory, (2) with a more or less permanent population, (3) ruled by a reasonably stable government, (4) which possesses the final power to make decisions, a power sometimes known as sovereignty. The next chapter discusses in some detail the first two elements of the state, territory, and population. The remainder of the book deals with the last two, the American government and how it exercises its power.

Government
Government is the agency which makes and administers the decisions that regulate social institutions. In the United States, as in all nation-states, there are many such institutions — churches, unions, businesses, social clubs, families, etc. Although it may be informal and based largely on custom, each

of these has some sort of government. We are concerned here, however, only with those governments which make and administer the decisions of the state.

The Growth of State Power

In comparison with other social institutions, the government of the state has increased most rapidly in importance. Today it provides the ultimate police power necessary for the protection of life and property. It receives much of the devotion once given to religion. It assumes the direction and support of education once in the hands of the church or family. It provides welfare services once supplied by private groups. And it determines the use of over a fourth of the gross national product. In short, the so-called negative state which "governed best" when it "governed least" has been replaced by the positive, active state performing many functions.

Indeed, the nation-state is becoming the most powerful of all social institutions. The family still has the greatest influence on the personalities of its children, but its stability is being shaken by rising divorce rates, new life-styles, and the generation gap. Loyalty to one's employer seems to be a thing of the past as does unquestioned devotion to one's religion. In fact, all institutional loyalties have lost much of their former strength. Yet despite the increase in political protests during the 1960s and early 1970s, disloyalty to one's country or rejection of its form of government is still generally regarded as unforgivable betrayal.

The state, then, has enormous power. We will soon turn to an analysis of power itself and of the resources necessary to exercise it. But first it would be desirable to look at the recent misuses of power and the resulting distrust of those who control it.

Corruption and Alienation

The death of democracy is not likely to be an assassination from ambush. It will be a slow extinction from apathy, indifference, and undernourishment.

Robert M. Hutchins

The sentiments expressed in the polls cited on page 2 indicate that while most people may still have a strong loyalty to the nation and its form of government, they distrust its political leaders. They feel cut off from the process of government, sensing that their faith in the system has somehow been betrayed. They believe they are powerless to control the institutions that affect their lives. This is the essence of what is often called *alienation.*

The Politician as Crook

Corruption is one of the major causes of alienation, recently dramatized by a single word: Watergate. Scarcely a week went by in 1973 and 1974 when television channels and newspapers did not sicken the American public with reports of new scandals, accusations of official misconduct, and charges of criminal deceit. The president to whom we gave more votes than anyone else in the nation's history resigned in disgrace. It was disclosed that two of the government's most secret bodies, the Federal Bureau of Investigation (F.B.I.) and the Central Intelligence Agency (C.I.A.), used their vast powers not only to fight domestic crime and foreign threats, but also to harass and discredit the political opponents of those in office.

Corruption in government is not limited to Watergate crimes. It seems like a spreading cancer, creeping into every branch and level of the political system. In 1974, two New York congressmen were found guilty of accepting money in return for political influence.[6] The same year, ten former or current state legislators in Illinois were indicted for similar offenses.[7] Other instances of misconduct are discussed in the following chapter and elsewhere in this book.

The Roots of Alienation

Corruption, of course, is not the only cause of alienation. Another contributing factor has been the "credibility gap" of the late 1960s—a belief that officials were not telling the truth, especially about the Vietnam war. In the mid 1970s, the situation has been worsened by the apparent inability of the government to cope with such basic problems as unemployment, prices, and crime rates which were too high and energy supplies which were too low.

Also contributing to the growing alienation of people is the "future shock" of change, the dizzying speed with which old and familiar attitudes have had to be readjusted or replaced. In little more than a generation, abortion was legalized, pot became popular, and Germany and Japan rose from destitute and defeated enemies to prosperous and peaceful allies. Television entered the living room, computers entered the office, blacks entered all-white schools, topless dancers entered bars, men entered outer space, and Richard Nixon, staunch foe of communists in America, entered Peking as a guest of the Communists in China. Within just four months, President Ford recommended a tax increase to fight inflation and then a tax cut to fight recession. Worst of all, perhaps, an economy of abundance suddenly became one of scarcity, and a politics of speech-making and baby-kissing became one of spying and burglary. Many people looked to their leaders to provide at least some cushion against these startling changes. But they often looked in vain, while the trauma of change joined with corruption, loss of credibility, and unsolved economic problems in further alienating people from their government. A big segment of the population had the feeling that somehow public officials were too powerful to control yet too weak or indifferent to solve the country's problems.

The Effects of Alienation

We have just attempted to explain some of the causes of alienation. Equally important are its effects. What happens when people lose faith in their government? Three things, all of them bad. First, this reduces participation in politics. Voter turnout at the 1972 and 1974 elections, which will be discussed further in Chapter 9, dropped to its lowest levels since the 1940s. A 1974 poll of college freshmen disclosed that only 36.6 percent, the lowest in 9 years, think it important to keep informed about political events. Only 12.5 percent want to try to influence political affairs themselves.[8] Since 61 percent of the total population seem to believe that what they think doesn't count much any more,[9] it is not surprising that many college students also "don't want to get involved." Many, no doubt, would follow the recommendation of Gordon Strachan, a former aide in the Nixon White House. He advised young people to "stay away" from government service. They don't have the necessary experience, he later explained, "to deal with such a crummy business." If this advice is heeded, however, the nation will surely lose the services of some of its most able and honorable citizens.[10]

Such a loss would lead to worse government, a second result of alienation. If good people are not involved in politics, corruption is likely to increase,[11] and even more problems are likely to go unsolved. It was the involvement of Rachel Carson, Ralph Nader, and Martin Luther King, Jr., along with thousands of others, that led to regulations on dangerous pesticides,[12] bans on automobile safety hazards, and new civil rights legislation. T. V. Smith, a philosopher and congressman, said it well: "Democracy is government by politicans for citizens who too often reward them with disdain. This disdain of politicians is a dangerous disease. . . . Politicians, of course, are not perfect—not yet. They may be improved and should be improved. . . . Disdain, however, is a poor improver. Understanding is much better. . . . From it will flow replacement of the weak and corrupt. From it will flow larger participation in politics by the strong and the good."[13]

The third effect of alienation is a decrease in the authority of government. If people disdain their political system, they will be less likely to obey even ordinary laws regulating things like fire hazards and traffic safety. This weakens the whole principle of rule of law which is so important in limiting excessive use of power in a democracy. It could also undermine government efforts in an emergency such as a flood or enemy attack, when respect for government authority might be the key to survival itself.

Idealism and Politics

[The ethics of democracy assume] not that man is good, but that he is capable of good; not that he is free from corruption, but that he is desperately sick of it.

Stephen K. Bailey

The Good Guys
That which is news, as any good reporter knows, is that which is unusual. It is not surprising therefore, that political corruption and scandal make the

front page. As a result, however, we too often forget the idealistic principles that guide the actions of many loyal government officials. We remember the resignations of Nixon and Agnew and the convictions of the Watergate conspirators. But we forget that if the system were totally immoral nothing would have happened to them. We also forget that Elliott Richardson and William Ruckelshaus resigned from office because of attempts to conceal the Watergate crimes. Archibald Cox was fired for trying to expose them. And a bipartisan majority of the House Judiciary Committee demanded impeachment because of them.[14]

More importantly, we forget that there are many examples of high standards of political morality. In 1956, Senator Francis Case (R–S.D.) reported that an oil lobbyist had offered a campaign contribution in return for opposition to a natural gas bill. As a result, the bill was vetoed and the oil company fined.[15] More recently, Senator Marlow Cook asked not to be named to the Banking and Currency Committee because of his investment in a Louisville, Kentucky bank. Representative Ken Hechler of West Virginia resigned an officer's commission in the Army Reserve (and lost $220 a month) when the House considered a military pension bill. Senator Charles Percy of Illinois put his $6 million fortune in a blind trust to avoid conflicts of interest. Representative Morris Udall of Arizona "relinquished his lucrative law practice" for the same reason.[16]

While generalizations about honesty in government are clearly risky, the testimony of Stephen K. Bailey, a political scientist and former mayor of Middletown, Connecticut bears repeating: "Power may corrupt, but it can also ennoble. The sense that you . . . are widely valued often creates . . . a desire to live close to the public expectation, a wish to become a kind of community example. . . . I have seen men utterly transformed by a judgeship."[17]

Moral Dilemmas
It is a mistake, however, to view political actions only in terms of corruption or honesty. There are a million shades of gray lying between those black and white polar opposites. The gray areas force us to deal with the essential moral problem of politics: how important must the ends (goals or objectives) be to justify the use of means or methods which are ethically objectionable? Bailey cites some concrete examples at the local level. If the appointment of a person less qualified than someone else is required to gain support for a much needed slum-clearance program, is such an appointment justified? If a single city must foot the bill for a county-wide ambulance service or lose such service entirely, should it be asked to pay what is obviously more than its fair share?[18] On the global level, should the Central Intelligence Agency help decide whether the use of espionage, assassination, and terror overseas (immoral means) are justified by the necessity for national security at home (a moral end)? Jeb Magruder, one of the Watergate defendants, admitted that he had failed to balance this delicate scale of ends and means. On the

subject of burglary and deceit, "although I was aware they were illegal," he conceded, "I agreed to using some activities that would help us in accomplishing what we thought was a . . . legitimate cause."[19]

There are no easy solutions to the moral dilemma of ends and means, but politicians must cope with it daily. They would be wise to remember the advice of Max Weber, the great German sociologist. He suggested that politicians must have a deep devotion to a cause (the end), accept responsibility for the things they do in advancing that cause (the means), and maintain a sense of proportion regarding both.[20]

In addition to the overriding issue of ends and means, there is a second moral dilemma in politics involving the use of compromise. For every great goal or noble cause to which one political leader is devoted, other officials are equally dedicated to quite different ones. Their objectives may conflict or there may be too little time or money to accomplish all of the goals. In such cases, does the "moral" official stick to his principles, yield not an inch, and end up with nothing at all? Or does he compromise and get a little more than existed, but not as much as he wanted? Sometimes politicians have to make a choice between two of their own important principles. Say a congressman favors increased federal aid to public schools but is opposed to government support for parochial schools. Assume further that the only school-aid bill with any chance of passage provides funds for both. What is he to do? Either way he votes, one principle must be sacrificed to advance the other. To compromise with others may be a mark of practicality or even of humility and good will. But to compromise one of your own ideals is often harder, for it requires the establishment of moral and political priorities.

American politics, for better or for worse, is full of such compromise. "When seen from the shining cliffs of perfection," as one writer observed, "compromise appears shoddy indeed. But when seen from some concentration camp of the only alternative way of life, the compromises of legislation appear but another name for what we call civilization. . . ."[21] We shall have more to say about this later on in the chapter.

The Politics of Hope

It may be too much to seek again what Senator Hubert Humphrey once called the politics of joy in the wake of tragedies so great as Vietnam and Watergate. But there is ample reason for Americans to practice the politics of hope, striving for the ideals necessary to a good society. If politicians are also doing this, perhaps they can be excused for occasionally using immoral means to attain great ends. But their own power or wealth is never a great end, never a sufficient excuse. No one knows whether higher standards of conduct will prevail in the future. No one knows if the finest ideals of democracy can ever be realized. But to give up hope on these objectives guarantees that they will never be reached. When black leaders of the 1960s admonished their followers to "keep the faith, baby" they were expressing a fundamental psychological truth: There is no progress without faith that progress is possible.

POLITICS AS POWER

The ideals that are dominant in a society are determined largely by the way power is distributed within it. So, too, is the effectiveness of government action to realize those ideals. Politics, in other words, can best be understood through an analysis of power. Therefore people talk about the international balance of power, the separation of powers among the three branches of government, the existence of a power elite, the power of big business, black power, the power of judicial review, the power base of a politician, and so on. Although each of these uses of power has a slightly different meaning, we can say in general that *power is the capacity to alter socially significant behavior.* It makes people do things which they might not do, or stops them from doing things which they might do. In other words, power involves a relationship between people. All the topics considered in this book can be interpreted in terms of power—how it is distributed, how it is obtained, and how it is used. We shall be concerned here with three main types of power—force, influence, and authority. Although these types will be defined separately, it is important to realize that in practice they often overlap. Force and influence are generally illegitimate without authority. And authority is often weak and ineffective when not backed up by force or influence.

Power as Force

The most obvious source of government power is its physical force. In this area, the government has almost a monopoly, for although private citizens may possess guns, they are subject to many legal restrictions. In contrast to the government, other social institutions seem weak. A church can make rules but can only expel those who defy them. An employer can issue orders but can at most fire a rebellious employee. Only the government can use force to compel obedience to its commands.

The U.S. seems to resort to force somewhat more quickly than many other nations. Since World War II, American military units have been sent to the Dominican Republic and Lebanon for possible battle action, and to Korea and South Vietnam for a total of eleven years of costly combat. At home, heavily armed police forces, national guard units, and prison guards have inflicted many casualties upon rioters and demonstrators at such places as Detroit, Kent State University, and the state prison in Attica, New York. In Los Angeles, police seeking to arrest members of the violent Symbionese Liberation Army (SLA) burned a home to the ground, killing the fugitives inside. During the 1968 Democratic National Convention, the streets of Chicago were the scene of what was later called a "police riot" against antiwar protesters.

If American police are unusually violent, they may simply be reflecting the high level of violence among the American people. The assassinations of John F. Kennedy, Robert F. Kennedy, and Martin Luther King, Jr., in the 1960s, and the attempted murder of George C. Wallace in 1972, altered the course of our political history. In addition, threats of violence from the SLA, Minutemen, American Nazis, Black Panthers, and other undergound groups pose a grave challenge to the government's monopoly of force. We shall examine this topic again in later chapters.

Power as Influence

Fortunately for human dignity, government can usually gain compliance without resort to force. Schattschneider points out that only "about 5 percent of all state and local government employees are police officers." He concludes that "the internal relations of American government are not characteristically forceable."[22] Instead, the government can often obtain the ends it seeks by the use of influence. Influence is a more subtle approach that involves rewarding people with what they want (like tax exemptions, jobs, or defense contracts). Influence also involves threatening to deprive people of what they have (such as drivers' licenses, business permits, teaching credentials, or prison paroles).

Of course, institutions other than the government also exert influence. This can be in their own private sphere, as when a business promotes one employee rather than another. Or it can be in the broad political sphere, as when a union criticizes a senator in its weekly newspaper. Since the process of giving (bestowing rewards) and taking (imposing deprivations) may involve jobs, prestige, or money, nearly everyone has some influence over at least a few people.

However, governments and large corporations today probably exert greater influence over people in part because of their enormous wealth. Governments can get farmers to plant more crops by guaranteeing them higher prices, for example. Politicians can often win votes by promising better public services. On the negative side, business can often lock people into jobs by depriving them of recommendations, stock options, or other company benefits if they quit. But anyone who exerts influence probably also has some measure of authority.

Power as Authority

No government could long survive if it had to rely solely upon force and influence. Policemen and prisons are too few and money and prestige too scarce. Instead, most governments endure because they possess authority.

Authority is that kind of power with which people voluntarily comply because they respect it as necessary, just, and therefore legitimate. If there is anything which might be called a "law" of politics, it is that when a government loses the respect of its people, it must increase the force necessary to maintain its rule. When too much confidence is lost, there eventually comes a time when the available force is just not enough to sustain power. Laws are obeyed, finally, because people believe they should be. It is this which converts power into authority, producing voluntary compliance.

Yet governments must share authority, as well as influence, with other institutions and private citizens. Some people believe so firmly in the moral doctrines of a church, the teachings of their parents, or the views of a television commentator that they occasionally act upon them unquestioningly. To command such uncritical respect is to possess some measure of authority.

As indicated earlier, however, all social institutions seem to be losing the respect necessary to exercise authority effectively. Churches are torn by internal disputes. Family ties have been weakened. The reliability of the news media is often questioned. The rising crime rate and growing political alienation reveal that even the government cannot expect uncritical cooperation.

The reasons for this decline of authority can be traced to the somewhat shaky foundations on which it rests. Three such foundations were identified by Max Weber.[23] The first, custom or tradition, has been undermined by a rapid change in behavior standards, especially as glamorized on television and in movies. A second basis for authority, the charisma or personal appeal of a strong and popular leader, seems oddly lacking in current American politics. Former President Nixon acknowledged his own lack of charisma. The personalities of his opponents, Senator Humphrey in 1968 and Senator McGovern in 1972, seemed to inspire as little enthusiastic devotion as that of his successor, President Ford. The final basis for authority is the "legality" of rules believed to be rational and just. In America, such rules stem from the Constitution and the actions of government officials authorized by it. Yet these too command less respect than they once did mainly as a result of government mistakes and misconduct in Watergate and Vietnam.

From one point of view, weakened authority is a good thing. It indicates that the people are less willing to unquestioningly comply with the demands imposed by others. It demonstrates a healthy kind of skepticism arising out of independent thought. But in another sense, grave dangers lurk behind this rejection of authority. It reveals a suspiciousness and distrust among citizens which undermines the desire to cooperate voluntarily. Thus it heightens the danger of a chaotic society which can be regulated only by the use of increased force or influence by those with the most might or money. Authority rests on mutual respect and confidence. Without authority, we are faced with either lawlessness or tyranny.

Political Resources: Tools of Power

In order to exercise any kind of power—force, influence, or authority—an individual or institution must possess certain tools or capabilities. If these tools are used to affect or enforce government policy, they are called political resources. For example, military weapons and police equipment are the major resources of force. Votes, money, jobs, and status are important tools of political influence. The Constitution, the Bible, laws, and custom are examples of authority resources.

Usually, both the type of power brought into play and the kind of resources used will be determined by the nature of a particular situation. In coping with a criminal, for example, the government will employ force and use police equipment. But many times a tactical choice must be made. In protesting compulsory busing to achieve racial integration ordered by a school board, a group might blow up the buses (force). Or they might elect a new school board (influence). Or they might challenge the school board decree in court (authority). When such a choice is available, the easiest course—but not necessarily the most effective—is often to invoke authority, because it entails less risk than force and is usually less costly than influence.

The Measurement of Power

The three broad types of power just described, along with the many political tools that can be used in exercising them, make overall power quite difficult to measure. In comparing the power of one person or group with that of another, however, at least three dimensions can be considered:[24]

1. The *degree* or extent to which behavior can be changed. If Smith can get Jones to make a $20 campaign contribution to a certain candidate, but Clark can persuade him to contribute $40, then Clark has more power over Jones than Smith does.
2. The *number* of people whose behavior can be changed. If Jones is the only person Clark can get to make a donation, but Smith can raise $20 from each of five other people as well, then Smith has more power over campaign contributors than Clark does.
3. The *range* or scope of behavior which can be changed. If Smith can get campaign contributions from six people, but Clark can, in addition, get one of them to write speeches for the candidate and bug the head-quarters of his opponent, then Clark has power over more types of behavior than Smith does. In the real world, for example, House Speaker Carl Albert has more power on a wider variety of issues over more House members than any individual committee chairman.

In attempting to make such comparisons, however, we must be careful of two complications. First, relative power often changes rather quickly. Clark, for example, might start drinking heavily or become ill. This is what happened to Wilbur Mills, chairman of the House Ways and Means Committee. His vast power, especially on tax bills, suddenly evaporated when he entered a sanitarium and was replaced as committee chairman. Second, someone with power may decide not to use it. Smith might take a vacation instead of soliciting campaign contributions. Or the president might decide not to veto a particular bill in order to avoid a showdown with Congress. It is unpredictable factors like these that make politics as much a creative art as an exact science.

OTHER VIEWS OF POLITICS

Not all political scientists are pleased with an emphasis upon power. They agree that power is an important part of politics, but insist that there are other views to consider. However, the view of politics as power, taken throughout this book, does not necessarily exclude these other views.

Politics as Compromise

We must be contented to secure what we can get. . . . It takes time to persuade men to do even what is for their own good.

Thomas Jefferson

In our pluralistic society, one noted for its many diverse groups, politics is often viewed largely as an instrument of compromise among them. Between white and black, Christian and Jew, labor and management, some sort of compromise must be reached. If we are to avoid civil war, there must be both an accommodation of interests and an agreement to disagree peacefully.

This conception of politics has been given a hard time in recent years. Compromise has been equated with betrayed principles, unethical deals, and a cynical sellout for the purpose of gaining power. Yet, as noted earlier, compromise reflects a tradition both long and strong in American politics. Henry Clay of Kentucky won his place in history books as "the Great Compromiser," postponing North-South conflict by authoring the Missouri Compromise of 1820 and the Compromise of 1850. John C. Calhoun justified in theory the kind of compromise that his Kentucky colleague practiced. Calhoun developed the concept of the *concurrent majority*. By this he meant that the government should adopt only those policies which had the support of a majority within each of the major sections or interest groupings of the nation.[25]

More recently, the political importance of compromise has been reflected in our major parties. Both the Republicans and Democrats have tried to gain power by forming coalitions of several and often differing groups. Due to the varied makeup of each party, most candidates must compromise in order to be nominated and elected. And, of course, the voter must compromise, too.

He is sometimes asked to choose between the "lesser of two evils." He is reminded that "God isn't running this year."

Politics as Continuity and Change

Another view of politics emphasizes mediation between the forces of stability and the forces of change. Some stability is essential and is related to our psychological needs for security and predictability. If you are a homeowner, for example, you need confidence that your property will not be seized. If you are an inventor, you want the assurance that your patent rights will be upheld by the courts.

Yet if stability is necessary, it is equally true that change is inevitable. The invention of new machines, like the train or airplane, has led governments to subsidize their development, to regulate the fares charged, and to establish requirements for the licensing of pilots. Changes in the relative influence of various groups have produced such legislation as that prohibiting racial discrimination in theaters and hotels. A shift in values and moral codes has forced changes in laws governing drinking and abortion.[26]

As already mentioned, many people look to their government to channel the direction of these changes, to minimize the violence, and to aid the victims. In this way, some degree of comforting continuity can be maintained. Sometimes, of course, changes have been stained with the blood of violence. It was thus that Americans displaced the native Indians, won independence, settled the western frontier, ended slavery, and secured the right to organize unions.

Politics as Group Dominance: Elitism and Pluralism

A variety of political observers with little else in common agree that governments are dominated by some sort of privileged minority or elite class. Marxists or communists see politics as the process by which this "ruling class" maintains its advantages relative to the rest of the people. They assert, moreover, that the ruling class is always an economic one consisting of those who own the nation's farms and factories, the means of production. They point to the use of police and even armies to protect this private ownership of property and to preserve the unequal distribution of wealth.

This theory was shared by non-Marxists such as Charles Beard. Beard was an American historian who saw the Constitution as a document designed to protect the economic interests of those who wrote it. His view was challenged by later scholars and is only accepted in part today.[27] More recently, sociologist C. Wright Mills criticized American politics because of its alleged control by a small "power elite" consisting mainly of corporate and military leaders.[28]

Other writers, sometimes called "democratic elitists," also assert that modern government is run by an "establishment." By this they mean a power structure composed of a relatively few leaders from big business, the unions, the professions, and the universities. Members of this establishment are said to possess much more than their fair share of such political resources as prestige, money, and specialized abilities. In addition, they are in close agreement on basic political issues and it seems impossible to remove them from their seats of power. Yet far from deploring this state of affairs, elitists believe it to be beneficial. They support their position by such arguments as these:

1. Political resources such as money, knowledge, and access to the mass media are—and always will be—unequally distributed.
2. The complexity of modern problems requires that policy decisions come from those with specialized training rather than from an ill-informed majority.
3. Most citizens know little about most public issues. But their ignorance helps stabilize the political system by minimizing dissent and maximizing the chances for peaceful compromise of existing differences.
4. The masses are less tolerant than the highly educated elites. They often tend to support selfish demagogues who seek to violate the rights of unpopular minorities.
5. Even if the government is democratically organized, the pressure groups which influence it decisively are not.
6. Democracy requires only that the governing elite be held accountable for its performance at the next election.

In contrast to the elitists, other scholars known as pluralists maintain that political power is actually shared by many different groups with different policy interests. Each group helps control decisions on matters of its special concern and all interact, compete, and sometimes ally with one another. In a very general way, however, both elitists and pluralists would agree that there is a governing class even in the most democratic of nations.[29] To pluralists perhaps that class is more democratic since it consists of so many groups competing for political resources and power.

Politics as Systems Analysis

A fifth view of politics is known as *systems analysis.* It is an attempt to understand the political system without the biases of the other viewpoints. It sees politics as a process through which public demands and expectations are transformed into official programs and policies. Borrowing the language of economics and mechanics, the demands are called "inputs" and the resulting policies are termed "outputs." The government is thus seen as a processing machine.[30]

The activities of parties and interest groups help create the inputs entering the political system, while laws, executive actions, and court decisions are the outputs. Usually, any kind of governmental output alters the later demands, opinions, and other inputs into the system through a feedback process. If policy outputs fail to cope with the inputs adequately (in other words, if the people aren't satisfied with government action), the whole system may be in danger. In general terms, systems analysis seeks to understand the relationship between environmental influences and the policies which the government pursues. This approach is diagrammed in Figure 1–1. As can be seen, it is based on a "cause and effect" assumption. Each influence (or input) encourages the government to take some action (or output) which alters (by feedback) the subsequent influences.

Politics as Institutions and as Behavior

For many years, political science emphasized the careful analysis of political institutions and their legal foundations. Considerable stress was placed on constitutional law as interpreted in America by the Supreme Court, while the organization of Congress, political parties, and executive agencies also received much attention.

In the 1950s, another approach known as behavioralism appeared more frequently in the research of political scientists. It stressed the politically significant behavior of individuals and groups more than formal structures, abstract theory, and legal authority. Behavioralism was characterized by (1) a reliance on ideas and research findings derived from other social sciences such as psychology, anthropology, and sociology; (2) the statistical measurement of the frequency of political actions, especially voting patterns; (3) an emphasis on the root causes and conditioning factors which may explain political events; and (4) an attempt to develop a "value-free," morally neutral method of political analysis.

The trend today seems to be away from strict behavioralism toward a combination of both old and new approaches. There is an insistence that research be relevant to current issues and that it be related to values, to ethical standards of right and wrong. In other words, any description of what *is* (empirical theory) should be associated with a conception of what *ought to be* (normative theory). With that in mind, this book will include a little history, philosophy, and law, as well as some study of political behavior, elite groups, and other elements from the several views of politics just discussed. Our overriding focus, however, will be the power approach, a view of politics centering on who holds power, how much, how it is distributed, and for what purposes.

ORGANIZATION OF POLITICAL POWER: VARIETIES OF GOVERNMENT

The distinctive features of American government can sometimes be seen more clearly in contrast with other types of political systems. Such a comparative analysis focusing on power will be undertaken in this section.

Figure 1-1. THE POLITICAL SYSTEM AS VIEWED BY SYSTEMS ANALYSIS

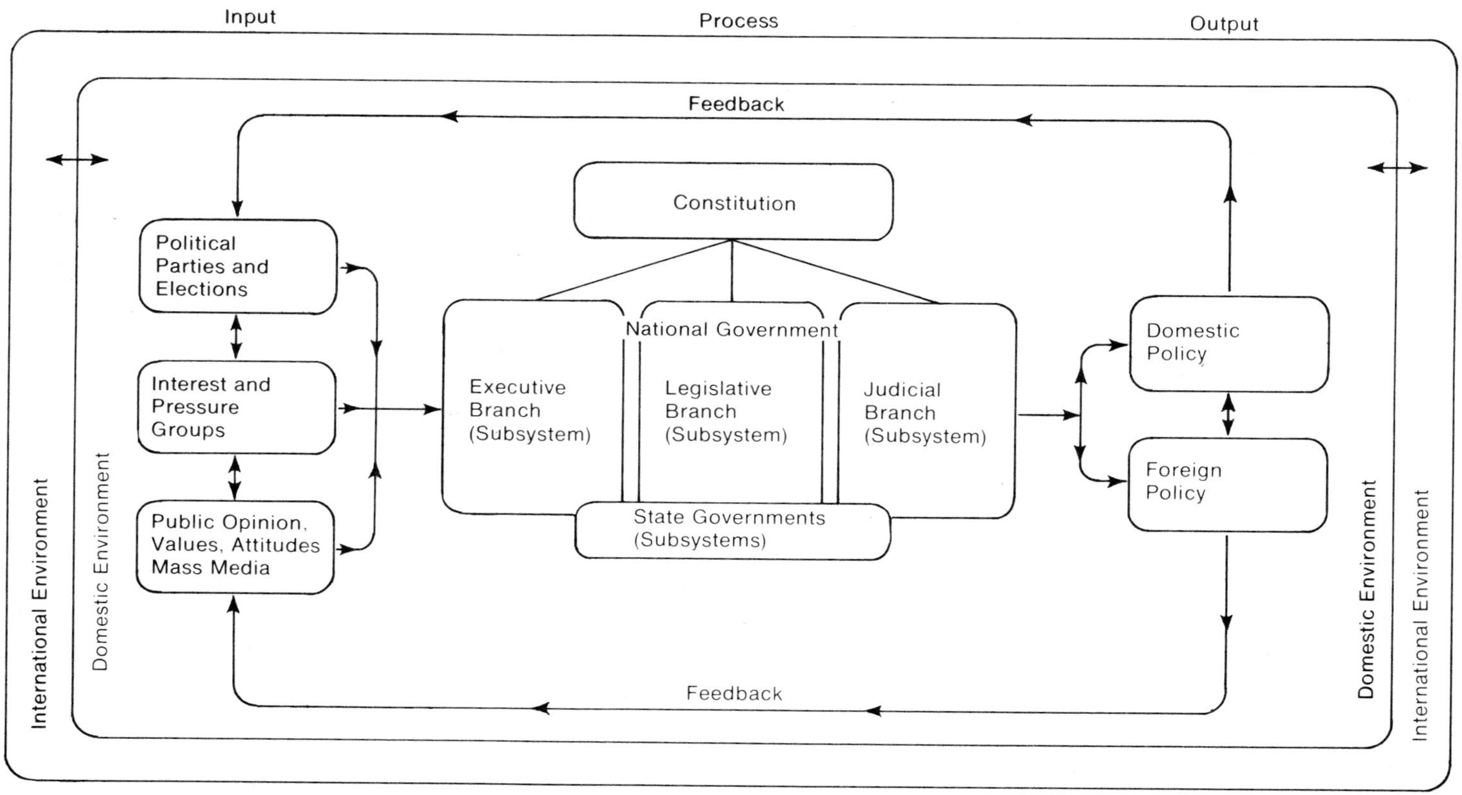

Input   Process   Output

International Environment

Domestic Environment

Domestic Policy

Foreign Policy

Feedback

Constitution

Judicial Branch (Subsystem)

National Government

Legislative Branch (Subsystem)

State Governments (Subsystems)

Executive Branch (Subsystem)

Feedback

Political Parties and Elections

Interest and Pressure Groups

Public Opinion, Values, Attitudes Mass Media

Domestic Environment

International Environment

Diagram by Janice Adleman, Instructor in Political Science at Oakton Community College, Morton Grove, Illinois.

Possessors of Power

Aristotle classified governments, usefully but somewhat crudely, into three broad categories based on who possessed ultimate power: government by one person, a few, or many. Today these types are often called dictatorship, aristocracy (or elitism), and democracy.

Dictatorship

Rule by one person was often carried out by hereditary kings. Even today, King Khalid of Saudi Arabia is a one-man ruler. But such absolute monarchies are dying out, and most of the remaining thrones in the world are occupied by persons, like Queen Elizabeth of Great Britain, who "reign but do not rule." They are constitutional monarchs who perform ceremonial functions as head of state but do not actually run the government. One-man rule in modern times, however, has been exercised by dictators such as Castro in Cuba, Franco in Spain, or Hitler in Germany. They have often swept into power on a wave of violence.

Aristocracy

Rule by a small, privileged minority of people is sometimes called government by an elite or an aristocracy. This type of government has many forms and holds most of the world's people in its sway. Indeed, pure dictatorships may not exist at all, since even a dictator depends upon his servants, advisers, and especially his police and army for continued power.

Some oligarchies have been based upon race, as is the case with the ruling white minorities in the Union of South Africa, Rhodesia, and certain areas of the American South. Others are based upon membership in an elite political party, like the Communist party in the Soviet Union. Still others, such as the military juntas ruling many countries in Asia, Africa, and South America, are aristocracies of career army officers. Theocracy is rule by a religious elite. It dominated Geneva, Switzerland, for a time as well as the early years of the Massachusetts Bay colony. Other common forms are plutocracy, government by the wealthy few, and various aristocracies of age and sex that have rewarded old men with political dominance. Among all the varieties of minority rule, however, government by the wise and just has been very rare.

Democracy

Governments chosen by and responsive to a majority of the adult population are called democracies. Most have emerged rather recently and they are still limited to relatively few nations. The term *direct democracy* was originally used to mean government in which all the people actually participate themselves, as in the ancient Greek city-states or the New England town meetings. This was contrasted with a republic—*representative democracy,* in which the government was run by representatives elected by the people. The U.S. today is sometimes called a democratic republic. But this label can obscure the underlying issue suggested earlier: Is any kind of real majority rule possible if elites possess most of the political resources?

Extent of Power

Broadly speaking, government power is either limited or unlimited. Unlimited power is often associated with dictatorships, while more limited power is frequently found in democracies.

Constitutionalism

Government power is limited where the governors as well as the governed must follow the "rules of the game," and where certain rights are guaranteed to minorities even against the majority. Written constitutions, like ours in America, usually contain a "bill of rights" designed to protect individual freedom. Governments that accept such limitations upon their own power are also referred to as "constitutional" even when there is no single document called a constitution, as in England.

Totalitarianism

Governments which reject any limitations upon their authority, either by law or practice, are called authoritarian, despotic, tyrannical, or totalitarian. The latter term implies a total monopoly of decision-making power by the ruling group. Such regimes severely limit individual freedom. They depend upon rigid censorship and control of mass media, a secret police, and the prohibition of all political parties except the one controlling the government. The regimes of Spain, Haiti, the Soviet Union, and the People's Republic of China seem to fit this definition fairly closely.

Territorial Distribution of Power

In most nations power is divided among several different levels of government. There are three possible relationships between the central or national level and the regional level of government, each reflecting a different distribution of power.

Unitary Governments

The unitary system is most common in relatively small countries or those having a rather similar population. In this form, the regional or local governments have only those powers which the national government chooses to give them. England, France, Italy, and China are leading examples of unitary systems. Moreover, if each of the fifty states in the United States is viewed as a separate political system, they too are unitary. Cities, counties, townships, and other units of local government have only the power which the various state governments give them.

Figure 1–2. METHODS OF DISTRIBUTING POWER TERRITORIALLY

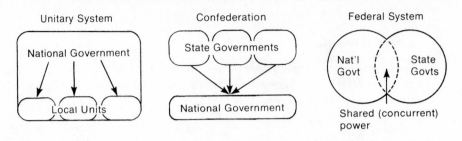

Note: The nature of the federal system in the U.S. is described more fully in Chapter 2. The exact division between national and state powers has caused bitter political controversy.

Confederations

The opposite of a unitary system is a *confederation.* Here, the national government possesses only those powers that the regional governments choose to give it. The first national constitution in America was called the Articles of Confederation. Under it, the central government was dependent upon the thirteen states for all the authority it exerted. This, indeed, was one of its major weaknesses for the states were reluctant to give up enough of their powers to make the confederal government effective. Today, confederations have become rather rare. With the possible exception of Yugoslavia and some Arab states, the leading example is the United Nations, functioning at the international level. The U.N. has some of the same weaknesses as the U.S. had under the Articles.

Federalism

The third plan for distributing power territorially within a nation is *federalism,* an American invention first implemented by our present Constitution. In this system, the central (national or federal) government and the regional (state) governments each have certain powers independent of one another and allocated by the Constitution itself. There is often cooperation between the two, but there is also competition for power in certain areas, for example, in education. In the event of a conflict, however, the national government normally prevails. In addition to this country, federal systems are found primarily in other large nations such as Brazil, Canada, Mexico, Australia, West Germany, India, and the Soviet Union.

Functional Distribution of Power

Every government performs two kinds of functions: it makes laws and it administers them. The passage of laws is a legislative function while carrying them out is an executive function. The relationship between those who pass the laws and those who administer them may take two broad forms.

Parliamentary Governments

If the same group is largely involved in the performance of both functions, we say that there is a *fusion of power,* usually called a *parliamentary* system. Such is the case in Great Britain, Canada, West Germany, Italy, and Israel among many other nations. In this form of government, the prime minister or premier must be an elected member of the legislative body (parliament) and so must all members of his cabinet. Usually, he is the head of the largest political party, or coalition of parties, in the legislature. He holds office only as long as he has the support of a majority of the lawmakers. But in his role as prime minister he is the chief executive, performing most of the same functions that the American president does.

Presidential Governments

In contrast, if one group is responsible for passing laws and another separate group for administering them, a *separation of powers* exists, often called a *presidential* system. This is the case in the United States, where the president and members of his cabinet are prohibited by the Constitution from serving at the same time in Congress. The president, moreover, normally serves for a fixed term of four years, whether or not he has the support of a majority in Congress.

It should be noted that there is usually a separate judicial branch to apply the laws. In the U.S. the same three separate branches — legislative, executive, and judicial — are found in each of the fifty state governments as well as in the national government.

The separation of powers principle is modified substantially in the American system, however, by formal and informal powers known as *checks and balances.* Each branch has various ways of checking and balancing the power of the other two branches. For example, the Supreme Court has the power to declare legislative or executive actions unconstitutional and the president has the power to select judges, subject to approval by the Senate. France, Mexico, the Philippines, and various South American countries also have modified presidential systems roughly comparable to the American one.

Combining the various terms just discussed, we may say that *the United States has a representative, democratic, constitutional, federal, presidential form of government.* Of course, many other combinations of the preceding characteristics are also possible.

Purpose of Power

The language of politics remains fairly cool when discussing the forms of government described above. But it heats up to the boiling point when the subject changes to the basic purposes of government and the philosophies on which they rest. Conservatives who view untested policies with suspicion are sometimes denounced as "fascist pigs." Liberals who criticize the existing society may be branded as "commie traitors." While labels may be less important than the actual policies or personalities to which they are applied, they are widely used and we therefore need to agree on their definitions.

Labels of the Left

Political views are frequently described in the oversimplified terms of liberal versus conservative, radical versus reactionary, or left wing versus right wing.

A liberal is generally someone who wants change or reform and who tolerates a wide diversity of viewpoints, including new and unpopular ones. Modern liberals usually favor a strong, active government that limits the economic freedom of business in the interests of consumers and employees. They also support government policies to improve the lot of the poor and the victims of discrimination. Especially since the New Deal of the 1930s, the Democratic party in America has usually been associated with such policies, often to the dismay of some of its more conservative members. As a result, the Democrats have developed voter support primarily among industrial workers, low-income groups, and such oppressed minorities as blacks and Mexican-Americans. Other ethnic groups and many intellectuals have also been attracted to the Democratic party because of its more liberal outlook.

The term radical is often associated with extreme liberalism and describes those who wish great changes, frequently accomplished through violent protest or revolution. Sometimes people who want a drastic reversal of liberal policies are also called radicals, although this use of the term is rather confusing. Generally, however, radicals would be included among leftists, or left-wingers, which is a broad category encompassing everyone from mild liberals to revolutionary Communists. The so-called New Left which gained prominence in the late 1960s, is characterized by its youth, its distrust of liberal politicians, and its taste for confrontation politics often involving demonstrations and sit-ins. The Progressive Labor party, the Black Panthers, and the Symbionese Liberation Army (SLA) can all be considered parts of the New Left. They tend to be anticapitalist, but often view the communist bureaucracy of the Soviet Union with equal suspicion.

The Old Left, defined very broadly, includes liberals, socialists, and American communists who are committed to the doctrines of Karl Marx, usually as interpreted by the Soviet Union. While socialists and communists are often confused, there are important differences between them. Most socialists, such as those in power in England and West Germany, believe in freedom of expression and democratic elections. They are often among the most vigorous opponents of communism. Communists, on the other hand, such as those controlling most of the nations of Eastern Europe, abolish opposition parties and exercise rigid censorship. Another difference is that socialism involves a belief in certain economic policies, emphasizing more equal distribution of wealth and more government services. Communism, however, is a total philosophy which assumes that economic conditions determine all of the political and cultural characteristics of a society. Finally, socialists favor government ownership only of basic industries such as transportation, mining, and steel. Communists would extend this to the entire economy.

Labels of the Right

At the other end of the political spectrum, as seen in Figure 1–3 are conservatives, reactionaries, or right-wingers. A conservative is one who wishes to conserve and perpetuate existing values and institutions. He or she is usually skeptical of abstract logic, preferring instead to depend upon experience and tradition, the "tried and true" as a guide for future action. Conservatives also tend to rely upon individual initiative, private enterprise capitalism, and state and local rather than national responsibility for solving social problems. They distrust government welfare programs and deficit (in the "red") spending because these supposedly destroy self-reliance necessary for both personal integrity and national strength. The Republican party has typically been associated with such ideas. Its main sources of support have been businessmen and independent farmers, both with a considerable stake in keeping existing conditions pretty much as they are.

Just as radicals are considered extreme liberals, so reactionaries may be described as ultraconservatives. They are not content with resisting new changes but fight for a return to what they believe to be the "good old days." Rightists or right-wingers are terms referring to a broad group that includes moderate conservatives as well as reactionaries. Examples of rightist organizations are Young Americans for Freedom (YAF), the John Birch Society, and the American Nazi party. These ultraconservatives usually endorse censorship, toughness toward criminals, superpatriotism, and sometimes racial or religious bigotry.

Fascism lies on the extreme right of the political yardstick. It originally described the theories of Benito Mussolini, the dictator who led Italy into World War II. Later, the term also included the ideas of the German Nazis headed by Adolf Hitler, as well as similar beliefs in other countries. Although fascism is not a systematic political philosophy, it emphasizes five basic concepts: inequality among people and races, extreme nationalism, a belief that will and instinct are superior to reason, a glorification of military strength, and dictatorial leadership.

Oddly enough, a look at the far edges of the Left and Right reveals certain similarities in the two extremes. Both are hostile to real freedom of choice. The Left feels this is in the interest of greater equality. The Right feels it serves the purpose of suppressing immorality and alien ideas. Moreover, both extremes tend toward dictatorship. Nevertheless, there are basic differences which are reflected in the way that liberals and conservatives view the world. The liberal sees men as basically rational and cooperative. These traits become obvious once education and a decent standard of living

Figure 1-3. THE POLITICAL SPECTRUM

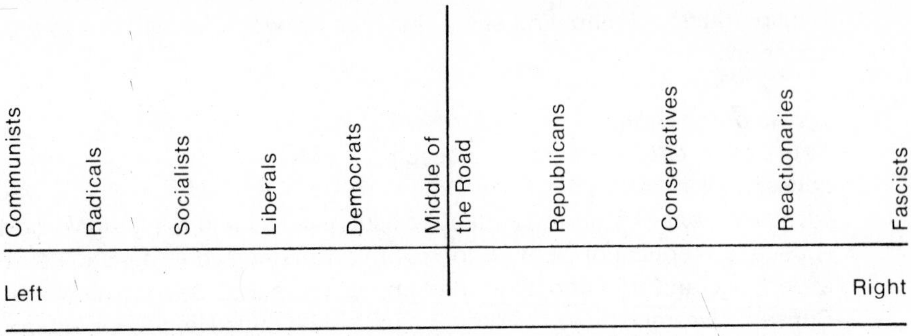

Communists	Radicals	Socialists	Liberals	Democrats	Middle of the Road	Republicans	Conservatives	Reactionaries	Fascists

Left   Right

have freed men from the dire effects of ignorance and poverty. Both tasks are government responsibilities according to liberals. Conservatives, on the other hand, see men as basically selfish and aggressive. Thus, they must be taught to obey established values and they must be restrained by firm control. For conservatives, these are the major tasks of government.

It is important to note, however, that most Americans do not think in terms of liberal and conservative, but are more interested in policies that work, no matter what labels they bear. It is not surprising, then, that the government's economic and social policy is really a mixed one. It is a combination of ideas from both the Right and the Left. We are gradually moving, however, toward the Left, toward a more active, positive role for the government in regulating economic and social relationships.

Notes

1. *Confidence and Concern: Citizens View American Government* (Cleveland: Regal Books/King's Court Communications, 1974), pp. 6–7. This pamphlet is a summary of a poll by Lou Harris and Associates.
2. Gallup Poll, *Los Angeles Times,* Oct. 14, 1973, Part IX, p. 4, and Feb. 3, 1974, p. 3.
3. *Confidence and Concern,* p. 8.
4. *Los Angeles Times,* Dec. 29, 1974, p. 4. The only one not connected with the government was the Reverend Billy Graham, a friend of both President Johnson and President Nixon.
5. "Politics" has many meanings. See, for example, Austin Ranney's discussion of the term in *The Governing of Men,* 3rd ed. (New York: Holt, Rinehart & Winston, 1971), pp. 4–6.
6. *Los Angeles Times,* Jan. 2, 1974, p. 9 and July 20, 1974, p. 2. They were Representatives Bertram L. Podell and Frank J. Brasco, both Democrats.
7. Ibid., Dec. 5, 1974, p. 18. They included six Republicans and four Democrats.
8. Ibid., Jan. 12, 1975, p. 12. The poll was conducted by the American Council on Education.
9. *Confidence and Concern,* p. 6.
10. *Los Angeles Times,* March 11, 1975, p. 7.
11. See Chapter 2, pp. 43–44 of this book.
12. Rachel Carson, *Silent Spring* (Greenwich, Conn.: Fawcett Publications, 1962).
13. T. V. Smith, *The Legislative Way of Life* (Chicago: The University of Chicago Press, 1940), pp. IX–X.
14. The Staff of the *New York Times, The End of a Presidency* (Toronto: Bantam Books, 1974).
15. Warren Weaver, *Both Your Houses* (New York: Praeger Publishers, 1972), p. 158.
16. Mark J. Green, James M. Fallows, and David R. Zwick, *Who Runs Congress?* (Toronto: Bantam Books, 1972), p. 161.
17. Stephen K. Bailey, "Ethics and the Politician," Karl A. Lamb, ed., *Democracy, Liberalism, and Revolution* (Palo Alto, Calif.: Center for the Study of Democratic Institutions, James E. Freel & Associates, 1971), p. 353.
18. Ibid., pp. 336–37 and 343.
19. *Los Angeles Times,* June 15, 1973, p. 23.
20. Max Weber, "Politics as a Vocation," excerpted by Michael Curtis, ed., *The Great Political Theories,* vol. 2 (New York: Avon Book Division, The Hearst Corp., n.d.), pp. 374–78.
21. T. V. Smith, p. 92.
22. E. E. Schattschneider, *Two Hundred Million Americans in Search of a Government* (New York: Holt, Rinehart & Winston, 1969), pp. 19–21.
23. Max Weber, pp. 372–73.
24. These criteria are taken from a somewhat longer list which Robert A. Dahl suggests for measuring influence in *Modern Political Analysis,* 2nd ed. (Englewood Cliffs, N.J.: Prentice-Hall, 1970), pp. 20–25.
25. John C. Calhoun, "A Disquisition on Government," in *Works,* Vol. I (Columbia, S.C., 1851; New York, 1853–55), p. 28.

26. Alvin Toffler, *Future Shock* (New York: Random House, 1970).
27. Charles A. Beard, *An Economic Interpretation of the Constitution* (New York: Macmillan Co., 1913). For divergent views, see Robert E. Brown, *Charles Beard and the Constitution* (Princeton, N.J.: Princeton University Press, 1955); Edmund S. Morgan, *The Birth of the Republic, 1763–89* (Chicago: University of Chicago Press, 1956); Forrest McDonald, *We the People: The Economic Origins of the Constitution* (Boston: Houghton Mifflin Co., 1965); and Jackson Turner Maine; *The Anti-Federalists: Critics of the Constitution, 1781–1788* (Chapel Hill: University of North Carolina Press, 1961).
28. C. Wright Mills, *The Power Elite* (New York: Oxford University Press, 1956). For diverse views on this issue, note the opinions of Dahl, Domhoff, Janowitz, and others in Normal L. Crockett, ed., *The Power Elite in America* (Lexington, Mass.: D. C. Heath & Co., 1970).
29. Peter Bachrach, *The Theory of Democratic Elitism* (Boston: Little, Brown and Co., 1967). See also Chapter 13 of this book, pp. 328.
30. David Easton, *The Political System* (New York: Alfred A. Knopf, 1953).

2 THE NATURE OF AMERICA:
Land, people, and political culture

"America is God's crucible, the great Melting-Pot where all the races of Europe are melting and reforming."

Israel Zangwill

Political systems are affected by both their physical and cultural environments. The physical environment is the geographic area of the state, its land, and its natural resources. It also includes the population, its characteristics, and its distribution. The cultural environment refers to the beliefs, expectations, traditions, values, and motivations of the people. Indeed, we cannot understand American politics unless we know a little about America—its land, people, and political culture.

GEOGRAPHICAL INFLUENCES

Robert Frost, one of America's great literary figures, was the first person ever asked to read a poem at a presidential inauguration. Squinting into the reflected glare of the winter sun, he spoke not of John F. Kennedy, about to take the oath of office, but of the United States itself. "The land was ours," the old poet rasped, "before we were the land's."[1] The words sink in slowly. We understand owning our land. Only later, gradually, do we realize that the land we own begins to mold us, determine our actions, change our thinking. The very word *land* means country or nation in several languages. Where we live, how far apart, the way we make our money—even how we govern ourselves depends, at least in part, upon the land.

Size and Location

Not a place upon earth might be so happy as America. Her situation is remote from all
the wrangling world. . . .

Thomas Paine

The most obvious geographical fact about America is that it is large. When a
country is large, it is almost essential that its government be decentralized.
It would be absurd, for example, to regulate hunting licenses in Hawaii from
a Washington office. Of course, where government services and controls are
widely dispersed, this leads to a dispersal of the power to make policy. Here
then is a major justification for our federal system.

Location used to be a geographic factor at least as important as size.
America's location between oceans 3000 miles wide on the east and 6000
miles wide on the west promoted a foreign policy known as *isolationism*.
Until this century, we made few international commitments and joined no
military alliances. Geographic isolation from international power centers
prevented foreign invasion and permitted national attention to be devoted to
the development of the continent. In other words, as Thomas Paine indicated,
America's location has contributed to its relative security. Even today if an
enemy were to invade our shores, the logistical problems of supply lines
thousands of miles long would probably make successful occupation
impossible.

Yet the world is smaller now, largely as a result of modern
communication, transportation, and weaponry. Isolationism fell victim to this
new reality. Its death was marked by the graves of American soldiers killed in
two world wars, in Korea, and in Vietnam. The jet and missile age has
required a reevaluation of America's international position. Although sea
power remains important, the air routes over the Arctic polar region have
surpassed it in significance. The United States, isolated for so long by its
location, now finds itself an air neighbor to the other great powers of the
world. In terms of American defense, the change is not an easy one. While
our security can be violated from nearly anywhere, we have insufficient
power to protect our interests everywhere. In the Middle East, Asia, and
Europe, hard choices must be made.

Resources: People of Plenty

The political significance of America's size and location is dwarfed by the
importance of its vast riches. In quantity, variety, and accessibility of natural
resources we have been greatly favored. In fact, the very abundance of our
resources has encouraged their rapid and wasteful depletion.

However, the extensive river systems, the level of rainfall, the availability
of reasonably flat farm land, and the length of the growing season have and
no doubt will continue to contribute to our economic wealth. The United

States grows a surplus of wheat, corn, rice, meat, and dairy products. In addition, we are a leading producer of copper, lead, sulfur, coal, iron, and magnesium. But known reserves of some of these minerals can support the current level of use for only a limited period. In total manufacturing output, the U.S. is also a world leader. It outproduces the Soviet Union, Japan, and Germany—its chief competitors.

To compare America's wealth with that of other nations, one must rely on reported production statistics for various commodities, and especially on the gross national product (GNP) per capita. GNP per capita shows the value of all goods and services produced in a country if the total were divided equally among its inhabitants. Figure 2–1 summarizes some of the comparative data. As can be seen, the U.S. ranks number one or two in each category. Yet there are other wealthy nations in the world too and, as footnote 1 shows, the differences in GNP between the "have" and the "have not" nations are very great. It is hardly surprising then that the United States and other wealthy nations have been the object of envious hatred among the "have-nots" of Asia, Africa, and Latin America.

Apart from this, wealth has another important political implication. Democracy seems to flourish best in wealthier nations. Poorer nations are often tempted to sacrifice majority rule and personal freedoms for economic development.[2] David M. Potter, in *People of Plenty*, pins down the particular effect of prosperity on politics in America. He argues that our economic surplus made it possible to improve the lot of the poor without hurting the rich. The widespread belief that equality could be attained by "leveling up" as well as by "leveling down" has made the appeal of revolution less and that of democracy greater to America's poor.[3]

Geography, Energy, and Politics

While nature has blessed America with an abundance of resources, the blessings are mixed with an abundance of problems as well. Petroleum was perhaps the most pressing of these in the mid 1970s. To put it briefly, our appetite exceeded our supply. Although the United States produced more petroleum than any other nation, its consumption was even greater. As a result, we found ourselves depending upon an increasingly unreliable supply of oil from the Arab countries in the Middle East.

The Energy Crisis
The fact that America produced too little oil to meet its needs prompted many political responses. Presidents Nixon and Ford pledged to work for "Project Independence" which would make the nation self-sufficient in supplying its own energy requirements. Congress approved construction of an Alaskan oil pipeline in spite of claims that it was dangerous to the environment. President Ford favored increased taxes on petroleum products

Figure 2–1. COMPARATIVE NATIONAL WEALTH

Rank	GNP Per Capita Nation	Amount	Electricity Nation	Volume²	Steel Nation	Volume³	Wheat Nation	Volume³	Crude Petroleum Nation	Volume⁴
1	Switzerland	$6,525	U.S.	1,853	U.S.S.R.	139	U.S.S.R.	86	U.S.	467
2	U.S.	6,127	U.S.S.R.	857	U.S.	133	U.S.	46	U.S.S.R.	400
3	Sweden	5,941	Japan	428	Japan	107	China	35	Saudi Arabia	285
4	Canada	5,309	West Germany	275	West Germany	48	India	26	Iran	249
5	Denmark	5,293	U.K.	264	U.K.	28	France	18	Venezuela	168
6	Kuwait	5,280	Canada	238	France	27	Canada	15	Kuwait	151
7	West Germany	5,160	France	163	China	25	Turkey	12	Libya	106
8	France	4,747	Italy	135	Italy	22	Italy	9	Nigeria	90
9	Australia	4,595	Poland	76	Belgium	16	Argentina	8	Canada	73
10¹	Luxembourg	4,569	East Germany	73	Poland	15	Pakistan	7	Iraq	71

¹Other GNP figures: Japan $3,848, U.K. $3,056; U.S.S.R. $890; Mexico $753; Brazil $495; Nigeria $150; India $98; Indonesia $84. For Kuwait, Mexico, Brazil, Nigeria, India, and Indonesia, figures are for 1972; for U.S.S.R., 1967; for all other nations they are 1973 figures.
²In trillions of kilowatt-hours.
³In millions of short tons.
⁴In millions of metric tons.
Source: U.S. Bureau of the Census, *Statistical Abstract of the United States: 1974.* For U.S.S.R. GNP, *Los Angeles Times,* Nov. 21, 1968, Part II, p. 5.

while many in Congress called for gas rationing. Meanwhile Secretary of State Kissinger hinted that the U.S. might have to resort to military force if we were again in danger of being "strangled" by an Arab oil cut-off.

Energy controversy has also intensified regarding the possible dangers of nuclear power plants and research was stepped up into the usefulness of solar and geothermal energy. Federal expenditures on energy projects were hiked by Congress from $4 million in 1973 to some $50 million a year later.[4] As fuel shortages combined with scarcities of sugar, meat, and other products, Americans began to realize that they were being squeezed between dwindling supplies and persistent demands. The inflationary result was a price too high for many to pay.

Geographic Politics

Politics affects the distribution of goods—oil, food, money, etc. These and other limited resources cannot meet all of the demands upon them. Thus, the political system is often used to establish priorities and to allocate resources. Some people, for example, may want tax dollars used to build a bridge across a river, while others may want the funds used to build a riverfront park. If there is not enough money to do both, the political process will determine which project to pursue.

Often such disagreements pit one region of a nation or state against another. When this happens, the output of the political process is usually some sort of compromise. It may take on the form of legislative "log-rolling" in which votes for a highway in one location, for example, are traded for future votes for a state college somewhere else. Similarly, on a global scale, countless rivalries between nations have also involved the geographic distribution of resources such as land, a warm water port, or oil. But because international relations are not always subject to political compromise, these rivalries must sometimes be settled by other means.

DEMOGRAPHIC INFLUENCES

The analysis of population characteristics—where people live, their race, sex, age, etc.—is known as *demography*. Since people are probably any nation's major resource, demographic factors deserve our consideration. Three seem particularly significant: the population's growth, its urbanization, and its diversity.

Growth: Plenty of People

The American population has increased more spectacularly than that of any nation in history.[5] From the nearly four million recorded in the first official census count in 1790, it rose to more than 211 million in 1974. Our vast geographic area is capable of sustaining this large population with relatively little crowding. While uninhabitable mountain and desert regions make population density figures somewhat misleading, it is nevertheless significant that the United States has an average of 58 inhabitants per square mile, compared with 216 in China, 245 in France, and 744 in Japan. At the other extreme there are 29 people per square mile in the Soviet Union, 22 in Argentina, and 6 in Canada. The world average is 72.

In terms of total population, America ranks fourth behind China, India, and Russia. We also rank fourth in total land area after Russia, Canada, and China. Although numbers alone cannot make a nation a formidable power, they are an important indication of its strength. Large numbers of combat troops, for example, are still a valuable military asset, as we recently saw in Korea and Vietnam. Moreover, a large population is better able to supply the manpower and the talent needed to utilize natural resources.

But exceptional population growth is not an unmixed blessing, for as we have seen it often strains the nation's geographic assets. Automobiles pollute the air, industrial wastes contaminate rivers and oceans, and an increasing population demands that the government permit the leveling of hillsides for housing tracts, schools, and shopping centers. Indeed commercial, residential, and recreational needs already imperil the environment to a substantial degree. More important perhaps, every additional person means the additional consumption of energy and raw materials which are already in short supply around the globe.

Bob Main, BBM

An example of human pollution: fishermen at the mouth of Rouge River in northern California when the salmon are running.

While most problems seem to grow worse, however, the danger of overpopulation in America seems to be decreasing. The birth rate began to drop rapidly in 1971, and in 1973 reached the lowest point in history. But even this apparently happy development had a few ominous by-products. Declining enrollments have closed schools and put teachers out of work in a number of cities. And the base of future workers who pay taxes and provide financial support for the social security retirement system will be smaller in years to come.

Urbanization: Cities and Suburbs

A popular song of World War I asked, "How ya gonna keep 'em down on the farm, after they've seen Paree?" The answer was—whether they had seen Paris or not—that you couldn't. In fact, the steady process of urbanization began long before World War I. By 1970, 74 percent of the population was urban. The reason for this massive shift away from rural areas was the desire for economic improvement. Thus, in most cases, it was a shift from farms to factories—the very essence of the industrial revolution. Indeed, urbanization

Figure 2-2. POPULATION GROWTH AND DISTRIBUTION

	Growth	Distribution
	1960–70	1970
Central cities	6.4%	31.4
Outside central cities (suburbs)	26.7%	37.2
Nonmetropolitan areas	6.8%	31.4
Entire nation	13.3%	100.0

Source: U.S. Bureau of the Census, *Statistical Abstract of the United States: 1974*, p. 17.

and industrialization have had political and legal results that cannot be ignored:

First, they reduced the percentage of the labor force which was self-employed and increased the proportion working for someone else. This led to the eventual passage of minimum-wage, worker's compensation, child-labor, and union-recognition laws.

Second, they helped create new industries which demanded and received government subsidies, tax advantages, and tariffs on imported goods to weaken foreign competition.

Third, they thrust upon city governments grave new problems in such areas as zoning, public health, transportation, recreation facilities, and pollution.

While the majority of Americans had moved to urban areas by 1920, there remain great differences among the states. As recently as 1970, for example, eight states were still predominantly rural. Vermont led (or trailed) the list, with only 32.2 percent of its population living in urban areas, while New Jersey had 88.9 percent, and California had 90.9 percent.[6]

Until recent years, urbanization conjured up thoughts of the big city— bright and bursting with opportunity. Yet the 1970 census reveals that rapid population growth is occurring not in the older central cities but in the suburban fringe areas that surround them. In fact, many core cities are losing population and may be in danger of losing their vitality as well.

Small Town Comeback

Just as the 1960s saw urbanization give way to "suburbanization" the early 1970s witnessed the largest rate of growth in nonmetropolitan areas. Calvin L. Beale, a prominent demographer for the Department of Agriculture, called it "the most dramatic demographic change I've seen in this country," with the exception of reversals in the birth rate.[7] Metropolitan counties grew by 2.2 percent between 1970 and 1973, while nonmetropolitan counties were growing by 4.1 percent.[8] The growth of resort industries, new manufacturing plants, and government installations have combined to give such areas as northern Michigan, central and western North Carolina, parts of southern Appalachia, and the Ozark plateau a period of renewed growth. At the same time, farm population which had dropped by nearly five percent a year in the 1960s, stabilized at a decline of less than one percent annually from 1970 to 1973.[9] More and more Americans, it seems, were living where they wanted to. A 1972 Gallup poll showed that 55 percent of the people would prefer to live in a small town or on a farm, compared with 44 percent who chose a city or suburb.[10]

The fact that small towns, far removed from metropolitan centers, are setting the pace for national growth is as encouraging a sign as the slowing of total population increase. "What it means," said Conrad Taeuber, former associate director of the Census Bureau, "is that by the year 2000 we won't have the degree of congestion that we would have had if we had continued with the growth rates of the 1960s."[11] But whether or not population actually becomes more dispersed—will depend largely on government action at the national, state, and local levels. The awarding of contracts, the construction of electric generators and highways, the funding of planned towns, and the passage of land use or zoning ordinances will determine to a considerable extent where people live in the future.

Diversity: A Mixed Blessing

As Franklin D. Roosevelt once reminded the conservative Daughters of the American Revolution, we are all immigrants or the descendants of immigrants. Even the ancestors of the Indians were probably Asians who made their way across the Bering Straits. Although one might think that America was relatively homogeneous until the arrival of Europeans, the Indian tribes actually displayed great diversity in language and life-style. The Spanish, English, Dutch, and French settlers contributed still more variety during the early colonial period, while later periods saw many Scandinavian immigrants. A multiracial society was guaranteed with the importation of African laborers beginning in 1619. In the late 1800s, thousands of Eastern European immigrants, many of them Jewish, added more religious diversity. Similarly, the Chinese immigrants of the 1870s and 1880s added a non-Western influence. All the immigrants came carrying, duty free, their ancestral prejudices and varied ethnic backgrounds which of course have had a profound impact on American politics. Even today the impact is still being felt. The demands of blacks, for example, have led to a white backlash. Political organizations formed by Indians, Mexican-Americans, Chinese-Americans, and other groups have mushroomed rapidly. And "bloc voting" by various ethnic groups still elects (and defeats) many a candidate. To understand American politics, therefore, one should know what sorts of people inhabit the country in the 1970s. What are their characteristics? Where did they come from?

Immigration Policy
For the first hundred years or so, America maintained an open door policy

Figure 2–3. MAJOR AMERICAN ETHNIC GROUPS

Group	Number	Percentage
English, Scotch, Welsh	31,006,000	15.3
German	25,661,000	12.7
Negro	22,810,000	11.2
Irish	16,325,000	8.0
Italian	8,733,000	4.3
French	5,189,000	2.6
Mexican	5,073,000	2.5
Polish	4,941,000	2.4
Spanish, Puerto Rican, Cuban, other Latin American	3,883,000	1.9
American Indians, Japanese, Chinese, other nonwhite	2,412,000	1.2
Russian	2,132,000	1.1
Austrian, Canadian, Swedish, other white	59,467,000	29.3
Not reported	15,216,000	7.5
Total	202,848,000	100.0

Source: Adapted from *Congressional Quarterly Weekly Report,* March 11, 1972, p. 532. Reprinted by permission of Congressional Quarterly, Inc. Figures are based on a Census Bureau sampling taken in March 1971.

with no significant restrictions on immigration into this country. Nevertheless during that period thousands of black Africans came here in chains, countless Indians were killed, and many Chinese were brought here under exploitative contracts to lay railroad tracks. After 1882, however, the situation changed. We find increased racial prejudice and fear on the part of American factory workers that they might lose their jobs to Asian laborers. This led to a prohibition of further immigration imposed by the Chinese Exclusion Act. It was the first time that any nation had been subjected to any restrictions whatsoever.

It took several decades, however, for the U.S. to adopt general limitations on the number of new immigrants. The Immigration Restriction Act of 1921, inspired by the antiforeign fervor after World War I, established the national origin quota system. This was designed—as amended in 1924—to keep the proportion of new immigrants from various nations the same as it was before 1890. The Act was justified as a measure to assist the assimilation or adjustment of new arrivals into American society. In fact, however, it discriminated against non-Protestants, since large numbers of Catholics and Jews had emigrated after 1890 from countries such as Russia, Poland, and Italy.

The U.S. soon added racial discrimination to this religious prejudice. In

1924, Asians were prohibited from becoming citizens and immigration was prohibited for all persons ineligible for citizenship. The U.S. also prevented the immigration of black Africans by refusing to classify Negroes as being of African origin.

Not until 1965 was the national origin quota system abandoned and the stains of ethnic bias removed. The new law establishes a maximum of 170,000 immigrants each year who may enter the United States from outside the Western Hemisphere. With exceptions, no more than 20,000 of this number may be admitted from any one country. Preference is given to those who have either relatives in the United States or special occupational skills needed by the American economy. The 1965 Act also includes another controversial change: Before its passage, immigrants from nations in the Western Hemisphere such as Canada and Mexico were admitted "quota free" in unlimited numbers. But present policy limits to 120,000 per year the number entering from these areas, in addition to the 170,000 from the rest of the world. Emergency legislation, however, can permit the entry of thousands more immigrants in cases of war, national disasters, or other circumstances which create large numbers of refugees. Thus, thousands of South Vietnamese refugees were admitted to the U.S. in 1975 as a result of Communist conquests.

It is important to note that accurate figures on immigration are difficult to obtain because of the number of aliens entering the United States illegally. Nearly 800,000 aliens were deported in 1974, but estimates indicate that more than 6 million may still be living here with an additional 2 million crossing the borders each year. Many live in poverty while others hold jobs which would otherwise reduce unemployment among American citizens.[12]

Figure 2–4. IMMIGRANTS, BY COUNTRY OF LAST PERMANENT RESIDENCE

Rank	Country	Annual Average Number of Immigrants, 1951–1960	Country	Number of Immigrants, 1973
1	Germany	47,776	Mexico	70,411
2	Canada	37,795	Philippines	30,248
3	Mexico	29,981	Cuba	22,537
4	Great Britain	19,549	Korea	22,313
5	Italy	18,549	Italy	22,264
6	Cuba	7,894	West Indies	21,641
7	Austria	6,710	Canada	14,800
8	Ireland	5,733	India	11,975
9	Netherlands	5,227	Great Britain	11,860
10	France	5,112	Greece	10,348
Total		251,547		400,063

Source: U.S. Bureau of the Census, Statistical Abstract: 1974, p. 99.

As indicated in Figure 2–4, the 1965 immigration law has had the effect of reducing the number of European immigrants and increasing those from Asia and Latin America. Between 1960 and 1970, the Cuban population in the United States rose 351 percent, and that of the Philippines 95 percent. Because of an increasing birth rate, the native American Indian population leaped 51 percent. All signs, in fact, indicate that the ethnic mix of the United States is changing substantially.

The Melting Pot

Early in our history, a French immigrant lauded "that strange mixture of blood . . . melted into a new race of men, whose labors and posterity will one day cause great changes in the world."[13] He thus became one of the first to set forth the now famous *melting pot thesis.* The diversity of the American people has no doubt exceeded his expectations, and the nation is far richer for it.

But this is only part of the story. Although we have woven the talents, skills, and values of many peoples into a rich and unique tapestry, we have yet to create a fabric of happy fellowship. While conceding that some ethnic groups (notably German-Americans) have diminished in solidarity, two leading scholars have concluded that the melting pot has actually melted very little. Rather, racial and religious groups—especially in the older cities— retain their separate identities and also their ethnic political power.[14] Indeed, we can see this quite clearly in the antibusing stand of the Irish Catholics in South Boston who do not want to send their children to school with blacks. Thus, on the one hand, we have a culture enriched by the exciting variety of diverse peoples. Yet, on the other hand, we are sometimes troubled by their persistent, occasionally violent rivalries. It should be noted, however, that conflict is a normal part of politics which the democratic process seeks to resolve peacefully.

THE POLITICAL CULTURE

It must, I think, be rare in a democracy for a man suddenly to conceive a system of ideas far different from those of his contemporaries; and I suppose that, even should such an innovator arise, he would have great difficulty in making himself heard. . . .

Alexis de Tocqueville

Americanism

The American polical system operates within a framework of related ideas and values which help to determine political behavior. Such influences are part of the political culture. Any leader who expects to be elected as well as respected must identify strongly with this culture. An important ingredient in it is the concept of Americanism which is our own variety of nationalism. Nationalism involves the identification of one's individual interests with the welfare of the entire nation. As a result, loyalty to the nation is a supreme allegiance, often overriding obligations to one's family, church, or political creed. Men and women submit to it willingly, they kill and are killed in the nation's wars, and they pay taxes to support it.

But how many Americans feel devotion and reverence for their country today? In the wake of Watergate, the Vietnam war, racial friction, rising crime, and falling employment, does Americanism remain a vital value? There are no certain answers to such questions, but a few statistics are pertinent. In 1963, 85 percent of Americans said they took more pride in their political institutions than in any other characteristic of the nation.[15] Ten years later, when respect for politics had dropped sharply, 74 percent of the people still gave the United States a "highly favorable" rating in a Gallup poll.[16] Among those with college backgrounds, however, that rating drew only a 65 percent response, while it received only 64 percent from younger adults aged 18 to 29, and 60 percent from nonwhites.

The remarkable thing, perhaps, is that most Americans remain as patriotic as they are. Why is this the case? The answer is largely historical. First, most Americans came to view their new homeland as a vast improvement over the rigid class structures and severe poverty of the lands from which they came. Second, the differences among Americans have inspired determined attempts to overcome them. Thus, free public education deliberately sought to Americanize the immigrants' children by teaching them English, American history, and patriotic customs.

In America, as in all countries, however, the glorification of nationalism can be dangerous. It allows public officials to divert attention from the validity of their policies by associating them with patriotic pride. Thus President Nixon pleaded for support of his Vietnam policy in April 1970 by reminding us that in the "proud history" of America we had never lost a war. Such nationalism, unfortunately, can increase the possibility of international conflict. Love of country can too easily become xenophobia, a fearful hatred of foreign peoples, as was skillfully accomplished in Nazi Germany.

Nevertheless, nationalism can serve more positive purposes. It can increase public confidence in the authority of the government and thereby reduce its need to depend on force. It can also contribute to internal unity and the desire for compromise. That is, it can encourage labor and business, black and white, the devout and the atheist to submerge their differences on behalf of the common good. This type of nationalism can clearly have beneficial effects on the political process.

Capitalism

While nationalism is strong in almost every country, capitalism is not. But it has had a very powerful influence on the American political system. Briefly described, capitalism is an economic system based on the ownership of

Automobiles—the foundation of our economy.

business by private individuals or corporations, rather than by the government. In 1776, Adam Smith argued in *The Wealth of Nations* that prosperity resulted from a government policy of *laissez-faire,* one that placed few legal restrictions upon the free competition of private business firms. A dozen generations of American capitalists have enthusiastically agreed that this policy would produce a higher standard of living for the entire society. The law of supply and demand would then be able to operate freely as a kind of "unseen hand" governing the economy. It would result in the manufacture of exactly those goods consumers wished to buy because only that would maximize sales and profits as well. Moreover, each company would be forced to produce the best possible product at the lowest possible price because if they did not their competitors would. Governmental activity could then be confined largely to the protection of life and property, with each individual left to compete in the free market on the basis of his own talents and initiative.

Even before Adam Smith put it in writing, this basic theory of capitalism dominated America. Its appeal was strengthened by its compatability with the Protestant ethic which stressed hard work, self-reliance, and thrift. Specifically, the disciples of John Calvin argued that the ability to accumulate earthly wealth was a probable indication of the grace of God that predestined one for eternal salvation. This religious theory, which also encouraged simple living, business shrewdness, and private profit, was first implanted in colonial

New England by the Puritans and has flourished in the American mind ever since.

Private capitalism was further strengthened in the last half of the nineteenth century by the spread of social Darwinism in America. This theory held that capitalistic competition for markets and jobs resulted in the "survival of the fittest." Society would be improved because its inferior members would gradually be eliminated through a process of natural selection. That is, they would be less able to compete in the free market for jobs, food, etc., and thus less able to reproduce. As for political programs, the implication was clear: Government should neither restrain the successful nor aid the failures because that would violate the laws of natural selection. With such ideas strongly embedded here, it is little wonder that social security and welfare programs have faced great resistance. Indeed, as recently as 1964, 79 percent of the American people were found to agree with the statement "We should rely more on individual initiative and not so much on government welfare programs."[17] It was partly because of this kind of attitude that the United States lagged far behind Germany, France, and England in instituting such programs as unemployment conpensation, retirement pensions, or Medicare.

Although modern times have brought about substantial changes in American capitalism, it remains the dominant theme in an economy now "mixed" with limited government ownership and Welfare State programs. However, the overriding strength of capitalism is indicated by the fact that American labor unions are the only ones in the world not committed to some sort of socialism as the best economic system.

Racism

Anthropology provides no scientific basis for discrimination against people on the ground of racial inferiority.

American Anthropological Association

The Commission on Civil Disorders, appointed by President Lyndon B. Johnson in 1967, received considerable criticism for its conclusion that riots in Los Angeles, Detroit, Newark, and other cities were essentially the result of white racism.[18] But racism has been a persistent ingredient of American culture throughout our history.

American Indians
The first victims of racism in America were, of course, the Indians. The Indian population in what is now the United States is estimated to have been over a million at the time Columbus arrived in the New World. Since then it has been substantially reduced due to contamination with disease, bloody massacres by the United States cavalry, and displacement to poorer lands farther west. Although the Indians at first received the white intruders with

hospitality, after several centuries of deceit and betrayal they fought back with vengeance. By that time, of course, the odds against them were overwhelming. Armed Indian resistance ended in 1890 at Wounded Knee, South Dakota, where several hundred Sioux, including many women and children, were killed.

However, the spirit of resistance was revived in 1973 at the same location. It is little wonder that the Indians are still resisting: the 1970 census revealed that of the 792,730 Indians living in the United States about 40 percent had incomes below the poverty level—the highest proportion of any ethnic group in America. Nearly half lived in cities, with the remainder in reservations and other rural areas. It was not until 1924 that Indians were made American citizens. They were not permitted to vote in Arizona and New Mexico, however, until 1948.

Afro-Americans

The first blacks were brought to America from Africa in 1619 as indentured servants. However, they soon became part of one of the most brutal systems of slavery the world has ever known. In many states it was against the law to teach slaves to read or write. Some profitable plantations derived most of their income from commercial slave-breeding. Theologians debated whether blacks had souls. More than 3000 blacks were lynched between 1882 and 1951.[19] Such discrimination has been among the most persistent and degrading forms of racism in America.

Asian-Americans

In addition to the legal discrimination against Asians already noted, several massacres of Chinese occurred in the West in the late 1800s. Although it was not always so violent, this discrimination continued. It was not until 1952 that the Chinese could be employed by state, county, or municipal governments in California. The Japanese were also targets of those who feared the "yellow peril." They were segregated in San Francisco public schools in 1906. Even worse, 110,000 Americans of Japanese origin were herded into "relocation centers" during World War II, although not one of them was found to actually be disloyal.

White Ethnics

The list of those discriminated against goes on and on, embracing Mexicans, Irish, Jews, Italians, Slavs, and others. Most of these ethnic groups *are* white. Yet they are still fair game because racists are constantly searching for new groups to tread upon. The basic insecurity of the racist mind seems to require that it be made to feel superior by having others feel inferior. Thus, exclusive schools, clubs, and many employers have long discriminated against Jews and other white ethnic groups as well as against blacks and Asians.

Equality

[Y]ears ago I recognized my kinship with all living things, and I made up my mind that I was not one bit better than the meanest of the earth . . . While there is a lower class, I am in it; while there is a criminal element, I am of it; while there is a soul in prison, I am not free.

Eugene V. Debs

In spite of the inequalities of racism, Americans have cherished the ideal of equality in very meaningful ways. In 1776 when Thomas Jefferson, a slave owner, asserted it to be "self-evident" that "all men are created equal," even a commitment to white equality was truly a revolutionary concept. We tried to meet that commitment by prohibiting titles of nobility in Article I and later by guaranteeing "equal protection" of state laws in Amendment Fourteen. Our basic constitutional system gives jurors, judges, legislators, and voters each an equal vote in making the decisions entrusted to them.

Nevertheless, there is considerable evidence of confusion and even opposition regarding the concept of equality. For example, in 1964 a major study reported 58 percent agreement with the statement that "we have to teach children that all men are created equal but almost everyone knows that some are better than others."[20] Clearly, we are not equal if equality means identity. People differ widely in strength, skill, ambition, and intelligence. Equality, however, does not mean that everyone must be exactly alike. Rather it means that each human being is as *inherently worthwhile* as the next, regardless of his race, his talents, or his title. This definition also implies a recognition that there is equality in the human condition: We are all similar in our biological needs for food, drink, and sex. We all require shelter and warmth. We all have emotional needs for approval and respect. We are all products of our genetic attributes, infant environment, and racial identity. Finally, we must all face inevitable death. Increasingly, each is dependent upon the other—butcher, mortician, plumber, and lawyer—in industrialized societies demanding ever more specialized divisions of labor. Equality assumes the similarities outweigh the differences.

These inherent human equalities have prompted the desire for equality in other areas of our life. In the U.S. we were fortunate to be more equal in material conditions than people of other nations. The open frontier with its available land and the absence of an old feudal aristocracy were immensely important here. They made it easier for us to translate our equality into political ideals and sometimes into political practice. Today we have come to think of practical equality as equality of opportunity.

Pragmatism

The true is the name of whatever proves itself to be good. . . .

William James

While Americans are not well known for their philosophical ideas, they are renowned for their practical accomplishments. They take frank pride in being "doers" not "thinkers." It is therefore appropriate that this country's most notable contribution to philosophy is *pragmatism,* the belief that the truth of an idea is best tested by its results. Abstract conceptions have validity, pragmatists contend, only in terms of their practical consequences.

This philosophy, developed and refined in the early years of the twentieth century by Charles Peirce, William James, and John Dewey, is an important part of political culture. Its roots go back to an earlier period when American frontiersmen were forced to devise practical means to cope with their immediate, and often vital needs. Gradually, we developed a faith in the process of trial and error for solving our problems.

Such pragmatic solutions stand out clearly in almost every part of our political system. Our major political parties are not ideologically oriented, for example. Rather, they consist of expedient and shifting group coalitions formed to win elections. Our legislative process, as we shall see in Chapter 10, is marked by continual compromise born of the lawmaker's concessions to his conscience, his colleagues, and his constituents. Even our courts, led by the great justices Holmes and Brandeis, have applied a sort of legal pragmatism which "follows the election returns" rather than abstract legal theory. Finally, the "mixed economy" of America, part government owned or regulated and part privately controlled, reflects the same practical preoccupation with final results rather than formal doctrine. In fact, our continuing preference for democracy itself shows a pragmatic concern with existing realities. As Winston Churchill said, democracy is the worst form of government—except for all the others that have ever been tried. Democratic politics is above all the art of the possible. Theoretically, it is not very neat; morally, it is sometimes corrupt. But, practically speaking, it usually works. As two prominent pollsters concluded: ". . . what seems to make the system continue to function as effectively as it does is its distinctly American pragmatism."[21]

Fair Play Versus Corruption

. . . [E]nds and means on earth are so entangled That changing one, you change the other too; Each different path brings other ends in view.

Ferdinand Lasalle

The attachment Americans have for pragmatism—for that which works—can lead dangerously close to a belief that "anything goes," that a good enough end, or goal, justifies even the worst means. But most Americans have rejected that belief. Instead, they seem to value fair play and doing things "according to Hoyle." They resent "dirty pool." In politics, this means that they want candidates to campaign fairly and officials to govern honestly. When Vice President Agnew said the criminal charges against him were the result of a "post-Watergate morality," he distorted thousands of years of history. The moral codes he was charged with violating are as old as the Old Testament itself. The truly remarkable thing is that most people continue to expect integrity in their leaders no matter how often they have been disappointed in the past.

However, some parts of the country seem to have higher standards of integrity than others. V. O. Key, an astute student of American politics, observed that "Communities develop, or so it seems, their own peculiar customs and attitudes toward electoral bribery and fraud. In one county, elections may be really as clean as a hound's tooth while an adjacent county over long periods maintains a record of consistent crookedness."[22] Some states such as Minnesota, Wisconsin, Oregon, and California have a reputation for generally "clean" politics. But certain rural areas in the South and several major cities in the North have a sorry history of nearly every known form of political corruption. And so do some presidential administrations.

Types of Corruption

To deal with the question of political morality as objectively as possible, a classification of corruption may be useful. There seem to be three types: selfishness which involves getting money or other material advantages dishonestly; deceit which entails lying to the people; and attempts to destroy the opposition which threaten the whole principle of democratic government.

Of these three varieties, selfishness has been the most common in the past. Party leaders or city officials in New York, Kansas City, and other areas, for example, frequently accepted money from underworld racketeers engaged in prostitution and gambling. Often politicians profited by buying land they knew the city would buy back at a higher price to use for parks and other public purposes. Sometimes they accepted pay-offs for granting business licenses or overlooking building code violations.[23] Fortunately, there is probably far less corruption of this sort in city government today than in the past.[24] At the state level, however, officials still sometimes profit by awarding highway construction contracts or liquor licenses and by depositing tax funds in certain private banks.[25] In the national government, the corruption of money has been far less common. Only during the Grant administration of the 1870s and the Harding administration of the 1920s have public officials reaped large profits from illegal activities.[26]

It is more difficult to determine whether deceit, the second type of corruption, has increased or decreased. We do know, however, that Lyndon Johnson created a huge "credibility gap" by misrepresenting an alleged attack by North Vietnamese patrol boats in the Gulf of Tonkin in 1964. This became a major justification for large-scale intervention of American combat forces. President Nixon, moreover, was responsible for false reports that the American bombing of Cambodia in April 1970 actually occurred over

Vietnam.[27] More recently, President Ford and his economic advisers may have deceived the public about the depth of the recession.

There is no doubt that television enables a president to communicate whatever he wants—true or false—more effectively than ever before. In fact, many of our executive leaders have such a command of the mass media that they can present their side of almost every story more rapidly and more persuasively than anyone else. In comparing the evils of various forms of corruption, Stimson Bullitt wrote that "the principal vice of money dishonesty is its degradation of public officials and the consequent loss of confidence in government." But, he went on, the "great moral problem of American politics is intellectual honesty. A free society cannot operate unless leaders tell the truth to the led."[28]

Certainly, not telling the truth was a major form of corruption in the Nixon administration as were its unprecedented efforts to destroy the political opposition. These included not only the break-in at the Democratic headquarters in the Watergate, but also the burglary of a doctor's office to obtain the psychiatric records of Daniel Ellsberg. Ellsberg was the man who had released a secret Pentagon history of the Vietnam war. The White House also put pressure on the I.R.S. to audit the tax returns of their critics, authorized F.B.I. wiretaps on unfriendly reporters, and maintained an "enemies list." Moreover, the Committee to Reelect the President (CREEP) made false accusations against leading Democratic presidential contenders during the Florida primary campaign. It also accepted illegal campaign contributions from big corporations.

Although this kind of power corruption was most rampant during the Nixon administration, it was not entirely new. Fraudulent vote counts have occurred for years in certain localities, as noted earlier. And Lyndon Johnson, as we shall see later, used the F.B.I. to gather secret data on people he distrusted.

Causes of Corruption

Why the Watergates? Why does corruption surface so often in a culture pledged to fair play? The blame lies with all of us. The observation of Adrian and Press about city government can be applied throughout our political system: "corruption may enter . . . , in the first place, as a result of the commonplace lack of interest in the operations of the city which permits lax administration. Dishonesty and irregularities breed a greater lack of interest and a cynicism which allows for more of the same."[29] This vicious circle is aggravated by the relatively low salaries of many public officials which make the temptation of illegal money harder to resist. Moreover, business and commercial interests are also at fault for they are usually more corrupt than government,[30] supplying the bribes which politicians take.

Finally, teachers and scholars are guilty, too. In the past twenty years, few books have said much, if anything, about corruption, civic virtue, or political morality.[31] As already noted, many authors dedicated to the behavioral goal of a value-free science of politics tended to reject moral judgments as unprofessional. However, such judgments must be returned to politics. As its respect for fair play declines, the authority of government diminishes.

Toward a Better Future

There is already considerable evidence that corruption will not be tolerated and that fair play remains a significant part of our political culture. First, there is the frequency with which corruption is being punished. In 1974 President Nixon was driven from office, and his pardon decreased President Ford's popularity. In 1973 Vice-President Agnew was fined and stripped of the right to practice law in his native state of Maryland. In 1975 Attorney General John Mitchell, along with top White House aides H. R. Haldeman and John Ehrlichman, received two-and-a-half to eight-year prison sentences for their roles in the Watergate conspiracy. In 1969 Justice Abe Fortas of the U. S. Supreme Court felt compelled to resign as a result of an apparent conflict of interest. Moreover, twenty-four members of Congress were indicted for crimes between 1900 and 1972, and 15 of them were convicted. In 1966 Bobby Baker, a top Senate staff member, and in 1971 Martin Sweig, an aide to Speaker of the House John McCormack, were sent to prison for tax evasion and bribery, respectively.[32] In 1973 a Federal District Court Judge and former Illinois governor, Otto Kerner, was sentenced to three years in prison for bribery, stock fraud, and other offenses. Although this is only a partial list, it is sufficient to show that high offices provide poor protection from dedicated prosecutors spurred on by an aroused public and a persistent press.

In spite (or maybe because) of the sins of the past, a second cause for hope can be found in the measures taken to discourage future corruption. In 1973 Congress passed the most extensive campaign reform law in its history, and at least nine states passed legislation dealing with the same problem in the post-Watergate period.[33] In the 1960s, both the Senate and the House created standing committees which have devised codes of ethical conduct. In the early 1970s, South Dakota, Kansas, Georgia, and Minnesota, among other states, developed improved methods for the removal of corrupt judges.[34]

It is too soon to tell whether this flurry of reforms will do any good. Clearly, however, they can produce no lasting benefits unless the whole society condemns corruption. The lessons of Watergate must be learned. To ignore the importance of decency and fair play is to risk the loss of that confidence and trust which permits democracy to persist. In the end, the values of the vast majority of the people will probably prevail. For as long as politicians spend huge sums of money on public opinion polls, as they do, the public will have a chance to determine the moral level of American government.

Political Culture: Past and Future

As we have just seen, American political culture is a blend of both positive and negative elements. It includes our special brand of patriotism, our preference for capitalism, our racism, our respect for equality, our tendency to practicality, and our efforts to keep fair play in the ball game. But each of these elements is constantly changing. The evolution of a common American political culture and the symbols which represent it has always been a dynamic and continuing process. The War of 1812, for example, produced the national anthem, the Uncle Sam symbol, and the successful defiance—for the second time—of English military might. Some twenty years later our political culture was strengthened by broadening its base. The administration of Andrew Jackson linked the welfare of the lower middle class to national prosperity and prominence, much as Washington and Hamilton had done for the commercial elite. Union victory in the Civil War was also important in bringing another subgroup, the Negroes, into our political culture. But in the last half century, America fell in love with its own prosperity and power. As we aspired to world leadership, we added devotion to an unexcelled standard of living and unmatched military might to our national self-image. How long can reality sustain this illusion? Not long. Vietnam and Watergate have burst some high-flying balloons.

Now more than ever our political culture is in a state of flux. It must adapt, it must come down to earth. But clearly it must not again sink below the horizon into the murky seas of racism, corruption, or arbitrary use of power.

POWER IN AMERICA

American society, like most others, has experienced sweeping changes in the redistribution of power. Much of it has shifted from East to West, from rural to metropolitan areas, and from a WASP monopoly to greater diffusion among ethnic groups. Yet despite these changes, the exercise of power continues to be determined largely by the availability of resources. Both economically and militarily, America's power resources are more limited than they once seemed to be. We have faced shortages of oil and other products. We have also found it increasingly difficult to compete successfully with a number of foreign manufacturers. In addition, the eight futile years of direct military involvement in Southeast Asia reveal that the conventional (nonnuclear) power of American armed forces is insufficient to shape world affairs to our own desires.

Moreover, wealth, a major element in political influence, is still distributed very unevenly. About a fourth of all American families earned less than $7,000 in 1972, while nearly a third earned $15,000 or more.[35] In 1971, the 10 percent of families with the largest income owned 74 percent of all family-owned corporation stock.[36] Political power, of course, involves skill, votes, and other resources in addition to money. How it is actually exercised depends largely on the form and limits of government established in the Constitution. This, then, is the subject of the following chapter.

Notes

1. From "The Gift Outright" in *The Poetry of Robert Frost,* edited by Edward Connery Lathem. Copyright 1942 by Robert Frost. Copyright © 1969 by Holt, Rinehart and Winston, Inc. Copyright © 1970 by Lesley Frost Ballantine. Reprinted by permission of Holt, Rinehart and Winston, Inc.
2. Seymour M. Lipset, *Political Man* (Garden City, N.Y.: Anchor Books, Doubleday & Co., 1963), pp. 31–45.
3. David M. Potter, *People of Plenty* (Chicago: University of Chicago Press, 1954), pp. 111–27.
4. *1975 Information Please Almanac, Atlas and Yearbook,* p. 430.
5. The source of statistical data here and elsewhere in "Demographic Influences" is U.S. Bureau of the Census, *Statistical Abstract of the United States: 1974,* pp. 815–17.
6. Ibid., p. 19.
7. *Los Angeles Times,* Nov. 15, 1974, Part 1A, p. 9.
8. *Statistical Abstract 1974,* p. 19.
9. *Los Angeles Times,* September 1, 1974, p. 14.
10. Ibid., December 20, 1972, Part VI, p. 10.
11. Ibid., November 15, 1974, Part 1A, p. 9.
12. *U.S. News & World Report,* Feb. 3, 1975, pp. 27–30.
13. Michel Guillaume St. Jean de Crevecoeur, *Letters from an American Farmer,* excerpted in Oscar Handlin, *Immigration as a Factor in American History* (Englewood Cliffs, N.J.: Prentice-Hall, 1959), p. 149.
14. Nathan Glazer and Daniel P. Moynihan, *Beyond the Melting Pot* (Cambridge, Mass.: M.I.T. Press, 1963).
15. Gabriel A. Almond and Sidney Verba, *The Civic Culture* (Princeton: Princeton University Press, 1963), p. 102.
16. *Los Angeles Times,* September 16, 1973, Part 1-A, p. 1.
17. Lloyd A. Free and Hadley Cantril, *The Political Beliefs of Americans* (New York: Clarion Books, Simon & Schuster, 1968), p. 30.
18. *Report of the National Advisory Commission on Civil Disorders,* (New York: Bantam Books, 1968), p. 203.
19. *Negro Year Book* (New York: Wm. H. Wise & Co., 1952), p. 277.
20. Herbert McClosky, "Consensus and Ideology in American Politics," *American Political Science Review* 58 (June 1964): 361–82.
21. Free and Cantril, p. 178.
22. V. O. Key, Jr., *Politics, Parties, & Pressure Groups,* 5th ed., (New York: Thomas Y. Crowell Co., 1964), p. 636 n.
23. Ibid., pp. 15 and 360–68.
24. Charles R. Adrian and Charles Press, *Governing Urban America* (New York: McGraw-Hill, 1968), p. 5.
25. Key, p. 505.
26. Joan Joseph, ed., *Political Corruption* (New York: Pocket Books, 1974), pp. 27–28 and 31–34.
27. Ibid., p. 52.

28. Stimson Bullitt, *To Be a Politician* (New York: Doubleday & Co., 1961), p. 128.
29. Adrian and Press, p. 41.
30. Bullitt, p. 127.
31. Some rare exceptions are the works cited in notes 25 through 32. Also Warren Weaver, *Both Your Houses* (New York: Praeger Publishers, 1972); Charles Frankel, *The Democratic Prospect* (New York: Harper & Row, 1962); and especially Edmond Cahn, *The Predicament of Democratic Man* (New York: Dell Publishing Co., 1961).
32. Mark J. Green, James M. Fallows, and David R. Zwick, *Who Runs Congress?* (Toronto: Bantam Books, 1972), pp. 143–65.
33. Richard J. Carlson, "Election Legislation," in *The Book of the States 1974–75* (Lexington, Ky., The Council of State Governments, 1974), pp. 28–29.
34. Alan V. Sokolow, "The State of the Judiciary," in *Book of the States 1974–1975*, pp. 116–17.
35. *Statistical Abstract 1974,* p. 382.
36. Marshall E. Blume, Jean Crockett, and Irwin Friend, "Stockownership in the United States: Characteristics and Trends," U.S. Department of Commerce, *Survey of Current Business,* November 1974, p. 17.

3 THE TWO-HUNDRED-YEAR LEGACY:
Constitutional development

Some men look at constitutions with sanctimonious reverence and deem them . . . too sacred to be touched. They ascribe to the men of the preceding age a wisdom more than human, and suppose what they did to be beyond amendment. . . . But I know also that laws and institutions must go hand in hand with the progress of the human mind. . . . Each generation . . . has (the) right to choose for itself the form of government it believes the most promotive of its own happiness.

Thomas Jefferson

In all but the most remote and simple societies, the winds of change batter against established institutions. Those without power struggle to wrench it away from those who control it. During America's bicentennial observance, we shall celebrate a change of this sort. We honor the daring revolutionaries who, two hundred years ago, seized power from the mighty English empire. They were the first people in modern times to succeed in such an undertaking. This chapter will describe how that transfer of power was accomplished, and how Americans allocated the power among themselves once they got it.

EARLY INFLUENCES

Our roots are sunk deep in the past. American government had already gone through three clear stages of development before the adoption of our present

Constitution. They were the colonial, the Revolutionary, and the Confederation periods. Each of these periods contributed significantly to the character of our current political system.

Colonial Development

In spite of Spanish, Dutch, French, and American Indian influences, our early history is essentially a child of English imperial expansion. From the establishment of Jamestown, Virginia in 1607 to the founding of Savannah, Georgia in 1733, England created the thirteen colonies and proceeded to rule them for more than a century and a half. During that time certain English traditions became so entrenched that they persist, in one form or another, up to the present time.

Common Law

One of these is the English common law tradition that now prevails in all American states except Louisiana, which still reflects its French origins. The common law was developed before the birth of legislative bodies by judges who traveled from place to place settling disputes in a common, or uniform, manner. The judges employed a combination of old Roman legal ideas, Catholic doctrines, prevailing customs, and their own ethical values. Strong reliance was placed upon *precedents,* or previous decisions in similar cases, to give the law consistency and continuity.

The common law also established rules of court *procedure* that we still consider essential to a fair trial. For example, it insisted that the burden of proof in criminal cases be placed upon the prosecution. It stated that defendants have such rights as trial by jury and access to legal counsel. It also determined certain *substantive* grounds of injury, such as contract violations or property damage, which enabled one person to sue another to gain compensation for losses.

Governmental Institutions

The colonial period laid the foundations for many later institutions. The separation of legislative and executive officials into distinct branches of government was one important idea which we used in our constitutional system. The establishment of bicameral (two-house) legislatures was another. And the creation of towns, counties, and other units of local rule was copied largely from English patterns.

Representative Government

At the time of the Revolution, eight of the thirteen colonies were royal ones. Their governors, and often members of the upper houses of their legislatures were chosen—directly or indirectly—by the English king. But the crown permitted members of the lower houses to be chosen by the voters. Thus, although property requirements limited voting rights to the upper class, part of the government even in royal colonies was representative of at least some of the people. The other types of colonies had even more elected representation.

The effects of this system were highly significant. First, in the elected lower houses native Americans such as Thomas Jefferson and James Madison gained the political experience and leadership training that they would later need. The lack of this kind of training ground in former Dutch, French, and Spanish colonies may help to explain the difficulty of establishing stable governments in those areas. Second, the election of some legislators gradually created a desire for the election of more government officials. Not only legislators, but also executive leaders and some judges were eventually to be elected by a broadening base of voters.

State Loyalty

Because the thirteen states existed first, people gave their loyalty to them and only later, grudgingly, did they transfer it to the nation as a whole. When English colonial policy became harsh in the 1760s and 1770s, Americans grew to hate national authority and to feel that decentralized government was best. Such attitudes help account for the extreme weakness of the central government under the Articles of Confederation, and the later compromise between state and national power in the Constitution.

Indeed, continuing devotion to decentralized rule is far from dead in the U.S. today. This can be seen when we speak (misleadingly but lovingly) of "states' rights." But we refer (far more fearfully) to "national power." It can also be seen in the number of votes given to recent candidates who emphasize states' rights such as Barry Goldwater in 1964 and George Wallace in 1968 and 1972.

To be sure, national patriotism now supersedes state loyalty in the hearts of most Americans. Some hope that the next step will extend our loyalty to embrace the entire human race. Yet, our global involvement since World War II has produced a reaction which looks inward to unsolved problems at the state and especially at the community levels. In fact, even many liberals and radicals who once believed that the national government had the final responsibility for solving nearly every problem are now beginning to change their tune. Thus, we may have made a complete circle, returning to the distrust of central power that was an inheritance from British rule.

The Revolutionary Heritage

Although the American Revolution spanned only six years, its principles have influenced not only our own government but also that of many other emerging nations ever since.

Independence

It has been two centuries since Thomas Jefferson wrote that "these United

Colonies are, and of Right ought to be Free and Independent States." Yet the freedom from foreign control proclaimed in our Declaration of Independence remains pertinent today. Indeed, the American revolutionary experience has much in common with the colonial struggles that have swept across Africa and Asia since World War II. The foundation for these struggles was often laid by underground conspiracies such as our Committees of Correspondence. These committees were set up by Samuel Adams to coordinate protest efforts and organize self-government in the various colonies. Like our own, most later revolutions also had their share of fiery propaganda similar to Thomas Paine's *Common Sense*. This pamphlet, written in 1776, did much to convince our colonists that revolution was justified. Even guerrilla warfare was pioneered by such men as Nathaniel Green and George Washington who learned it the hard way from the Indians. It has been copied by rebel forces ever since. Finally, in many other lands as in America, the struggle was basically one of colonial farmers fighting for their independence from more industrialized European nations.

Not only did the American colonies serve as a model of revolutionary techniques, but our government also later encouraged foreign independence movements. In the 1820s, when Latin Americans sought to free themselves from Spanish rule, the United States gave support through the Monroe Doctrine which warned against European intervention there. Nearly a century later, President Woodrow Wilson proclaimed the right of national self-determination as one of our aims in World War I.

In recent years, however, American dedication to the cause of independence has been undermined. This is largely the result of our far-ranging commercial investments, our alliances with colonial powers, and our fears that "wars of national liberation" are actually tools of communist imperialism. Our embarrassment was heightened in 1946 when Ho Chi Minh quoted from Thomas Jefferson in proclaiming the independence of Vietnam from French rule. Our dilemma was that Ho happened to be a Communist.

Was It a Revolution?
In the old struggle between the forces of stability and the forces of change, there is no doubt that the war for American independence was a victory for the latter. It replaced the authority of the king and Parliament with a devotion to home-grown governments which sprang from native soil. It transferred power over more than three million Americans from one side of the Atlantic to the other. It was a triumph of treason which created our own radical political tradition that continues to be deeply disturbing to today's conservatives.

But was it really a revolution? That word conjures up many different visions and is defined in many different ways. The war was begun for the limited purpose of forcing the English to repeal certain laws that the colonists didn't like. Although these included restrictions on freedom of assembly in Massachusetts, they had to do primarily with economic matters such as trade and manufacturing restrictions and taxes.[1] At the beginning, most colonists only wanted to assert their rights as Englishmen to participate in decisions on these matters. Many of the revolutionary leaders were actually wealthy, conservative businessmen and farmers. They were members of the upper class who did not want to destroy the status quo or overturn the system. Rather they probably wanted to improve it both in order to protect their own economic position and to better that of the rest of society.

It is for such reasons that some writers argue, with considerable merit, that the events of the 1770s were not a true revolution. They did not, these writers say, significantly alter the existing power relationships among social classes in America. We were already a basically middle-class country,[2] but most of our leaders, both before and after the Revolution, were members of the elite. It took several more decades, probably until the time of Jackson, for the people to really acquire and know how to use political power.

Yet in many ways we did have a revolution, although against an external, not internal, enemy. Several major characteristics of revolutions were present here—violence, the creation of new political institutions, speed of change. In the long run, perhaps, the most revolutionary aspect was the relationship between the people and their government set forth in the Declaration of Independence. "Governments are instituted among men," that document states, to safeguard the rights of the people to "Life, Liberty and the pursuit of Happiness." They derive "their just powers," it goes on, "from the consent of the governed." Most important of all, if a government no longer serves the purposes for which it was instituted, "it is the Right of the People to alter or to abolish it. . . ." Quite literally, those were fighting words. They still are, for they embody a vision of society in which the people's power over the government is superior to the government's power over the people.

New American Governments

As independence became the major objective of the Revolution, its success required that new state and national governments be set up. During the Revolutionary War, most colonies drafted new constitutions as independent states. These first state constitutions reacted strongly against the excessive power of the old royal governors. Thus, they created strong state legislatures and weakened the authority of the new state governors, especially with respect to money matters and appointment powers. As a result, the governors of many states today still have too little authority to meet their responsibilities effectively.

At the national level we needed to create new governmental machinery, too. But again people were reluctant to surrender any of their newly won state power to a strong central government. The Second Continental Congress, consisting of delegates representing the various states, directed the war effort, but lacked a secure legal status. Hence a committee was appointed to draft a formal constitution. This, the Articles of Confederation, was approved by all thirteen state legislatures and went into effect in 1781.

The Articles of Confederation

As we saw, the British Empire was a unitary system of government in which the colonies had only as much authority as the central government chose to give to them. In overreacting to what they considered a tyrannical system, the American colonists created a Confederation in which the territorial distribution of authority was exactly the opposite. That is, the central government was limited to only that authority given to it by the thirteen states.

The New Government

Nevertheless, under the Articles the national government was delegated some important responsibilities. It could establish a postal system, make treaties, maintain a navy, and govern all territories outside the jurisdiction of the various states. In its eight-year existence, however, the powers that the national government lacked were more significant than those which it possessed. Since it could neither tax nor enlist troops into the army, it was dependent upon the states for both money and manpower, the two prime power resources of any political system. Moreover, it could not prevent the states from coining money or from setting up their own tariffs and trade barriers. Thus, financial chaos among the states resulted.

The structure of the national government under the Articles consisted of a one-house, or *unicameral,* legislature in which each state had one vote regardless of its population. The Confederation possessed no independent executive branch and no court system. In addition, any amendment that might strengthen it required the unanimous approval of all thirteen state legislatures. Predictably, the Articles were never amended.

Failure of the Confederation

The Confederation had the misfortune of being born during a war that caused both the state governments and the Congress to incur heavy debts. The poor farmers, forced to foot the tax bill, were already hard pressed to make their mortgage payments. They staged bitter and sometimes violent demonstrations. In 1786 the militia was called out in New Hampshire to counter angry demands for the printing of more paper currency. In Massachusetts it was called out to suppress Shays' Rebellion, an uprising designed to prevent the courts from ordering farm foreclosures.

There were other problems too. The Confederation's Congress could not guarantee American territory against British and Spanish claims. Moreover, it was unable to get the states to make the contributions needed to pay the troops and the holders of government bonds. It was also difficult to find foreign markets to replace those temporarily lost in England, and state-imposed trade barriers reduced the volume of goods sold within the country. Finally, there was a fear among bankers, land speculators, and other creditors that many states would follow the example of Rhode Island. That state had adopted an inflationary currency policy to enable the poor to repay their debts in money worth less than that which they initially borrowed.

Confronted with the inability of the Confederation to cope with these crises, some politicians began to think about creating a stronger national government. Having won a revolution against a central government we thought was too powerful, we created one under the Articles which failed because it was too weak. The chief importance of this first national constitution was in the mistakes it taught us to avoid when we tried again.

THE CONSTITUTION

[When the Constitution was written,] there was a holy Roman emperor, Venice was a republic, France was ruled by a king, Russia by a czar and Great Britain had only the barest beginnings of a democracy.

All these proud regimes and scores of others have long since passed into history and among the world's powers the only government that stands essentially unchanged is the federal union put together in the 1780s . . .

John Gardner

In May 1787, fifty-five delegates came together in Philadelphia for the purpose of improving the Articles of Confederation. Most of them quickly agreed, however, to start from scratch in drafting a new document. They knew it would be impossible to get the unanimous state approval required to amend the Articles. And they were further encouraged by a decision to bar the press and public from their convention.[3] The result of their work was the Constitution of the United States.

The Constitutional Convention

The Delegates
The men who wrote our Constitution left the imprint of their minds, personalities, and interests upon it. As a group, they had certain characteristics which seem highly significant: (1) Their average age was only forty-two. The delegates' youth may have contributed to their willingness to try new methods and to expand national power. (2) They were a very well-educated group, with practical backgrounds in numerous areas of public life. Many had served in diplomatic and military posts, seven as state governors, and thirty-nine in Congress. In short, they were seasoned politicians, adept in the skills of compromise and tactical maneuver.[4] (3) The delegates represented a relatively wealthy professional and commercial elite. Although small independent farmers made up a huge majority of the population, they found themselves almost unrepresented in the convention. (4) Conservatism is often defined to include a distrust of the masses of people, and by this standard the delegates were largely conservative. Elbridge Gerry, more liberal than most, asserted that the "evils we experience flow from the excess of

democracy." Edmund Randolph of Virginia argued that "our chief danger arises from the democratic parts of our (state) constitutions."[5]

George Washington was the presiding officer of the convention and many men made valuable contributions to its work. But it was James Madison, an obscure young Virginia state legislator, who is commonly regarded as the "Father of the Constitution." Probably the most scholarly of the delegates, Madison proposed the basic framework of the government, kept the most complete notes on the convention proceedings, and wrote many of the superb *Federalist Papers* urging that the Constitution be ratified.

The Agreements

With relative ease the delegates agreed that the power of the national government would be enlarged to include the authority to tax, raise an army, regulate interstate and foreign commerce, regulate the value of currency, and control navigable rivers. The result, of course, was to diminish the relative power of the states.

This shift of authority required a more elaborate structure for the national government. To guard against despotism, a separation of powers among three distinct branches was established. It was decided that the legislative branch should be bicameral, and that an independent chief executive and national court system should be created. But there were still important controversies to be resolved.

The Disputes

Quite early, the Virginia delegation introduced a draft constitution which provided that representation in both houses of the bicameral legislature be based on population. The small states feared that if they were outvoted in the legislative branch they would be helpless victims of large-state tyranny. Thus, from New Jersey came an alternative proposal for a unicameral Congress with one vote for each state. The deadlock between the proponents of the Virginia Plan and those of the New Jersey Plan was finally broken by the acceptance of Benjamin Franklin's compromise as presented by the Connecticut delegation. Known as the Great or the Connecticut Compromise, it provided for a bicameral Congress, giving each state two votes in the upper house or Senate, while apportioning seats in the lower chamber, or House of Representatives, on a population basis.

This solution, however, produced another major dispute concerning taxes which were also to be levied according to population. But the South did not want slaves fully counted in determining its tax burdens, while the North did not want slaves fully counted in determining the number of representatives southern states would have. Eventually a compromise emerged by which each slave was counted as three-fifths of a person for both purposes. This, of course, was changed by the fourteenth Amendment.

Still another controversy concerning the manner of electing the chief executive resulted in the electoral college, one of the strangest political devices ever invented. This device, which we shall discuss fully in Chapter 11, prevented the distrusted masses from directly electing their president. Instead, he was to be chosen by a group of special electors appointed as each state saw fit. The number of electors from each state would be equal to the total of that state's senators and representatives in Congress. Although it has been modified by Amendment 12 and by the rise of political parties, the electoral college is still a subject of great controversy today.

The final problem confronting the delegates was perhaps the most difficult: they has written a new constitution for a country which already had one. It was obvious to them that there was no hope of gaining approval from all the states, as required for amendments to the existing Articles. Rhode Island had not even sent anyone to the convention. The delegates felt that other state legislatures would also oppose the Constitution since it would transfer substantial power from them to the new national government. Their solution was as daring (and illegal) as the problem was difficult. They decided to ignore the Articles and have the new Constitution take effect when approved by specially elected ratifying conventions in nine of the thirteen states. Opponents of the Constitution later claimed that as a result of this decision they had been framed by "the framers" at Philadelphia.

Ratification

The ratification process was not an easy one. Those opposing the Constitution consisted mostly of small farmers who were untroubled by state trade barriers and delighted with inflated state currencies that aided in the payment of their debts. These opponents or anti-Federalists leveled four main attacks upon the Constitution: (1) It was a tool of wealthy interests to be used against the small farmers. (2) It created a danger of tyranny by transferring too much power from the states to the national government. (3) It contained no Bill of Rights to protect the individual citizens. (4) It was an illegal document since the Constitutional Convention was called only to amend the Articles.

The supporters of the Constitution responded in a series of eighty-five essays appearing first in New York newspapers and later in book form. Written by Alexander Hamilton, James Madison, and John Jay, *The Federalist* (or *The Federalist Papers*) evaluated the weaknesses of the Articles and argued very persuasively for a strong national government as created by the proposed Constitution. Not only did this work win support for ratification, but it is today considered one of America's finest contributions to the literature of political theory.

Another and possibly crucial factor in getting the Constitution approved was that its supporters agreed that a Bill of Rights was needed. They pledged to add one by amending the Constitution once it had been ratified.

The "Wonderful Work": Seven Pillars of Wisdom

The American Constitution is the most wonderful work ever struck off at a given time by the brain and purpose of man.

William E. Gladstone

The Constitution of the United States established a basic organization of government which had never before been tried anywhere. The framers in Philadelphia wrote a document consisting of only a preamble and seven articles. It was brief, essential, and flexible. This Constitution has endured for nearly two centuries, longer than any other in recorded history. More significantly, it has proved responsive to the needs of whatever group has gained control of the government. In the 1790s, for example, wealthy commercial interests got the new government to tax the farmers in order to create a National Bank which then loaned money to manufacturers. Yet, in the nineteenth century that same government, yielding to farm pressures, built canals and gave away land to encourage agricultural expansion. In this century, industrial labor was able to extract from the government minimum wage laws and social security benefits. Like the delicate machinery in a fine car, the political system created by the Constitution has responded to the desires of the driver, proceeding at varying speeds and only occasionally changing directions.

Constitutional Amendments

If a constitution can be altered too easily, its authority as the basic law is diminished and it cannot provide needed stability and continuity. If, on the other hand, it is too difficult to amend, its own rigidity may doom it to an early death. The authors of our Constitution provided four different amendment methods in Article V. One of these, passage by a two-thirds vote in the Senate and House of Representatives followed by ratification by three-quarters of the state legislatures, has been used for all amendments but the Twenty-first. Altogether the document written in 1787 has been changed only sixteen times since the first ten amendments providing the Bill of Rights were added in 1791. Nothing speaks more eloquently of the work of the framers. The subject matter of each of the original articles and of the amendments is shown in Figures 3–1 and 3–2.

The Unwritten and the Living Constitution

If one interprets a constitution to include all that determines the basic structure of government (as the British do), then there is more to the United States Constitution than its short text. Under such a definition, our Constitution has other sources, some of which (again as in the English case) are unwritten.

First, there are certain national institutions and procedures that have become deeply entrenched through custom and tradition. These include the two-party system, pressure groups, the president's cabinet, and the congressional committee system for handling legislation. They are as important as many provisions of the Constitution itself, although they can probably be altered more easily by changing usage.

Second, certain actions by state governments have had such an effect upon national politics as to be of constitutional importance. The selection of presidential electors by the voters rather than by state legislatures, the abolition of property ownership as a voting requirement, and the nomination of congressional candidates by primary elections rather than by party conventions are all results of state action.

Third, various parts of the Constitution have been supplemented by acts (or statutes) of Congress. Article III gives Congress the authority to create lower courts and Article II allows it to create executive departments. The result has been a government bureaucracy of great complexity and power. To the bones of constitutional structure, statutory elaboration has attached awesome muscles. Some would argue that it has added considerable fat as well.

Fourth, presidential action has at times altered the emphasis of certain parts of the Constitution, and perhaps even distorted their intent. Thus, recent presidents have used their constitutional authority as commander-in-chief of the armed forces to render congressional power to declare war almost irrelevant.

Finally, the Supreme Court, as the final interpreter of the Constitution, has made many vital decisions. "The Constitution," former Chief Justice Charles E. Hughes once wrote, "is what the judges say it is."[6] Of course, the judges may—and do—reverse their own interpretations, thus creating a living, evolving constitution.

BASIC CONSTITUTIONAL PRINCIPLES

Although the U.S. Constitution is relatively short, it is not always easy to understand. Thus, it is helpful to isolate the basic constitutional principles and discuss them separately. The following four principles provide a key to understanding the American political system.

Federalism: The Middle Ground

The American system of federalism is perhaps our greatest political invention. It provides a middle ground between the extremes of confederation and unitary government by giving authority to both the national and the state levels. It forbids either from taking away the power of the other, yet it permits a wide arena for cooperation and joint action.

Figure 3–1. AN OUTLINE OF THE ORIGINAL CONSTITUTION

Preamble:	**Attributes Constitution to "We the People"**
	States purposes of Constitution
	Contains no enforceable provisions
Article I:	**Legislative Branch** (see Ch. 10)
	Bicameral Congress: Senate and House of Representatives
	Membership and methods of selection
	Legislative procedures
	Powers and limitations on powers
	Limitations on state governments
Article II:	**Executive Branch** (see Ch. 11)
	President and vice-president
	Selection by electoral college
	Conditions of service
	Powers
Article III:	**Judicial Branch** (see Ch. 12)
	Supreme Court and provision for lower courts
	Selection and service of judges
	Powers
	Trial by jury guaranteed
	Treason defined
Article IV:	**Intergovernmental Relations**
	Obligations of states to one another
	Admission of new states
	Obligations of national government to states
Article V:	**Amendment Procedures**
Article VI:	**Supremacy of Constitution and Miscellaneous**
	Basis for judicial review
	Assumption of prior debts
	Prohibition of religious qualifications for public office
Article VII:	**Procedure for Ratifying Constitution**

Figure 3–2. AN OUTLINE OF AMENDMENTS TO THE CONSTITUTION

Amendment	Subject	Year of Ratification
1[a]	Guarantees freedom of expression and of religion	1791
	Prohibits establishment of state religion	
2[b]	Protects states' power to maintain armed militias (national guard)	1791
3	Prohibits housing soldiers in private homes	1791
4[b]	Protects right to privacy from unreasonable searches and seizures	1791
5[b]	Limits criminal prosecution (grand jury)	1791
	Prohibits two trials for same crime (double jeopardy)	
	Prohibits forced confessions (self-incrimination)	
	Guarantees due process of law	
	Limits power to take private property (eminent domain)	
6[b]	Criminal trial procedures guaranteeing rights:	1791
	To a speedy and public trial	
	To an impartial jury	
	To cross-examine witnesses	
	To subpoena witnesses	
	To legal counsel	

7	Guarantees jury trial in civil cases	1791
8[b]	Prohibits excessive bail and fines	1791
	Prohibits cruel and unusual punishments	
9	Guarantees to the people rights not otherwise listed	1791
10	Protects powers reserved to the states	1791
11	Reduces judicial power of national courts, modifying Article III (adopted to counteract Supreme Court decision)	1798
12	Changes method of electing vice-president, modifying Article II	1804

After Amendment Twelve, more than sixty years elapsed before the three Civil War amendments were adopted, largely to protect black people against oppressive legislation passed by white-controlled state legislatures.

13	Prohibits slavery	1865
14[c]	Establishes citizenship by birth in U.S.	1868
	Guarantees due process of law against state interference, incorporating most of Bill of Rights as limitations upon state as well as national power	
	Prohibits denial by states of equal protection of the laws (adopted partially to counteract Supreme Court decision)	
15	Prohibits denial of right to vote because of race	1870

After another forty years, Amendments Sixteen through Nineteen were adopted within seven years. Although dissimilar in content, they were all products of the Progressive movement which early in this century urged reform in all levels of government.

16	Permits national income tax levied without regard to state population, modifying Article I (adopted to counteract Supreme Court decision)	1913
17	Requires U.S. senators be elected directly by voters, modifying Article I	1913
18	Prohibits manufacture, sale, or transportation of alcoholic beverages	1919
19	Prohibits denial of right to vote because of sex	1920
20	Reduces period of time between election and start of term for national officials	1933
21	Repeals Amendment Eighteen	1933
22	Limits president to two terms	1951
23	Gives Washington, D.C. electoral votes in presidential elections	1961
24	Prohibits denial of right to vote because of failure to pay poll taxes	1964
25	Establishes procedure to select vice-president to fill vacancy in that office	1967
	Establishes procedures for vice-president to become acting president in the event of presidential disability	
26	Prohibits denial of right to vote because of age to those eighteen or more	1971

[a]See Ch. 4
[b]See Ch. 5
[c]See Ch. 6

The Division of Powers

The authority of the national government stems largely from Article I, Section 8 of the Constitution. This section deals with the powers of Congress. But it involves the executive and judicial branches as well since they administer laws passed by Congress and apply them in individual cases. In the first seventeen paragraphs of Article I, Section 8 are the *enumerated powers* expressly given to Congress (also called *delegated* or *expressed* powers). The eighteenth paragraph grants broad authority to make laws "which shall be necessary and proper" to carry out the powers specifically listed. This final grant is often called the elastic clause because it expands the powers of Congress by allowing it to exercise *implied powers.*

The United States Supreme Court established the doctrine of implied powers in a decision written by our third and most influential Chief Justice, John Marshall. In the case of *McCulloch* v. *Maryland* in 1819 Marshall upheld the power of Congress to create a National Bank even though that was not one of the enumerated powers. This case became the precedent for the immense expansion of national power that has since taken place.

As a result of such expansion certain enumerated powers have had a much greater impact on our lives than others. The power to tax, for example, implies the power to spend. Hence, it justifies such programs as Medicare to pay hospital costs for the elderly, farm price supports, and subsidies to airlines and other private companies. Similarly, the power to regulate interstate commerce implies the authority to pass laws on racial discrimination in restaurants and hotels, on kidnapping, minimum hourly wages, and consumer protection.

Although the national government possesses this great range of implied and expressed powers, the Tenth Amendment states that all other powers, unless specifically prohibited elsewhere in the Constitution, "are reserved to the States respectively, or to the people." Traffic regulations, marriage and divorce requirements, public schools, building codes, gambling laws, the licensing of lawyers and doctors—all these are exercises of the *reserved powers* of the states. They may not be so dramatic as the federal government's powers, but they provide the day-to-day necessities of civilized life. It should be noted that some of these reserved state powers are actually exercised by local governments. But the latter have only those powers granted to them by the states because each state taken alone is in fact a unitary system.

Cooperative Federalism

As the national government has expanded its activities, it has intruded into matters of state jurisdiction. The result has been the growth of an area of *concurrent powers,* exercised jointly by national and state authorities. Thus, federalism has become a sharing as well as a division of power.

In recent years, federal aid has become an increasingly important area of joint cooperation. This form of assistance to state and local governments permits Congress to help finance activities in areas, such as education, where it actually has no other constitutional authority. Few expenditures in our history have risen so rapidly as federal aid. In 1965, it amounted to less than eleven billion dollars, but by 1974 it had quadrupled to an estimated forty-eight billion dollars. While such aid accounted for only 8.2 percent of state and local revenues in 1942, this more than doubled in the next thirty years, reaching 18.7 percent in 1972. In nine states, over 25 percent of their revenue came from this source. Quite significantly, five of these were among the ten poorest states in per capita personal income.[7]

It should be noted that there are usually two strings attached to federal financial assistance. One is that the state or local governments receiving it put up some minimum amount of matching funds to help finance the same projects. The other is that these projects meet certain nationally determined standards. In 1972, however, Congress passed a far-reaching program of revenue sharing that did away with these strings. The new grants of national tax money are given to state and local governments to be used largely as they wish. This revenue sharing has three broad purposes: First, it is an attempt to save local governments from bankruptcy. Second, it seeks to decentralize control over public funds by transferring certain spending decisions from the national government to the states, counties, and cities. Finally, it shifts some of the financial burden of state and local government services from local property tax sources to more equitable federal income tax sources.

Intergovernmental Relations: The Jealous Partners
The numerous relationships among several levels of government obviously require certain ground rules, some of which are found in Article IV of the Constitution. This article sets forth three obligations of the states to one another. As our society has become more mobile, the importance of these interstate obligations has increased greatly. They are: (1) The "full faith and credit" clause which requires each state to honor the contracts, deeds, marriages, wills, and court orders (including financial settlements) authorized by the legal processes of all other states. (2) The "privileges and immunities" clause which prohibits states from unjustly discriminating against citizens of other states. They may, however, charge students from other states higher college tuition fees on the grounds that they have not helped to pay the state taxes which largely finance these institutions. States may also require newly arrived professionals (such as doctors or lawyers) to satisfy their own standards in order to practice. (3) Each state should return escaped criminal suspects to the states from which they fled. This process of *rendition* or *extradition,* is generally voluntarily applied by state governors. However, the national courts have declared they are powerless to enforce it, since no constitutionally guaranteed individual rights are at stake.

Article IV also requires that the national government assume three obligations to the states. First, it must see to it that each state has "a republican form of government." The Supreme Court has held that whether or not a state has this form of government is a "political question" which must be determined by Congress or the president, not by the courts. The second obligation, protection of the states against invasion, has very fortunately never had to be tested.

By far the most important of the national responsibilities to the states has been the protection against domestic violence whenever states have asked for such assistance. Racial conflict on the streets of Detroit and Newark, for example, led President Johnson to send in army units at state request. Much more controversial, however, has been the presidential dispatch of troops against the wishes of state officials. President Cleveland sent troops into Chicago in 1894 to end a railroad strike and resume mail transportation. Similarly, President Eisenhower dispatched armed forces to Little Rock, Arkansas in 1957, and President Kennedy sent them to the University of Mississippi in 1963. Both men were trying to avert violence which threatened to block racial integration in the schools. On all three of these occasions, however, national action was justified not by Article IV dealing with intergovernmental relations but by Article II authorizing the president to see to it that laws (including federal court orders) "be faithfully executed."

Another important field where the federal government has a role in state affairs is the area of interstate agreements known as compacts. As Article I, Section 10 is interpreted, states may make such compacts only with the approval of Congress. Dozens of these are now in effect. Compacts involving oil conservation and convicts on probation or parole include most of the states. Other compacts deal with such matters as interstate boundaries, rivers or bridges, forest fire prevention, and cooperative use of state-supported medical and dental schools. The New York Port Authority, one of the biggest business enterprises in the world, was created by an interstate compact between New York and New Jersey.

Assessment

The federal division of power, like any compromise, has both assets and liabilities. Some of the assets are: (1) It permits unity on matters affecting the whole nation, such as foreign policy, while allowing diversity with respect to more personal matters such as gambling and liquor laws. (2) By dividing power between national and state officials it provides a barrier to possible dictatorship. (3) States may act independently as "social laboratories" in which new policies can be tested without damaging other states. (4) Policies can be more readily tailored to local conditions and interests. (5) State officials can gain experience which will prepare them to serve more effectively in the national government later. (6) It permits the election of a large number of public officials personally engaged in a kind of participatory democracy.

Offsetting these advantages of federalism are several liabilities: (1) It results in unequal opportunities since rich states can provide better schools, hospitals, and other services than poor states. (2) A division of power can mean mutual jealousy and sometimes bitter disputes over where national power ends and state power begins. (3) It often produces delay in the solution of problems by fostering "buck-passing" between national and state officials. (4) Differences among state laws in such fields as taxes and traffic regulations are often confusing or unfair to citizens who move across the country. (5) Fragmentation of authority makes it easier for powerful pressure groups concentrated in certain states to gain great influence. (6) State boundaries, the offspring of history, have rendered many states too small, and others too large, for maximum administrative efficiency.

Separation of Powers: Ambition Versus Ambition

Although the Founding Fathers intended to create a stronger national government, they had mixed feelings about it. In fact, they took a dim view of human nature and feared that more centralized power heightened the danger of its abuse. Their solution was to increase the authority of the national government but at the same time to separate it among three groups of officials—legislative, executive, and judicial. Each of these groups was given the means to check and balance the power of the other two. "Ambition," in Madison's words, was "made to counteract ambition."[8] All fifty state governments are structured in much the same way.

The Three Branches

The separation of powers provided in Articles I, II, and III of the Constitution applies to both personnel and function. In terms of personnel, no one (with the exception of the vice-president) can serve in more than one branch at a time. In terms of function, each branch is given control in its own area: Congress passes the laws; the president and the executive branch administer them; the courts interpret them in individual cases. This idea was borrowed from Montesquieu, a French theorist who had urged the separation of powers to give each group of officials enough independent authority to limit the power of the other two.

Checks and Balances

American constitutional theory assumes the three branches to be equal in authority. To assure this in practice, the framers, as we said, gave each one certain checks with which to balance the power of the other two. This modifies the separation of powers principle substantially, since it means that each branch shares some of the functions of the other two. Considerable cooperation among the branches is required, therefore, if the government is to function effectively. The Senate, for example, must approve presidential appointments and treaties. The president may veto acts of Congress. And the courts may declare actions of the other two branches unconstitutional.

Judicial Review

Perhaps the most controversial and unique of the interbranch checks is this last one, known as the power of judicial review. The Constitution does not give the courts this authority, and there is some disagreement over whether most of the framers intended them to have it. Hamilton, however, in No. 78 of *The Federalist,* supported judicial review and others agreed. The issue was of no practical importance until 1803 when, in *Marbury* v. *Madison,* the Supreme Court delcared a congressional law unconstitutional for the first time. The Court's opinion, written by Chief Justice Marshall, relied largely on the "supremacy" clause of Article VI to justify its decision. That article states that "This constitution, and the laws . . . which shall be made in pursuance thereof . . . shall be the supreme law of the land . . . ." Marshall asserted quite simply that the law in question came in conflict with the Constitution and was hence invalid. There were those who contended passionately that it was unconstitutional to declare a law unconstitutional, but they cried out in vain.

As the Court's prestige increased, the precedent established in *Marbury* v. *Madison* became more deeply entrenched. Judicial review has now been used to invalidate more than one hundred national and about eight hundred state laws. It has also been applied to dozens of executive acts by officials ranging from rookie policemen to the president of the United States. Judicial review has made American courts the most powerful in the world. Indeed, some people feel that it makes the judicial branch superior to the other two. Others feel that it is undemocratic because it allows nine appointed judges to invalidate the acts of all our elected representatives.

Assessment

The separation of powers possesses several merits. First, like federalism, it helps prevent the concentration of too much power in the hands of too few people. After the administration of Franklin D. Roosevelt, and especially during the Johnson and Nixon years, there were fears that the power of the president had become too great for the judicial and legislative branches to control. The Nixon resignation, however, quieted such fears. Coming on the heels of a Supreme Court decision requiring Nixon to release White House tapes and a congressional impeachment hearing, it demonstrated the continued vitality of the separation of powers. Another merit of this system is that it helps balance the sometimes conflicting claims of majority rule and minority rights. It does so by permitting periodic elections of the two "political" branches as well as lifetime tenure, free from majority pressure, for the judicial branch.

There are, however, certain liabilities resulting from the separation of powers. First, governmental delay and even deadlock may result when the branches are controlled by opposing political parties. In 1976, this had been the case for 13 of the last 25 years. Second, responsibility is so dispersed that the people may wonder who is to blame for what. Too often, the president and Congress point fingers of blame at one another for failure to deal promptly with such problems as unemployment and the energy shortage.

Both federalism and separation of powers relate to government structure. Both fragment government authority, the first territorially and the second functionally. The other two constitutional principles to be examined, freedom and democracy, involve not the structure of government but its relationship with the people whom it governs.

Freedom: The People's Rights

If there is any principle of the Constitution that more imperatively calls for attachment than any other it is the principle of free thought — not free thought for those who agree with us but freedom for the thought that we hate.

Justice Oliver Wendell Holmes

Freedom of speech, press, and assembly as well as freedom from unjust convictions and imprisonment were established by common law and the English Parliament long before American independence. Indeed, the Revolution was fought, and the new government was set up, partly to protect these freedoms. It is little wonder then that several provisions of the original Constitution along with Amendments One through Nine, Thirteen, and Fourteen entrench freedom as a major principle in American society.

Natural Rights
The idea that citizens have certain rights, for example the right to possess property and to express their opinions, goes back to ancient Greece and Rome. This idea was elaborated in 1689 by a famous English philosopher, John Locke, who wrote that mankind lived initially in a "state of nature" governed only by "natural law." Natural law, Locke argued, is self-evident, the product of universal and unchanging reason. Its most important principles are that all men are born free and that they are endowed with certain "natural rights" to life, liberty, and property. Man's freedom and his rights are inalienable; that is, they cannot be taken away. In order to protect these rights, especially when they involve property disputes, people formed a "social compact" or contract, which created government. And, according to Locke's most radical idea, if that government does not protect their natural rights, the people may revolt against it and form a new one which will. With only minor changes, this was the philosophy and the justification for revolution which Jefferson wrote into the Declaration of Independence.

Assessment
Governments play complex roles in relation to individual freedom. They may, as Locke hoped, protect freedom from the murderer, bully, or crook. Or they may themselves be the biggest bullies of all. Restrictions on government

power and the protection of liberty are actually two sides of the same coin. We should also remember that freedom can be jeopardized by both private and public power. In many ways, the pressures of social conformity and the demands of employers or families can seriously erode the freedom of individuals. But the power of the state to restrict freedom is even greater. The state can imprison or kill. Yet we cannot endorse unrestricted freedom. Each one of us must lower his voice occasionally so that another may be heard. In our increasingly complex society, this means that some degree of discipline and restraint is necessary. It is the price society demands for efficiency, fairness, and perhaps even for survival.

Democracy: The People's Power

Sometimes it is said that man cannot be trusted with the government of himself. Can he, then, be trusted with the government of others? Or have we found angels in the form of kings to govern him? Let his history answer this question.

Thomas Jefferson

In its modern context, the simplest definition of democracy is majority rule. As such, democracy makes two basic assumptions about mankind: (1) That most people are basically good and rational, and thus capable of knowing their own and society's best interests. (2) That a majority of them will vote to elect representatives who will serve these interests.

Both assumptions make democracy theoretically possible, but certain other procedural conditions are necessary for it to exist in practice. For example, in the early decades of American government suffrage (the right to vote) was restricted by property-ownership requirements in some states. Racial and sexual barriers to suffrage persisted much longer. Even those who could vote were permitted to elect few of the real decision-makers. The Constitution originally required that U.S. senators be selected by state legislatures, a practice which continued until the ratification of Amendment Seventeen in 1913. The president was elected by an electoral college which, in most states, was also chosen by state legislatures until the 1820s. Judges were, and still are, appointed. Thus, only the House of Representatives—one half of one of the three branches—was initially subject to direct popular control.

Now that most of these procedural obstacles have been swept away, can we conclude that democracy will permanently flourish? Not necessarily. Democracy is not a hardy, garden-variety perennial that one can plant and then forget. Instead, it is a rare species, so delicate that it withers quickly without rich supporting soil. In fact, democracy needs many different kinds of environmental supports.

Social Supports
A democratic society is one in which families, churches, organizations, and

schools embody at least some democratic principles. From these major social institutions, individual citizens learn their attitudes and values. If social institutions are controlled dictatorially or if they discourage respect for human dignity and for minorities, then prospects are dim for political democracy. The inability of Germany to maintain a democratic government prior to World War II, for example, has been attributed in part to attitudes developed in the traditionally authoritarian German family. Conversely, the growth of democracy in America has been associated to some degree with the fact that many early New England churches were democratically controlled by local congregations. Some form of participatory democracy in the home, classroom, and job bolsters the chance for successful democracy in city halls, state capitals, and in Washington, D.C.

Economic Supports

It was observed earlier that democracies seem to flourish best in fairly wealthy countries, where there is not a constant struggle for mere existence. Normally, people can't get the information they need to make intelligent political decisions unless they can read. And they can't read unless they live in a country rich enough to maintain free public schools. In modern times, of course, a wealthy educated nation is also a highly industrialized one. Industrialization produces a large middle class which appears to provide the stability necessary for democracy. If a nation consists mainly of the very rich and the very poor, there will be no moderating force to encourage the compromises on which democracy thrives.

Psychological Supports

There are a number of psychological factors which may help to explain the relationship between democratic attitudes and certain personality traits. Among the traits thought to be associated with democracy are self-esteem (a good feeling about oneself which enables one to believe that others are "good folks" too), an open ego (warm, trusting, and friendly), and a multivalued orientation rather than concern with a single interest (such as safety or wealth) for which one might sacrifice democratic procedures.

Cultural Supports

Crucial to the survival of democracy is a culture in which its basic values are widely shared. If a society is sharply divided about such fundamental principles as religious freedom, equality, or the protection of personal property, these issues may have to be settled by bullets rather than by ballots. In other words, democracy can tolerate disagreements on some issues only because there is agreement on the most basic ones.

The cultural value most central to democracy is the belief in the dignity and worth of the individual. As E. E. Schattschneider, one of America's most distinguished political scientists, wisely observed:

To put it very blunty, democracy is about the *love* of people . . . : *each is a human being, infinitely precious because he is human.* . . . The democratic concern for people is not selective; it is not reserved for good or admirable people only. Democracy is about all kinds of people—good, bad, wise, stupid, white, black, brown, yellow, ungrateful, disorderly, lazy, the worst as well as the best. . . . Democracy does not turn its back on anybody.[9]

Majority rule itself pays tribute to the importance of each individual. We want people to vote because that is the best way yet devised to guarantee that their interests will be served by the government. But the equal worth of each human being is not merely a convenient assumption for counting votes. It also commits us to equal opportunity and justice under the laws. Democracy, than, is more than a device to decide who will rule. It is dedicated to the individual not merely as a means, but an ultimate end.

Democracy and Freedom

Democracy cannot survive without a commitment to freedom. Therefore, majority rule should not (though it sometimes does) override minority rights. Unless the majority permits the minority freedom of expression, people may be deprived of both the knowledge and the choices necessary to make a wise decision on public policy. Without a choice, without alternative policies and personnel, the people have no way to keep the government accountable to their wishes. Moreover, as long as today's minority is free to become tomorrow's majority, it is likely to accept the verdict of the voters without resorting to violence.

Assessment

Even under the best conditions, democracy is not a simple system. Sometimes the freedom of the individual conflicts with the will of the majority. Sometimes it conflicts with the legal equality of all citizens. Each generation must meet these and other contradictions in some way.

In America, democracy must accommodate itself to federalism and to the separation of powers, both of which fragment power. Although this protects freedom by limiting power, it also requires a majority of the people to elect more representatives, perhaps, than they can intelligently evaluate. As a result, an alert press, competitive parties, and effective pressure groups must sometimes act on behalf of the public as watchdogs to help hold officials accountable for their performance.

But as we have seen, the social, economic, psychological, and cultural conditions of democracy indicate that it is not merely a political system: It is a state of mind, a pattern of relationships in our institutions, a luxury product of an affluent economy. The critics of democracy sometimes contend that it is so lofty and so broad an ideal that it can never be attained. To some, it is little more than propaganda used by a small group of elites to conceal their own political dominance. Others admit that democracy is feasible but undesirable: It works too slowly and produces mediocrity resulting from compromise.

The proponents of democracy counter these arguments on both theoretical and practical grounds. Theoretically, they assert that if democracy is visionary, at least it is a vision that summons the best and noblest of human hopes. Practically, they concede that democracy is an ideal that is realized only by degrees. But they point out that the most democratic societies are those that came out on top in both world wars, those that are most productive, and those that best fulfill the individual's need for recognition.

THE ROLE OF THE STATES

The American federal system requires vigorous governments in the 50 states as well as in Washington, D.C. Fortunately, such vigor seems to exist. It was reported, for example, that many states acted much more quickly than the national government in 1973 and 1974 in at least two major areas of public concern. To cope with the energy shortage, fifteen of them adopted gasoline rationing plans. To restrict the corrupting influence of money in politics, thirty enacted campaign finance laws.[10]

Since state budgets are growing more rapidly than the national one, such action is necessary if the public is to get its money's worth. Between 1950 and 1972, federal tax revenue increased by less than three and a half times, while state and local governments boosted their tax intake by nearly five times.[11] The Texas state government increased its spending by 532 percent in just 20 years.[12]

Thus, although the expanding activities of the national government were capturing most of the headlines, state governments were also greatly increasing their powers. The explanation for this lies in three facts crucial to an understanding of American federalism. The first is that the expansion of national power has not, for the most part, been at the expense of the states. It has occurred, instead, in such areas as social security programs and farm price supports in which no level of government had previously been active. Second, as noted earlier, the reserve powers clause in Amendment Ten permits the states to do anything which the Constitution does not prohibit. Thus, state powers have grown considerably in such newer areas as community colleges, expanded universities, the licensing of professions, and environmental protection. Finally, states create and control all the authority exercised by cities, counties, and other units of local government. It is at this level in such areas as land use, fire regulations, business licensing, and police protection that the citizen feels the impact of government most frequently.

State Constitutions

Just as the U.S. Constitution defines the structure of the national government, so also do the fifty state constitutions establish the organization of state government. In addition, they set limits upon the powers of local governments. The complexity of these tasks is indicated by the length of state constitutions. While it is true that many contain needless detail, it is striking that the constitution of Georgia has about 500,000 words, that of Okalahoma 63,000, and that of Texas 54,000.[13] By contrast, the U.S. Constitution contains only about 33,000 words.

The basic constitutional structure of state governments, with many modifications, is much like that of the national government. Each state government has a separation of powers among three branches. Each has a bill of rights limiting government power in the interests of individual freedom. Each provides for democratic election procedures. While Massachusetts has had but one constitution dating back to 1780, most states have adopted several during their history. Montana's second constitution took effect in 1973 and Louisiana's eleventh in 1975. Whereas the federal Constitution has been formally amended only 26 times, California's has grown by 392 amendments, South Carolina's by 417, Texas' by 343, and New York's by 249.[14] In all states, the legislatures may propose constitutional amendments, and in all but Delaware a vote of the people is required to ratify them.

Local Government in Metropolitan Life

It is in the great metropolitan areas that crime is most common, racial tension most dangerous, pollution most poisonous, and transportation most slow. In their struggle with some of the worst problems confronting the nation, local governments are often handicapped by three major burdens. One is a lack of funds, partly due to the movement of industry and major shopping centers away from the central cities and into the suburbs. As a result, where needs are often the greatest, property taxes produce the least funds. Second, many states have been unwilling to give their local governments the amount of authority or "home rule" which they need to function effectively. Finally, the tremendous number and overlapping jurisdictions of local government units in most metropolitan areas make a coordinated attack on various problems almost impossible. An area south of Seattle, for example, is ruled more or less by 36 local governments, and there are 78 separate cities in Los Angeles County alone. The extent of this problem is indicated by Figure 3–3.

There are two bright spots, however, in this otherwise gloomy picture. One is a renewed interest in urban problems as reflected in revenue sharing and other federal programs. The second is the movement toward local government consolidation as seen most dramatically in Miami, Nashville, and Indianapolis.

Figure 3–3. NUMBER OF GOVERNMENTS, 1972

Governments	
National	1
State	50
County	3,044
City	18,517
Township	16,991
School District	15,781
Special District	23,885

Source: U.S. Bureau of the Census, *Statistical Abstract of the United States: 1973*, p. 412.

POWER AND THE AMERICAN CONSTITUTIONAL SYSTEM

The American constitutional system is a variation on universal political themes. If we interpret these themes in terms of power, we can see some of the paradoxes presented by our historical development. The Revolution signified rebellion, change, and freedom — a challenge to authority. But the Constitution adopted thirteen years later symbolized stability, order, and authority itself. The protection of individual rights, federalism, and the separation of powers have limited power more than in almost any other country. Yet our national and state governments have continuously increased their power. However, political influence has also been more widely diffused among the people through the gradual extension of voting rights and direct elections. Thus, our two-hundred year legacy, like our Consitution, has been a gradual development of political checks and balances. Most importantly, the Constitution itself has provided the institutions and procedures which have at least checked and usually balanced the power of the officials controlling them.

Notes

1. There are many adequate histories which provide necessary background for the developments described thus far. See, for example, Carl N. Degler et al., *The Democratic Experience,* 3rd ed. (Glenview, Ill.: Scott, Foresman and Co., 1973), pp. 24–37.
2. Louis Hartz, "Democracy without a Democratic Revolution," *American Political Science Review* 46 (June 1952): 321–42.
3. In footnote 15 of his famous decision in the case of *U.S.* v. *Nixon* in 1974, Chief Justice Warren Burger noted that "without secrecy no constitution of the kind that was developed could have been written."
4. Stanley Elkins and Eric McKitrick, "The Founding Fathers: Young Men of the Revolution," *Political Science Quarterly* 76 (June 1961): 202–16; and John P. Roche, "The Founding Fathers: A Reform Caucus in Action," *American Political Science Review* 55 (December 1961): 799–816.
5. Quoted in J. Mark Jacobson, *The Development of American Political Thought: A Documentary History* (New York: D. Appleton-Century Co., 1932), pp. 41 and 43.
6. Quoted in Saul K. Padover, *The Living U.S. Constitution* (New York: Mentor Books, The New American Library, 1953), p. 58.
7. U.S. Bureau of the Census, *Statistical Abstract of the U.S.: 1974,* pp. 253 and 387.
8. *The Federalist* No. 51. Exact authorship is undetermined, and it is possible that it was written by Hamilton rather than Madison.
9. E. E. Schattschneider, *Two Hundred Million Americans in Search of a Government* (New York: Holt, Rinehart and Winston, 1969), pp. 43, 45–46.
10. *Los Angeles Times,* March 14, 1975, p. 4.
11. *Statistical Abstract 1974,* p. 245.
12. *Los Angeles Times,* June 30, 1974, Part IV, p. 3.
13. *The Book of the States 1974–1975* (Lexington, Ky.: The Council of State Governments, 1974), p. 23.
14. Ibid.

Bibliography

CHAPTER ONE **THE NATURE OF POLITICS**

Dahl, Robert A. *Modern Political Analysis.* 2nd ed. Englewood Cliffs. N.J.: Prentice-Hall, 1970.

Easton, David. *The Political System: An Inquiry into the State of Political Science.* New York: Alfred A. Knopf, 1953.

Ebenstein, William. *Today's Isms.* 6th ed. Englewood Cliffs, N.J.: Prentice-Hall, 1970.

Eulau, Heinz. *The Behavioral Persuasion in Politics.* New York: Random House, 1963.

Joseph, Joan, ed. *Political Corruption.* New York: Pocket Books, 1974.

Lasswell, Harold D. and Abraham Kaplan. *Power and Society.* New Haven, Conn.: Yale University Press, 1950.

Murphy, Robert E. *The Style and Study of Political Science.* Glenview, Ill.: Scott, Foresman and Co., 1970.

Ranney, Austin. *The Governing of Men.* 3rd ed. New York: Holt, Rinehart & Winston, 1971.

CHAPTER TWO **THE NATURE OF AMERICA**

De Tocqueville, Alexis. *Democracy in America.* Translated by Phillip Bradley. New York: Alfred A. Knopf, 1945.

Free, Lloyd A. and Cantril, Hadley. *The Political Beliefs of Americans.* New York: Clarion Books, Simon & Schuster, 1968.

Hofstadter, Richard. *The American Political Tradition.* New York: Alfred A. Knopf, 1959.

Lipset, Seymour M. *Political Man.* Garden City, N.Y.: Anchor Books, Doubleday & Co., 1963.

Myers, Henry A. *Are Men Equal?* Ithaca. N.Y.: Cornell University Press, 1945.

Potter, David M. *People of Plenty.* Chicago: University of Chicago Press, 1954.

Smith, Adam. *The Wealth of Nations.* New York: Everyman's Library, E. P. Dutton & Co., 1957.

Steinfield, Melvin, ed. *Cracks in the Melting Pot.* 2nd ed. Beverly Hills, Calif.: Glencoe Press, 1973.

U.S. Bureau of the Census. *Statistical Abstract of the United States.* Published annually. Washington, D.C.: U.S. Government Printing Office.

CHAPTER THREE **THE TWO-HUNDRED-YEAR LEGACY**

Beard, Charles A. *An Economic Interpretation of the Constitution of the United States.* New York: Macmillan Co., 1913.

Brown, Robert E. *Charles Beard and the Constitution.* Princeton, N.J.: Princeton University Press, 1956.

Corwin, Edward S. and Peltason, Jack W. *Understanding the Constitution.* Rev. ed. New York: Dryden Press, 1958.

Farrand, Max. *The Framing of the Constitution of the United States.* New Haven, Conn.: Yale University Press, 1913.

Grodzins, Morton. *The Federal System.* Englewood Cliffs, N.J.: Prentice-Hall, 1960.

Hamilton, Alexander, et al. *The Federalist.* New York: Everyman's Library, E. P. Dutton & Co., 1929.

Kammen, Michael G., ed. *Politics and Society in Colonial America.* New York: Holt, Rinehart & Winston, 1967.

Roche, John P., ed. *Origins of American Political Thought.* New York: Torchbooks, Harper & Row, 1967.

PART TWO

THE PEOPLE'S RIGHTS

My definition of a free society is a society in which it is safe to be unpopular.
Adlai E. Stevenson

The activities known as "Watergate" have dramatized the necessity for protecting the rights of the people against the power of the government. Two hundred years after a Revolution freed us from the tyranny of British rulers, American rulers were forced out of office for their own tyrannical behavior.

Those who wrote the Constitution recognized such a danger. They knew that a government powerful enough to serve the people effectively was also powerful enough to take away their rights. As a result, the Constitution protects freedom of expression (discussed in Chapter 4), assures suspected criminals of a fair trial (Chapter 5), and requires legally equal treatment of all persons (Chapter 6).

These protections of the people are often divided into two broad categories: substantive rights and procedural rights. Substantive rights are those such as religious freedom which cannot be taken away by law. Procedural rights are those such as protection from telephone wiretapping which limit the means used to enforce the law. A law prohibiting all brothers from talking to one another, for example, would be a bad law substantively, no matter how fairly it might be enforced procedurally. Similarly, a good law prohibiting drunken driving would be procedurally intolerable if the home of every licensed driver were searched each night for alcoholic beverages. Moreover, substantive rights limit legislative bodies while procedural rights limit the power of executive and judicial officials. Although the Supreme Court once seemed to give preference to certain substantive rights, it now makes little distinction as to the importance of these two types of constitutional protections.

4 Freedom of Expression:
First things first

Those who won our independence by revolution . . . believed that freedom to think as you will and to speak as you think are means indispensable to the discovery and spread of political truth; that the greatest menace to freedom is an inert people; that public discussion is a public duty. . . .

Louis D. Brandeis

It is no coincidence that the First Amendment to the Constitution protects the freedoms essential to democracy: religion, speech, press, assembly, and petition. These are the very lifeblood of a free society, and the authors of the Bill of Rights were simply putting first things first.

Most of these specific freedoms are dependent upon one another. Freedom of religion, for example, entails the freedom to assemble in church congregations. Freedom of speech without freedom of assembly is nothing but the right to talk to oneself. And freedom of the press is often necessary to petition the government effectively (meaning to protest or request official action). Such close relationships enable us to refer to all five of these rights as freedom of expression. Clearly a democracy requires this freedom in order for citizens to form their own opinions and to make a choice among opposing candidates and policies.

Nevertheless, in guaranteeing the five freedoms of expression, our government has consistently held that they are not limitless. Such a position raises a number of crucial questions. Who is to decide what limits on freedom are permitted? For what purposes may these limits be imposed? What standards or rules should be used to determine the nature of the limits?

There is so much controversy surrounding these questions that only the first can be answered with much certainty. It is the courts that decide what limits can be placed on constitutionally guaranteed freedoms. But in making such decisions, even the wisest of judges disagree. Their disagreement is a fundamental one. It involves a basic political conflict that can be phrased in many ways: liberty versus order; individual freedom versus majority rule; personal or minority rights versus the safety of society or the state. "Liberal" judges, such as those who dominated the Supreme Court under Chief Justice Earl Warren (1953–1969), tend to stress liberty by expanding the area of First Amendment freedoms. "Conservative" jurists, usually in a majority on the Court before 1954 and after Nixon's appointment of four new justices between 1968 and 1972, tend to restrict it.[1]

When choices must be made between liberty and order, i.e., between enlarging and restricting the freedoms protected by the Constitution, these choices will inevitably be affected by the power resources arrayed against each other. On the side of liberty is the authority of the words in the First Amendment and the principles for which we have fought in several wars. On the side of order, quite often, is the influence of public opinion, fearful of unpopular ideas, as well as the police, prosecutors, and other agents of government force. It is no surprise that judges, regardless of their theoretical commitment to freedom, frequently bend to the superior power enlisted in defense of order. Nevertheless, over the years the Court has been able to maintain a reasonable balance, as we shall soon see.

THE SEPARATION OF RELIGION AND POLITICS

It does me no injury for my neighbor to say there are twenty gods, or no God. It neither picks my pocket nor breaks my leg.

Thomas Jefferson

Religion has touched nearly every part of American life. It has influenced our literature, music, art, and recreational activities. Among twelve leading nations, a 1968 Gallup poll showed that the U.S. ranked highest in belief in God (98 percent of Americans) and in life after death (48 percent).[2] For more than a decade, over 40 percent of Americans have attended a religious service each week.[3] Even without an established church such as is found in many other countries, the United States may be one of the most religious nations in the world.

Freedom from Religion:
The "Establishment" Clause

In view of its pervasive influence in other areas, it is not surprising that religion has also had a strong impact upon American politics. Thirty-seven states still have "blue laws" which require the closing of businesses on Sunday.[4] The armed forces employ thousands of chaplains. Legislative bodies throughout the nation begin each day's session with a prayer. Even our official currency affirms that "In God We Trust."

But all of these examples may be carry-overs from the past. It is more difficult to assess the likely future of religion as a factor in American politics. The election of John F. Kennedy in 1960 as our first Catholic president may have signaled either an increase in tolerance or a decrease in the importance of religious matters to voters. Such a decrease may be inferred from the fact that church attendance has dropped by 9 percent since 1958 and by 20 percent among adults under twenty-nine years of age. On the other hand, political issues continue to surface, such as abortion or aid to Israel, which have unmistakable religious overtones.

The Secular State

Yet American government is commanded by the Constitution to remain neutral on religious issues. It appears that the framers of the Constitution wished to create a political system which was essentially secular or nonreligious in nature. In the first place, the Constitution makes no mention of a Supreme Being. Secondly, Article VI clearly stipulates that "no religious Test shall ever be required as Qualification to any Office or public Trust under the United States." Finally, the First Amendment opens with the words "Congress shall make no law respecting an establishment of religion. . . ."

The phrasing of this "establishment" clause is significant. It does more than simply prohibit an established church—an officially favored one receiving tax support. It goes further to ban legal aid for religion in general, thus separating church from state. There are two major reasons for this. Most important is that European history was marred by many tragic wars fought over what help governments were to give in support of religious principles.

Figure 4-1. AMERICAN RELIGIOUS PREFERENCES[1]

Denomination	Percentage of Population	Denomination	Percentage of Population
Protestant	66.2	Roman Catholic	25.7
Baptist	19.7	Jewish	3.2[2]
Methodist	14.0	Other religions	1.3
Lutheran	7.1	No religion	2.7
Presbyterian	5.6	Not reported	0.9
Others	19.8		

[1]Based upon 1957 responses to the only government census of religious preference.
[2]About 40 percent of all American Jews live in New York City where they constitute about one fourth of the population.
Source: "American Religious Preferences" from *This U.S.A.* by Ben J. Wattenberg with Richard M. Scammon. Copyright © 1965 by Ben J. Wattenberg. Reprinted by permission of Doubleday & Company, Inc. and A. D. Peters & Co.

Our Founding Fathers wished to avoid such "holy wars." A second reason for separation of church and state was the dislike that some of our early leaders felt toward organized churches of the day. "In every country and in every age," Jefferson once wrote, "the priest has been hostile to liberty."[5]

In addition to the constitutional restrictions, religious influence in America is partly neutralized by the wide diversity of beliefs. The expression of almost any religious sentiment is bound to antagonize many people holding contrary views. Candidates for public office should remember that more than sixty separate religious denominations in the U.S. have memberships in excess of 50,000 people.

Confusion on the Court

The Supreme Court of the United States, as final arbiter of what government can and cannot do, has been faced with many hard decisions on religious matters. How much encouragement can laws give to organized religion without violating the First Amendment's prohibition of religious establishment? Upon occasion, the judges have ruled that this clause merely prevents legal preference for one religion over another, what is known as the "preferred position" doctrine. But most of the time the Court favors the "wall of separation" between church and state which bars assistance to all religions. The difficulty in making some of these decisions, however, is indicated by their closeness. In 1947, in the case of *Everson* v. *Board of Education of Ewing Township, N.J.,* the Court upheld by a 5–4 vote the constitutionality of a school district providing bus transportation for pupils attending parochial schools as well as for those attending public schools.[6] In 1968, a six-member majority approved a New York law supplying nonreligious textbooks for parochial schoolchildren. In this case, *Board of Education* v. *Allen,* the Court distinguished between state aid primarily for the benefit of students themselves (such as books) and aid that constitutes direct assistance to religion.[7] Three years later federal aid to construct church-owned classrooms not used for religious purposes was approved 5–4. But state subsidies for teachers' salaries in church schools were considered direct assistance and invalidated 8–1. In 1970 seven justices sustained the constitutionality of tax exemptions for church property.[8]

In *Zorach* v. *Clauson,* a 6–3 decision in 1952, the Court held that public school students could be released part of the regular school day for the purpose of receiving religious instruction in the church or synagogue of their choice.[9] Only four years earlier the Court ruled that "released-time programs" for religious purposes were a violation of the establishment clause if the religious instruction took place on public school property.[10]

Prayer in the Schools

The most controversial cases in this area have dealt with religious observances conducted as a part of the daily routine in public schools. The leading case is *Engel* v. *Vitale* in which the Supreme Court ruled that a nondenominational prayer written by the New York State Board of Regents and recited in every public school classroom was unconstitutional – even though no student was forced to join in saying the prayer. Justice Hugo Black, who wrote the majority opinion, believed that the prayer constituted that kind of state-endorsed religious activity prohibited by the First Amendment. It is not "the business of government," he wrote, "to compose official prayers."[11] Standing alone, Justice Potter Stewart wrote a dissenting opinion stating that he saw nothing unconstitutional in "letting those who want to say a prayer to say it."[12]

Only a handful of decisions in our entire history have met with attacks as bitter as those against the *Engel* case. Even though Justice Black took great pains to point out that he saw nothing objectionable in *studying* religion, or in nondevotional or nonworship activities such as singing Christmas carols, over a hundred congressmen introduced constitutional amendments specifically to permit prayer in the public schools. But the following year, 1963, the Supreme Court handed down two more decisions consistent with its ruling in *Engel*. In one, *Abington School District* v. *Schempp*, a Pennsylvania law requiring portions of the King James Version of the Bible to be read in all public schools each morning was declared unconstitutional. In the other, *Murray* v. *Curlett*, a Maryland law authorizing classroom use of the Lord's Prayer met the same fate.[13] Such laws encouraged not merely religion, but the Christian religion. While outraged criticism followed the *Engel* decision, the *Schempp* and *Murray* decisions were openly defied. An estimated 30 percent of all public schools had required religious observances prior to 1962. As late as 1966 nearly 13 percent were continuing them in deliberate disobedience of the Supreme Court.[14]

In 1973 another important decision on religion and school laws was made in the case of *Committee for Public Education and Religious Liberty* v. *Nyquist*.[15] This time the Court declared unconstitutional state laws providing tuition aid or tax credits to the parents of children in church schools. Writing for the majority, Justice Powell set forth a three-part test that laws must meet if they are to steer clear of the establishment prohibition. They must have a "secular purpose," neither "advance nor inhibit religion," and avoid excessive "government entanglement with religion." These standards may guide the courts for a long time. However, they may forecast a gloomy future for parochial schools looking forward to government help pledged by politicians of both parties. Even before the *Nyquist* decision, Catholic school enrollment had dropped by nearly 2 million students since 1965, largely as a result of financial problems. Public schools supported by taxes absorbed the additional pupils, but many of them also found this financially difficult.

**Freedom of Religion:
The "Free Exercise" Clause**

In addition to prohibiting the establishment of religion, the First Amendment also contains another clause guaranteeing "the free exercise thereof." This means that everyone has the right to believe and to practice any religion he chooses. Yet, just as the establishment clause is not absolute, so also the "free exercise" clause has exceptions. Here we approach a vital principle of human existence: Society is so complex and our values often so contradictory that there is no freedom guaranteed in the Constitution which can be absolute—all have permissible limits.

The Limits of Free Exercise

In 1878 the Supreme Court placed some limits on freedom of religion by upholding a law prohibiting polygamy, even though the Mormon religion at that time endorsed plural marriages.[16] Similarly, there seems little doubt that states can prohibit such practices as human torture or sacrifice or the use of drugs like LSD, even though they may be sanctioned by religious groups. In a 1905 case, a Massachusetts law compelling vaccinations against smallpox was upheld, regardless of contrary religious convictions.[17]

Most of these cases involved the use of the so-called police power of the states (one of the powers reserved to the states by the Tenth Amendment) to protect the health, safety, morals, and welfare of the people. Unfortunately, the protection of the majority sometimes runs counter to complete religious freedom for a minority. When such a conflict arises the judges are forced to decide between two parts of the Constitution.

The Extent of Free Exercise

Yet the Court has still guaranteed minorities wide latitude in their exercise of religious freedom. A relatively small church, the Jehovah's Witnesses, has brought about thirty cases to the Supreme Court. As a result it has won the right to distribute religious literature without a permit, to expound religious views even to people offended by them, to sell religious tracts without payment of the license fees often required by municipalities, and to refuse to salute the flag on grounds of religious doctrine.[18] A 1972 decision upheld the right of members of the Amish church to prohibit their children from attending high school.[19] These cases produced sharp disagreement among Supreme Court justices and in a few instances represent reversals of previous decisions. Like all human beings, judges change their minds. When they do, the meaning of the Constitution also changes.

Religion and the Draft

American draft laws have always provided exemption from military service to those who were opposed to war on the grounds of religious belief. Such persons were classified as "conscientious objectors," or C.O.'s, and were excused from normal military duty to perform some humanitarian service. During the unpopular Vietnam conflict, claims for C.O. classification increased dramatically, resulting in a major Supreme Court decision in the case of *Welsh v. U.S.*[20] This case ruled that a C.O. classification, under the

First Amendment, must be made available to those sincerely opposing war on philosophic, moral, and sociological grounds, as well as to those whose motives were religious. In 1971, however, the Court upheld the refusal of a draft board to grant C.O. status to a person opposed only to the Vietnam war, but not necessarily to other wars.[21]

FREEDOM OF SPEECH, PRESS, ASSEMBLY, AND PETITION

Government itself tends to dislike freedom in general because it obstructs the exercise of arbitrary power, and freedom of speech and of the press in particular because they are the instruments which expose official mismanagement and misconduct.

Senator Sam Ervin

Like freedom of religion, other varieties of freedom of expression have also been limited by the courts. By imposing most of these limits, the courts are attempting to serve one of five specific purposes. These are to prevent the overthrow of the government by prohibiting subversive propaganda; to avert riots by permitting "disorderly conduct" or similar arrests; to protect personal reputations through slander and libel suits; to promote orthodox sexual morality by antipornography measures; and to minimize public inconvenience by allowing restrictions on parade and meeting permits. Such limits on freedom of speech, press, assembly, and petition are discussed in some detail in the following pages.

Freedom of Speech

A function of free speech . . . is to invite dispute. It may indeed best serve its high purpose when it induces a condition of unrest, creates dissatisfaction with conditions as they are (and strikes) at prejudices and preconceptions.

Justice William O. Douglas

Private citizens can restrict speech in whatever ways they wish in their own homes. But as the Supreme Court interprets the First Amendment, the government cannot render the American people tongue-tied unless some rational standard or doctrine can justify such a limitation. It is not enough that laws have a worthwhile purpose such as preventing riots. In addition, their objectives must be reconciled with the Constitution. Over the years, the Court has applied four major standards to test the constitutionality of laws restricting, or having a "chilling effect" upon, freedom of speech. These judicial rules or doctrines are usually known as "clear and present danger," "bad tendency," "grave and probable danger," and "balancing" tests. Some, as we shall see, permit more freedom than others.

Clear and Present Danger

This doctrine, set forth in the case of *Schenck* v. *U.S.* in 1919, was used to uphold the conviction of a man charged with violating the World War I Espionage Act.[22] That law prohibited, among other things, statements intended to interfere with the armed forces. Schenck, who had urged resistance to the draft, invoked the First Amendment rights to freedom of speech and press in arguing that his conviction was unconstitutional. The Supreme Court voted unanimously against him. In an opinion written by Justice Oliver Wendell Holmes, one of the nation's most famous jurists, the Court based its decision on three assumptions: (1) The Constitution guarantees freedom of expression but not freedom of action. (2) Expression is often designed to provoke action. (3) When expression creates "a clear and present danger" that illegal action will occur, it loses its constitutional protection. This "clear and present danger" doctrine, while not always followed by the Court, has influenced most of its decisions in cases involving verbal attacks upon the government or its policies. Under such a standard, freedom of expression is protected up to that point at which it results in an obvious (clear) and immediate (present) threat of "substantive evil" (serious crime) that the state has the power to prohibit.

Bad Tendency

The "clear and present danger" test, in actual application, has often protected a wider area of expression than the other standards. In *Gitlow* v. *New York,* for example, the Court utilized what has come to be known as the "bad or dangerous tendency" doctrine.[23] Over the dissents of Justices Holmes and Brandeis, this doctrine held that free expression lost its constitutional protection if it merely created a *tendency* toward illegal acts. In other words, this decision made it easier for the government to suppress criticism.

Grave and Probable

The balance between personal freedom and state power was adjusted again in 1951. The case, *Dennis* v. *U.S.,* involved the prosecution of eleven top leaders of the American Communist party.[24] They were tried under the Smith Act which prohibited the advocacy of violent revolution. The Supreme Court majority upheld the conviction of these defendants using a diluted version of the "clear and present danger" test, sometimes called the "grave and probable" doctrine. Under this doctrine there was sufficient cause to limit free expression if it created a probable danger of some grave evil. In the early 1950s, more than seventy other Communists were convicted under the Smith Act. But in 1957 such prosecutions nearly ceased when the Supreme Court reversed itself in *Yates* v. *U.S.*[25] This decision stated that the First Amendment protected all political expression except that which urges "one to *do* something . . . rather than merely to *believe* in something." The emphasis upon incitement to action rather than abstract advocacy moves the

Court closer to the "clear and present danger" test as originally stated by Holmes.

Balancing

It should be noted, however, that in 1950 the Supreme Court temporarily abandoned the "clear and present danger" rule entirely. Instead, in the case of *American Communications Association* v. *Douds,* it held that government restrictions on freedom of speech and assembly must be balanced against the seriousness of the evil that the government is trying to prevent.[26] In this case, the evil to be prevented was politically inspired strikes by Communist-led labor unions.

While all four of the tests just described are somewhat subjective, the last seems to depend most on the interpretation, and perhaps the biases, of the Supreme Court. To avoid this, a few justices, notably William O. Douglas and the late Hugo Black, have rejected all doctrines that limit freedom of expression. They have interpreted the First Amendment literally and view freedom of speech as an absolute, unqualified constitutional right.

It is important to note, moreover, that when freedom is exercised by those who are generally feared and disliked, the Court is most likely to uphold restrictions upon it. Several of the cases just mentioned, for example, involved left-wing radicals and took place during times of extreme public hostility toward communist sympathizers. Some of these cases also involved subversive propaganda, that is, propaganda which might lead to the overthrow of the government. Thus, the question being raised was this: Should those who would destroy freedom of expression be permitted to use it to come to power?

Free Speech and Public Order

Congress and the state legislatures have occasionally restricted freedom of speech not only to punish subversive utterances but also to minimize the chances of panic, fighting, and riots. Justice Holmes gave a partial endorsement to such efforts when he wrote that no one has a right to falsely shout "Fire!" in a crowded theater. In other words, one man's freedom of speech should not endanger another man's safety. In the same vein, Holmes once remarked that "your right to swing your arms ends where my nose begins."

Yet it is easier to devise clever phrases than it is to distinguish speech that is constitutionally protected from that which is not. In 1942 the Supreme Court held that calling a policeman a "damned Fascist," and "God-damned racketeer" was so likely to invite violence as to lose its First Amendment protection.[27] Yet seven years later, by the narrowest of margins, it reversed a breach of peace conviction of a speaker who denounced Jews and other minorities in highly offensive terms. Should violence break out, as it did in the latter situation, the Court apparently believed that the violent ones, and not the speaker, should be punished.[28] Another significant case involved a black speaker who denounced the president and the mayor of Syracuse, New York as "bums," and also urged that Negroes "rise up in arms and fight" for equal rights. By a 5–3 vote, the Court upheld the "disorderly conduct" conviction of this Syracuse man.[29] But it reversed a breach of the peace conviction against 187 blacks who marched to the South Carolina state capital carrying banners proclaiming "Down with Segregation," and chanting "We Shall Not Be Moved." This time, only Justice Clark dissented.[30] In all of these cases the constitutional rights to free speech came in conflict with the authority of the state to prevent riots (implicit in Amendment Ten). That is, the conflict was between constitutional *law* and public *order.* Although the Supreme Court has drawn some very fine lines in such cases, it has often come down on the more conservative side of public order.

Symbolic Speech
Whereas antiriot or antisubversion laws tend to restrict freedom of speech, the courts have recently accepted a doctrine which tends to expand it. This is the concept that silent, nonverbal communication can be used to transmit ideas in a sort of symbolic speech protected by the First Amendment.

The concept of symbolic speech was used successfully in California to protect nude dancers from prosecutions for lewd conduct. The more important case of *Tinker* v. *Des Moines,* however, involved not only civil rights, but also student rights. Here the Supreme Court held that wearing black arm bands to class as a gesture of antiwar sentiment was protected by the First Amendment even if school officials prohibited it. This 1969 decision[31] slightly offset an earlier ruling that the public burning of draft cards was not a constitutional exercise of freedom of expression.[32] Thus, the extent of constitutionally protected symbolism is still largely undetermined.

Freedom of the Press

The Government's power to censor the press was abolished so that the press would remain ever free to censure the Government. . . . Only a free and unrestrained press can effectively expose deception in Government.

Justice Hugo Black

In two recent and dramatic cases, the First Amendment guarantee of freedom of the press again proved its priceless worth. The cases came about when high government officials lied about the history of U.S. involvement in Vietnam, and when President Nixon attempted to conceal the involvement of White House aides in "covering up" Watergate facts. Without the courage and persistence of the reporters and publishers of the *Washington Post, New York Times,* and other newspapers, these deceptions might never have been revealed.

Yet they were revealed largely because the courts have consistently refused to allow government censorship of the press. In the landmark case of

Near v. *Minnesota*[33] the Supreme Court ruled that censorship before publication, or what is called "prior restraint," is normally unconstitutional. It can only be undertaken to prevent revelations endangering national security such as the description of future troop movements. Possible abuse of this press freedom can be prevented, the Court argued, because publishers can be sued or prosecuted *after* publication, for such things as libel or obscenity.

The prohibition of "prior restraint" was further strengthened by the 1971 Pentagon Papers case involving a secret history of the Vietnam war. Here, the Court ruled 6–3 that the government could not suppress the publication of the documents provided to newspapers by Daniel Ellsberg.[34] Their publication at this point did not endanger national security. Thus it was not subject to prior restraint.

The Movies Go to Court

In 1952 the Supreme Court expanded the constitutional guarantee of freedom of the press to encompass motion pictures. It did not, however, protect them against "prior restraint." Movies can, therefore, be censored in advance,[35] although only a few states have done so. But the Court has refused to ban films either on the ground that they are "sacrilegious" (treating religion with "contempt, mockery, scorn and ridicule") or because they depict "sexual immorality (adultery, in this case) as desirable."[36] To date, the Court has approved of film censors but has reversed nearly every act of censorship brought before it.

Freedom of the Press Versus Trial by Jury

Just as with freedom of speech or religion, freedom of the press may also conflict with other parts of the Constitution. It can at times interfere with the right to trial by an impartial jury, guaranteed in Amendment Six. If the media inflame emotions or reveal prejudicial information about a pending trial, it may be impossible to find open-minded jurors who can render an impartial verdict based only on evidence disclosed in court.

The English tend to solve this problem by contempt of court actions against the press. But American courts have not tended to limit freedom of the press in this way. Instead, they have overturned guilty convictions when they found the juries to be brainwashed by earlier publicity.[37] On the constitutional level, these conflicting rights must somehow be compromised. On the practical level, we need a press capable of exercising responsible self-restraint.

Freedom of the Press Versus Slander and Libel

A person's reputation is his most valuable possession. At stake may be his job, his friends, even his family. Slander and libel laws help protect individuals from irresponsible accusations. Slander is an oral, and libel a written, statement which maliciously injures the reputation of another person. Most court cases involving such statements are brought under state civil codes. These permit the person allegedly injured to sue the person who supposedly made the damaging statement for a certain amount of money.

Now, if a person is threatened with a slander or libel suit, that will surely inhibit his freedom of expression. Yet the courts have held that laws in this area do not violate the First Amendment because they were a part of the common law long before that amendment was proposed. Those who wrote the Bill of Rights, judges contend, would surely have prohibited libel and slander laws expressly if that had been their intention.

There is less danger of being successfully sued for libel if you criticize a public figure rather than an unknown citizen. This is the essence of the Court's decision in *New York Times* v. *Sullivan*.[38] In that case a libel judgment in favor of a Montgomery, Alabama city official was set aside on the grounds that "erroneous statement is inevitable in free debate" and that discussion of public issues "should be uninhibited, robust, and wide open." In *Associated Press* v. *Walker* the Court expanded this same doctrine to protect those who write about prominent citizens engaging in debate on vital public issues.[39] A 1974 decision, on the other hand, made it easier for private citizens to win a libel suit against the press. They no longer have to prove malice on the part of writers or publishers, only that the accusations were made without reasonable efforts to check out the facts. Thus, while the press in this country is virtually free to criticize public officials, it cannot claim that it is serving democracy when it makes libelous statements against a private individual.

Obscenity: The Uncertain Crime

The reserved powers of the states have always included the "police power" necessary to protect, among other things, public morality. Thus, states tended to punish the sale or distribution of sexually explicit books and pictures since the early 1800s. In 1873 the national government joined the crusade against obscene materials by banning them from the mails. Although the exact definition of obscenity was rather vague, American courts usually followed the Hicklin obscenity test. This test hinged upon "whether the tendency of the matter . . . is to deprave and corrupt those whose minds are open to such immoral influences and into whose hands a publication of this sort may fall." Thus, the Hicklin standard barred everyone from access to publications which might have an undesirable influence on anyone.

Not until 1957 did the Supreme Court confront the conflict between obscenity laws and freedom of expression. The landmark case, *Roth* v. *United States,* upheld a conviction for sending obscene materials through the mail.[40] It asserted that "obscenity is not within the area of constitutionally protected speech or press." Yet this case had the effect of permitting open distribution of previously obscene materials. It had this effect because it explicitly rejected the Hicklin doctrine and established a new test of obscenity: "Whether to the average person, applying contemporary standards, the dominant theme of the material taken as a whole appeals to prurient interest." "Prurient interests" were defined to include "lustful thoughts," or "a shameful or morbid interest in nudity, sex or excretion."[41] Thus the *Roth* decision made obscenity a dynamic concept, shaped by changing standards recognized by "average" people.

The Permissive Society
The *Roth* case was the crack in the censorship wall which later widened to an open door. In 1959, for example, the Court held that a bookseller could not be convicted unless he knew he was selling an obscene publication. Seven years later, in *Memoirs* v. *Massachusetts,*[42] it was decided that no publication could constitutionally be deemed obscene unless it was "utterly without redeeming social value."[43] The most permissive decision of all came in the 1969 case of *Stanley* v. *Georgia.* Here the Supreme Court upheld the right to *possess* admittedly pornographic films in one's own home. In 1971, however, a divided Court upheld prohibitions against the mailing or importation of obscene materials.[44]

By 1973 the impact of the four conservative justices appointed to the Supreme Court by President Nixon was imprinted even more strongly on the doctrine of obscenity. In *Miller* v. *California,* a 5–4 decision modified the rules established in *Roth* in order to crack down more harshly on allegedly pornographic materials.[45] The "community standards" by which offensive works were to be judged were now defined locally, rather than nationally. Presumably, this was to safeguard the innocence of small-town America against the corrupting influences of "Las Vegas or New York City." Moreover, material no longer had to "without redeeming social value" to be punished as obscenity. It was enough that it depict or describe sexual acts specifically prohibited by law and that it lack "serious literary, artistic, political, or scientific value." The fear that magazines and movies would have to be tailored to the tastes of the most prudish parts of the country as a result of the *Miller* decision was partially allayed by a 1974 decision, *Jenkins* v. *Georgia.* In that case the movie "Carnal Knowledge" was declared not obscene, even though jurors in Albany, Georgia, had ruled otherwise. This movie was acceptable because according to the *Miller* standard it did not depict sexual acts specifically prohibited by law. All that seems clear from these decisions is the difficulty the Supreme Court has had in dealing with obscenity. The justices will probably continue to see a lot of X-rated movies and what is obscene will continue to lie largely in the eyes of these judicial beholders.

Freedom of Assembly

Freedom of assembly has generally had to endure more restrictions than freedom of speech or press. This is because assembly often entails physical demonstrations such as marches and picketing. Local governments, therefore, may require permits or licenses for rallies and parades so long as these are granted on an impartial basis. A permit application for a peace march, in other words, must be treated the same as one for an armed forces parade. If freedom of assembly is unconstitutionally denied by a permit agency such as a park department or police commission, the legal remedy is to seek a court order requiring the permit rather than to assemble without it.[46]

A more difficult problem in this area was posed by thirty-two students from Florida A. & M. University. These students entered the jail grounds in Tallahassee to protest both racial segregation in the prison and the earlier arrest of some fellow students. Police arrested the protesters under a "malicious trespass" law. At issue was whether trespass laws may be applied to restrict assembly on public as well as private property. In a 5–4 vote, the Court held that they could.[47]

Picketing is another important form of assembly particularly in labor disputes. It has generally been constitutionally protected if the picketers do not block the entrances of the institution picketed. The Court has ruled, however, that a shopping center may bar distributors of antiwar leaflets from its premises, but may not bar labor pickets.

Freedom of assembly also includes the right to associate in organizations based on common beliefs. This right was upheld for college students when the Supreme Court reversed a decision by the president of Central Connecticut State College. The president sought to deny campus recognition to a group affiliated with the left-wing Students for a Democratic Society (SDS).[48]

Freedom of Petition

The First Amendment right to "petition the Government for a redress of grievances" was designed to guarantee the people some access to government officials. That is, it provided a medium of communication with those in charge. Increasingly, large groups of citizens hire professional lobbyists to contact officials in their behalf. Most recent court cases involving the right to petition have arisen from congressional attempts to regulate this lobbying activity.[49] Such activity will be discussed in considerable detail in Chapter 7. It should be noted, however, that the right to petition guaranteed in the First Amendment is not related to initiative petitions. These are petitions by which some states permit proposals to be placed on the ballot for approval by the voters.

THE FUNCTIONS OF FREEDOM

[T]he ultimate good desired is better reached by the free trade in ideas . . . the best test of truth is the power of the thought to get itself accepted in the competition of the market.

Oliver Wendell Holmes

It is disturbing that the strong emphasis on freedom of expression found both in the Constitution and in many court decisions seems to have relatively little support among Americans. Surveys during the past two decades indicate that about three-fourths of the people would not allow groups to organize peaceful antigovernment demonstrations. Sixty percent would prohibit speeches against churches or religion. Forty-five percent would forbid socialists from publishing newspapers. And 36.7 percent believed that "a man oughtn't to be allowed to speak if he doesn't know what he's talking about."[50]

Moreover, only 21 percent of Americans know much about the Bill of Rights according to a 1945 poll.[51] Even fewer are familiar with the Declaration of Independence. Only one person out of fifty would sign it when it was circulated in the form of a typed petition to a sample group of people in 1970.[52] There seems to have been a failure of political socialization, that is, a failure of families, schools, and other institutions to teach new generations the political values upon which democracy depends. The ultimate importance of freedom of expression clearly requires renewed emphasis. We can provide some of that emphasis by looking at the vital functions of freedom in our society.

Human Dignity: Are Natural Rights Self-Evident?

The Declaration of Independence contends that it is a self-evident truth that governments were created to protect, among other things, the natural right to liberty. The chief problem with this natural rights philosophy is that it cannot be empirically proved. No one can feel or see the rights that are claimed. Rather, he must just accept them on faith. Whether or not there is a natural right to liberty, the *theory* of natural rights elevates the individual to a position of supreme importance. It assumes that he *has* rights and that the state is supposed to protect them. Moreover, it assumes that society exists for the purpose of enhancing his dignity, rather than he for the purpose of serving its needs.

Indeed, the characteristic of democracy which most sets it apart from communist or fascist regimes is this belief that there is no greater good than the dignity and welfare of the individual. Love and compassion may lead him to sacrifice for others. But if he has freedom, his own integrity and worth can never be bartered away in behalf of some abstract class, creed, or flag. Freedom is essential, then, because without it the individual is stripped of his basic dignity and subject to the control of others. The belief in natural rights may be necessary to freedom, just as freedom is necessary to human dignity. But like the belief in God, a belief in man's dignity requires an act of faith.

Social Progress: The Search for Truth

A strong case for individual freedom can also be made on the basis of its social contributions. This line of reasoning was expressed most influentially by the great English philosopher John Stuart Mill. In his long essay, *On Liberty,* Mill defended freedom of expression as necessary to the search for truth on which human progress depends. Through the clash and combination of differing viewpoints, he believed, new insights are possible. Even the challenge of bad ideas is socially valuable, he argued. Bad ideas can stimulate the further improvement of good ones and can make the truth easier to see by comparison.

Indeed, history has shown that it is often difficult to distinguish truth from falsity, good ideas from bad ones. Socrates and Jesus, perhaps the two most honored figures in the Western world, were put to death because their ideas were believed to be wrong. Galileo was forced to retract a scientific truth of unsurpassed importance (that the earth revolves around the sun) in order to escape the same fate. Even the wisest of men sometimes suppress the wrong ideas. Thus, *On Liberty* has proved its worth many times. Yesterday's "dangerous lies," such as biological evolution, have become accepted parts of today's "truth." Freedom is clearly a prerequisite for maximum progress.

Personal Improvement and Intellectual Growth

Once limits are put on discussion people do not develop their capacities. They cease to learn and become saturated with the prevailing orthodox creed.

William O. Douglas

In a free society, there are many opinions among which we must choose. Such choices are often difficult. They require maximum use of our intellect. But the very freedom which makes choice necessary, also gives us the practice which makes wise choices possible. Just as a child learns to walk by standing, stepping, and falling, over and over, so we learn to make wise choices by choosing over and over, finally learning from our mistakes.

John Dewey, known as a pragmatist, was also a leading defender of freedom as essential to personal growth and mental development. "Learning by doing," as his theory was often described, is impossible in a totalitarian society. There choice is not available and one does only what he is ordered to do. Freedom, on the other hand, exercises the mental muscles. It forces each individual to confront, and take responsibility for, his own decisions.

Types of Freedom: Freedom *From* and Freedom *To*

The discussion thus far has focused upon but one kind of freedom—the minimizing of governmental or social restraint. Vital as this is, freedom is too complex a concept to be confined to so narrow a definition. There are actually several different conditions which various people call "freedom." One, surely, is the relative lack of external control just mentioned. Another is the absence of compulsive drives, as when one is "free" of nicotine or alcohol. Both of these are essentially negative freedoms. They are freedom *from* something. Equally important is freedom of opportunity—a more positive condition that involves the freedom *to* make a choice among two or more realistically available options. One is not really free to choose between law school and medical school if one lacks the money to attend either one.

Moreover, we must be aware that the different types of freedom can come in conflict. Freedom *to* may limit freedom *from,* or vice versa. For example, as we discussed earlier, freedom *to* make an inflammatory speech may limit freedom *from* dangerous riots. Or to put it differently, one person's freedom may limit another's. The freedom to have a party extending until 3:00 A.M. in a crowded apartment building limits the freedom of other tenants to sleep. The freedom to manufacture a car or cigarets may restrict the freedom to breathe clean air. The freedom to sell your house to whom you wish (say a white family) limits the freedom of others (say a black family) to buy a house they can afford. Dewey stated the issue plainly:

There is no such thing as the liberty or effective power of an individual, group, or class, except in relation to the liberties, the effective powers, of *other* individuals, groups and classes. . . . [L]iberty is always a *social* question, not an individual one.

This poses one of society's most difficult dilemmas: Whose freedom is to prevail? There is no easy answer or pat formula, but two solutions are available. One is the traditional democratic solution of counting noses: Restrict the freedom of the minority in the interests of the majority. The other, more difficult to apply, is to determine which of the conflicting freedoms is most important. This is a subjective test. Try applying it to the examples just cited and you will see how hard that decision can be.

In the final analysis, we must remember that the minority *must always* be free to become a majority. This is precisely what happened in the Watergate affair. What started out as minority media opinion could become, in the environment of free expression, majority public opinion demanding nothing less than the resignation of the president. Such is the ultimate political consequence of freedom of expression in a democracy.

FREEDOM AND POWER

The drama of American politics lies largely in two opposing processes: the exercise of power by the government over the people and by the people over the government. Freedom affects both of them. First, the constitutional guarantee of freedom of expression is a limitation on government power. They are two sides of the same coin. The Constitution exalts the free mind and commits the government to no creed but tolerance. Yet both logic and day-to-day experience teach us that if we are to keep our freedom, we must rely upon our own power as well as upon constitutional protection. The less power we exercise—in votes, or money, or knowledge—the easier it is for the government to restrict our freedom.

Just as freedom of expression limits the power of government, so it exerts power over the government. As we saw in the turmoil over Vietnam and Watergate, the force of free expression can be very great. But such freedom gives more power to some than to others. Freedom of expression for carpenters or clerks has far less effect upon society than freedom for writers or teachers. As used by newspaper editors or television commentators, free expression can actually form public opinion, win votes for political candidates, or alter the decisions of government agencies. But such people serve us all if they use their freedom to relay facts, expose corruption, and propose alternative policies among which average citizens may make a choice. If they deceive us occasionally, the remedy lies partially in our own good sense.

One further point must be made. The kind of power which freedom of expression makes possible for those who control the mass media is not based on force. It is primarily authority along with considerable influence which derives not from guns but from respect gained largely through intelligence, reliability, and logical persuasion.

Nevertheless, it is not only to those with a mass audience that freedom of expression is valuable. For most Americans its greatest benefits are felt mainly in terms of the human dignity which it affirms and the personal and intellectual growth which it makes possible. But freedom also confers potential power upon us to influence the government. And our history from the time of the Revolution to Vietnam and Watergate has shown that when Americans feel strongly they can act upon that potential. Most of the time we allow our leaders to exercise power for us but we must not forget that ultimately that power lies in our own hands.

Notes

1. The four new, more conservative justices appointed by Nixon were Warren Burger, Harry Blackmun, Lewis Powell, and William Rehnquist. Justices William O. Douglas, William J. Brennan, and Thurgood Marshall are the liberals from the Warren Court. Justice Potter Stewart has sometimes been voting with the liberals, while Justice Byron White has often been in a swing position, shifting between the conservative and the liberal sides and causing many cases to be decided by a 5 to 4 vote.
2. George Gallup, *Los Angeles Times,* Dec. 28, 1968, p. 19. Note that 89 percent of Americans said they believe in God, up 4 percent since 1948, and 73 percent in life after death, up 5 percent. By 1973, belief in God had dropped back to 84 percent but belief in the devil increased to 48 percent. Ibid., April 4, 1974, p. 1.
3. *Los Angeles Times,* March 20, 1972, p. 9, and Jan. 13, 1974, Part VII, p. 7.
4. *Gallagher* v. *Crown Kosher Supermarket of Massachusetts,* 366 U.S. 517. In this case, the Supreme Court upheld the constitutionality of Sunday-closing laws on nonreligious grounds. Supreme Court decisions are usually documented this way. "U.S." refers to *United States Reports,* the official volumes containing the full text of Court opinions. The first number indicates the volume and the last, the page on which the case begins.
5. Saul K. Padover, ed. *Thomas Jefferson on Democracy* (New York: Random House, 1965), p. 167.
6. 330 U.S. 1 (1947).
7. 392 U.S. 236 (1968).
8. *Tilton* v. *Richardson,* 403 U.S. 672 (1971), *Lemon* v. *Kurtzman,* 403 U.S. 602 (1971).
9. 343 U.S. 306 (1952).
10. *Illinois ex rel McCollum* v. *Board of Education,* 333 U.S. 203 (1948).
11. 370 U.S. 425 (1963). The case illustrates our religious diversity, since it was brought by five parents—two Jews, a Unitarian, a member of the Ethical Culture Society, and a nonbeliever.
12. 370 U.S. 445 (1962). The prayer itself was quite short: "Almighty God, we acknowledge our dependence upon Thee, and we beg Thy blessings upon us, our parents, our teachers, and our country."
13. The two cases were decided together, 374 U.S. 203 (1963).
14. Prof. Richard B. Dierenfield's figures, in Charles H. Sheldon, ed., *The Supreme Court: Politicians in Robes* (Beverly Hills, Calif.: Glencoe Press, 1970), p. 84.
15. 413 U.S. 756 (1973).
16. *Reynolds* v. *U.S.,* 98 U.S. 145 (1878).
17. *Jacobson* v. *Massachusetts,* 197 U.S. 25 (1905).
18. *Lovell* v. *Griffin,* 303 U.S. 444 (1938); *Cantwell* v. *Connecticut,* 310 U.S. 296 (1940); *Murdock* v. *Pennsylvania,* 319 U.S. 105 (1943); *West Virginia State Board of Education* v. *Barnette,* 319 U.S. 624 (1943).
19. *Wisconsin* v. *Yoder,* 92 S.Ct. 1526 (1972).
20. 398 U.S. 333 (1970).
21. *Gillette* v. *U.S.,* 401 U.S. 437 (1971).
22. 249 U.S. 47 (1919).
23. 268 U.S. 652 (1925).

24. 341 U.S. 494 (1951).
25. 354 U.S. 298 (1957).
26. 339 U.S. 382 (1950).
27. *Chaplinski* v. *New Hampshire,* 315 U.S. 568 (1942). "Resort to epithets or personal abuse," the Court said, "is not in any proper sense communication of information or opinion safeguarded by the Constitution."
28. *Terminiello* v. *Chicago,* 337 U.S. 1 (1949).
29. *Feiner* v. *New York,* 340 U.S. 315 (1951).
30. *Edwards* v. *South Carolina,* 372 U.S. 229 (1963). The dissenting opinion observed that "to say that the police may not intervene until the riot has occurred is like keeping out the doctor until the patient dies."
31. *Tinker* v. *Des Moines Independent Community School District,* 393 U.S. 503 (1969).
32. *United States* v. *O'Brien,* 391 U.S. 367 (1968).
33. 283 U.S. 697 (1931).
34. *New York Times Company* v. *United States,* 403 U.S. 713 (1971).
35. *Times Film Corp.* v. *Chicago,* 365 U.S. 43 (1961). The vote was 5–4.
36. *Burstyn* v. *Wilson,* 343 U.S. 495 (1952) and *Kingsley Pictures* v. *Regents of the University of New York,* 360 U.S. 684 (1959). The vindicated film in this case was a screen adaptation of *Lady Chatterley's Lover.*
37. Two major cases in point involve a former aide to the U.S. Senate, *Estes* v. *Texas,* 381 U.S. 532 (1965) and a well-known doctor accused of murdering his pregnant wife, *Sheppard* v. *Maxwell,* 384 U.S. 333 (1966). On this topic, see the discussion by Henry J. Abraham, *Freedom and the Court* (New York: Oxford University Press, 1967), pp. 127–32.
38. 376 U.S. 254 (1964).
39. 388 U.S. 130 (1967). In another case decided with this one, *Curtis Publishing Co.* v. *Butts,* the Supreme Court upheld a $460,000 libel suit won in a lower court by Butts, athletic director of the University of Georgia, against the *Saturday Evening Post,* a magazine which had accused him of giving pregame information to the University of Alabama football team.
40. 354 U.S. 476 (1957).
41. The definitions are cited and discussed in Eberhard and Phyllis Kronhausen, *Pornography and the Law* (New York: Ballantine Books, 1959), pp. 147–48.
42. *Smith* v. *California,* 361 U.S. 147.
43. 383 U.S. 413 (1966). The "memoirs" are those of a "Woman of Pleasure," a book more commonly known as *Fanny Hill.*
44. 89 S.Ct. 1243.
45. 413 U.S. 15 (1973).
46. *Poulos* v. *New Hampshire,* 345 U.S. 395 (1953).
47. *Adderley* v. *Florida,* 385 U.S. 39 (1966).
48. *Healy* v. *James,* 408 U.S. 169.
49. For a good discussion of this subject, see the editor's essay in Robert F. Cushman, ed., *Cases in Civil Liberties* (New York: Appleton-Century-Crofts, 1968), pp. 490–92. This casebook is one of the best, containing condensations of many Supreme Court decisions, along with interesting editorial commentary.
50. Herbert McCloskey, "Consensus and Ideology in American Politics," *American Political Science Review* 58 (June 1964): 367. See also Rita James Simon, *Public Opinion in America: 1936–1970* (Chicago: Rand McNally, 1974), pp. 117–18.
51. Robert E. Lane and David O. Sears, *Public Opinion* (Englewood Cliffs, N.J.: Prentice-Hall, 1964), p. 61.
52. *Los Angeles Times,* July 5, 1970, p. 2. Two called it "Commie junk," one "the work of a raver," another "rubbish," and yet another "meaningless."
53. John Dewey, *Philosophy of Education* (Totowa, N.J.: Littlefield, Adams Co., 1956), pp. 112–13.

5 THE DEFENDANT'S RIGHTS:
Criminal justice in America

Two of the great purposes of the Constitution, listed in its Preamble, are to "establish justice" and to "insure domestic tranquility." Nearly two hundred years later, we still have a long way to go to achieve a just and peaceful society.

Crime does pay.

James S. Campbell (National Commission on the Causes and Prevention of Violence)

While "justice" can mean many different things, most people would agree that it involves what we do with criminals. For every one hundred crimes reported, only about 20 people are arrested, five are convicted, and two are sent to prison. In terms of "domestic tranquillity," the number of serious crimes per 1000 people tripled between 1960 and 1974 (from 11 to 34).[1] Yet these frightening figures seem like good news when compared with a Gallup poll revealing that about one out of every three people living in a central city had been mugged, robbed, or burglarized during the last year.[2]

Such statistics show the difficulty of catching criminals and the still harder problem of preventing their crimes in the first place. But justice requires even more than this. It demands that the government not violate the law in the process of enforcing it. It recognizes that every defendant has rights, because some may be innocent and all are human beings. Perhaps the most important of these is the right to due process of law. Without due process, no government can establish justice. Without justice, domestic tranquillity is drowned in a flood of turmoil and violence.

DUE PROCESS OF LAW

No person shall be deprived of "life, liberty, or property, without due process of law." The Constitution says this twice, once in the Fifth Amendment, limiting the power of the national government, and again in the Fourteenth Amendment, restricting state governments. No phrase in the Constitution is more vague or sweeping, and its repetition makes it no easier to understand. One can begin to gather its meaning only by looking at the actual cases to which the Supreme Court has applied it over the years. These fall into three main areas: the procedures used by law-enforcement officers, the kinds of laws that may be passed, and the rights which must be protected against both national and state governments.

Procedural Due Process

From the time the words were first heard, in fourteenth-century England, due process of law was recognized as a limit on the methods or procedures that the government could use against its citizens. Someone could be deprived of life, liberty, or property by the common methods of punishment: execution, imprisonment, or fine. But these penalties could not be employed except through lawful procedures.

Five centuries have passed, however, and we are still trying to define lawful procedures. In 1952, for example, the Supreme Court held that a man could not be convicted on the basis of evidence obtained by holding him down and pumping his stomach. Yet even in that case, *Rochin* v. *California,*[3] the Supreme Court ruled that Rochin had been denied due process without defining the term. Instead, Justice Frankfurter merely related it to such general concepts as "civilized conduct," "a sense of justice," and "the community's sense of fair play and decency." By contrast, in later cases the Court found that it was not a denial of due process to take blood samples from suspected drunk drivers.

The idea of due process is not limited only to criminal matters. In 1975, for example, the Supreme Court decided in the case of *Goss* v. *Lopez* that public-school students could not be suspended without "some kind of hearing."[4]

Substantive Due Process

For many years, it was assumed that due process was related only to the *procedures* used to enforce laws and not to the laws themselves. As such, it restricted the executive and judicial branches of government, but not legislative bodies. Gradually, however, the courts began to declare laws unconstitutional because they believed their content or *substance* took away life, liberty, or property, regardless of the procedures used to enforce them.

Labor-Management Relations

Between 1900 and 1925, this idea of substantive due process was used mainly to benefit business corporations at the expense of their employees. Laws limiting the hours employees could work per day, guaranteeing a minimum wage for women, and protecting the right of workers to join unions were considered violations of the due process clause.[5] Although it is hard to believe today, in all these cases the Supreme Court held that it was unconstitutional to deprive workers of their "liberty" to work long hours, at low pay, without union assistance. Moreover, since corporations are also legal "persons," they too are protected by the due process clause.

Abortion and the Court

The business-oriented use of substantive due process gradually disappeared as later court decisions overruled earlier ones. But the Supreme Court gave this doctrine new meaning in two stunning decisions which declared many state laws prohibiting abortion to be unconstitutional. In *Roe* v. *Wade* and *Doe* v. *Bolton*[6] the Court decided by a 7–2 vote that the right to have an abortion, at least during the first three months (or trimester) of pregnancy, was part of women's privacy protected by the guarantee of liberty in the due process clause. During the second trimester of pregnancy, the Court ruled that states can set abortion regulations which are necessary to protect the health of the mother. After that, abortions can be prohibited entirely "except when it is necessary to preserve the life or health of the mother."

These decisions triggered an explosion of conflicting emotions. Feminists cheered them as recognition of a woman's right to control her own body. "Right to life" groups blasted them as legalized murder and pleaded for a constitutional amendment to reverse them. But for better or worse, the doctrine of substantive due process had survived.

Due Process and Incorporation

The due process clause in the Fifth Amendment did not restrict the power of state governments. This is because the Supreme Court decided in 1833 that the entire Bill of Rights (Amendments One through Ten) limited the powers only of the national government.[7] But the Civil War changed all that. Congress, controlled by Northerners, realized that the white-dominated southern states presented a threat to the rights of newly freed slaves. Thus, they proposed the Fourteenth Amendment which also contained a due process clause specifically applied to states. In practice, this limits the power of all states in order to safeguard the rights of all persons—black or white.

But the due process clause in the Fourteenth Amendment has been held by the courts to have a broader meaning than the one in the Fifth Amendment. Beginning with the case of *Gitlow* v. *New York* in 1925[8] the Supreme Court has ruled that due process required state governments to respect most of the rights which are guaranteed in the Bill of Rights against action by the national government. This is sometimes known as the incorporation doctrine. That is, the Fourteenth Amendment, by judicial interpretation, now absorbs or incorporates within the meaning of "due process" such other guarantees as freedom of speech, protection against unreasonable searches and seizures, and the right to trial by jury.

In determining exactly which rights are protected from state interference, Supreme Court justices have often disagreed. They have usually relied on the rule of Justice Benjamin Cardozo, who said in *Palko* v. *Connecticut*[9] that any part of the Bill of Rights that was essential to "a scheme of ordered liberty" was incorporated into the due process clause of Amendment Fourteen. Over the years, the only rights not incorporated are found in Amendments Two, Three, Seven, and in the grand jury clause of Amendment Five. Thus, the double standard which protected certain rights against abuse by the national government but not the state governments has largely disappeared.

Laws, Not Men

Finally, in view of all these changes and incorporations, what does "due process of law" mean? Like other vital phrases in the Constitution, it is too broad and majestic a concept to be restricted by an exact definition. But it comes very close to providing a guarantee that we have a government of laws and not of men. While laws are made, enforced, and applied by men and women, the power of such government officials is limited by the higher law of the Constitution. In theoretical terms, the agents of the law must not be permitted to violate it. In practical terms, they must not use more force than is necessary to perform their duties, nor use public offices for private purposes. If only the members of Richard Nixon's White House staff had respected these requirements of due process, they would not have brought dishonor to themselves or to the political profession.

PROTECTING THE SUSPECT

The common law which the American colonists brought with them from England required the government to assume that people were innocent until it had proved them guilty. In practice, this meant that a person is entitled to certain protections both when he is a mere suspect and after criminal charges have been filed. We turn now to those provisions of the Constitution designed to protect potential defendants, beginning with the three contained in Article I.

The Writ of *Habeas Corpus*

The constitutional guarantee of the writ of *habeas corpus* is designed to protect the most basic of all rights in a free society. This is the right not to be jailed unfairly. A writ is a court order and the writ of *habeas corpus* (once called the "great writ") is an order usually directed to prison officials. It requires them either to release someone held in custody or to show cause why the inmate should be charged with a crime. Thus it prevents indefinite imprisonment without trial merely "on suspicion," or as a weapon against political opponents.

The Constitution contains no provision relating this writ to the states. But Article I, Section 9 provides that the national government not suspend it "unless when in Cases of Rebellion or Invasion the public Safety may require it." Since the Civil War, the writ has been suspended only in Hawaii when martial law (military rule) was declared during World War II.

No *Ex Post Facto* Laws

The old adage that "ignorance of the law is no excuse" obviously cannot be applied to laws not yet passed. The citizen cannot be expected to know today what may be declared illegal tomorrow. This elementary logic underlies the unconstitutionality of *ex post facto* laws. Such laws make some action a crime that was not a crime when the action was performed. Or they make it easier to convict someone of a crime committed previously. Or retroactively they increase criminal punishments.[10] Motorists, for example, could not be arrested for driving without seat belts on January 1, if the law requiring them was not passed until January 2. Article I, Section 9 forbids Congress from passing such laws and Section 10 forbids the states from doing so.

No Bills of Attainder

"Equal justice under law," one of man's highest goals, is the motto inscribed on the Supreme Court building in Washington, D.C. A society that has one law for the rich and another for the poor, one for me and another for you, is clearly unjust. The ban on *bills of attainder,* laws which punish specific persons or groups without a conviction in court, was meant to prohibit such unequal justice. Such laws are specifically forbidden in Article I, Sections 9 and 10. Certain laws have been declared unconstitutional bills of attainder even though they were not criminal statutes in the usual sense of that term. These include a law withholding salary from three allegedly subversive government employees and a law prohibiting Communists from serving as officers of labor unions.[11] However, the claim that the placement of Japanese-Americans into detention camps during World War II constituted a bill of attainder (while no action was taken against German-Americans) was not upheld by the courts.

The prohibitions on both *ex post facto* laws and bills of attainder restrict legislative bodies in the kinds of laws, or statutes, they may pass. As a result they are among the few substantive rights, as distinguished from procedural ones, that apply to criminal justice.

Policing the Police: The Right to Privacy

A policeman's lot is not a happy one!
William S. Gilbert

An old English proverb says that "A man's house is his castle." But if the police are given maximum authority to ensure domestic tranquillity, they will occasionally batter down the castle walls. The two horns of this dilemma, adequate power for the police and reasonable privacy for the people, deserve brief examination.

The Thin, Blue Line

Confronted with a soaring crime rate, our society must rely more and more on the police. Certainly, the police are the first line of defense against criminals. But it is often a thin, blue line, considering the lack of respect and support from other segments of society.

In many ways, the lot of the "cop" appears to be getting worse. Underpaid and often undereducated, his job is among the most dangerous in the world. In 1968 patrolmen's pay in big cities averaged about $7500 a year. This was only two-thirds that of union plumbers and far less than police received thirty years earlier relative to other occupations. Whereas in 1940 over half of the police recruits in New York City were college graduates, this proportion had fallen to about 5 percent by 1969. Other cities showed similar trends.[12]

In spite of poor pay and preparation, however, police have had to face ever greater challenges. The crime rate climbed steadily in the 1960s, dropped slightly in 1972, then spurted upwards 6 percent in 1973 and an astonishing 17 percent in 1974.[13] The police, unable to check the rising tide of lawlessness, were often its victims. In 1960, 48 policemen were killed, 88 in 1964, and 153 in 1972.[14]

As crime continued to increase, so did its political importance. In 1968 Congress passed a Safe Streets Act creating a Law Enforcement Assistance Administration (LEAA) to supervise federal grants for the "war on crime." As a result, federal expenditures for crime reduction, which were $857 million in 1970, tripled by 1973. Moreover, between 1965 and 1973, cities of more than 100,000 people increased their maximum salaries for police patrolmen by considerably more than the increase in the cost of living—from an average of $6900 to $12,300.[15] And as every level of government poured more money into police work, city voters chose former police officials as mayors in Philadelphia, Minneapolis, and Los Angeles.

Yet all of these efforts seemed inadequate. Part of the problem, perhaps, was a lack of national leadership. In the first six years of its existence, the LEAA had no administrator at all for 18 months and four different ones in the remainder of that period.[16] Moreover, the Justice Department itself had five different Attorney Generals in the same period. Frustrated by the government's inability to deal with crime effectively, many people began to demand that we stop "coddling crooks," "handcuffing the cops," and even that we "curb the courts" in their leniency toward criminal defendants. As a result of President Nixon's judicial appointments, it was clear that the courts were getting the message. Many of their decisions after 1972 gave police and government prosecutors more power in relation to suspected criminals. But there is another side to this story, called privacy.

The Fourth Amendment: Protecting the Castle

The poorest man may in his cottage bid defiance to all the force of the crown. It may be frail; its roof may shake; the wind may blow through it; the storms may enter; the rain may enter—but the king of England cannot enter.

William Pitt the Elder

The word "privacy" is not mentioned in the Constitution, but provisions designed to guarantee it are an important part of our Bill of Rights, and especially of the Fourth Amendment. A police sergeant, therefore, has no greater authority to enter an American home than the king (or queen) has to enter an English cottage. Justice Brennan spoke for the Supreme Court majority when he wrote that "The overriding function of the Fourth Amendment is to protect personal privacy and dignity against unwarranted intrusion by the State."[17]

But what intrusions are unwarranted? It is a hard question, and even the Fourth Amendment is not very specific. "The right of the people," it says, "to be secure . . . against unreasonable searches and seizures, shall not be violated, and no Warrants shall issue, but upon probable cause, . . . and particularly describing the place to be searched, and the persons or things to be seized."

Clearly, the provision involving warrants, which are court permits authorizing police action, is designed to limit law enforcement procedures. It is generally agreed that a search or seizure (including an arrest) without a warrant is unreasonable *except* in one of the following circumstances:

1. When the crime is committed in the presence of a policeman (or other person making a "citizen's arrest").
2. When there is "probable cause" to believe that a felony (or major crime) has been committed, and there is no time to get a warrant.
3. When there is probable cause to make an arrest and when a search of the person is necessary to prevent the destruction of evidence or to seize weapons which might endanger the arresting officer.

On many occasions, these rules are easy enough to apply. If a patrolman hears a gunshot from inside an apartment followed by a bloodcurdling scream, most people would agree that he has probable cause to suspect a crime and that the building should be entered—warrant or not. Yet there are borderline cases in which decisions about what constitutes probable cause would confound even the wisest of judges. But it is the police officers on the scene who must make instant choices in an atmosphere of grave danger. If an officer decides there is no probable cause, a criminal may escape. If he decides there is, a court may disagree and release the suspect.

Three Supreme Court cases decided in 1968 indicate some of the complexities involved. In the major one, *Terry* v. *Ohio*, police "stop-and-frisk" procedures were upheld with respect to a suspect whose behavior indicated he might be about to hold up a store.[18] Similarly, the Court approved another frisking without a warrant when a policeman discovered burglar tools on a suspect who was tiptoeing down an apartment hall. These cases indicate Court approval of at least modified searches when there was enough cause to suspect criminal activity, although not necessarily probable cause for arrest. Yet the Court reversed another conviction on the grounds that the mere fact that a defendant had talked to known drug addicts did not justify his being searched (successfully) for narcotics.[19]

Most arrests, however, can take place without a warrant,[20] because there is probable cause. This provision of Amendment Four was specifically applied to the states, as well as to the national government, in *Mapp* v. *Ohio*.[21] That Supreme Court decision also applied the so-called exclusionary rule to state as well as federal courts. This highly controversial rule prohibits materials unconstitutionally seized from being used as evidence in criminal court prosecutions. This does not apply to evidence found in cars or other moving vehicles, however, because no warrant is needed to search them if there is probable cause for an arrest.[22] But even when there are sufficient grounds for an arrest without a warrant inside a house, the police must confine their search for evidence to the suspect and the area within his reach. Warrants must usually specify items to be seized, although officers entering a home with a warrant to search for one object (for example, forged checks) may seize something else (draft cards belonging to others), but only if possession of the latter is itself a crime.[23] The implication for drug or marijuana users is clear and ominous. Finally, it should be noted that police entry into a private home, even without a warrant, is permissible if it can be justified in terms of "practical considerations of everyday life."[24] Loud noises or suspicious smells coming from a late night party, for example, are probably sufficient to justify such action.

Taking the Fifth: Self-Incrimination
Closely related to the Fourth Amendment is a provision in Amendment Five which specifies that "No person . . . shall be compelled in any criminal case to be a witness against himself . . . ." This protection against forced self-incrimination has become one of the best known of our constitutional rights. One may "take the Fifth" in refusing to answer any questions about oneself whether they are posed by police, prosecuting attorneys, legislative committees, or any other government officials. An exception in which

persons *may* be compelled to testify about their own activities occurs when they are offered immunity from prosecution for testimony regarding related criminal behavior by others.

Police Brutality: The "Third Degree"

Although a refusal to reveal facts about one's self is obviously a protection of privacy, it may also jeopardize one's safety while being questioned by police. A clear purpose of the Fifth Amendment is to prevent the police from getting confessions by force, the so-called third degree. Yet such techniques seem to persist in the privacy of a few police-station back rooms. Forced confessions once involved physical torture, replaced in many instances with psychological pressures including the loss of sleep, deprivation of tobacco, use of bright lights, and promises of leniency if the suspect confesses. Police training manuals have also advised the use of false claims that an accomplice had confessed or that nonexistent evidence had been obtained.[25]

Pretrial Procedure

The usual procedure in an arrest varies somewhat from state to state but it generally entails *detention* by a police officer, often only for the purpose of asking questions.[26] Next, assuming the answers are unsatisfactory to the officer, the suspect is transported to the police station. There he or she is *booked* and thus saddled with a police record. Within about forty-eight to seventy-two hours after arrest and booking, the suspect is brought before a magistrate, or judge, for a *preliminary examination.* During this period between booking and examination, most police questioning takes place. As a result of such questioning, "as many as 40 percent of those arrested are released without being charged before a magistrate."[27] If there is sufficient evidence for charging, however, one will be *arraigned* and ordered to stand trial. Arraignment can come about either through a complaint from a private citizen, the police, a prosecuting attorney, or a grand jury.

In the long process just described, the police have viewed pretrial confessions as essential to effective crime control. They believe that about 80 percent of all felony convictions result largely from such confessions.[28] But what legal guarantees does the suspect have in protecting himself against attempts to extract confessions? The answer has been clarified in a series of recent Court decisions.

The Supreme Court held in 1964 that the Fifth Amendment's prohibition of forced self-incrimination applies to both state and national governments.[29] In the 1966 landmark case of *Miranda* v. *Arizona,*[30] it decided that a confession could not be admitted as evidence unless the suspect was first informed of his constitutional rights to remain silent and to obtain legal counsel. The *Miranda* decision did result in fewer confessions. It was attacked on the grounds that it tends to protect the guilty and restricts the police too severely. The arguments in its defense are that it protects the individual from invasion of privacy and painful police coercion. It also encourages more thorough police investigation. An Indian policeman put it well when he said, "It is far pleasanter to sit comfortably in the shade rubbing red pepper in some poor devil's eyes than to go about in the sun hunting up evidence."[31] But perhaps the strongest argument for the right to remain silent is that it helps prevent the conviction of innocent people. In 1964, in New York City alone, three men confessed to murders, under police questioning, of which they were later proved innocent.[32]

The defense of the Fifth Amendment is not meant to suggest that the police are trying to send innocent people to jail. However, the police are expected to solve more crimes than they can adequately investigate. Their prestige and promotion depend upon their producing a culprit for almost every crime. Under these conditions, they naturally try to get the quickest confession from the most probable suspect. The people need protection from the police not because they are evil but because they—like all officials to whom we grant vast powers—are human.

Technological Tyrants

The framers of the Bill of Rights no doubt believed that the prohibitions on unreasonable searches and forced confessions were sufficient to protect the privacy and dignity of suspects. But they could not anticipate twentieth-century technology which has produced such skilled snoopers as electronic eavesdropping devices.

The Supreme Court met the problem of telephone wiretaps as early as 1928. In the case of *Olmstead* v. *U.S.* it held, 5 to 4, that wiretaps were constitutional because they involved no seizure of material things nor any physical trespass.[33] In 1961 and 1967, however, the Court began to retreat from the *Olmstead* ruling.[34] In the case of *Katz* v. *U.S.*, it held that the Fourth Amendment's prohibition against seizing things without a warrant extended to intangible things such as conversations.[35] The constitutionality of wiretapped evidence was thus rejected entirely, even though obtaining it involved no physical entrance or trespass. In 1968, Congress got into the act by passing the Omnibus Crime Control bill which in effect repealed a 1934 law outlawing electronic eavesdropping. The new legislation authorized judges to issue warrants permitting the use of both wiretapping and listening devices or "bugs." Clearly, in its eagerness to fight crime, Congress was responding to political pressures, but it was all too eager to pass the buck back to the courts for delicate decisions involving constitutionality.

Today the bugging business seems to be flourishing with the blessings of court warrants. Between 1969 and 1972, the number of authorized bugs and telephone wiretaps rose from 301 to 855. Most of these involved gambling and drug cases investigated by state officials.[36] But, even in cases involving an attempt by internal or domestic groups to overthrow the government, the Supreme Court has ruled that a warrant is necessary before electronic spying can take place.[37]

The threat of government intrusion upon private affairs is also heightened by another technological tool. This is the use of computers that are capable of recording, combining, and exchanging information about individual citizens almost instantly. The army, for example, has the criminal and "loyalty" records of seven million servicemen, contractors, and civilian employees, as well as extensive data on anti-Vietnam war protestors. Moreover, it was acknowledged in 1974 that the Federal Bureau of Investigation (F.B.I.) had spied on many "extremist" and some moderate political groups. The Internal Revenue Service (I.R.S.) and the Central Intelligence Agency (C.I.A.) were also used for similar purposes.

We are faced, it seems, with a pollution of our privacy often associated with totalitarianism. It is not only government agencies which have pried into our conversations, financial records, and political attitudes. They have been joined by such private peekers as banks, credit agencies, and psychological testing experts.[38] These threats to privacy, whatever their origins, challenge the integrity of everyone. They also threaten the progress of a nation which has depended upon the inventiveness of people who were a little bit different. Einstein, for example, seldom wore socks. The computers might go crazy with that one.

The Difficult Choice

When hampered by constitutional restrictions in their attempts to enforce the laws, the police and prosecutors sometimes become frustrated. One must finally face the sad truth that crime detection and personal privacy are sometimes incompatible. The police search, arrest, and question many innocent people sometimes with too little regard for their constitutional rights. Yet many more who are subjected to the same treatment are indeed guilty. In short, if we want all criminals captured, the rights of some innocent people will be sacrificed. But if we want the rights of all innocent people preserved, some criminals will escape. No one ever claimed that it was easy to run a society which promised "liberty and justice for all."

Privacy and the Presidency

If the government becomes a law-breaker, it breeds contempt for law; it invites every man to become a law unto himself; it invites anarchy.

Justice Louis Brandeis

In 1973, a growing disillusionment with politics was heightened by the revelation that individual privacy had been threatened as much by the presidency as by the police. During the Senate hearings on "Watergate," the news broke that between 1969 and 1971 President Nixon had authorized F.B.I. wiretaps on many people. These included political columnist Joseph Kraft, three other newsmen, and thirteen government officials, some of whom were on Henry Kissinger's National Security Council staff. Such measures were defended on the grounds that they were necessary to determine who had been "leaking" secret information to the press. Yet that kind of spying without a warrant had been ruled unconstitutional in the 1972 case cited earlier.

Bad as wiretapping was, burglary was worse. On September 3, 1971, agents from a White House investigation team called the "Plumbers" unit, broke into a psychiatrist's office to obtain damaging information about Daniel Ellsberg. Ellsberg was the man who had exposed the secret Defense Department history of American involvement in Vietnam. These were among the acts concealed by President Nixon for which, had he not resigned, he surely would have been impeached. Nixon, perhaps the most shy and secretive of all our presidents, was brought down, in part, for invading the privacy of others.[39] Yet Nixon staunchly defended the privacy of the presidency, as we shall see in the discussion of executive privilege in Chapter 11.

"To Keep and Bear Arms": A Right or a Wrong?

One of the most misunderstood provisions of the Constitution is Amendment Two. This amendment seems to guarantee "the right of the people to keep and bear arms." The fact is, however, that this right was actually designed to guarantee to the states the authority to maintain their own military and police forces. This is indicated by the seldom quoted opening words of the Second Amendment: "A well regulated Militia, being necessary to the security of a free state. . . ." What is really meant, therefore, is that the national guard, sheriffs' deputies, and other state law enforcement officers have a right to carry guns. In other words, the Constitution did not give the national government a complete monopoly on the use of force.

While many people believe that private citizens *should* also be allowed to own firearms, this issue is essentially a political one on which the Constitution remains silent. Only after the assassinations of President John F. Kennedy, Dr. Martin Luther King, Jr., and Senator Robert F. Kennedy did gun control become a major public issue. President Lyndon B. Johnson requested more stringent national restrictions on guns. The resulting legislation did place severe limits on mail order and other interstate sales of firearms. It also prohibited the sale of guns to convicts and minors. But it did not require that gun owners be licensed or that the firearms themselves be registered.

These last two restrictions were strongly opposed by the National Rifle Association, a powerful pressure group, as well as by certain extremist groups on both the left and right. They all insist that they need guns for hunting, target shooting, or self-defense. Opposing them and favoring some type of licensing or registration are several prominent police officials, the U.S. Conference of Mayors, Common Cause, and various church groups.

By the fall of 1974, the Gallup poll reported that 71 percent of people throughout the nation also favored the registration of all firearms.[40]

The issue of gun control touches emotions rooted deep in our soil. Americans have been a frontier people, used to relying on self-defense and fond of glorifying the cowboy, sheriff, and even the daring crook. That the issue will not soon disappear is suggested by the fact that gun controls are weaker here than in any other major nation. There are at least thirty-five million rifles, thirty-one million shotguns, and twenty-four million hand guns in civilian possession.[41] Moreover, the percentage of murders committed with guns rose from 55 in 1964 to 66 in 1971.

A Constitutional "Catch-All": Amendment Nine

One of the least used guarantees of the Constitution is found in Amendment Nine. It assures us in very general terms that the people have other rights in addition to those specifically stated. Although it is not clear exactly what these other rights include, there are many possible examples. One expects to be able to choose his occupation, for example, or the color of his shoes, without government interference. Of course, a constitution which tried to list all these rights would be ridiculous.

The most important case involving Amendment Nine is *Griswold* v. *Connecticut*.[42] This case declared unconstitutional a state law prohibiting the use of birth-control devices. The decision produced six different opinions by the justices. The only one endorsed by three justices stated that the law violated a right of marital privacy—such as Amendment Nine was designed to guarantee.

PROTECTING THE ACCUSED

Procedural fairness and regularity are . . . the indispensable essence of liberty.

Justice Robert Jackson

Thus far we have been concerned with those constitutional provisions which protect the people in their homes, on the street, or in the police station. We come now to the nation's courtrooms and the rights of those who must stand trial as criminal defendants.

Prelude to Prosecution

To be a defendant in a criminal trial is usually a traumatic experience. It forces the accused person to endure psychological stress and social embarrassment, in addition to considerable costs in time and money. Ideally, then, no one should be tried unless he or she is guilty. But this ideal, like most others, can never be fully attained. At least the American legal system attempts to make sure that no one is tried without good cause.

Trial Without Error

The Fifth Amendment provides that no person can be tried for a serious crime except through "indictment of a grand jury." A grand jury is a group of about two dozen citizens which can issue formal criminal accusations known as *indictments*. These bring suspects to trial when the grand jury has found that the evidence against them, as presented by police and prosecutors, indicates probable guilt. In practice, grand juries are most important in criminal cases against government employees and prominent private citizens. It was a federal grand jury that brought the "Watergate defendants" to trial in 1974 and named President Nixon as an unindicted coconspirator.

In many states, however, grand juries have been abolished. In other states, they serve only as a sort of public watchdog, investigating local government agencies such as the welfare department or coroner's office. The reference to them is one of the few provisions of the Bill of Rights which the Supreme Court has held not to be binding on the states. Even in the most serious crimes, therefore, states may bring persons to trial either through grand jury indictments or through charges, brought by prosecuting attorneys, known as bills of information or *true bills*.

No Excessive Bail

Anglo-American law insists that no person be considered guilty of a crime unless proven so in a court of law. The burden of proof is on the government prosecutors. The defendant has no obligation to prove his innocence.

This presumption of innocence raises a difficult problem: Since a suspect is presumed innocent until proven guilty, he should not have to remain in jail until his trial. Yet if he is released, he needs to be motivated to reappear for the trial rather than to run away. Therefore, *bail* is required—an amount of money which the defendant must deposit with the court before he can be released from jail. If he shows up for the trial the bail money is returned. But if he has "jumped bail" and evaded prosecution, a warrant for his arrest is immediately issued by the judge.

Amendment Eight prohibits excessive bail, the amount of which depends on the seriousness of the alleged crime and the defendant's previous record. If a person can't raise bail, it is often still possible to get out of jail by paying a lower fee to a bail bondsman who then posts the bail for him. In some cases, judges allow a defendant to be released without bail on his *own recognizance*. But in cases where the crime is quite serious, they may also deny bail and keep the accused in prison until the trial.

A Fair Trial

The Sixth Amendment contains as impressive a list of defendants' rights as can be found anywhere in the world.

How Fast Is Speedy?

Its first command is that "the accused shall enjoy the right to a speedy . . . trial." The longer it takes to bring a man to trial, the less reliable will be the memory of key witnesses and the greater likelihood that they will have died or disappeared. But how fast is speedy? In an age of increasing crime and overworked courts, the only reasonable answer is "as soon as possible."

The courts have usually held that this requirement has been met if there has been no deliberate delay in bringing a case to trial. In some areas, however, they have set six-month limits. In 1974 Congress passed a law, effective in 1979, which would free defendants in federal criminal cases if they were not tried within 100 days of their arrest. In the meantime, speed is encouraged by trying criminal cases before civil ones. Speed is also promoted by statutes of limitations prohibiting prosecutions, except in murder cases, if no arrest warrant has been issued within a certain period of time.

How Exposed Is Public?

The Sixth Amendment also demands public trials. This is on the assumption that secret, or "star chamber," trials are less apt to be fair than those spotlighted by publicity. But judges can clear the courtroom if spectators disrupt the proceedings. Moreover, photographs and live radio and television coverage of a trial are almost always banned as too distracting.

Confrontation

An additional right of the defendant is "to be confronted with the witnesses against him." Here the theory is that his accusers, testifying under oath and subject to cross-examination, will be more likely to tell the truth.

This provision has prohibited secondhand, hearsay testimony but it has also limited the use of secret witnesses (sometimes called "faceless informers" or "stool pigeons") by the prosecution. If such persons were forced to appear in court, they might later be murdered by criminals who had confided in them. Although their testimony, often paid for by the police, is sometimes unreliable, it can also be very valuable especially in crime syndicate cases. If necessary, police have provided protection to enable threatened witnesses to testify in court.

Another problem involving the right to confront witnesses is raised by defendants whose behavior makes if difficult to maintain order in the courtroom. This gained national attention in the 1969 trial of Bobby Seale, a defendant in the case involving riots at the 1968 Democratic National Convention. At that trial, the judge ordered Seale to be chained and gagged because of his insulting shouts. Judge Hoffman apparently believed that he could not constitutionally remove Seale from his own trial. But the Supreme Court later ruled in another case that such action is permissible under certain extreme circumstances.[43]

The Right to Subpoena Witnesses

Since the prosecution may call witnesses in its effort to prove guilt, Amendment Six also gives the accused the right "to have compulsory process for obtaining witnesses in his favor." Subpoenas are the compulsory process available. They are court orders requiring people upon whom they are served to appear in court to answer questions (not involving their own possible guilt) about the alleged crime. If the person subpoenaed does not testify, the judge may rule him in contempt of court and punish him, without trial, by fine or imprisonment.

The Right to Legal Counsel

No Sixth Amendment right has been more strengthened by recent court decisions than the right to professional legal advice. In 1963 the *Gideon* v. *Wainwright* decision applied it to state as well as federal courts.[44] Then, in 1964 the Court ruled in *Escobedo* v. *Illinois*[45] that legal counsel had to be provided when the defendant requested it at the time of his arrest, and not solely for trial. The 1966 *Miranda* decision required the police not only to inform the defendant of his right to remain silent, but also to tell him, before questioning, of his right to be represented by an attorney. A 1972 decision required that legal counsel be made available to anyone threatened with even a single day in jail.[46]

Yet how can the accused obtain legal counsel? He may, of course, hire his own lawyer. But the *Miranda* decision also insisted that he be told that an attorney will be provided for him free if he cannot afford to hire one. This can be done in one of two ways. In federal courts, and in most state courts, the judge can appoint a private attorney to represent the defendant. Or he may appoint a public defender. In most big cities, public defenders' offices have been created and staffed by full-time lawyers paid on the same basis as those working in the prosecuting attorney's offices. These public defenders, who represent only the poor, seem to provide better legal counsel than had been available in such cases.

The extension of the right to legal counsel to more and more situations occurred primarily in the 1960s while Earl Warren was Chief Justice of the Supreme Court. By the mid-seventies, however, it was clear that most of the precedents in criminal proceedings set by the "Warren Court" would be expanded no further. With the addition of the four conservative justices appointed by President Nixon, the Court ruled, 5 to 4, that a person who had not been formally accused of a crime had no right to a lawyer during a lineup of suspects at a police station.[47] In 1974, it ruled 6 to 3 that the right to legal counsel did not extend to prisoners facing disciplinary hearings.

No Double Jeopardy

With few exceptions, criminal defendants may be tried only once for a single act. This is the result of the Fifth Amendment's assurance that no person shall be "twice put in jeopardy of life or limb." The exceptions are: (1)

Persons in the armed forces are subject to both military and civilian law. There are situations, therefore, permitting both a military court martial and a prosecution in a regular state court for the same offense. (2) If a person has broken both national and state laws, he or she could theoretically be tried in both courts. In practice, however, this seldom happens. (3) A person may be tried twice for the same crime if the first conviction resulted from some unconstitutional procedure and if, on appeal, a higher court orders a new trial. Hence convicted criminals are not just set free on some technicality, as is often supposed. Many of them are again found guilty at the second trial where great care has been taken not to violate any of their rights.

Trial by Jury

Trial by jury is mentioned three times in the Constitution. Article III establishes it, Amendment Six specifies an impartial jury, and Amendment Seven extends the right from criminal cases to civil cases involving more than $20. Sir William Blackstone, an eighteenth-century English legal scholar, wrote that ". . . the trial by jury ever has been, and I trust ever will be, looked upon as the glory of the English law."[48]

Yet jury trials are not required. They are simply a right the accused may exercise, except in minor cases, if he wishes to do so. Either a judge or a jury may render the verdict, and the defendant makes the choice. If judges are corrupt or prejudiced, then trial by jury is vital. But if judges are honest, competent, and fair—which seems to be the prevailing view today—then trial by jury is not essential. In fact, this right is being used less and less. Judges now render the verdict in 40 percent of criminal cases and there is evidence that their decisions are frequently the same as juries would have made.[49]

As long as jury trials exist, however, the constitutional requirement of an impartial jury is of vital importance. That guarantee is enforced in a number of ways:

1. If a defendant has received so much bad publicity that it would be impossible to find jurors who are not already biased against him, then the judge can issue a *change of venue.* This is an order transferring the trial to some other area where there has been less coverage of the case by TV, radio, and the press.
2. No group may be systematically excluded from jury duty because of race, sex, nationality, or attitude toward capital punishment (the death penalty).
3. Attorneys for both defense and prosecution may disqualify prospective jurors after questioning them. These *voir dire* examinations permit an unlimited number of disqualifications for adequate cause, such as being related to a witness. They also usually permit from five to thirty "peremptory" challenges of prospective jurors for which no explanation need be given.

In 1970 the Supreme Court upheld the constitutionality of Florida's six-member jury, upsetting a centuries-old tradition that juries must consist of twelve persons. A more important issue was whether juries could hand down a verdict in criminal cases by less than the unanimous vote established by common law custom. This issue was resolved in 1972 when a Louisiana law that permitted convictions by a 9–3 margin was upheld. Only a few states now allow similar verdicts but defendants throughout the country fear that more will follow.[50]

OF CRIME AND PUNISHMENT

I should like to be able to love my country and still love justice.
Albert Camus

Justice, certainly, is the goal of American criminal courts. But what is justice? If a defendant, having utilized all of the constitutionally guaranteed rights described above, is still convicted, what should become of him? Like other peoples, Americans still aren't quite sure what to do with their criminals. The oldest theory is that they should be punished according to their crime. This follows the Old Testament rule of "an eye for an eye, a tooth for a tooth." It is a concept rooted in revenge.

Another concept of punishment assumes that its purpose is not for revenge but rather to discourage or deter others from committing crime. Those holding this opinion often believe that the harsher the penalty, the more effective its deterrent value. A newer theory, however, is that convicts should be punished only to the extent necessary to reform them. In other words, we want to make sure that they have been changed or rehabilitated enough so that they won't commit crimes again after their release.

Who Are the Criminals?

Before discussing what to do with criminals, it would be well to find out who they are. But that is not easy since less than one-fourth of all crimes lead to arrests. We do know, however, that cities of over 250,000 population have a crime rate six times higher than those with populations under 10,000. Moreover, from police records we can gather some characteristics of the "typical" criminal. In 1972, out of every 100 persons charged with serious crimes, 82 were males and 75 were under 25 years of age. Eight out of every 13 were white and it seems nearly certain that an overwhelming majority were poor. Of those in local jails, more than half had incomes under $3,000 per year.[51]

Types of Sentences

No Cruel and Unusual Punishment
Although the Constitution contains many provisions aimed at helping

criminal defendants, it includes only one for the person finally convicted. This is the Eighth Amendment's prohibition against cruel and unusual punishments. The courts have never said precisely what such punishments are. But their decisions indicate a belief that the severity of sentences should be related to the seriousness of the crime.

In *Robinson* v. *California*,[52] the Court ruled that *any* criminal punishment for being a narcotics addict was cruel and unusual. While a state may punish possession or use of narcotics, addiction was held to be an illness, not a crime. In *Powell* v. *Texas*,[53] however, the conviction of a chronic alcoholic for being drunk in a public place was sustained. Such decisions show the difficulty the Court has had in deciding what is cruel and unusual and what is not.

Capital Punishment

Before June 29, 1972, never in American history had as many as six hundred people owed their lives to a single court decision. Those saved were 517 murderers, 79 rapists, and 4 armed robbers. What had happened, of course, was that the death penalty had been declared unconstitutional in the case of *Furman* v. *Georgia*.[54] This decision applied to all persons then on death row. They were an intriguing group: 329 blacks, 257 whites, 10 Mexican-Americans, 2 Puerto Ricans, and 2 Indians.

The historic decision was announced in conflicting voices. The vote was 5-4, nine different opinions were written, and the long-term impact was far from certain. Two justices seemed to believe the death penalty to be a cruel and unusual punishment under almost any circumstances. Three others objected to the arbitrary standards by which some felons were doomed to death while others found guilty of the same offenses were given lesser sentences. The four dissenters were again the new Nixon appointees. Most of the justices, however, expressed no opinion regarding situations in which laws might give the judge or jury less choice in imposing the death sentence. Many states responded to the Court decision by passing new laws *requiring* the death penalty for certain offenses. Their constitutionality was to be decided in future court cases.

Those who defend the death penalty claim that it is a deterrent to murder and that it has been approved by centuries of religious tradition and legal precedent. Critics argue that the death penalty is immoral, and of questionable deterrent value. They point out that in eleven of the fifteen states where it was abolished before the *Furman* decision, the homicide rate was below the national average. Finally, opponents of capital punishment argue that it has been unequally imposed. A disproportionate number of its victims are poor, black, and male. Nevertheless, in 1974 a Gallup poll showed that 63 percent of the public still favored the death penalty for convicted murderers.[55]

Imprisonment

Until recently, it was generally agreed that the easiest way to deal with convicted criminals was to lock them up. Yet by the end of September 1971, prison violence at San Quentin, California and Attica, New York had resulted in nearly fifty deaths of inmates and guards. Suddenly attention was focused on such issues as prison overcrowding, abuse by guards, and poor facilities for recreation and job training. Of the jails maintained by local governments in 1970, 86 percent had no facilities for exercise, 89 percent lacked education programs, and 49 percent lacked medical care.

In addition to its inadequacies, prison is expensive. In part this is due to the number of people imprisoned, more than 360,000 in 1970 or about one person out of every 570 Americans. It can also be attributed to the relatively long sentences imposed in this country in comparison with most other Western nations.[56] For the 9883 federal prisoners released for the first time in 1972, the average time served was almost nineteen months. The cost of all government correctional programs amounted to more than $2.2 billion per year.[57]

Even this price would be cheap enough if imprisonment rehabilitated the criminal. Yet the evidence indicates that this is not the case. One expert found that "two-thirds of the men and women now imprisoned are repeaters."[58] Another notes that in Oklahoma those convicts receiving short sentences committed proportionately fewer crimes upon their release than those who had been imprisoned longer.[59]

All too often, it seems, prolonged imprisonment further hardens or brutalizes criminals. It also allows them to become more skillful by exchanging ideas with one another. And it contributes to homosexuality by cutting them off from contact with the opposite sex. Perhaps the worst indictment of prison is that "85 percent of the nation's crime is committed by repeaters."[60] It is little wonder then that even former Attorney General William B. Saxbe has concluded that criminal rehabilitation is "a myth."[61] Although it can be argued that not enough resources have gone into our prison system to give it a fair test, current evidence indicates that it fails miserably as a "correctional" system.

One further damning criticism is that prison terms depend too much on the whims of the judges who impose sentences. In 1974, an experimental survey of 50 federal district court judges showed wide differences in the way they would treat the same defendants. A factory worker found guilty of bank robbery would have received twenty years in prison from one judge and three from another. An extortion conviction drew sentences ranging from 10 years imprisonment to a $5000 fine with no time in prison or on probation.[62]

The criticisms of imprisonment as a method of punishment lead logically to an examination of the major alternatives, probation and parole.

Probation and Parole

In most states, judges may release convicted persons on probation, rather than sending them to prison. Probation involves certain restrictions on their travel, associations, and behavior during a specified period. It also places

The inadequacy of our prison system and rehabilitation programs is mirrored in the faces of these prisoners.

them under the supervision of a probation officer. More than 70 percent of the persons convicted in California state courts in 1971 were kept out of jail in this way, along with 44 percent of those convicted in federal courts in 1972.[63]

Parole is an arrangement similar to probation by which persons already in prison are released if they meet certain requirements and agree to report periodically to parole agents. The requirements generally involve good behavior while in prison. Parole boards in each state, usually appointed by the governor, have the right to free prisoners from their state's penitentiaries. The U.S. Parole Board, consisting of eight members chosen by the president, makes the decisions for federal inmates. Most of the latter are eligible for parole after serving one-third of their sentences. But less than a third are actually released before their time is up.[64]

Probation and parole have clear advantages over long imprisonment. They permit the convict to earn a living, enjoy normal sex relations, and live with his family. They also minimize correctional expenses for the taxpayer. Their success is somewhat difficult to assess, however. It seems related to the types of persons selected for such treatment and the adequacy of their supervision. Of prisoners paroled in New York, New Jersey, and California, between 40.5 and 50.9 percent had violated the conditions of their parole within three to five years.[65]

In general, while probation has been criticized mainly for allowing dangerous criminals to run loose, parole has been condemned for different reasons. It has been argued that parole boards too often forbid prisoners from having legal assistance when seeking release. They also tend to rely too heavily on the unchallenged testimony of prison guards. Moreover, they sometimes deny inmates information in their prison files, or they fail to inform them why parole is denied, or what is necessary to obtain it. And, like judges, parole boards have too much latitude in determining the fate of those who must come before them. The U.S. Parole Board, however, made a significant reform in 1973. It published guidelines for the length of time prisoners should serve for various crimes before it would consider their applications for release.[66]

The Crime Crisis

The system of criminal justice in America does not protect the lives and property of the people as effectively as it once did. And in spite of considerable progress, it still does not protect the rights of criminal defendants as well as it someday might. There have been failures at every step of the process. Let us consider some of the evidence.

First, slums, ghettos, broken homes, drug addiction, inadequate education, job shortages, and other basic causes of crime still exist.[67]

Second, even the officially reported crime rate does not fully reflect the seriousness of the problem. A 1974 survey by the Census Bureau found that in our five largest cities only one-half to one-fifth of all crimes were actually reported to the police.[68]

Third, arrests and convictions fall far short of even the reported crimes. As shown by the figures at the beginning of this chapter, the chances of being arrested if you commit a crime are about one in five and the chances of being convicted are only about one in twenty.[69]

Fourth, the evidence just discussed seems to demonstrate that imprisonment does not rehabilitate criminals but, on the contrary, brutalizes them still more.

Finally, and most significantly, whether and to what degree a lawbreaker is punished depends to a great extent on the infinite variations in human character and judgment. The police, for example, exercise some initial choice in deciding whom to arrest, whom to merely "warn," and sometimes from whom to accept a payoff. Next, the prosecuting attorney or grand jury has considerable latitude in deciding whether the person arrested should be brought to trial. The judge then determines what bail, if any, will be required of the defendant to get out of jail until the trial occurs. "Plea bargaining," discussed in Chapter 12, may then occur among attorneys of varying skills and scruples. This determines whether the accused will plead guilty to a lesser offense than the one first charged by the prosecution. If the case goes to trial, a judge or jury must consider conflicting evidence, assess the truthfulness of opposing witnesses, and render a verdict. If a guilty verdict is handed down, the judge can often decide to suspend the sentence, inflicting no punishment whatsoever. Or he may place the convict on probation, or give him a prison sentence which can vary in length by several years. If a prison sentence is imposed, the way in which the time is served (in solitary confinement, for example) may depend on the prison warden. Finally, the date of the prisoner's release can be determined by a parole board or possibly by a pardon or commutation from the president or governor.[70] Throughout this whole process, of course, the potential for human whim and error is very great and very disturbing.

In view of these serious failures and inconsistencies, is it still possible to speak of real criminal justice in America? Can the government still be described as one of laws and not of men? There are no easy answers, but we can say that justice is relative and that the American variety looks pretty good when compared to that of many other countries. Our system depends on the collective judgments of many impartial, though imperfect, humans. That is certainly better than depending on the biased judgments of a few, equally imperfect, ones.

JUSTICE AND POWER

As we have just seen, the task of establishing justice is two-fold. It requires a proper relationship between the government and the people, as well as among the people themselves. In other words, the citizen must first be protected from abuse by his government. Second, the government must protect him from abuse by his fellow citizens. The first requires some restrictions on the government's use of force, especially by police officials. The second may require the expansion of government force to cope with the increasing crime rate.

This dilemma in regulating the proper use of force can be resolved only by looking more closely at the relationship between power and justice. Force is the most obvious form of power—about as subtle as a rifle shot. It can serve the cause of justice only if it is controlled by another more intangible kind of power—the authority of the laws. But if those laws are not applied by the courts in a fair and impartial manner, they lose the respect upon which their authority depends. They are then no longer just.

When authority is undermined by the biased and unequal application of the law, it is often because illegal or unfair influence has been used to gain special favors. It was the suspicion of unfair influence that inspired the criticism of President Ford's pardon of ex-President Nixon in 1974. This contributed to the growing distrust of American justice. The government, however, can seldom maintain a standard of justice higher than the ethical level of the people it governs. Perhaps the most hopeful sign for our nation's future is the growing demand that influence must not be used to buy legal favors, that the authority of laws must control the use of force, and that justice must, in that way, be made more perfect.

Notes

1. U.S. Bureau of the Census, *Statistical Abstract of the U.S., 1973,* p. 152.
2. Ibid., p. 146, and *Los Angeles Times,* Jan. 14, 1973, and Oct. 4, 1974.
3. 342 U.S. 165 (1952).
4. A discussion of the case by Fred M. Hechinger appears in the *Los Angeles Times,* April 13, 1975, Part XI, p. 3.
5. *Lochner* v. *N.Y.,* 198 U.S. 45 (1905), *Adkins* v. *Children's Hospital,* 261 U.S. 525 (1923), and *Adair* v. *U.S.,* 208 U.S. 161 (1908).
6. 410 U.S. 113 and 410 U.S. 179 (1973).
7. *Barron* v. *Baltimore,* 7 Peters 243 (1833).
8. 268 U.S. 652 (1925).
9. 302 U.S. 319 (1937).
10. The leading case in this matter is an old one, *Calder* v. *Bull,* 3 Dallas 386 (1798).
11. *U.S.* v. *Lovett,* 328 U.S. 303 (1946) and *U.S.* v. *Brown,* 381 U.S. 437 (1965).
12. Jerome H. Skolnick, *The Politics of Protest,* A report to the National Commission on the Causes and Prevention of Violence (New York: Clarion Books, Simon & Schuster, Inc., 1969), pp. 151–54 and 384. Low educational backgrounds are noted also for new policemen in Berkeley, California and Washington, D.C.
13. *Los Angeles Times,* March 31, 1975, p. 1.
14. *Statistical Abstract 1974,* p. 152.
15. *Statistical Abstract 1974,* p. 158.
16. *Los Angeles Times,* August 28, 1974, p. 1.
17. *Schmerber* v. *California,* 384 U.S. 757 (1966).
18. 392 U.S. 1 (1968).
19. The cases were *Peters* v. *New York,* involving burglary; and *Sibron* v. *New York,* narcotics, 20 L. Ed. 2d 917 (1968).
20. Paul W. Tappan, *Crime, Justice and Correction* (New York: McGraw-Hill, 1960), p. 329.
21. 367 U.S. 643 (1961).
22. *Carroll* v. *U.S.,* 267 U.S. 132 (1925).
23. *Harris* v. *U.S.,* 331 U.S. 145 (1947).
24. In this connection, see *Johnson* v. *U.S.,* 333 U.S. 10 (1948) and, more importantly, *Brinegar* v. *U.S.,* 338 U.S. 160 (1949).
25. Fred E. Inbau and John E. Reid, *Criminal Interrogation and Confessions* (Baltimore: The Williams & Wilkins Co., 1962), p. 28.
26. Questionable police practices sometimes occur at this point. See Diane Schroerluke, *Police Personnel Complaints and Redress Remedies* (Berkeley, Calif.: American Civil Liberties Union, Berkeley-Albany Chapter, 1970). Mimeographed.
27. Ed Cray, *The Big Blue Line* (New York: Coward-McCann, 1967), p. 73, and A. C. Germann, Frank D. Day, and Robert R. J. Gallati, *Introduction to Law Enforcement* (Springfield, Ill.: Charles C Thomas, 1962), pp. 164–65.
28. Cray, p. 70.
29. *Malloy* v. *Hogan,* 378 U.S. 1 (1964).
30. 384 U.S. 436 (1966).
31. Cited in Robert F. Cushman, ed., *Cases in Civil Liberties* (New York: Appleton-Century-Crofts, 1968), p. 242.
32. Cray, pp. 77–82.

33. 277 U.S. 438 (1928). In dissent, Justice Holmes called wiretapping a "dirty business."
34. *Silverman* v. *U.S.*,365 U.S. 505 (1961) and *Berger* v. *New York,* 388 U.S. 41 (1967).
35. 389 U.S. 347 (1967).
36. *Statistical Abstract 1973* p. 157.
37. *U.S.* v. *District Court,* 407 U.S. 297 (1972).
38. "The Assault on Privacy," *Newsweek,* July 27, 1970, p. 16.
39. Staff of *The New York Times, The End of a Presidency* (Toronto: Bantam Books, 1974), pp. 32, 47–48, 229, 320–21.
40. In 1975, President Ford proposed a ban on handguns known as "Saturday-night specials."
41. The National Commission on the Causes and Prevention of Violence, *To Establish Justice, to Insure Domestic Tranquillity* (Toronto: Bantam Books, 1970), p. 158.
42. 381 U.S. 479 (1965).
43. *Illinois* v. *Allen* 397 U.S. 337 (1970).
44. 372 U.S. 335 (1963). An intriguing account of the case appears in Anthony Lewis, *Gideon's Trumpet* (N.Y.: Random House, Inc., 1964).
45. 378 U.S. 478 (1964).
46. *Argersinger* v. *Hamlin,* 407 U.S. 25 (1972).
47. *Kirby* v. *Illinois,* 406 U.S. 682.
48. Quoted by Justice Black, *Reid* v. *Covert,* 354 U.S. 1.
49. Justice Harlan, in dissent, *Duncan* v. *Louisiana,* 20 L. Ed. 2d 491 (1968), and Harry Kalven and Hans Zeisel, *The American Jury* (Boston: Little, Brown & Co., 1966).
50. The ruling affected only state court procedures; federal court verdicts must still be unanimous. *Johnson* v. *Louisiana,* 406 U.S. 356 (1972).
51. *Statistical Abstract 1974,* pp. 154–55 and p. 163.
52. 370 U.S. 660 (1962).
53. 20 L. Ed. 2d 1254 (1968).
54. 92 S.Ct. 2726 (1972).
55. Gallup Poll, *Los Angeles Times,* November 4, 1974, p. 5.
56. *Crime and the Law* (Washington, D.C.: Congressional Quarterly, 1971), pp. 11–14. The prisoner figure includes 21,000 in federal prisons, 185,000 in state prisons, and 160,000 in local jails. And Hoyt Gimlin, "Street Crimes in America," *Editorial Research Reports on Challenges for the 1970's* (Washington, D.C.: Congressional Quarterly, 1970), p. 78.
57. *Statistical Abstract 1973,* p. 155.
58. Gimlin, p. 78.
59. Ronald L. Goldfarb, *Washington Post,* reprinted in *Los Angeles Times,* July 26, 1970, Section G, p. 1.
60. Reo M. Christenson, *Challenge and Decision,* 3rd ed. (New York: Harper & Row, 1970), p. 221.
61. *Los Angeles Times,* October 1, 1974, p. 4.
62. Ibid., September 12, 1974, Part 1-B, p. 1.
63. *Statistical Abstract 1973,* p. 160 and *Los Angeles Times,* January 14, 1973, Part II, p. 2.
64. *Statistical Abstract 1973,* p. 166 and *Los Angeles Times,* August 27, 1972, Sec. B, pp. 2–3.
65. Tappan, p. 749.
66. *Los Angeles Times,* November 23, 1973, p. 3.
67. See the interview with James Vorenberg, Executive Director of the Commission on Law Enforcement, *Los Angeles Times,* September 4, 1974, Part II, p. 5.
68. *Los Angeles Times,* April 15, 1974, p. 1.
69. *Statistical Abstract 1973,* p. 152.
70. See Ch. 11, p. 277.

6 EQUAL JUSTICE UNDER LAW:
Of dreams deferred

I have a dream.
               Martin Luther King, Jr.

What happens to a dream deferred?

Does it dry up
like a raisin in the sun?
Or fester like a sore—
And then run?
Does it stink like rotten meat?
Or crust and sugar over—
like a syrupy sweet?

Maybe it just sags
like a heavy load.

Or does it explode?
               Langston Hughes*

Human equality is the often unspoken assumption underlying many rights guaranteed in the Constitution. This chapter is devoted to the broad concept of equality, and to the gap that still exists between that ideal and the realities of American life.

EQUAL PROTECTION OF THE LAWS: JUSTICE IN BLACK AND WHITE

Following the "due process" clause in the Fourteenth Amendment is another crucial clause which says that no state shall "deny to any person within its jurisdiction the equal protection of the law." In the last quarter of a century, no part of the Constitution has had a more explosive impact on American life than this one.

A Color-blind Constitution

For 90 years, the Supreme Court interpreted the Fourteenth Amendment in a way that gave little help to black Americans—the very group it was designed to aid. In 1883, for example, after white supremacists regained control of most southern states, the Court declared unconstitutional much of the 1875 Civil Rights Act. This act had prohibited racial discrimination in restaurants and other "public accommodations."

Separate but Equal
In 1896, the Court upheld, in the famous case of *Plessy* v. *Ferguson,* a Louisiana law requiring separate but equal railroad coaches for black and white passengers.[1] Such a law, the Court said, did not deny Negroes their constitutional right to equal protection. The result of this "separate but equal" doctrine was to permit the spread of "legal" segregation of blacks and whites to almost every area of southern life. This included schools, theaters, restaurants, courthouses, rest rooms, and marriage chapels, as well as railroad coaches. Only Justice John Marshall Harlan sounded a dissenting cry, largely ignored for over half a century. "Our Constitution," he wrote, "is color-blind."

A Segregated Nation
Whether or not the Constitution was color-blind, most white Americans had no such eye trouble. While the South relied chiefly on segregation laws to keep the races apart, the North was a bit more subtle. White businessmen simply refused to serve blacks or employ them in any prominent positions.

Moreover, the Supreme Court continued to set forth the separate but equal doctrine. In 1899 it approved a high school only for whites on the plea that the county in question could not afford another one for blacks.[2] In 1927 it sanctioned the requirement that a Chinese student attend a school for blacks rather than one for whites closer to her home.[3] Not until 1940 did the

Court require school boards to pay black teachers as much as white ones of equal training and experience.[4]

Most shameful of all was the example set by the national government, which became increasingly discriminatory. During Woodrow Wilson's admininistration, the number of black presidential appointees dropped from thirty-one to nine. Moreover, segregation of offices and toilet facilities was suddenly introduced for employees of the Post Office, the Treasury, and the Navy. The armed forces were not integrated until the administration of President Truman (1945–53).[5] Finally, at the pinnacles of power, no cabinet position escaped Caucasian control until 1966. At that time, President Johnson designated Robert C. Weaver as Secretary of the newly created Department of Housing and Urban Development. The next year Thurgood Marshall became the first black on the Supreme Court. Mexican-Americans, Asian-Americans, and American Indians are still waiting for their chance.

The Decline of Compulsory Segregation

All this time, however, the "equal protection" clause remained in the background. Occasionally it was invoked in discrimination cases. Back in 1886 the Supreme Court used it to decide that San Francisco business licensing laws were unconstitutionally discriminating against Chinese laundry operators.[6] Much later, it was invoked to permit black people to vote in Democratic party primary elections,[7] serve on juries,[8] and attend previously all-white state law schools.[9]

But it was not until 1954 that the Fourteenth Amendment began to fulfill its initial promise of racial justice. In that year, the landmark case of *Brown* v. *Board of Education of Topeka* overturned the separate but equal doctrine.[10] This *Brown* decision produced profound changes in American society. First, its immediate result was to declare racial segregation in the public schools to be an unconstitutional violation of the equal protection clause. Second, it established a precedent for ending racial segregation in all government facilities, such as public parks, beaches, prisons, and municipally owned buses.

Third, the *Brown* decision constituted a moral victory for blacks. It began a period of rapidly rising expectations embodied in the civil rights movement led by Martin Luther King, Jr. During the next few years blacks made some major gains, but by 1965 the gap between expectation and actual change caused many hopes to fade. As a result, certain parts of the civil rights movement were converted into a crusade for "black power."

A fourth effect of the *Brown* decision was to increase tensions between the South, where racial prejudice was most obvious, and the rest of the nation. In 1957 President Eisenhower had to send troops into Little Rock, Arkansas to enforce a court order requiring the integration of a local high school. Five years later, President Kennedy responded the same way to insure the enrollment of James Meredith, the first black ever admitted to the University of Mississippi.

Although the Court's desegregation order is still the subject of bitter dispute, there is considerable evidence to support the belief that separate educational facilities are inherently unequal. Twelve years after the *Brown* decision, a report on *Racial Isolation in the Public Schools* was issued by the United States Commission on Civil Rights. The report was based largely on a 1966 study of thousands of black students in the ninth and twelfth grades.[11] It concluded that racial segregation in schools tends to lower students' achievement and restrict their ambition. After black students were placed in integrated schools, they showed improved academic progress. The chief reason for this seems to be the superior educational backgrounds of their classmates' parents and the resulting higher occupational goals of the classmates themselves.[12]

Busing and the Future

The *Brown* decision left three crucial questions unanswered regarding school desegregation: Is compulsory busing an appropriate means of integrating black and white students? Is segregation based on neighborhood residential patterns, rather than on legal requirements, also unconstitutional? Is it necessary to disregard school district boundaries if that is required to end racial segregation?

In April 1971 the Supreme Court held that busing was an appropriate method of correcting school segregation.[13] Four months later, however, ten school buses were firebombed in Pontiac, Michigan to protest court-ordered desegregation in that city. Whether because of prejudice against blacks, fear for the safety of students, or a sentimental attachment to neighborhood schools, politicians soon learned that opposition to "forced busing" was a surefire vote getter. Following the lead of Governor George Wallace of Alabama, President Nixon persuaded Congress in 1972 to restrict the use of federal funds for busing. But the issue was not dead. Violence flared again in 1974 in South Boston. There eight black children were injured as angry whites tried to block court-ordered busing used to bring better racial balance to South Boston High School. As a result of the Boston situation, the busing issue again became very heated. It is interesting to note that on a national basis in 1970 more than 4 out of 10 pupils took the bus to school each day, apparently with little resentment.[14] Yet by 1974 a poll showed that nearly 7 out of 10 Americans were opposed to busing when required for school desegregation.[15] Meanwhile, however, we are haunted by two nagging questions: Why was there no white outcry against compulsory busing used to keep schools segregated for so many years? Moreover, what other methods can help both black and white children overcome generations of bigotry if segregated neighborhoods still prevent them from getting to know one another?

As demonstrated in Pontiac and South Boston, the tragedy of racial friction has shifted from the South to the North. There, school segregation tends to mirror housing segregation. It has not been established by law as *de*

Police were required to protect black students bused to South Boston High School, Boston, Massachusetts, January 8, 1975.

jure or legally compelled segregation, but rather by racially separated neighborhoods or *de facto* segregation. At least two members of the Supreme Court, Justices Douglas and Powell, have concluded that *de facto* segregation is just as unconstitutional as that compelled by law *(de jure).*[16] For three other justices, the decisive factor is whether continued segregation is deliberately fostered through the drawing of school boundaries and the location of new schools. In any event, the line between *de jure* and *de facto* segregation seems to be fading. The North can no longer look South with smug self-righteousness.

For twenty years after the *Brown* decision, the Supreme Court applied the equal protection clause in a relentless attack on segregation within individual school districts. But if one district is "overwhelmingly black in all of its schools, surrounded by . . . suburban school districts overwhelmingly white . . . ,"[17] then real integration within a district is impossible. This was the situation confronting the Supreme Court in the 1974 case of *Milliken* v. *Bradley,* involving Detroit and its suburbs. The Court's decision in this case marked the first clear-cut reversal of its twenty-year devotion to the cause of integrated education. With Justice Stewart joining the four Nixon appointees, the Court ruled 5 to 4 that the constitutional doctrine of desegregation did not require school districts to be combined. Nor did it require busing across school district boundaries or between suburbs and central city. Since the racial distribution of the Detroit area is similar to that of other large metropolitan regions, it seems that this decision will have the effect of legalizing *de facto* segregation in many of our cities. Thus it is not surprising that a moderate black leader, Roy Wilkins of the National Association for the Advancement of Colored People (NAACP), called it "the way to apartheid, the South African equivalent of strict racial separation."[18]

Racial Politics

Governments exist to protect the rights of minorities. The loved and the rich need no protection.

Wendell Phillips

Discrimination by the government is prohibited by the Constitution. But discrimination by private groups can only be banned through laws passed by our elected representatives. Ultimately, then, it is popular prejudice, partially reflected in voting behavior, which determines how much equality really exists in the United States.

The many causes of racial prejudice are too complex to evaluate thoroughly here, but they include bias in print and on television, psychological needs, and economic competition. Bias in books and the mass media has been reduced considerably as a result of more careful use of the language and more favorable depictions of black people. For example, black men are no longer called "boys" or shown holding only menial jobs like janitor or garbage man. Nevertheless, the psychological need to boost one's ego by looking down on someone "worse" does not seem to have lessened in our society.

Economic considerations probably play a large role in this. After World War II, two researchers found that veterans who slid downward in socioeconomic status (those who had to take poorer jobs, for example) showed greater prejudice than those who were more successful.[19] Nearly twenty years later a new survey found that racial prejudice was most prevalent among the troubled "middle Americans" who were hardest hit by inflation, high taxes, and rising unemployment. "The more precarious a family's hold on economic security," the study revealed, "the more menaced it feels by . . . black militancy."[20] In light of the economic recession of the mid 1970s, such a finding could be disturbing for the future of race relations in America. But it is encouraging to know that the reduction of racial prejudice may be a very positive by-product of increased economic prosperity for all Americans.

Another hopeful sign is that public opinion polls showed an unmistakable increase in tolerance toward ethnic minorities in the late 1960s. Between 1967 and 1969, for example, the percentage of Americans who would vote for a Jew for president jumped from 82 to 86. Those willing to vote for a Negro climbed still more, from 54 to 67 percent.[21] Even in the area of mixed marriages, tolerance has increased. In 1967 a unanimous Supreme Court declared state laws prohibiting racial intermarriage (miscegenation) to be an unconstitutional violation of both the equal protection and due process clauses.[22] But in 1968 an international Gallup poll found that 72 percent of Americans opposed white-nonwhite marriage. This was the highest percentage in any of the thirteen nations surveyed.[23]

By 1972, however, opposition to black-white marriages had dropped to 60 percent and the number of such marriages in the U.S. had increased to about 65,000.

State Action

By 1947 eighteen states had prohibited racial discrimination in privately owned restaurants, hotels, and theaters.[24] By 1962 twenty-one states, beginning with New York in 1945, had passed laws forbidding racial discrimination in employment. Moreover, discrimination in at least a portion of the housing market had been barred in nineteen states and fifty-five cities by 1963.[25] However, a 1972 Supreme Court decision upheld the power of a state, if it wished, to issue liquor licenses to private lodges (the Moose, in this case) which refused to serve black guests.[26]

Population Changes and Political Power

It should be noted that these state prohibitions against racial discrimination were found only in the northern and western states. This may be explained largely by the steady movement of black people from the South to other sections of the country, and from rural areas to urban ones. The percentage of all blacks residing in the eleven southern states dropped from 77 in 1940 to 52 in 1972. The four cities with the largest black population in 1972 were northern ones: New York, Chicago, Detroit, and Philadelphia. Moreover, the 1960 census revealed that for the first time in American history a higher percentage of blacks than whites had urban homes.[27]

One effect of such population changes was to increase black political power. To begin with, voting restrictions were fewer in the North and West than in the South. Because black voters were more heavily concentrated in cities, they were better able to elect black candidates and influence the passage of civil rights laws. As a result of the 1974 congressional elections, there were seventeen blacks in the House of Representatives, more than at any time since the Reconstruction period following the Civil War. All were Democrats from big cities. In 1967 Edward W. Brooke, Republican from Massachusetts, became the first black senator in this century. Such encouraging progress, however, should not obscure the fact that even now blacks, with 11 percent of the population, have less than 4 percent of the members of Congress.

In state governments, the situation is similar. Two lieutenant governorships, in California and Colorado, are the top posts held by blacks.

At the local level, however, there were 108 black mayors in 1974, up 31.7 percent from a year earlier. These included mayors of such major cities as Los Angeles, Detroit, Atlanta, and Raleigh, North Carolina.[28] At all levels of government, the total number of black elected officials more than doubled between 1968 and 1972.[29]

Other ethnic minorities also won important victories at the ballot box in the mid-1970s. Asian-Americans have done relatively well in Hawaiian politics for many years. But it was not until 1974 that Norman Mineta of California became the first Asian-American elected to Congress from the mainland. The same year Raul Castro became the first Mexican-American governor of Arizona, and Jerry Apodaca the first Spanish-surnamed governor of New Mexico since 1918.

Congressional Action

Congress, lagging behind many of the states, did not enact a national civil rights law until 1957. That law was followed by several others over the next decade. The 1957 act created the United States Commission on Civil Rights. It was authorized to investigate both voting discrimination prohibited by the Fifteenth Amendment, as well as violations of the Fourteenth's equal protection clause. The Civil Rights Act of 1960 allowed the federal courts, in suits filed by the attorney general, to declare persons qualified to vote. Many of the persons were blacks who had been prevented from voting in southern states because of their race.

Taken together, the 1957 and 1960 laws opened the discrimination door a crack, but it was the passage of the 1964 Civil Rights Act that seemed to unhinge it completely. This law followed the often violent sit-ins and marches of the early 1960s which dramatized the need for further congressional action. Against a background of tension and fear, President Kennedy, on June 19, 1963, submitted to Congress the proposal which was the basis for the 1964 Civil Rights Act. It was passed by Congress exactly one year later, but only after the man who initiated it was assassinated.

The Civil Rights Act of 1964

The sweeping new law was divided into eleven parts or titles, two of which are particularly significant. Title II prohibits discrimination based on race, color, religion, or national origin in restaurants, gas stations, theaters, stadiums, hotels, and similar public accommodations. Title VII forbids discrimination based on race, color, religion, sex, or national origin in employment practices. There were also several other important provisions in the 1964 act. One makes a sixth-grade education sufficient proof of literacy for purposes of state voting requirements. Another cuts off federal financial assistance from programs, including schools, which practice discrimination. A third allows the U.S. attorney general to bring suit against schools defying court decisions on desegregation. But the 1964 act still did not deal effectively with discrimination at the polls.

The Battle for the Ballot

The Fifteenth Amendment, adopted in 1870, was supposed to have prohibited voting requirements based on race. Yet many states, especially in the South, showed great skill in getting around it. Some state laws imposed ridiculously complex "literacy tests" as a prerequisite for voting, and there were "white primary" elections which excluded blacks from the selection of party candidates. Poll taxes also kept poor people (including most blacks) from the ballot boxes. And certain states still had "grandfather clauses" which suspended other voting requirements if one's grandfather had been able to vote. Of course, the grandfathers of most blacks had been slaves and thus had not been able to vote.

Over the years several of these devices were declared unconstitutional, but many blacks still could not vote. President Johnson, therefore, asked for additional legislation. With an expanded Democratic majority resulting from the 1964 elections, Congress responded favorably with the Voting Rights Act of 1965. Its major provision permitted the national government to appoint voting examiners. These examiners could register persons to vote in any area where there was a state literacy requirement and less than 50 percent of the persons of voting age had actually voted in the last election. Under these circumstances, the state literacy tests were suspended. The act also prohibited poll taxes as voting requirements in state elections. In this area, it supplemented the Twenty-fourth Amendment which had forbidden poll taxes in the election of national officials.

The 1965 Voting Rights Act is perhaps the most effective civil rights legislation ever passed. As a result of it, the percentage of blacks registered to vote in the eleven southern states zoomed from 36 to 65 between 1964 and 1968.[30] While there were only thirty-six black state legislators in the entire nation in 1960, their number grew to 238 after the 1972 elections. Lounds County, Alabama exemplifies the dramatic change. In the spring of 1965, it had not a single registered black voter. In the fall of 1970, it elected a black sheriff.[31] In 1975, the Voting Rights Act was broadened to aid Mexican-Americans by requiring that ballots in certain areas be printed in Spanish.

Further Congressional Action

Ironically, the civil rights laws also stimulated more violent bigotry. After the passage of the 1965 act, many people were arrested, and some wounded, during voter registration drives in various southern states. On April 4, 1968, Martin Luther King, Jr., was assassinated in Memphis, Tennessee. He was attempting to gather support for a strike of that city's predominantly black rubbish collectors. Frustration over the death of Rev. King, winner of the Nobel Peace Prize and the most influential black man in America, caused serious riots in several major cities. Partly as a result, the civil rights movement became more militant, and Congress passed another civil rights law.

The Civil Rights Act of 1968 included harsh penalties for those who crossed state lines to incite a riot or who interfered with a person's exercise of his civil rights. The act also contained a fair housing provision. But this turned out to be unnecessary because the Supreme Court ruled that a one-hundred-year-old law actually barred discrimination in disposing of all property. In 1972 another law prohibited job discrimination by state and local government agencies.

Racial Realities

Any attempt to assess racial attitudes and progress toward equality in the 1970s requires a look at the real conditions of minority life in the U.S.

Employment

In spite of persistent obstacles, nonwhite Americans (mostly black) seem to be making important advances in the struggle for better jobs. Between 1960 and 1971, for example, the total number of professional and technical jobs increased by 49 percent, while the number of blacks holding down these positions jumped by 128 percent.[32] Perhaps the employment provisions of the 1964 Civil Rights Act have really begun to pay off. Improvement in this area may also be due to Executive Order 11246 issued by President Johnson in 1965. This required all employers with federal government contracts (employing about one-third of all workers in the nation) to take "affirmative action" in seeking out minority group employees.[33] Although such action does not usually require the employment of a minimum "quota" of minorities, it has resulted in widespread charges of "reverse discrimination," especially against white males. Many jobs have gone to women, to blacks, and to other minority group employees instead of to equally qualified white men.

In some occupations, however, racism still seems more deeply rooted than in others. Just four percent of police officers throughout the nation are members of racial minorities, for example, and only one percent of all airline pilots.[34] Asian-Americans, sometimes regarded as the most successful minority, are substantially underemployed in the construction, electronic, and printing industries in the San Francisco area.[35] Contrary to general opinion, Jews have been largely excluded from top jobs in the fields of banking and public utilities.[36]

Many minorities have indeed been hired for jobs previously reserved for whites. But statistics indicate that this may be a kind of "tokenism" that gives only well-publicized positions to nonwhites. For most years since 1960, total nonwhite unemployment rates have been at least twice as high as those for whites.[37]

Income

Like employment, income figures have revealed substantial racial variations. In 1972, for example, the median family income for the entire nation was

$10,350. At the same time, WASPs (white Anglo-Saxon Protestants or those of English, Welsh, or Scottish ancestry) averaged a thousand dollars higher, while the median for Spanish-surnamed families was only $7,600 and for blacks $6,860.[38] In 1973, similar figures were: whites, $12,595; Cuban-Americans, $11,191; Mexican-Americans, $8,434; blacks, $7,269; and Puerto Ricans, $6,779. Average black family income, which had reached 61 percent of the white figure in 1969, dropped to 58 percent four years later.[39] In 1970 American Indian families trailed all ethnic groups with a median income of $5,832.[40]

Education

In 1964, over 90 percent of the black students in seventeen southern and border states were still attending all-black schools.[41] Progress was so slow primarily because the 1954 *Brown* decision ordered desegregation to proceed "with all deliberate speed." The Supreme Court recognized that practical problems were worse in some districts than in others and would take time to solve. The result was that further lawsuits were required to integrate school districts that refused to do so voluntarily.

The years since 1964 have seen great changes, however. Spurred by threats to cut off federal funds and by court decisions that condemned too much slowness, the pace of southern desegregation speeded up. In an ironic switch, by 1973 there was more racial integration in southern schools than in northern ones. While 46 percent of all black students in the South were attending schools with a white majority, the figure was only 28 percent in the North and West.[42] More surprising was the reluctance of Casper W. Weinberger, Secretary of Health, Education, and Welfare, to cut off federal aid to northern school districts that were slow in developing integration plans.[43] Southern school boards might well have been amazed at such discriminatory patience by a leading federal official. It should be noted that where busing has been used for integration purposes, better race relations have often resulted. But, despite the study referred to earlier, there seems to be little resulting change in student achievement.[44]

Mexican-Americans or Chicanos are the second largest racial minority in the U.S. Their problems are also obvious in the field of public education. Of the 1.4 million Chicano schoolchildren in Colorado, Texas, New Mexico, Arizona, and California, nearly half (635,000) are attending predominantly Mexican-American schools. Moreover, while Chicanos comprise 17 percent of the public school enrollment in these five southwestern states, they account for only 10 percent of the school board members, 4 percent of the teachers, and 3 percent of the school principals.[45] The U.S. Civil Rights Commission reported in 1972 that 80 percent of Chicano students were receiving education which showed little respect for their culture or the Spanish language. American Indians are faced with educational disadvantages that are even greater. Ten percent of those over age fourteen have never been to school at all and more than half never completed the eighth grade.

But there have been some educational changes affecting America's minorities. In 1974, in the case of *Lau* v. *Nichols* the Supreme Court unanimously held that San Francisco public schools must provide bilingual and bicultural instruction for Chinese-speaking students. This decision may have broad implications for Puerto Rican, Mexican, and other minority students. Never before had the Court insisted that our varied backgrounds and native tongues deserve special educational attention.

There was another issue in higher education, however, that was still plaguing the courts in 1975. Was it constitutional for universities, in an attempt to assist racial minorities, to use lower entrance requirements for them than for whites? An earlier case involving admission policies at the University of Washington Law School was resolved on a technicality that evaded the basic question of this apparent "reverse discrimination."

Housing

Today, as we have seen, segregated schools are chiefly the result of segregated neighborhoods. These have persisted in spite of the fact that local laws prohibiting blacks from living in certain areas were declared unconstitutional in 1917.[46] Also, "restrictive covenants" barring blacks, Asians, and Jews from certain neighborhoods were invalidated in 1948.[47]

These legal advances, however, did little to stop increasing residential segregation in many urban areas. The black population of central cities increased 31.6 percent between 1960 and 1970, while the white population, fleeing to the suburbs, dropped 1.3 percent.[48]

Among the most segregated cities in 1970 were Shreveport, Louisiana and Dallas, Texas with Newark, New Jersey not far behind. Racially integrated housing, on the other hand, was most widespread in Cambridge, Mass., East Orange, New Jersey, and the San Francisco Bay area.[49]

The causes of housing segregation are too complex to analyze completely here. But one that deserves mention is the widespread belief, almost totally false, that if a black family moves into a white neighborhood, property values will fall. Except for a brief period in which white homeowners, inspired by this myth, try quickly to sell their houses, this is simply not true. A study of 10,000 home sales over a five-year period in San Francisco, Oakland, and Philadelphia, showed that property values are usually at least as high in racially integrated areas as in all-white ones.[50] The opposite belief is often fostered by real estate salesmen, called "block-busters," who spread the rumor in order to sell more houses.

EQUAL PROTECTION OF THE LAWS: ONE MAN, ONE VOTE

A leading authority on constitutional law has observed that "Negroes would probably constitute a minority of those who have invoked the equal protection clause against discriminatory treatment."[51] Indeed, the largest group to benefit from this clause is not racial but geographic—those who live in and around the nation's major cities.

Rural Dominance

Farm interests have dominated American government for most of our history. This was quite proper until urban dwellers began to outnumber the rural population shortly before 1920. But the situation persisted until the 1960s and still may, to some degree.

Legislative Apportionment

Perhaps the chief reason for the great political power of rural areas lies in the way seats in Congress and the state legislatures were distributed or apportioned. The United States Senate, with two members per state, gives farmers an enormous advantage. This is because the small states, mostly rural, have as many votes as bigger ones with huge metropolitan centers. The fifty-two senators from the twenty-six smallest states represent fewer people than the four senators from California and New York.[52] This imbalance, or malapportionment, of Senate seats will not improve unless there is a major population shift back to rural areas. Nothing can be done about it legally since the only provision of the Constitution which cannot be amended, according to Article V, is the one which guarantees an equal number of senators from each state.

The state legislatures themselves have been responsible for drawing boundaries of districts from which their own members are elected. They also determine the boundaries for congressional districts from which members of the U.S. House of Representatives are chosen. Since state legislatures were initially under farm control, it is not surprising that they apportioned these districts in such a way as to keep their own jobs and sometimes to help elect their friends to Congress. Consequently, while rural areas were losing thousands of people to the lure of the city and its suburbs, they were able to retain most of their legislative seats.

Gerrymandering

State legislators have been in the habit of drawing election district boundaries to their own advantage for at least a century and a half. The weirdly shaped results became known as *gerrymanders,* after Governor Elbridge Gerry of Massachusetts. Gerry signed a reapportionment bill in 1812 containing a district whose shape resembled a salamander. More will be said about gerrymandering in Chapter 11. Here it will suffice to say that until 1962 the Supreme Court considered it a political issue that the Constitution intended to be decided not by the courts but by the popularly elected legislative and executive branches.

". . . People, not trees or acres"

After refusing to rule on it in a 1946 case,[53] the Court decided sixteen years later in *Baker* v. *Carr*[54] that legislative apportionment *was* subject to judicial attention. If equal numbers of voters could not elect equal numbers of legislators, they could scarcely expect the constitutionally guaranteed "equal protection of the laws." The *Baker* case involved the lower house of the Tennessee legislature. It was interpreted by the courts to require that at least one house of all state legislatures be chosen from equally populated districts.

Two years later, in *Wesberry* v. *Sanders,* the *Baker* decision was broadened. The Court voted, 6–2, that state legislatures must also apportion congressional districts in a way that permitted equal numbers of people to elect equal numbers of U.S. representatives.[55] Completing the process, the Court ruled in 1964 that the "equal protection" clause required *both* houses of a state legislature to be elected from districts with approximately the same population. The key case, *Reynolds* v. *Sims,* produced the "one man, one vote" formula. This held that a person's vote in any district should have as much influence in electing a candidate as any other person's vote in another district. As Chief Justice Earl Warren put it: "Legislators represent people, not trees or acres."[56] One man, one vote was extended still further in *Avery* v. *Midland County,* a case from Texas. It demanded the same standards in the selection of "a city council, school board, or county governing board,"[57] as had been established for state and national legislators (except U.S. senators).

Eight years after the *Baker* decision, ninety-five of America's ninety-nine state legislative bodies had been reapportioned to meet the one man, one vote standard.[58] Similar progress occurred in congressional redistricting. The result has been a vast increase in the political power of the cities and suburbs at the expense of rural areas.

EQUAL PROTECTION IN OTHER AREAS

The importance of the "equal protection" clause extends even beyond questions of race or legislative apportionment. It also affects the relative legal status of men and women, citizens and aliens, rich and poor, married and single.

Sexism and the Law

Women are an oppressed class
    Redstockings Manifesto

Whether women are oppressed, as radical feminists often insist, may depend on the definition of that term. But there can be no doubt that our life experiences depend largely on our sex. To this degree, at least, ours is a "sexist" society. Few women hold positions as powerful decision makers. Clare Boothe Luce, a distinguished former playwright, congresswoman, and ambassador, pointed out that in 1974 there was but one woman among the 1,366 members of the New York Stock Exchange.[59] While women held 40 percent of all professional and technical jobs in the U.S. in 1973, they accounted for only 2 percent of all engineers, 4 percent of architects, 5 percent of lawyers and judges, and 9 percent of physicians.[60] In some occupations, women have even lost ground. In 1963, for example, there were 168 women bank presidents in the country, but by 1973 their number dropped to 40.

Worst of all, working women make less money than men who have similar jobs, and this discrepancy is widening. The median income of women working full-time was 63.9 percent of that of their male counterparts in 1955. But it had slipped to 57.9 percent in 1972.[61] Yet the percentage of women in the total labor force has increased. In 1972, 55 percent of single women and 42 percent of married women were working outside their homes, a rise of 4 percent over the preceding five years.[62]

Political Progress

In 1869 Wyoming became the first state to give women the right to vote. But it was not until 1920 that the Nineteenth Amendment to the Constitution extended this right to women throughout the nation. In the half century since then, however, they enjoyed little political success. No woman has ever been nominated for the presidency or vice-presidency by a major party, and none has ever been appointed to the Supreme Court. Only three have served in a president's cabinet, and only three more have won election to the U.S. Senate.

In 1974, however, there was a turn in the tide of female political fortunes. Ella T. Grasso's victory in Connecticut made her the first woman ever elected governor who did not succeed her husband in that office. At the same time, Susie Sharp of North Carolina became the first female chief justice of a state supreme court. In San Jose, California Janet G. Hayes became the first woman ever elected mayor of a city with a population of more than a half a million. The U.S. Senate remained an all-male bastion, but women picked up two additional seats in the House of Representatives, giving them a total of 18. Fourteen were Democrats and four were Republicans. In races for state legislatures, women won more than 120 new seats, boosting their percentage of total legislative membership from 6 to 8. New Hampshire led the nation, with women comprising more than 25 percent of the state's legislature.

Legal Evolution

Until recent years, laws pertaining to women reflected the prevailing notions of male superiority. In the nineteenth century, such laws prevented wives from owning property or even serving as legal guardians of their own children. Early in this century, they provided "protection" for the "weaker sex" by limiting the hours women could work and the weights they could lift. In 1963, however, a genuine concern for legal equality was reflected in an act of Congress requiring equal pay for equal work (if women could find such jobs). The next year, as we saw, Title VII of the Civil Rights Act banned discrimination in employment by sex as well as by race. And the 1965 executive order requiring affirmative-action programs by firms with government contracts resulted in more job opportunities for women as well as for ethnic minorities.

Two additional laws were passed by Congress in 1972 which advanced the march toward equality. The Equal Employment Opportunity Act allowed the government to bring job discrimination suits in federal courts. It also required state and local government agencies to end job discrimination. In addition, education amendments were enacted which prohibited sex discrimination in most colleges and universities.

Proof that women were beginning to enjoy the fruits of congressional legislation could be seen in three cases decided by federal district courts in 1974. In one, the General Electric Company was found guilty of violating the 1964 Civil Rights Act by denying disability benefits to pregnant employees. In another, Northwest Airlines was required to give back pay to stewardesses who had been grounded or fired for being overweight and to those who had been paid less than male cabin attendants. In the most far-reaching of the three cases, nine major steel companies and the steelworkers' union agreed to $30.9 million in back pay for 40,000 workers, including 4,000 women, who had been the victims of racial or sex discrimination. This employee back pay was expected to average $770 per worker. The companies involved also pledged to fill 25 percent of certain future job openings with women and another 25 percent with members of minority groups.[63]

Spurred by the women's liberation movement, state legislatures also took action in the early 1970s on a variety of feminist issues. At least 16 states now have laws prohibiting sex discrimination by stores or financial institutions in granting consumer credit. In addition, more than 10 states have now added equal rights amendments to their constitutions.[64]

Women, the Constitution, and the Court
From the time the women's liberation movement gathered momentum in the late 1960s, one of its major objectives was an equal rights amendment (ERA) to the U.S. Constitution. Such an amendment was first proposed more than forty years ago. Its language was clear and simple: "Equality of rights under the law shall not be denied or abridged by the United States or by any state on account of sex." By 1972, the ERA had finally won the necessary approval of two-thirds of both houses of Congress. It was then sent to the state legislatures for ratification. By 1975, it needed approval in only four more states to become the Constitution's twenty-seventh amendment.

It should be noted that the proposal was not a women's rights, but an

© Bettye Lane

Bella Abzug addresses NOW members gathered to demonstrate for ERA in Federal Plaza, Washington, D.C.

equal rights, amendment. It cut both ways. Women might derive new benefits, but they might lose such old advantages as draft exemption and superior claims to alimony and child custody.

For a time, it seemed to some that the Fourteenth Amendment's equal protection clause might make the new addition to the Consitution unnecessary. In 1971, the Supreme Court declared that an Idaho law preferring males over females in the administration of wills was an unconstitutional denial of equal protection of the laws.[65] That unanimous decision implied that distinctions based on sex, like those on race, were "suspect" classifications. A 1973 case involving dependents of women in government service supported this interpretation. But in 1974 the Court upheld a Florida law giving widows tax exemptions that were denied surviving husbands. It was clear, then, that the new amendment would make a difference.

Citizens and Aliens

The ancient Greeks classified foreigners, or noncitizens, as "barbarians." Today we call them aliens, but the implication of inferiority is similar. Its result was that many states denied the 4 million aliens living in the U.S. most welfare benefits, prohibited them from holding government jobs, and excluded them from the practice of law and other professions. Between 1971 and 1973, the Supreme Court declared that each of these discriminatory policies violates the Constitution.[66] This is because the Fourteenth Amendment states that no "person," not no "citizen," may be denied equal protection of the laws.

Money and the Law

The law, in its majestic equality, forbids all men to sleep under bridges, to beg in the streets, and to steal bread—the rich as well as the poor.   Anatole France

The equal protection clause has erased from the law book more distinctions based on race and citizenship than on wealth. But the early 1970s brought progress in this area as well. In *Tate* v. *Short* the Supreme Court ruled that states could not imprison poor defendants merely because they could not afford the fines paid by the richer ones for the same crime.[67] Similarly, it has prohibited the payment of property taxes as a requirement for voting in bond elections and the payment of a filing fee as a requirement to run for office.[68]

In a related area, it is worth noting that for most of our history divorce has been a luxury available only to those with enough money to meet the necessary legal fees and court costs. In 1971, however, the Court held that no state could refuse to grant a divorce "solely because of inability to pay."[69] Unlike most of the cases discussed in this chapter, that decision was based not on the equal protection clause, but on the due process clause.

Marriage and the Law

Whatever its other characteristics, marriage is a legal condition with far-reaching legal effects. The Supreme Court, however, has held that the absence of marriage cannot be used as an excuse for denying illegitimate children the equal protection of laws providing for workmen's compensation benefits, welfare assistance, or child support payments.[70] Yielding still more to modern morality, a six-man majority overturned a Massachusetts law prohibiting the distribution of birth control materials to unmarried persons.[71] Yet the Court would bend only so far. In 1974 it upheld a local zoning regulation aimed at "hippie" communes which prohibited more than two unrelated persons from occupying the same single-family house.

The Future of Equal Protection

While the coverage of the equal protection clause has been broadened greatly since its adoption in 1868, there are a few distinctions it has not erased. Thus far, the Court has not prohibited most legal distinctions favoring adults over children, heterosexuals over homosexuals, or couples over communes. Also, it voted 5–4 in 1973 that the equal protection clause did not prohibit greater tax support for some school districts than for others in the same state.[72] If the general trend of equal protection cases continues, however, that decision may someday be reversed. The Supreme Court seems determined that legal distinctions between groups of people be rational classifications caused by some compelling government interest.

EQUALITY AND POWER

Perhaps the greatest paradox in American society is the constitutional commitment to legal equality in the face of immense inequalities in political power. As long as people vary in wealth, education, status, and other political resources, the struggle for equal treatment will go on. Yet fairness and equality, in life as well as in law, stem not only from official policy but from the widely shared conviction that all humanity is precious. Unless constitutional safeguards protect each of us, the rights of all of us may someday be in danger.

These constitutional rights are sometimes abused in the rough and tumble of legislative and executive procedures. Their chief protection, therefore, has come primarily from the courts. The courts must generally reflect the values of society. But federal judges, appointed to life terms, are usually less vulnerable to the pressures of political influence.

Notes

1. 163 U.S. 573 (1896).
2. *Cumming* v. *County Board of Education,* 175 U.S. 528 (1899).
3. *Gong Lum* v. *Rice,* 257 U.S. 78 (1927).
4. *Allston* v. *School Board,* 112 Fed. 2d 992 (1940).
5. Leslie H. Fishel, Jr., and Benjamin Quarles, eds., *The Negro American* (Glenview, Ill.: Scott, Foresman and Co., 1967), pp. 390, 484–85.
6. *Yick Wo* v. *Hopkins,* 118 U.S. 356 (1886).
7. *Nixon* v. *Condon,* 286 U.S. 73 (1932).
8. *Norris* v. *Alabama,* 294 U.S. 587 (1935).
9. *Sweatt* v. *Painter,* 339 U.S. 629 (1950).
10. 347 U.S. 483 (1954).
11. James Coleman et al., *Equality of Educational Opportunity* (Washington, D.C.: U.S. Government Printing Office, 1966).
12. U.S. Commission on Civil Rights, *Racial Isolation in the Public Schools* (Washington, D.C.: U.S. Government Printing Office, 1967).
13. *Swann* v. *Charlotte-Mecklenburg County Board of Education,* 402 U.S. 1 (1971).
14. U.S. Bureau of the Census, *Statistical Abtract of the United States, 1973* (Washington, D.C.: U.S. Government Printing Office, 1974), p. 129.
15. *Los Angeles Times,* November 4, 1974, p. 6.
16. *Keyes* v. *School District,* 413 U.S. 189 (1973).
17. *Milliken* v. *Bradley,* 94 S.Ct. 3112 (1974).
18. *Los Angeles Times,* August 21, 1974, Part II, p. 7.
19. Bruno Bettelheim and Morris Janowitz, "Prejudice," *Scientific American* (October 1950): 11–13.
20. *Newsweek,* October 6, 1969, p. 32, 45. The Archie Bunker stereotype is a bit unfair in the opinion of several recent observers.
21. These figures are from Gallup polls reported in the *Los Angeles Times,* June 4, 1967, Section G, p. 2, and April 3, 1969, p. 31.
22. *Loving* v. *Virginia,* 388 U.S. 1 (1967).
23. *Los Angeles Times,* November 11, 1968, p. 6. Sweden with 67 percent, was highest in approval. "A slight majority" of American Negroes approved of mixed marriages, "but as many as three in ten disapproved."
24. Gustavus Myers, *History of Bigotry in the United States,* ed. Henry M. Christman (New York: Capricorn Books, G. P. Putnam's Sons, 1960), p. 443.
25. United States Commission on Civil Rights, *Freedom to the Free* (Washington, D.C.: U.S. Government Printing Office, 1963), pp. 132–33, 144.
26. The case involved K. Leroy Irvis, a Pennsylvania legislator. *Moose Lodge* v. *Irvis,* 407 U.S. 163 (1972).
27. *Statistical Abstract 1971,* pp. 16, 21–24, 27.
28. *Los Angeles Herald Examiner,* April 24, 1974, p. A-5.
29. U.S. Bureau of the Census, *The Social and Economic Status of the Black Population in the United States, 1972* (Washington, D.C.: U.S. Government Printing Office, 1973), p. 100.
30. *Statistical Abstract 1971,* p. 365.

31. *Los Angeles Times,* November 29, 1970, Sec. F, p. 8, and January 9, 1975, Part I-A, p. 2.
32. *Time,* June 17, 1974, p. 20.
33. Richard P. Nathan, *Jobs & Civil Rights* (Washington, D.C.: U.S. Government Printing Office, 1969), pp. 2, 92–98.
34. *Los Angeles Times,* January 21, 1974, p. 4, and November 12, 1974, p. 4.
35. Ibid., June 4, 1974, p. 12.
36. *Time,* November 25, 1974, p. 19 and *Los Angeles Times,* October 28, 1974, p. 28.
37. *Social and Economic Status of the Black Population,* p. 38.
38. Ibid., p. 17; and *Los Angeles Times,* May 13, 1973, p. 13.
39. *Los Angeles Times,* July 24, 1974, p. 12, and August 7, 1974, Part II, p. 1.
40. *The Sacramento Bee,* August 28, 1973, p. A-3.
41. *Statistical Abstract 1970,* p. 118.
42. *Los Angeles Times,* May 13, 1974, p. 18.
43. Ibid., September 7, 1974, p. 1.
44. Ibid., March 22, 1972, p. 12; and Neal Justin, *Changing Education,* Summer 1974, pp. 36–38 and *Racial Isolation in the Public Schools,* passim.
45. U.S. Civil Rights Commission, United Press International (UPI) release, *Los Angeles Times,* August 21, 1970, p. 11.
46. *Buchanan* v. *Warley,* 245 U.S. 60 (1917).
47. *Shelley* v. *Kraemer,* 334 U.S. 1 (1948).
48. *Statistical Abstract 1971,* p. 16.
49. These conclusions are derived from block-by-block tabulations evaluated by Karl Taeuber of the University of Wisconsin. *Los Angeles Times,* October 25, 1974, p. 19.
50. Luigi Laurenti, *Property Values and Race* (Berkeley, Calif.: University of California Press, 1960).
51. Robert F. Cushman, *Cases in Civil Liberties* (New York: Appleton-Century-Crofts, 1968), p. 541.
52. Glendon Schubert, ed., *Reapportionment* (New York: Charles Scribner's Sons, 1965), p. 169.
53. *Colegrove* v. *Green,* 328 U.S. 549 (1946).
54. 369 U.S. 186 (1962).
55. 376 U.S. 1 (1964). *Wesberry* did not impose the equal population rule on the basis of the "equal protection" clause of Amendment Fourteen. Rather it was on the basis of Article I, Section 2, which requires that members of the House of Representatives be elected "by the People"—presumably in equal numbers.
56. 377 U.S. 533 (1964).
57. 390 U.S. 474 (1968).
58. *The Christian Science Monitor,* July 23, 1970, p. 1. Only the South Carolina and Alaska lower houses and both houses of the Oregon legislature were apportioned so fairly before 1962 as to require no change. There are only ninety-nine legislative bodies at the state level because Nebraska has a unicameral legislature.
59. *Los Angeles Times,* September 15, 1974, Part IV, p. 14.
60. *U.S. News & World Report,* October 8, 1973, p. 42.
61. Ibid.; and *Congressional Quarterly Weekly Report,* March 18, 1972, p. 599.
62. *Statistical Abstract 1973,* p. 222.
63. *Newsweek,* April 24, 1974, p. 88; and U.S. Department of Labor, *Monthly Labor Review,* June 1974, pp. 69–70 and 73–74. For an excellent series of articles on "Women in the Workplace," see *Monthly Labor Review,* May 1974.
64. Beatrice Rosenberg and Ethel Mendelsohn, "Legal Status of Women," *The Book of the States, 1974–1975* (Lexington, Ky.: The Council of State Governments, 1974), pp. 402–10.
65. *Reed* v. *Reed,* 404 U.S. 71 (1971).

66. *Graham* v. *Richardson,* 403 U.S. 365 (1971), *Sugarman* v. *Dougall,* 93 S.Ct. 2842 (1973), and *In Re Griffiths,* 93 S.Ct. 2851 (1973).
67. 401 U.S. 395 (1971).
68. *Phoenix* v. *Kolodziejski* 399 U.S. 204 (1970) and *Bullock* v. *Carter* 405 U.S. 134 (1972).
69. *Boddie* v. *Connecticut* 401 U.S. 371 (1971).
70. *Weber* v. *Aetna Casualty & Surety Co.,* 406 U.S. 164 (1972), *New Jersey Welfare Rights Organization* v. *Cahill,* 93 S.Ct. 1700 (1973), and *Gomez* v. *Perez,* 409 U.S. 535 (1973).
71. *Eisenstadt* v. *Baird,* 405 U.S. 438 (1972).
72. *San Antonio Ind. School District* v. *Rodriquez,* 93 S.Ct. 1278 (1973).

Bibliography

CHAPTER FOUR **FREEDOM OF EXPRESSION**

Abraham, Henry J. *Freedom and the Court.* New York: Oxford University Press, 1967.
Chafee, Zechariah, Jr. *Free Speech in the United States.* New York: Atheneum Publishers, 1969.
Clor, Harry M., ed. *Censorship and Freedom of Expression.* Chicago: Rand McNally & Co., 1971.
Cushman, Robert F., ed. *Cases in Civil Liberties.* New York: Appleton-Century-Crofts, 1968.
Meiklejohn, Alexander. *Free Speech and Its Relation to Self-Government.* New York: Harper & Row, 1948.
Mill, John Stuart. *On Liberty.* Chicago: Gateway Edition, Henry Regnery Co., 1955.
Sheldon, Charles H., ed. *The Supreme Court: Politicians in Robes.* Beverly Hills, Calif.: Glencoe Press, 1970.

CHAPTER FIVE **THE DEFENDANT'S RIGHTS**

Campbell, James S., et al. *Law and Order Reconsidered.* A Staff Report to the National Commission on the Causes and Prevention of Violence. New York: Bantam Books, 1970.
Casper, Jonathan D. *The Politics of Civil Liberties.* New York: Harper & Row, 1972.
Cray, Ed. *The Big Blue Line.* New York: Coward-McCann, 1967.
Crime and the Law. Washington, D.C.: Congressional Quarterly Service, 1971.
Fellman, David. *The Defendant's Rights.* New York: Holt, Rinehart & Winston, 1958.
Inbau, Fred E., and Reid, John E. *Criminal Interrogation and Confessions.* Baltimore: The Williams and Wilkins Co., 1962.
Summers, Marvin R., and Barth, Thomas E., eds. *Law and Order in a Democratic Society.* Columbus: Charles E. Merrill Publishing Co., 1970.
Tappan, Paul W. *Crime, Justice and Correction.* New York: McGraw-Hill, 1960.

CHAPTER SIX **EQUAL JUSTICE UNDER LAW**

Baker, Gordon E. *Rural Versus Urban Political Power.* Garden City, N.Y.: Doubleday & Co., 1955.
Fishel, Leslie H., Jr., and Quarles, Benjamin, eds. *The Black American.* Glenview, Ill.: Scott, Foresman and Co., 1970.
Myers, Gustavus. *History of Bigotry in the United States.* Edited by Henry M. Christman. New York: Capricorn Books, G. P. Putnam's Sons, 1960.
Schubert, Glendon, ed. *Reapportionment.* New York: Charles Scribner's Sons, 1965.

Seib, Shirley M., ed. *Revolution in Civil Rights,* 3rd ed. Washington, D.C.:
Congressional Quarterly, Inc., 1967.

Silberman, Charles. *Crisis in Black and White.* New York: Random House, 1964.

U.S. Commission on Civil Rights. *Racial Isolation in the Public Schools.* Vol. 1.
Washington, D.C.: U.S. Government Printing Office, 1967.

PART THREE

POLITICAL BEHAVIOR

The only thing necessary for the triumph of evil is for good men to do nothing.

Edmund Burke

A democracy does what a majority of the people wants it to do. Effective methods of communication, therefore, are essential to a democratic government, so that a majority on any particular issue can inform government officials of its wishes. The next three chapters describe the most effective communication channels available in American politics. Chapter 7 stresses public opinion, describing how opinions are formed and then transmitted to the government through pressure groups. Chapter 8 deals with political parties which serve not only to elect officials, but also to help formulate policy choices. Of course, communication is a two-way process. Thus, Chapter 9 considers the campaigns in which politicians attempt to communicate with the people, and the voting process by which the people respond with their choices of leaders and policies. In all three of these chapters, we are dealing with the human behavior that links the citizens to the government. It is this behavior which transmits policy choices back and forth between the people and the politicians.

7 THE PEOPLE'S INFLUENCE:
Public opinion and pressure groups

If there is no struggle, there is no progress. Those who profess to favor freedom, and yet [oppose] agitation, are men who want crops without plowing up the ground. They want the rain without thunder and lightning. . . . Power concedes nothing without a demand. It never did and never will.

Frederick Douglass

Power is a two-way street. Government can change the behavior of the people, and in a democracy the people can also change the behavior of government. But what changes do the people want and how can they get them? This chapter gives us some clues. The chapter begins with the assumption that a democratic government responds to public opinion rather than to the views of individual citizens. Public opinion, in turn, is developed through group pressures. It is communicated to lawmakers and other officials largely by group lobbying. It is with these closely related topics that we will be concerned in this chapter.

THE NATURE OF PUBLIC OPINION

Democracy has been described as a government chosen by and responsive to a majority of the adult population. This is simply another way of saying that it rests upon public opinion. The latter is defined as the beliefs shared by large numbers of people on issues of general importance. For such public opinion to be effective, it must reflect the basic values common to the group and apply them to particular issues.

Political Socialization: The Development of Attitudes

How do people get their opinions? How are the attitudes and values that make up their political culture transferred from one generation to the next? The answers to these questions lie in the study of political socialization, a relatively new research area.

The Family

While many parents are worrying about the "generation gap," there is considerable evidence that most children—at least in political matters—have views quite similar to those of their elders. One study, for example, showed that only 12 percent of the people whose parents were both Democrats identified themselves as Republicans.[1] The influence of the older generation, moreover, is felt at an early age. Greenstein found that by the age of ten over 60 percent of a group of Connecticut children were able to express a party preference. This was true even though only "little more than a third . . . could name even one (leader) of either of the two major parties."[2]

All political ideas tend to either strengthen established values, or to promote change by challenging them. There is little doubt that ideas obtained in the family and in elementary school are generally of the former variety. Children seem to have viewed the American government as the next best thing to Disneyland. They have often attributed to government officials qualities of power and goodness usually reserved for saints. A study of pupils in grades three through eight in the Chicago area showed that from 70 to 84 percent of them agreed that "The government usually knows what is best for the people."[3] Adult dissatisfaction with the Vietnam war, however, forced a reexamination of some of these ideas. A study released in 1971 confirms family influence on children's political views. But it also shows that as a result of such influence 45 percent of elementary school pupils doubted whether the president was always telling the truth about the conflict in Southeast Asia.[4]

The Schools

"Nationalistic values," as two observers have written, "permeate the entire school curriculum. . . ."[5] Indeed, schools have generally contributed to an overly idealistic picture of American politics. For example, in Los Angeles County a study concluded that "the United States as portrayed in high school social studies textbooks would seem very near paradise for a man who was blind to economic and social facts."[6] The most commonly used texts are more objective than was once the case, however. A study of students in three Boston area high schools showed greater support of democratic ideals as a result of a semester course in civics. But the effects of the course depended in large part on the nature of the community in which it was taught.[7] Political influence in the schools goes beyond the impact of textbooks and subject matter, of course. In sports and other extracurricular activities, patriotic customs convey to students the political beliefs of their elders. That's what the socialization process is all about.

Peer Groups

But Americans are influenced by more than family and school. They seek and usually share the opinions of their friends and fellow workers, their peers. One study showed that 88 percent of those whose three best friends were Republicans voted Republican. And 85 percent of those whose best friends were Democrats voted Democratic.[8] It is difficult to tell, of course, whether our choice of friends determines our political views or vice versa. In either case, the desire to belong or to be accepted may make one's social circle into a sort of filter, straining out those ideas that are unacceptable to the group as a whole.

The Mass Media: Spreading Information

A new form of "politics" is emerging. . . . The living room has become a voting booth. Participation via television in Freedom Marches, in war, revolution, pollution, and other events is changing *everything*.

Marshall McLuhan

Newspapers, magazines, radio, television, and other elements of the mass media are also sources of political socialization. Although their impact is not so personal as that of a parent, teacher, or friend, they reach a far larger audience.

Newspapers

Thomas Jefferson wrote to a friend in 1816 that "Where the press is free, and every man able to read, all is safe."[9] Although newspapers may not be so important as they were in Jefferson's time, some of the evidence suggests that they are still quite influential. For example, the paid circulation of daily papers today is over sixty-three million.[10] And some newspaper reporters have been responsible for dramatic political stories in the last few years. Bob Woodward and Carl Bernstein of the *Washington Post* uncovered White House involvement in the Watergate affair and thereby helped to drive Richard Nixon from office. Jack Anderson, with a column appearing in more than 700 newspapers, revealed facts that contributed to the defeat of two senators, Thomas Dodd of Connecticut and George Murphy of California. He also exposed a possible connection between the International Telephone and Telegraph Company's contribution to the Republican National Committee and the settlement of an antitrust suit.[11] Other "fearless reporters" have struck frequent terror into the hearts of corrupt local politicians. Finally, newspapers also influence people indirectly because they are widely read by "opinion makers" such as politicians, authors, teachers, and clergymen.

On the other hand, radio and television have replaced newspapers as a prime source of information for most Americans. Thus, the impact of the press on election results is probably less important than it once was. As one indication of this, although most newspapers usually endorse Republican party candidates, the Democrats controlled Congress for all but four years between 1930 and 1976. In 1960, John F. Kennedy was elected president with the support of less than one third of the nation's daily newspapers. Even those that did support him had only 16 percent of the total daily circulation.[12] But while most editorial writers support Republican candidates, the working reporters who write the front-page stories tend to favor the Democratic party.[13] They may—as former President Nixon once charged—slant their stories to reflect that bias.

Three other trends in the newspaper field also require brief mention. First, the total number of papers declined by over eight hundred between 1950 and 1974 largely because of increased operating costs and resulting mergers.[14]

Second, an increasing percentage of newspaper space is filled by syndicated material sold to hundreds of papers throughout the country. The same news stories written by reporters for the Associated Press (AP) and United Press International (UPI) appear in hundreds of papers. A similar situation exists with respect to the work of editorial cartoonists and political columnists. Because of the increase in such syndicated material less space is devoted to locally produced journalism. The result may be that the public receives more information about national and international affairs but less about state and local political issues.

A third closely related trend is that there has been a notable decrease in locally owned newspapers. This is not only because there are fewer newspapers but also because many of those that remain are owned by the same corporation. Such newspaper chains often control other mass media outlets as well. The most famous is that founded by William Randolph Hearst which "includes 12 newspapers, 14 magazines, three television stations, six radio stations, a news service, a photo service, a feature syndicate, and Avon paperbacks."[15] Another communications giant is the Knight chain which owns papers in Miami, Detroit, Akron, and Charlotte.

All of these developments are parts of the same problem: more and more people are getting information and attitudes from fewer and fewer sources. To some extent, a similar situation exists with respect to magazines.

Television and Radio
Television and radio stations have not been given the special freedom guaranteed to the press by the First Amendment. They are licensed by the Federal Communications Commission and are more closely regulated by the

government than newspapers. For example, television and radio stations are required by the FCC to give equal time to opposing candidates. They are also required to honor the *fairness doctrine* in presenting both sides of important issues.

It is generally agreed that television now reaches more people than any other medium. It is the only one of the mass media that reaches the child early enough and often enough to rival his family in shaping values and molding opinions. Moreover, television is the most important single vehicle for campaign propaganda. In 1960, it had a decisive role in the Kennedy-Nixon presidential race. The two candidates met in four nationally televised face-to-face debates. After the first of these, public opinion polls showed that Kennedy picked up 4 percent of the probable vote, taking a narrow lead which he never lost.[16]

A poll of more than 1000 top leaders in business, government, labor, education, the mass media, and religion ranked television as the third most powerful institution in the country in 1975. It was topped only by the White House and the Supreme Court. Newspapers placed seventh, magazines came in thirteenth, and radio fifteenth. All the mass media ranked above the cabinet, the military, and organized religion.[17] Among the general public, 65 percent of the people rely on television "a great deal" in getting political news. Fifty-two percent depend on newspapers, 39 percent on radio, and 25 percent on news magazines.[18]

There are signs, however, that television's impact is not unlimited. The general public is realizing that this medium is even more monopolized than newspapers. Three networks, NBC, CBS, and ABC, have a virtual stranglehold on national and international news. Moreover, the opinions and attitudes developed by any individual over a lifetime form a sort of filter. This filter permits us to see primarily what we wish to see, whether on television or in direct observation. Thus, we often do not perceive those impressions which might challenge our values or beliefs to any great degree.[19]

Public Opinion and Political Activity

Our government rests on public opinion. Whoever can change public opinion can change the government.

Abraham Lincoln

If Lincoln was correct—and some think he exaggerated—it is important to understand how public opinion is formed and how it can affect political behavior. This involves a number of questions for which no reliable answers are available: Do teachers, parents, and others understand the cultural values they are trying to impart in the socialization process? Do they do a good job of imparting them? Do the commentators for the mass media report news events accurately and objectively? Most important of all, does the public opinion resulting from all this represent the real judgment of the people or views passed on by elite "opinion makers" in educational institutions and TV studios?

Public opinion in the United States is further complicated by two other considerations. First, there are numerous "publics" here with opposing interests. On many issues, rich and poor, black and white, or men and women may have very different views. In some cases, these diverse views may stem from differences in the ways in which these groups were socialized. Second, the public majority holding an "opinion" on one subject, such as oil drilling or school busing, may be composed of different people from the majority with an opinion on price controls or Cuban policy. Many "publics" produce many "opinions."

Public Knowledge

The concept of public opinion assumes that a large segment of the public does have an opinion on significant issues. Although some surveys show that most people know very little about political matters,[20] Americans may not be as ignorant as was once thought.[21] On such domestic issues as minimum wages and medical benefits, for example, one study concluded that "the public is not only reasonably well informed . . . but has on many occasions led or prompted the Congress or the president toward passage of a program that might otherwise have been delayed for months or years."[22]

Public Opinion Polls

Even if a great majority of the people have both knowledge and an opinion about a particular issue, they may be powerless to influence government officials unless they can convey that opinion to them. Reliable public opinion polls, developed by George Gallup and Elmo Roper in the 1930s, are probably the best method yet devised to serve that purpose. Such polls are based on interviews with about 1500 people from all parts of the country. The people are chosen at random and match the proportions of women, blacks, old people, etc., in the total population. Although they are quite accurate, polls have been criticized for encouraging politicians to follow public opinion rather than to stand by their convictions. But Richard Scammon, a former head of the Census Bureau, has praised them for giving voice to those whose opinions would not otherwise be heard. Community leaders, pressure group officers, and wealthy campaign contributors have no difficulty in getting the ear of their elected representatives. Public opinion polls, Scammon contends, are "the last refuge of the little guy."[23]

Political Action

There is no doubt that political candidates pay close attention to public opinion, as we shall see in Chapter 9. It is difficult to tell, however, what effect it has on them once they get in office. A member of Congress, for example, will probably look most carefully at polls, and at letters received from the folks back home, if he was elected by a narrow margin and has to face reelection in a few months. Although public opinion could never determine the exact content of a law, it probably could prevent government action which was in flagrant defiance of the people's wishes.

Naturally, public opinion is most important when it is translated into political behavior. What an individual actually does will be determined not only by his or her political resources (time, money, role, skills), but also by the strength or intensity of his or her opinions about public matters. Thus, the intensity of public opinion is as important as its content. If Jones thinks Smith would be a good governor, but doesn't believe this with much intensity, he may not even bother to vote. But if Green believes this very strongly, she will not only vote for Smith but probably also campaign for him. Indeed, politicians often plan their campaigns more to increase the intensity of convictions than to change them. Public opinion polls sometimes acknowledge the importance of intensity by asking respondents whether they "strongly favor," "mildly favor," "mildly oppose," or "strongly oppose" a particular candidate or proposal. The distinctions indicate the kind of behavior which is likely to follow.

The factors that determine the intensity of public opinion are the same as those that determine its content (family, friends, media, etc.). But there is an additional factor involved here—a sense of political efficacy or power. In other words, if one believes that what one does can make a difference, one is more likely to do it.

In the period of political disillusionment after Watergate, there seems to be a general feeling among the American people of powerlessness, alienation, and reduced efficacy. Harris polls show that those who believe that "What you think doesn't count much anymore" increased from 37 percent in 1966 to 61 percent in 1973.[24] This sense of powerlessness is reflected in a low level of political activity. Only 62 percent of the people voted in the 1972 presidential election. Only 33 percent contributed financially to a political campaign. Only 25 percent have ever written a letter to their U.S. senator. Finally, only 14 percent campaigned or worked actively for a congressional candidate.[25] If public opinion has little effect on the government, it may be because so few people act upon their opinions. When individuals do not act, however, groups usually do.

GROUP POLITICS

The United States has a population so vast that the voice of the individual can easily get lost. Much political participation, therefore, involves groups of individuals. These groups are bound together by mutual needs and common interests in attempting to influence the government. Moreover, government policy concerns itself almost entirely with groups such as veterans, dairy farmers, unions, etc., instead of with the individual citizen. Therefore, the analysis of group politics is essential to an understanding of modern democracy.

Types of Groups

One must first determine which groups are politically relevant. Such groups are based on some common *interest* as a result of which their members are affected by certain government policies in the same way. Indians, miners, or doctors fit this description. Occasionally certain groups of people such as students or women suddenly become politically relevant interest groups when they realize they have been singled out for special government action. All interest groups can be subdivided into unorganized (or informal) and organized (or formal) groups.

The Importance of Organization

Unorganized groups tend to be relatively powerless in influencing the conditions that affect their lives. Children, the insane, and poor people are examples, each exerting little political clout. Indeed, some of the most important political changes in our history have come about when previously unorganized groups "got themselves together" through formal organization. Slavery was ended only after those who opposed it formed abolition societies. The workday was shortened after laborers unionized. And civil rights laws were passed after minority groups organized.

But what conditions are needed for effective group organization? Six factors are important:

1. Group consciousness: The members must realize that they are a group with common interests and desires.
2. Leadership: At least a few members must possess the knowledge, dedication, and popularity to create the organization and state its goals.
3. Communication: There must be a way for the members to communicate with each other through phone calls, meetings, newsletters, or the mass media.
4. Money: It may not take much, but there must be some to pay postage and other costs of communication.
5. Hope: A sense of hopelessness dims the prospects for effective group action. Any sign of improvement — any "light at the end of the tunnel" — may produce what has been called a revolution of rising expectations and inspire more unified group effort.
6. Ideology: Most people will sacrifice very little — not even organizational dues — on behalf of a common cause unless it can be justified by some idea or doctrine. This may be as simple as "brotherhood" or "justice." But it is necessary to legitimize the organization, to assure the members that it is "right."

The important organized interest groups discussed later in this chapter possess, in varying degrees, these basic characteristics.

Membership Groups and Reference Groups

For a long time foreign observers have commented on the strong tendency of Americans to seek group associations. These associations may involve membership and dues, such as unions or clubs. Or they may be ones that the individual respects and identifies with, even though he or she does not belong to them. The former are *membership groups* and the latter *reference groups*. The influence of a membership group is more or less obvious, but the importance of reference groups requires a few more words.[26] A reference group is one from which a person derives his values or standards, whether he belongs to it or not. People often adopt the opinions of a reference group because they admire its members or obtain psychological benefits from it. Some white people, for example, support predominantly black organizations, while many blacks adopt the values of white society.

Primary Groups and Secondary Groups

In some groups, people have regular face-to-face contact with each other. These are *primary groups,* and they include family, local congregation, and co-workers. As a rule, such primary groups have a greater influence on our political ideas than the *secondary groups* of which we are also members. The latter are bigger, more impersonal, and may involve little or no face-to-face contact. The United States Chamber of Commerce, the Catholic Church, and the National Rifle Association are examples of secondary groups.

Ingroups and Outgroups

There seems to be a tendency to divide people into "we" and "they" or — as the sociologists would put it — into ingroups and outgroups. One generally distrusts the "outs" to which one does not belong, but shares the opinions of the "ins" to which one does belong.

Economic Pressure Groups

In politics, as in nearly everything else, the wheel that squeaks the loudest gets the grease. *Pressure groups are organized interest groups that attempt to influence government policy.* They are among the biggest wheels in the American political machine. Their squeaks rarely go ungreased by some sort of government service. Among the major pressure groups are those that represent the chief elements of the American economy — business, labor, agriculture, and the professions.

The Nation's Business

Of those who speak for business, the National Association of Manufacturers (NAM) and the U.S. Chamber of Commerce are the most prominent. The NAM, founded in 1895, consists of large industrial corporations — what might loosely be called big business. The Chamber of Commerce, established in 1912, is made up chiefly of retail merchants and small business firms.[27] While these two groups occasionally differ, they share a basic conservatism. This leads them to join in opposition to most welfare programs, to the higher taxes necessary to pay for such programs, and to most proposals made by labor unions.

Each type of business also maintains its own specialized pressure group. The American Petroleum Institute, for example, has assisted oil companies and mineral producers in obtaining depletion allowances from Congress that result in lower taxes for the oil industry. The National Association of Real Estate Boards has lobbied hard for government-guaranteed loans for home buyers. And the Association of American Railroads has fought for approval from the Interstate Commerce Commission to raise freight rates.

The interests of these specific pressure groups sometimes clash, however. Natural gas and electric power companies are potential foes, for example. This is because stiffer government regulation of one gives the other an advantage in the competition for a larger share of the stove and oven market. Similarly, the American Trucking Association and the Air Transport Association take opposing views on the issue of highway construction funds. Most individual companies do not attempt to influence government policy directly, but work instead through the pressure groups with which they are affiliated. It would be naive, however, to assume that America's corporate giants have no direct influence on government policy, especially regarding such issues as military contracts and antitrust prosecution.

Figure 7–1. AMERICA'S LARGEST CORPORATIONS

1973 Rank	Company	Net Profit[1]
1	American Telephone & Telegraph	$2,947
2	Exxon Corp. (oil, petroleum)	2,443
3	General Motors	2,398[2]
4	International Business Machines	1,576
5	Texaco, Inc. (oil, petroleum)	1,292
6	Ford Motor Co.	907
7	Mobil Oil Corp.	849
8	Standard Oil of Calif.	844
9	Gulf Oil	800
10	Sears, Roebuck & Co. (retail sales)	679
11	Eastman Kodak Co.	636
12	du Pont de Nemours, E. I. (chemicals)	586
13	General Electric Co.	585
14	International Telephone & Telegraph	521
15	Standard Oil of Indiana	511

[1]In millions of dollars
[2]The net profits of each of the three largest corporations exceeded the total revenues of 38 of the 50 state governments in 1972. The top 15 corporations all had greater profits than the revenues of 10 states. U.S. Bureau of the Census, *The Statistical Abstract of the United States: 1974,* p. 258.
Source: Reprinted from *The World Almanac & Book of Facts 1975,* p. 94 with permission of Newspaper Enterprise Assn., Inc.

The Unions

The first enduring labor alliance was the American Federation of Labor (AFL) formed in 1886. It was an association of highly skilled workers, such as carpenters and machinists, organized into trade or craft unions. The AFL, as some have put it, was the aristocracy of the labor movement. Not until half a century later, in the midst of America's Great Depression, were the poorer, unskilled workers unionized in the Congress of Industrial Organizations (CIO). This was a federation of industrial unions such as the United Steelworkers which welcomed all employees, skilled and unskilled alike, working in the same industry.

After some twenty years of rivalry, competition between the craft and the industrial unions declined enough to allow a merger. The single giant labor federation, the AFL-CIO, was formed in 1955. Although it includes more than a hundred groups, neither the Teamsters Union nor the United Auto Workers (UAW), now the two largest unions in the nation, belongs to the AFL-CIO. Other major independent unions are the United Mine Workers and the International Longshoremen's and Warehousemen's Union.

There are now about twenty million union members in the U.S. This is about one quarter of the total labor force.[28] Automation has cut heavily into the jobs available in many of the industries which were once most effectively unionized. Such industries include newspaper printers and typesetters, sheet metal workers, and musicians. However, there has been union growth among farm laborers, white-collar workers, and government employees such as

Figure 7—2. AMERICA'S LARGEST LABOR UNIONS

	1960 Membership	Present Membership	Change
Teamsters	1,484,400	2,020,000	Up 36%
Auto Workers	1,136,100	1,350,000	Up 19%
Steelworkers	1,152,000	1,200,000	Up 4%
Brotherhood of Electrical Workers	771,000	977,295	Up 27%
Machinists	898,100	900,000	Up 0.2%
Carpenters	800,000	808,000	Up 1%
Laborers	442,500	650,000	Up 47%
Retail Clerks	342,000	650,000	Up 90%
Meat Cutters*	436,000	550,000	Up 26%
State, County, Municipal Employees	210,000	525,000	Up 150%
Communications Workers	259,900	500,000	Up 92%
Service Employees	272,000	480,000	Up 76%
Hotel, Restaurant Employees	443,000	450,000	Up 2%
Ladies' Garment Workers	446,600	442,300	Down 1%
Operating Engineers	291,000	400,000	Up 37%

*Meat Cutters figures include those for former Packinghouse Workers Union, now merged.
Source: *U.S. News & World Report*, February 21, 1972. 1960 figures, U.S. Department of Labor; 1971 figures, union sources as reported to U.S. News & World Report, Inc.

social workers and teachers. The old distinction between craft and industrial unions has become blurred and some unions are diversifying their membership. Thus, the Teamsters Union once consisted only of wagon and truck drivers, but now it embraces many warehouse and processing employees, taxi drivers, airline workers, and people in other occupations as well.

For the most part, unions have been politically liberal. They have worked hard for larger pensions and medical care through the social security program. They have also supported the passage of civil rights laws, higher minimum wages and lower maximum hours, and more expenditures for public schools. Union leadership, however, is somewhat divided about its proper political role. Some officials like George Meany, president of the AFL-CIO, seem content to concentrate on such bread-and-butter issues as higher wages and job security for those already unionized. As part of the "establishment," they dine at the White House and usually support the administration's foreign policy. In contrast, men like the late Walter Reuther of the UAW and Cesar Chavez of the United Farm Workers, have had a broader vision of organizing the poor and the powerless.

The Voices of the Farmer

The major agricultural pressure group is the rather conservative American Farm Bureau Federation. It was founded in 1919 and has a membership of about a million and a half. Its members are found largely in the corn and cotton belts of the Midwest and South. They include many of the richest and largest farmers in the nation. The Farm Bureau has enjoyed very close relations with agricultural agencies in both the national and state governments.[29] The National Grange, the oldest of the major farm groups is more moderate. It is strongest in the East and has about half the membership of the Farm Bureau. The National Farmers Union is the most liberal and the smallest of the three groups with about 250,000 members. Most of them live in the wheat, dairy, and cattle country of the Midwest and Great Plains states.[30]

The chief concerns of nearly all farm organizations are government-guaranteed prices, acreage restrictions, and tariffs or quotas on foreign imports. Even on these issues, however, the views of farm groups reflect opposing economic interests. Corn farmers naturally want high grain prices and poultry farmers want low ones. Similarly, citrus growers may favor free international trade because of their large export market, but dairy farmers or beef producers may want trade restrictions because of the competitive threat of foreign imports.

Two overriding and related issues now confront American agriculture. One is the displacement of small, privately owned family farms by far larger ones owned by business corporations. These "factories in the field" have become so highly mechanized that there were fewer than half as many farm workers in 1973 as there were in 1950.[31] The other major development is the rapid unionization of farm laborers, first by the United Farm Workers, AFL-CIO, and later by the Teamsters. This has led to demands for government-conducted elections to decide which group will represent the workers in bargaining with farm owners.

The Professions

Many professional organizations are very influential pressure groups. Most lawyers, for example, belong to the American Bar Association (ABA). Through the ABA they influence such matters as the appointment of judges, court organization and procedure, and—to a lesser extent—changes in certain legal codes. The American Medical Association (AMA) represents a large precentage of the nation's medical doctors. The AMA successfully opposed tax-supported medical care (Medicare) for more than fifteen years. It continues to restrict the supply of doctors and to exert great influence on health legislation.

There are also associations of barbers, morticians, insurance salesmen, teachers, and many others. These groups are permitted by state laws to establish entrance requirements for new members of their professions. Like the ABA and AMA, most of them tend to be somewhat conservative, at least in protecting their own interests.

Ethnic Solidarity: Lumps in the Melting Pot

America has never confronted squarely the problem of preserving diversity.
Michael Novak

Economic interests share the stage of group politics with many organizations representing Americans of various races and national origins. The very existence of these organizations suggests that the "melting pot" which was supposed to blend Americans into a smooth mixture has been cold for a long time.

"If you're white, you're all right"

White groups can be divided into those based on prejudice and those designed to promote the interests of a particular ethnic group. The former include the Ku Klux Klan, formed after the Civil War and still existing, the American Nazis, and the Christian Nationalist Crusade. They also include the white Citizens' Councils that led the southern attack on racial integration in the 1950s and 1960s.[32] These organizations are nearly always antiblack, usually anti-Jewish, and often anti-Catholic. They are seldom capable of exerting nationwide influence, however.

Among the white groups, the most important are those representing the so-called white ethnics. As that term is popularly used, it refers to almost all whites except White Anglo-Saxon Protestants (WASPs), the group which has supplied the leaders of most of our major institutions. The strongest white ethnics in this country are probably the Irish, Poles, and Italians.

Two recent authors have observed that "in their search for respectability, the Irish ceased being Irish and started acting like WASP Americans."[33] They, like the Germans, Dutch, and Scandinavians, have been almost totally assimilated into American society and have enjoyed much of its prosperity. Through church organizations and such cultural traditions as St. Patrick's Day, however, many Irish maintain their sense of ethnic identity. Sometimes, as in the 1974–75 school busing dispute in South Boston, the Irish also struggle to maintain "their" schools and neighborhoods against the inroads of others.

Whereas nearly a third of all Irish workers hold "prestige" jobs, that is true of only a sixth of all Polish workers.[34] Along with other Slavs, Polish Americans are the least assimilated of the white ethnic groups. There are five Polish daily newspapers published in the U.S., and regular Pulaski Day observances in Chicago, Detroit, and other cities with large Polish populations. Politically, Slavs are organizing in such groups as the Southeast Community Organization in Baltimore and the Calumet Community Congress in Lake County, Indiana. In Detroit a Black-Polish Conference has been created to reduce friction between these two groups. The Polish National Alliance, while not politically oriented for the most part, has more than 300,000 members.

Like Poles, Italians in the U.S. tend to be working-class city dwellers. One-third of them live in the Greater New York area. The Italian population in the Midwest and in California is also rather substantial, but it remains low in the South, perhaps due to early hostility. In 1891, eleven Italians were lynched in New Orleans. More recently, like many Poles, the Italians have been "caught between the bulldozers of urban renewal and the encroaching territorial demands of the black ghetto."[35] The feeling of ethnic pride among Italian-Americans was shown on June 26, 1971 when 100,000 people crowded New York's Columbus Circle to celebrate the "unity day" proclaimed by the Italian-American Civil Rights League.

There are two closely related reasons for isolating this discussion of white ethnics. One is that many ethnics live lives significantly different from those of the dominant WASPS in our society. The other is that their economic status and political behavior is often different as well. In 1970, slightly over half of all Americans had lower-class or blue-collar jobs.[36] But this was true of about two-thirds of all Italian-Americans (and in Connecticut at least, of three-quarters of Polish-Americans). White ethnics, who are mostly Catholic or Jewish, also allocate their votes differently from WASPS, as shown in Figure 7–3.

Jews are often excluded from lists of white ethnics, probably because they are mainly a religious group and have come to America from many different nations. Although they are in better shape economically than other ethnics, Jews are haunted by memories of anti-Semitic prejudice and persecution that far exceed the worst fears of any other group. Jews tend to vote Democratic more heavily than Irish, Polish, or Italian Catholics, but

Figure 7–3. NIXON PLURALITY BY GROUP, 1968 AND 1972

Group	1968	1972
All Voters	+ 1%	+22%
Protestants	+14%	+36%
Catholics	−26%	+ 6%
Irish	−31%	+ 6%
Italians	−10%	+16%
Slavs (including Poles)	−25%	¹
Jews	−68%	−32%
Blacks	−89%	−74%
Spanish-Speaking	−77%	−46%

¹Not available.
Source: Mark R. Levy and Michael S. Kramer, *The Ethnic Factor: How America's Minorities Decide Elections* (New York: Simon & Schuster, 1973), p. 123. Copyright © 1972, 1973 by the Institute of American Research, Inc. Reprinted by permission of Simon & Schuster, Inc.

somewhat less solidly than blacks or Spanish-speaking Americans. Moreover, while the political preferences of Protestants (mostly Republican) and Catholics (mostly Democratic) vary according to income, it is surprising to find that high-income Jews vote Democratic as overwhelmingly as low-income Jews. Organizationally, Jews are represented by the half-million member B'nai B'rith, along with its politically active Anti-Defamation League, as well as by the American Jewish Congress. In addition, the more militant Jewish Defense League has demonstrated against anti-Semitism practiced in the Soviet Union.

"If you're brown, stick around"
The five million Mexican-Americans, most of whom have some Indian ancestry, constitute the second largest racial minority in the United States. In a sense, they have a double disability. First, they often can be identified by their physical characteristics. Second, their Spanish language environment, especially in areas near the Mexican border, makes it difficult for them to learn English.

Some of the other problems confronting Mexican-Americans, concentrated in the southwestern states, are similar to those of the 1.75 million Puerto Ricans living principally in New York, and the 565,000 Cubans residing mainly in Florida. All persons of Latin American origin average three years less schooling and a 30 percent smaller family income than other Americans. Moreover, Mexican-Americans, and all other workers of "Spanish origin," had an unemployment rate of 7.5 in 1973. This was more than three percent higher than white workers and less than two percent below the figure for blacks.[37]

Chicanos, as most younger Mexican-Americans prefer to be called, have developed new organizations and leaders in their struggle for equal opportunity. In south Texas, where Mexican-Americans are a majority in

Cesar Chavez, head of the United Farm Workers, leads California grape pickers in a strike.

·twenty-six counties, a political party, *La Raza Unida* (The United People), has elected two mayors. In Crystal City, Texas the "spinach capital" of the nation, this party won a majority on both the city council and the school board.[38] In California's rich San Joaquin Valley, Cesar Chavez, the head of the United Farm Workers, AFL-CIO, brought more gains for migratory laborers in five years than they had achieved in the preceding fifty. There are also older organizations such as the League of United Latin American Citizens which function much like other pressure groups.

The diversity of these and many other Mexican-American organizations reflects differences and divisions among the people themselves. First of all, there is a problem of identity involving what to call themselves—Mexican-Americans, Chicanos, Spanish-Americans, Latins, browns, or something else. Secondly, as with white ethnics, blacks, and other minorities, Americans of Latin origin disagree on their final goals. Most want full integration or assimilation into the mainstream of Anglo society. But a smaller number seek progress as a separate subculture within the nation as a whole. Thirdly, there are more tangible differences. Some Mexican-Americans have been in this country for many generations, while 17 percent are foreign born. Some speak little Spanish, while 47 percent speak little English.[39] Some are legal entrants into the U.S., while others are *wetbacks* who crossed the border illegally. Yet with few exceptions, Mexican-Americans are united by a common religion, a common cultural heritage, and common problems. Not the least of these is aloof toleration by the dominant Anglo society. At best, "browns" have been permitted to "stick around."

"If you're black, get back"

Some of the difficulties confronting blacks in America have been examined in Chapter 5. The present discussion is confined to the organizations that deal with such difficulties. But their significance goes beyond the black community, since they have inspired other minorities to seek solutions to their own problems in similar ways.

The first important civil rights organization to work for racial justice was the National Association for the Advancement of Colored People (NAACP), founded in 1909. The organization's greatest contribution has been its legal leadership in getting segregation laws declared unconstitutional. The National Urban League, formed in 1910, has been largely concerned with equal opportunity in housing and employment. In recent years, the executive directors of both organizations, Roy Wilkins of the NAACP and the late Whitney M. Young, Jr., of the Urban League, have become well known. Both of these men represent the moderate and responsible leadership that has linked white liberals to the black community, and the black community to the decision makers who hold political power.[40]

Another important black organization has been the Congress of Racial Equality (CORE), founded in the 1940s. This group developed nonviolent civil disobedience as an effective technique for fighting racial segregation. By the mid-1960s, however, CORE lost much of its initial white pacifist support because it abandoned nonviolence in the face of increasingly brutal reactions by white racists.

But CORE did influence the founding of the Southern Christian Leadership Conference (SCLC). Prior to the assassination of Dr. Martin Luther King, Jr., in 1968, the SCLC was largely a reflection of his magnetic leadership. He was a scholar, influential among intellectuals, and a preacher, effective in mobilizing the angry masses. His SCLC was born in 1957 after the Montgomery bus boycott. This was touched off when Mrs. Rosa Parks was denied a vacant seat in the front of a bus in December 1955. Subsequently, the SCLC engaged in massive marches and illegal sit-ins, persevering in the face of billy clubs, electric cattle prods, and police dogs. Through it all, the SCLC succeeded in capturing the essence of that which seemed "best" in the civil rights movement.[41]

The Student National (formerly Nonviolent) Coordinating Committee (SNCC or "Snick") was another significant black group. Under the leadership of Stokely Carmichael, it was the first major civil rights organization to embrace the slogan and ideology of "Black Power." This idea was also vigorously supported by the late Malcolm X, once a Black Muslim leader. Black power signaled the temporary abandonment of racial integration as a major black objective. Instead, it sought the election of black officials to represent black ghettos and black ownership of businesses in black neighborhoods.[42] Whether blacks want full integration or whether they want power to control their own affairs as a racially separate group, one thing is obvious — blacks will "get back" no longer.

The Red Agony

Informed observers point out that native Indians suffer greater deprivations than any other ethnic group:

The indicators of Indian suffering are appalling. Their life expectancy is 44 years, compared with 71 for white Americans. The average income for each Indian family living on a reservation — and more than half do — is only $1,500. The average years of schooling are 5.5, well behind that of both the black and the Mexican-American. Some officials rate 90 percent of reservation housing as substandard. Unemployment ranges from 20 percent on the more affluent reservations to 80 percent on the poorest.[43]

These statistics apply to a total reservation population of over 425,000. But in spite of their numbers, Indians have been unable to form groups strong enough to bring about any substantial changes in their situation. The reasons for this include geographic dispersion, tribal diversity, ignorance, feelings of futility, and a pronounced shyness common among Indian cultures. Some of these same reasons may also account for the fact that the suicide rate among young Indians is three times the national average.[44]

Yet there are some bright clouds on the horizon. For the first time in this century, President Johnson appointed an Indian to head the Bureau of Indian Affairs and President Nixon followed suit. Furthermore, in 1970 Congress abandoned the "termination" policy of the 1950s designed to lure Indians off the reservations.[45]

More importantly, there have been signs of organizational activity among Indians themselves. In 1961, for example, Indians from ninety tribes met to issue a "Declaration of Indian Purpose."[46] An Indian Patrol has been formed in Minneapolis in an attempt to minimize police mistreatment, and there is a Congress of American Indians headquartered in Washington, D.C.

An increased impatience and a growing militancy is apparent among at least a portion of the Indian population. It is directed in part against the loss of water rights on Indian land. But the most dramatic display of the new activism was the seizure of a trading post and church in Wounded Knee, South Dakota by members of the militant American Indian Movement (AIM). Demanding that the Senate Foreign Relations Committee hold hearings on broken treaties with the Indians, more than 200 AIM members occupied the buildings for nine weeks in 1973. It is clear that the problems resulting from white injustice to the "native Americans" have not gone away. And they will probably become more pressing in the future due partly to the fact that a high birth rate has resulted in a 50 percent increase in the Indian population since 1960.[47]

Asian-Americans; A "Yellow Peril"?
Americans of Asian ancestry—Japanese, Chinese, Filipinos, and Koreans, in order of their numerical strength in this country—have generally stayed out of politics. Their lack of involvement can be attributed to many factors, including their fear of white resentment and their small numbers. Even in the San Francisco—Oakland region, with its world-famous Chinatown, Chinese-Americans constitute only about 2 percent of the population.[48] In Hawaii, however, the situation is different. There, Asian-Americans comprise over three-quarters and Japanese-Americans about two-thirds of the state legislature.

As with the Indians, an additional reason for the political inactivity of Asian-Americans is their fragmentation. Chinese, Japanese, Filipino, and Korean communities in this country are geographically isolated from one another. Each group has unique problems and dissimilar outlooks. They came to the U.S. during different time periods, entered various occupations in different proportions, and reflected the rivalries that existed between their native countries.

The result of all these factors has been the emergence of very few pressure groups which specifically voice the needs and desires of Asian-Americans. By far the most important organization is the Japanese-American Citizens League (JACL), founded in 1930. The JACL maintains direct lobbying relationships with officials in Washington.[49]

While nearly all Asian-Americans identify solidly with the United States, they remember the World War II internment of Japanese-Americans in concentration camps. They are also aware of the hostility which some Americans expressed toward the admission of Vietnamese refugees in 1975. They know, too, of the economic and social problems that remain unsolved. In San Francisco's Chinatown, for example, the rate of substandard housing is over three times the city average and the rate of suicide is three times the national average.[50]

Figure 7–4 LEADING STATES IN MINORITY POPULATION

Rank	Indians	Japanese	Chinese	Mexicans	Negroes
1	Oklahoma	Hawaii	California	California	New York
2	Arizona	California	Hawaii	Texas	Illinois
3	California	Washington	New York	New Mexico	Texas
4	New Mexico	Illinois	Illinois	Arizona	California
5	North Carolina	New York	Massachusetts	Colorado	Georgia

Sources: Computed from U.S. Bureau of the Census, *Statistical Abstract of the United States: 1971*, pp. 27 and 31; *The New York Times Encyclopedic Almanac, 1971*, p. 288, and *The World Almanac and Book of Facts, 1972* (New York: Newspaper Enterprise Association, 1971), p. 149.

"Sexual Politics": The Women's Liberation Movement

Few social movements in our history have received as much publicity as the struggle of the female majority to attain equal rights. With steady persistence, the feminists have gained a grudging acknowledgment that American society, like others, is dominated by men. Along with nationalism, racism, and the other ideological influences that have shaped American politics, sexism has been an important factor in our society. Let us briefly consider the many years of struggle against it.

In 1848 the first organized attempt to improve the status of women produced a women's rights convention in Seneca Falls, N.Y. Progress was slow, however, and not until 1920 did the Nineteenth Amendment forbid sex discrimination in voting booths throughout the nation. Even this was only after long decades of effort and agitation — and the arrest of women who chained themselves to the White House fence.

The extension of voting rights to women began a period of general apathy regarding the relative roles of the sexes. For forty years only the National Federation of Business and Professional Women's Clubs and a few smaller groups worked actively, though quietly, for equal opportunity. A turning point came in 1963 with the publication of Betty Friedan's *The Feminine Mystique.* In 1966 this was followed by the formation of NOW, the National Organization for Women. Within a few years more militant groups such as Bread and Roses, Female Liberation, and SALT (Sisters All Learning Together) were established. Of these, NOW is the largest, least militant, and most broadly based — what some have called the NAACP of women's liberation. In 1971 the National Women's Political Caucus was formed in Washington, D.C. to encourage the election and appointment of more women to public office. In 1974 labor union women organized to unify their influence in job-related matters.

The goals of the feminist movement are numerous, varied, and in some cases basic to family structure. They include free child-care centers, the elimination of sexist school books, and more school counselors who will encourage girls to pursue traditionally "male" professions. Paternity leaves for new fathers, social security coverage for homemakers, equal job opportunites and salaries, and a fair division of child rearing and household responsibilities are also among the goals of the women's liberation movement. The United Nations proclaimed 1975 to be women's year. But women's own organizations will probably advance their causes far more than conferences called by the U.N.

Years of Our Lives: The Young and the Old

Groups comprised of one age level were once thought to be politically unimportant, with few common interests affected by government action. During the 1960s, however, young college students formed a number of organizations to fight tuition increases, administrative aloofness, U.S. involvement in Vietnam, and other causes relevant to their generation. As the most well known of these organizations, the Students for a Democratic Society (SDS), split into radical factions, student activism appeared to decline. It seems to have been replaced, in the 1970s, by greater student emphasis on the development of their own individual potentials.

The trend among younger people was accompanied by others involving older people. As the birth rate began to drop, the median age of the population started to creep upward in 1972. By 1974, about one in every 10 Americans—some 21 million people—was over the age of 65. Moreover, older citizens began to form effective pressure groups to work for such things as property tax exemptions, higher social security benefits, and tougher standards for nursing homes. The largest of these groups is the American Association for Retired Persons, claiming over 7 million members, and the AFL-CIO–backed National Council of Senior Citizens, with about half that number. The smaller, more militant Gray Panthers is attempting to work with students in an alliance against "ageism," a middle-aged prejudice against both the young and the old.[51]

Groups in the Government

Pressure groups are usually thought of as private organizations seeking government action or trying to prevent it. But governments themselves consist of people. These people, like other citizens, often have conflicting interests. As a result, there are pressure groups within the government as well as outside it.

Government Employees
One of the most important government groups is the American Federation of State, County, and Municipal Employees, the fastest growing union in the nation. Others are the American Federation of Government Employees, the American Federation of Teachers, as well as unions for letter carriers, firefighters, and social workers.

While the right of such public employees to strike against the government is still a subject of heated dispute, the fact is that they are striking more often. Postal workers, schoolteachers, air-traffic controllers, and even police officers and doctors have all engaged in work stoppages of one kind or another. Sometimes these have been under the guise of mass sick-ins. From 1958 through 1965, there were no more than fifty work stoppages by government employees in any single year. But in 1968 the figure climbed to 254, and in 1972 it reached 375.[52]

Level Against Level
Not only do government employees lobby against their employers (with work stoppages only a fraction of that activity), but various levels of government

lobby against each other as well. The National League of Cities, for example, attempts to get increased assistance from the state and national governments. Sometimes it is joined by the Council of State Governments in seeking to influence Washington policy makers. Moreover, a number of states and large cities have their own lobbyists working for them in Washington.[53] Even at the same level of government, various federal departments and agencies vie with one another for funds and other benefits bestowed by legislative bodies.

The Politics of Shared Attitudes

In our pluralistic society, there are many pressure groups concerned with a wide variety of interests other than occupation, race, sex, and age.

Veterans' Groups
After World War I, returning servicemen formed the American Legion. This is one of the nation's most influential lobbies with a membership now exceeding two and one-half million. The Veterans of Foreign Wars, about half the size of the Legion, is the second largest such group. The Disabled American Veterans ranks third. The major objectives of all three include pensions, educational assistance, and other GI benefits. The Legion has also lobbied for larger military appropriations and a more militant foreign policy.

Foreign Policy Groups
A wide variety of small but often influential organizations are interested in altering America's international outlook. Some, such as the American Friends Service Committee, are committed to pacifism. Others, such as the Council for a Livable World and the Committee for a Sane Nuclear Policy (known often as SANE), have worked for disarmament. In contrast to these is the highly nationalistic Daughters of the American Revolution. Also there are other groups committed to the interests of a particular foreign country, such as the National Council of American-Soviet Friendship founded in the 1940s.

Ideological and Issue Groups
Ideological groups are found on both sides of the political spectrum. At the far right are the Minutemen and the John Birch Society, both staunchly anticommunist. At the far left are the Symbionese Liberation Army and Young Socialist Alliance. Liberal groups such as the Americans for Democratic Action, National Council of Churches, and the Urban Coalition are closer to the center. Common Cause, a nonpartisan lobby established in 1970, takes few stands on policy issues but has stressed reforms in campaign financing and congressional procedures.

Many other groups have interests involving one or only a few issues. For example, the Sierra Club and various conservation groups lead the ecological crusade. The American Civil Liberties Union concentrates on defending First

Amendment rights, but has recently taken some left-wing stands on public issues. Public service law firms, such as that organized by Ralph Nader, work for the defense of consumer interests against careless manufacturers and ineffective government regulation. Still more specialized are the Right to Life (antiabortion) Committee, National Rifle Association, and Gay (homosexual) Liberation Front. Altogether, 309 organizations attempting to influence legislation were registered with Congress in 1972.[54]

LOBBYING TECHNIQUES

We come now to what is perhaps the most important question of this chapter: How can the groups just described obtain their objectives? There are three broad means available. Pressure can be exerted through access, confrontation, or violence.

The Politics of Access: Traditional Methods

Most pressure groups in the United States exert influence on government policy by gaining access to government officials. This involves the communication process called lobbying. The pressure group spokesmen who engage in it are termed lobbyists, although some prefer more elegant titles such as legislative counsels or advocates. The fragmentation of governmental power resulting both from federalism and from the separation of powers gives lobbyists many different points of potential access at which they can direct their influence.

The Lobbyists
Lobbyists come from all walks of life. But their backgrounds often fall into three broad categories. Some are pressure group members who have worked their way up in their organizations. Others are lawyers who have a legal specialty coinciding with the interests of a particular group. Still others are former public officials who have been defeated in seeking reelection.[55] Some of these lobbyists work only for a single pressure group, often one with which they have had a lifetime association. Others, however, are for hire and may represent as many as twenty-five different organizations.

Whatever their background, it is essential for lobbyists to know the problems of the groups they represent. A lobbyist for the Farm Bureau, for example, knows more about international wheat prices, the average size of farms, and the amount of money spent on agricultural research than most members of Congress. Moreover, lobbyists for the larger pressure groups are assisted by Washington office staffs that include statisticians, attorneys, and other specialists. It would be a foolish lawmaker indeed who did not avail himself of the vast information that lobbyists are eager to make available about proposed bills.

In human terms, the most effective kind of access to public officials is through personal trust and friendship. This, of course, results in considerable socializing between lobbyists and legislators. The purpose of entertaining legislators, however, is not bribery. Rather, it is a discussion of pending legislation at greater length and in a more informal atmosphere than is possible in their offices or the capitol building lobbies (the origin of the term "lobbyist"). In any event, few public officials trade their votes for a pitcher of martinis or a few days of fun. Most are too honest. Some have a higher price.

Legislative Contacts

A more serious means of access for lobbyists comes through committee testimony or the authorship of bills. In both state legislatures and Congress, bills are referred to appropriate legislative committees which usually hold open public hearings. Lobbyists are among the most frequent witnesses giving testimony at these hearings. It is there, perhaps, that they perform their two most valuable services to our political system. They contribute to better legislation by transmitting their specialized knowledge. And they act as direct channels of communication between the thousands of group members for whom they speak and the most powerful government decision makers in our national and state capitals. The benefits to the organizations themselves are also very great. Committee testimony permits lobbyists to argue for or against those bills which most directly affect their organization, in front of those legislators most likely to determine passage or defeat.

Occasionally, lobbyists will not only affect the passage of bills, but will also assist in writing them. The Association of American Railroads drafted legislation exempting freight rate agreements from antitrust laws, for example. Unions shaped part of the language in the National Industrial Recovery Act of 1933. Most legislators, especially those who are not lawyers, do not personally write the bills they introduce. They are too busy, or lack the technical vocabulary required. As a result, even though the idea for some new law is their own, they may seek assistance in drafting the exact language from sympathetic lobbyists who have been urging such legislation anyway.

Campaign Contributions

Much of the money required for political campaigns comes from pressure groups. They contribute not because it will guarantee that the candidate, if elected, will always vote the way they wish, but because it will at least assure access to him. Few lawmakers slam down the receiver when they get a phone call from the group that contributed $5000 to their last campaign. Before the 1974 elections the following amounts were given by leading pressure groups to federal and state candidates: AFL-CIO: $1.4 million; American Medical Association: $792,697; National Association of Realtors: $272,092; and National Association of Manufacturers: $257,996.[56]

There are, however, certain general rules that govern financial contributions from pressure groups. First, help is given to individual candidates rather than to political party organizations. The reason for this is that lobbies want to retain some influence regardless of which party controls the government. In the 1970 congressional races, the Committee on Political Education (COPE) of the AFL-CIO endorsed 341 Democrats, one Independent, and nineteen Republicans.[57] Sometimes, the same pressure group may quietly contribute funds to two opposing candidates, if the views of both are acceptable, just to cover its bets. In the 1974 campaign for the California governorship, official reports show that both the California Medical Association and a wine industry pressure group did precisely that.

Another rule governing campaign contributions is that pressure groups support their friends, rather than trying to buy off their enemies. There are two reasons for this. If a contribution is made in hopes of changing the vote of a legislator on some important bill, then the fine line between bribery and campaign support becomes even more blurred and criminal prosecution might result. A second consideration is that it often costs little more to elect a candidate who agrees with you than to bribe one who doesn't.

A last principle of financial donation is to give support to the incumbent when in doubt. He has already compiled a voting record. This is probably a better indication of his intentions than the promises of the challenger. Also he usually has a better chance of winning simply because he has the greater power and publicity of one already in office. Moreover, his experience and seniority will probably make him a more effective ally than a green, first-term legislator. According to Common Cause, in the 1972 congressional elections incumbents of both parties received twice as much money from large pressure groups as their challengers.[58]

Mobilizing the Public
In addition to legislative contacts and campaign contributions, pressure groups try to influence government officials indirectly through the manipulation of public opinion. This can be done by urging group members to write or wire their state legislators or congressmen, asking them to vote a certain way on a particular bill. In 1971 various environmental protection groups, led by Friends of the Earth, launched such a campaign to defeat further appropriation for the costly supersonic transport plane. Senator Clinton Anderson (D–N.M.), a former supporter of the SST, changed his vote because, he said, "I read my mail."[59]

Pressure groups can also attempt to gain support from the broader public through advertising campaigns in the mass media. These are sometimes quite ambitious, especially when designed by professional public relations firms. Such appeals are more often calculated to win general sympathy than to influence action on a particular bill. For example, in 1975 the Teamsters Union placed full-page ads in a number of national magazines stressing the many important and highly skilled jobs held by their members.

Executive and Judicial Influence
Lobbying is usually associated with attempts to influence the passage of laws. But it can also involve access to the executive agencies that administer

the laws and to the courts that apply them. This type of influence is used most often by business and professional organizations. Television industry lobbyists, for example, keep a close eye on the FCC, especially when they are under attack. The American Medical Association is widely credited with preventing the appointment of a liberal doctor, John F. Knowles, to the post of Assistant Secretary of the Department of Health, Education, and Welfare in 1969.

Lobbyists also pay attention to the judicial branch. Few political battles in recent history have equaled that fought by labor unions and civil rights groups to block two of President Nixon's appointments to the Supreme Court. AFL-CIO President George Meany denounced the nomination of G. Harrold Carswell as a "slap in the face" to blacks. And the lobbyist for the NAACP gave highly critical testimony before the Senate Judiciary Committee considering the appointment. Such methods succeeded in preventing Carswell's confirmation by the Senate. They also helped defeat Clement F. Haynesworth, Nixon's earlier Supreme Court nominee, who like Carswell was considered by many to have an antiliberal bias.

Most lobbying activity directed toward the courts, however, is not so dramatic. It entails the submission of written arguments known as *amicus curiae* ("friend of the court") briefs by parties not directly involved in a case. These are often used to persuade judges that a particular law or executive act is unconstitutional. The NAACP has often used such briefs in its struggle against racial segregation. Between 1945 and 1960, for example, the Supreme Court ruled as the NAACP wished in fifty cases. These included one case that declared racially discriminatory real estate deeds to be unenforceable. The ACLU has also successfully used *amicus curiae* briefs in its opposition to restrictions on individual freedom.[60]

Reservations and Regulations
Lobbying techniques contribute to the democratic ideal of popular control over government by providing a link between millions of group members and government officials. Yet such access politics poses some real perils. While the power of some pressure groups tends to be counterbalanced by the power of others, this is not always the case. Some interests don't get represented, and others get overrepresented. Even when opposing groups are equally well organized, one side is often much better financed than its opposition.

There are no foolproof remedies for these problems. In part this is because of the First Amendment's guarantee of the right to petition the government. But Congress has shown some sensitivity to the situation. It has prohibited the use of corporation profits and union dues for direct campaign contributions. It also passed a Regulation of Lobbying Act in 1946 which requires lobbyists to register and file financial reports four times a year. Although this act has many loopholes, it brought to light far more data on pressure group politics than had ever before been available. The AMA alone, for example, spent over one million dollars on lobbying in each of three years. The AFL-CIO, Farm Bureau, and National Association of Electric Companies have each spent more than half a million dollars in a single year.[61] Access politics is clearly an expensive business.

The Politics of Confrontation: Lobbies in the Streets

When traditional lobbying seems to work so well, why would certain groups resort to street demonstrations which often entail clashes with the police? One answer is that the usual pressure group tactics are sometimes unsuccessful.[62] Other explanations are indicated below.

Challenge and Change

Confrontation techniques may seem desirable if a group is small, poor, or disenfranchised. If it is small, few lawmakers will pay much attention to what it wants. This preoccupation with numbers is one of the characteristics of a democratic society. Yet a group can sometimes compensate for its meager numbers by dramatic actions that demonstrate the intensity of its convictions. To do this successfully, it must gain a wide audience for its grievances. It must also appeal to a kind of moral authority. Thus, the opposition to the Vietnam war was small in 1965. But a series of rallies, teach-ins, and marches attracted such wide television and newspaper publicity that by 1968 they had helped reverse the tide of public opinion.

A poor group, regardless of its size, is also forced to rely upon the politics of confrontation to influence government policy. Vivid illustrations of such actions were the sit-ins and mass marches of the civil rights movement in the early 1960s.

If a group does not enjoy the right to vote, like some migratory laborers, dramatic demonstrations might also be the only means of making themselves heard. Thus Cesar Chavez, leader of the migratory farm workers, staged several fasts in recent years, and organized mass marches as well.

Similarly, women demanding the right to vote in the early part of this century utilized picketing and protest demonstrations to win the sympathy of those who were already enfranchised. Students, many of whom were too young to go to the polls, have also used such techniques in trying to advance their causes.

Civil Disobedience

One form that confrontation politics may take is civil disobedience. This is a deliberate violation of the law that entails nonviolent acts designed to bring about social change. It usually also involves a willingness to accept whatever punishment the law may impose.

Civil disobedience, both as a theoretical concept and as a deliberate tactic, owes much to Henry David Thoreau. In 1849 this American writer published a short book, *On Civil Disobedience*. The book justified his refusal to pay a tax as a protest against the Mexican War. In it he argued that it was morally wrong to obey an unjust law. Each citizen, Thoreau said, must measure government policy against the dictates of his own conscience. Justifiably or not, civil disobedience has played a notable role on the American political stage. The successful sit-down strikes of auto workers in 1937 were carried on in defiance of a court injunction. More recently, this tactic was popularized by Dr. Martin Luther King, Jr. He was inspired in part by the example of Thoreau and in part by Mahatma Gandhi of India. CORE, SNCC, as well as the SCLC defied segregation laws in the struggle for civil rights. Thousands of young men have chosen federal penitentiaries rather than the U.S. Army. Nothing dramatizes one's convictions more convincingly than the willingness to risk jail for them.

The Politics of Violence: From the Barrel of a Gun

The outcome of the 1968 presidential race may well have been decided five months before the general election. It was then that Sirhan B. Sirhan assassinated Senator Robert F. Kennedy. This was on the night of his victory in California's presidential primary. A single bullet nullified millions of ballots.

A Decade of Death
Senator Kennedy's death marked the climax of one of the bloodiest decades in our history. It led President Johnson to appoint a Commission on the Causes and Prevention of Violence. There was much for this commission to study. Since 1960 Medgar Evers, (head of the Mississippi NAACP), President John F. Kennedy, Malcolm X (leading "Black Power" spokesman), George Lincoln Rockwell (American Nazi party boss), and Martin Luther King, Jr., had also been killed. Race riots had left 34 dead in Los Angeles, 23 in Newark, and 43 in Detroit. Dozens of other cities were shaken by similar, smaller riots. And the 1968 Democratic National Convention brought bloody battles to the streets of Chicago. Violence, both political and nonpolitical, was increasing steadily. By 1973 the murder rate had reached 9.3 per 100,000 people in the United States. This compared with 3.3 in West Germany, 2.6 in Israel, 2.2 in Japan, 0.6 in Sweden, and 0.4 in England and Wales.[63] A comparative international study revealed that in the 1960s the U.S. ranked twenty-fourth among 114 nations in "total magnitude of strife" and first among the seventeen Western democracies.[64]

The 1970s also got off to a tragic start with the deaths of two students in Jackson, Mississippi and four at Kent State University in Ohio, at the hands of law enforcement officers. A few months later, forty-two persons died in the Attica, New York prison revolt. In 1972 Governor George Wallace came within inches of death from another assassin's bullet.

The Quest for Causes
What has gone wrong? How can this tragic toll be explained in a nation whose Constitution is designed, in part, "to insure domestic tranquility"? The

answers are entangled in a complex web of history and current social movements. Some of the historical roots of American violence may be our revolutionary heritage, the brutal legacy of slavery, our lawless frontier tradition, and the attempt to exterminate native Indians. Frictions generated by ethnic and racial diversity, by unusually intense conflict in labor-management relations, and by the population pressures accompanying urbanization may also account for the extent of violence in our history. More recently, American violence has been explained in terms of the polarization of opinion on the Vietnam war, the relative ease of acquiring guns, the increasing permissiveness in bringing up children, the lurid use of violence by the mass media, and archaic prison conditions. Psychologically, a rapid rise in the aspirations of oppressed peoples, their need to prove their manhood, and the fears and frustrations involved in rapid social change may also promote a tendency toward violence.

From a practical political standpoint, the crucial question is: Does violence work? In totalitarian states such as the Soviet Union, it is almost certain to be totally unsuccessful. But, ironically, in free societies such as ours violence may result in some beneficial change. Who can say whether voting rights or educational and job opportunities for blacks have been expanded because of—or in spite of—the bloodshed on city sidewalks? But if violence buys some progress, it does so at a high price. In addition to death, it tends to produce a backlash of resentment and repression against those believed to have started it. Freedom and justice may then become trampled in the rush for law and order. Violence has an endless appetite, devouring friend and foe alike. It may come to liberate, but it stays to dominate.

PUBLIC OPINION, PRESSURE GROUPS, AND POWER

The user . . . of the house will even be a better judge than the builder . . . and the guest will judge better of a feast than the cook.

Aristotle

Since democratic government is supposed to be controlled by public opinion, the primary duty of the citizens is to form opinions. While public opinion is no doubt shaped by the values, beliefs, and biases of all the diverse groups in our society, it consists basically of many individual opinions. Therefore, the obligation to form one's own opinions about what government should or should not do is an individual one. Yet there is a substantial percentage of the people who answer "don't know" or "undecided" to questions asked by pollsters about government policy. If that percentage were to increase markedly, then democracy—uncertain and difficult at best—would become absolutely impossible. A system based on majority rule obviously cannot function if the majority has no opinions on political issues.

The most important reason for each citizen to form his or her own opinions, however, is not that the system depends on it, but that the welfare of the citizen demands it. Government bureaucracy may abound with thousands of experts on a wide variety of subjects. But only each person can have a valid opinion on the chief purpose of government — whether or not it has served the welfare of the individual. Aristotle's analogy, quoted above, remains one of the best arguments for democracy. "The user" must decide how well the "house of government" is built.

Yet it is not easy to form a set of rational opinions about public issues. One should begin, perhaps, by identifying the chief sources of one's own political socialization. Did political attitudes come largely from parents, friends, teachers, or others? What factors influenced *their* values, biases, and preferences? How reliable are the mass media or other sources which reinforce one's values and provide information about current developments?

One must also take into account the importance of the groups to which one belongs and the way in which they are affected by government policy. An opinion regarding college tuition, for example, is largely determined by one's group interest as a student or as a taxpayer. But one must also recognize that the legitimate interests of different groups may conflict. The students' desire for an education they can afford may conflict with the taxpayers' desire for lower taxes. Yet if only one group is exercising political power, the interests of the other group will probably be ignored. One must, in short, define one's own interests in terms of the groups to which one belongs before developing opinions that are useful in promoting one's own welfare.

The next step, of course, is to convert opinion into government policy. This involves the exertion of individual and collective influence on the government. Individually, one can contact senators, representatives, or other appropriate officials. One can also write letters to magazines and newspapers in order to enlarge public support for a particular position. Collectively, people can work through pressure groups which represent their opinions. Or — if there aren't any — they can form such groups.

Two warnings are appropriate, however, to those plunging into the swirling currents of group politics. First, the interest groups themselves should be democratically controlled. If the people have no power over their own occupational, ethnic, religious, or other organizations, there is no hope that they can control their government. It is important to note that of all the pressure groups discussed in this chapter, only labor unions are required by law, specifically the Landrum-Griffin Act of 1959, to have free and democratic elections of officers. To keep pressure groups working for the interests of their members requires more than the payment of dues. It demands attendance at meetings and requires the time, parliamentary skill, leadership ability, and good will of a large portion of the membership.

Secondly, pressure groups must be warned that although many of their interests can be advanced only at the expense of other pressure groups, such competition among them must be fair. If force or fraud or other overwhelming power is employed, the game is over. At worst, the losers may be destroyed and, at best, the victors may win what is left of a bitter, divided country. All groups have a common interest that transcends their differences: The game of politics must go on, played by the rules of mutual respect, with advances and retreats but no permanent winners. To guarantee that all interest groups are able to exert some continuing influence, it is essential that no one of them monopolize power over all government officials. And the government, as an institution, must refrain from permanent alliances with any of the pressure groups that seek to dominate it.

Notes

1. Angus Campbell, Gerald Gurin, and Warren E. Miller, *The Voter Decides* (New York: Harper & Row, 1954), p. 99.
2. Fred I. Greenstein, *Children and Politics* (New Haven: Yale University Press, 1965).
3. David Easton and Jack Dennis, "The Child's Image of Government," *The Annals of the American Academy of Political and Social Science* 361 (September 1965): 47.
4. *Los Angeles Times,* October 17, 1971, Sec. F, p. 2. The research was under the direction of Professor Howard Tolley.
5. Richard E. Dawson and Kenneth Prewitt, *Political Socialization* (Boston: Little, Brown and Co., 1969), p. 147.
6. Will Scoggins, *Labor in Learning* (Los Angeles: U.C.L.A., Institute of Industrial Relations, 1966), p. vii.
7. Edgar Litt, "Civic Education, Community Norms, and Political Indoctrination," *American Sociological Review* 28 (February 1963): 69–75.
8. V. O. Key, Jr., *Politics, Parties, and Pressure Groups,* 5th ed. (New York: Thomas Y. Crowell Co., 1964), p. 120.
9. Saul K. Padover, ed., *Thomas Jefferson on Democracy* (New York: Pelican Books, Penguin Books, 1946), p. 89.
10. U.S. Bureau of the Census, *Statistical Abstract of the United States: 1974* (Washington, D.C.: U.S. Government Printing Office, 1975), p. 506.
11. *Time,* April 3, 1972, p. 40.
12. *New York Times,* November 4, 1960, p. 24.
13. Seymour Martin Lipset, *Political Man* (Garden City, N.Y.: Anchor Books, Doubleday & Co., 1963), pp. 339–40. This was true both in the mid-1930s and mid-1950s.
14. *Statistical Abstract 1974,* p. 507.
15. G. William Domhoff, *Who Rules America?* (Englewood Cliffs, N.J.: Prentice-Hall, 1967), p. 81.
16. See Hugh A. Bone and Austin Ranney, *Politics and Voters* (New York: McGraw-Hill, 1963), p. 38, Table 8.
17. *U.S. News & World Report,* April 21, 1975. In a similar 1974 poll, television ranked first.
18. These are the results of a poll taken by Louis Harris and Associates reported in *Confidence and Concern: Citizens View American Government* (Cleveland: Regal Books/King's Court Communications, 1974), p. 19.
19. Joseph T. Klapper, *The Effects of Mass Communication* (New York: The Free Press, 1960), pp. 8–15.
20. See, for example, Bernard Hennessy, "A Headnote on the Existence and Study of Political Attitudes," in *Political Attitudes and Public Opinion,* ed. by Dan D. Nimmo and Charles M. Bonjean (New York: David McKay Co., 1972).
21. John C. Pierce and Douglas D. Rose, "Nonattitudes and American Public Opinion," *American Political Science Review,* June 1974, pp. 626–49.
22. Rita James Simon, *Public Opinion in America: 1936–1970* (Chicago: Rand McNally, 1974), p. 222.
23. Quoted in *Los Angeles Times,* June 18, 1970, p. 27.
24. *Confidence and Concern,* p. 6.

25. Ibid., p. 20.
26. Heinz Eulau, *The Behavioral Persuasion in Politics* (New York: Random House, 1963), pp. 53–54.
27. Harmon Zeigler, *Interest Groups in American Society* (Englewood Cliffs, N.J.: Prentice-Hall, 1964).
28. Estimates based largely on data in *Statistical Abstract 1974,* p. 365. Much of the material in this section reflects the insight of Paul Perlin, a former member of the Executive Board of the International Longshoremen's and Warehousemen's Union.
29. Theodore Lowi, "How the Farmers Get What They Want," *The Reporter,* May 21, 1964.
30. Key, pp. 31–40.
31. *Statistical Abstract 1974,* p. 344.
32. For a general survey of racist groups, consult Gustavus Myers, *History of Bigotry in the United States,* ed. and rev. by Henry M. Christman (New York: Capricorn Books, Random House, 1960). For more detailed recent information, see George Thayer, *The Farther Shores of Politics* (New York: A Clarion Book, Simon & Schuster, 1968), Part One.
33. Mark R. Levy and Michael S. Kramer, *The Ethnic Factor: How America's Minorities Decide Elections* (New York: Simon & Schuster, 1973), p. 123.
34. Ibid., pp. 125 and 143.
35. Ibid., pp. 165–66.
36. *Statistical Abstract 1973,* p. 233.
37. Robert V. McKay, "Employment and Unemployment Among Americans of Spanish Origin," *Monthly Labor Review,* April 1974, p. 16.
38. *Los Angeles Times,* August 23, 1970, Sec. F, p. 3.
39. *The World Almanac and Book of Facts, 1972* (New York: Newspaper Enterprise Association, 1971), p. 656; and *Statistical Abstract 1971,* p. 29.
40. For background information on the NAACP and Urban League, see Arna Bontemps, *One Hundred Years of Negro Freedom* (New York: Dodd, Mead & Co., 1961), Chs. 9–13; and Langston Hughes, *Fight for Freedom, the Story of the NAACP* (New York: Berkley Publishing Corp.,1962).
41. For a brief summary of post-World War II civil rights organizations, see *Report of the National Advisory Commission on Civil Disorders* (New York: Bantam Books, 1968), pp. 223–36.
42. The most detailed and sophisticated analysis is in Stokely Carmichael and Charles V. Hamilton, *Black Power* (New York: Vintage Books, Random House, 1967).
43. *Time,* February 9, 1970, p. 16.
44. *Los Angeles Times,* July 5, 1970, Sec. G, p. 3.
45. *Christian Science Monitor,* July 14, 1970, p. 13.
46. Wilcomb E. Washburn, ed., *The Indian and the White Man* (Garden City, N.Y.: Anchor Books, Doubleday & Co., 1964), pp. 400–407.
47. Laurence Urdang, ed., *Associated Press Almanac 1975* (Maplewood, N.J.: Hammond Almanac, Inc., 1974), p. 241.
48. Alfred H. Song, "Politics and Policies of the Oriental Community," Eugene P. Dvorin and Arthur J. Misner, eds., *California Politics and Policies* (Reading, Mass.: Addison-Wesley Publishing Co., Inc., 1966), p. 389, Table 14–3.
49. Bill Hosokawa, *Nisei: The Quiet Americans* (New York: William Morrow & Co., 1969), pp. 198–99, and passim.
50. *Newsweek,* February 23, 1970, pp. 57–58.
51. *Newsweek,* September 16, 1974, pp. 53–54.
52. *American Teacher,* May 1970, p. A-6, and *Statistical Abstract 1974,* p. 369.
53. Congressional Quarterly Service, *Legislators and the Lobbyists,* 2nd ed. (Washington, D.C.: Congressional Quarterly, 1968), p. 63. The states are California,

Florida, Illinois, Indiana, Maryland, Massachusetts, New York, Ohio, Pennsylvania, Texas, and West Virginia. The cities are New York, Los Angeles, San Francisco, Boston, Dallas, New Orleans, San Diego, and Seattle.

54. *Congressional Quarterly Weekly Report,* August 19, 1972, p. 2069.
55. Between 1946 and 1967, twenty-three former senators and ninety former representatives served as lobbyists for one or more pressure groups. *Legislators and the Lobbyists,* pp. 45–49.
56. *Los Angeles Times,* October 28, 1974, p. 4. The figures cover only the amounts given prior to October 14, 1974. Thus, actual contributions up to election day were probably even greater.
57. *The Washington Lobby* (Washington, D.C.: Congressional Quarterly, 1971), pp. 49–50.
58. *Los Angeles Times,* October 23, 1974, p. 4.
59. *The Washington Lobby,* p. 108.
60. Henry J. Abraham, *The Judicial Process* (New York: Oxford University Press, 1962), pp. 209–12.
61. *Legislators and the Lobbyists,* pp. 28–31.
62. Lewis Anthony Dexter, *How Organizations Are Represented in Washington* (Indianapolis: The Bobbs-Merrill Co., 1969), especially Ch. 7.
63. *The New York Times Encyclopedic Almanac, 1972,* p. 231, and *Statistical Abstract 1974,* p. 147.
64. Hugh Davis Graham and Ted Robert Gurr, *Violence in America* (New York: A Signet Book, The New American Library, 1969), pp. 775–76. This is an official report to the presidential commission on violence.

8 GOVERNMENT BY THE PEOPLE:
Political parties

He who refuses to rule is liable to be ruled by one who is worse than himself.

Plato

People cannot expect to get what they want from government simply by supporting their favorite pressure groups. Important as these groups are, citizens who wish to maximize their political influence must also engage in political party activity and vote as intelligently as they can.

Both pressure groups and parties are essentially voluntary organizations. Both provide opportunities for the people to exert power over government action. But parties differ from pressure groups in the goals they seek, the functions they perform, and the way they are organized. Figure 8–1 presents some of these major differences.

PARTY SYSTEMS

Political parties play a crucial role in governments all over the world. Nevertheless, they aren't mentioned in the U.S. Constitution. Washington and Madison opposed the formation of parties as a matter of principle. They feared that people might develop greater loyalty to them than to the nation as a whole. Yet even before Washington left the presidency, the seeds of the first two parties had already been planted.

The Functions of Parties

Political parties would not have lasted so long or spread so widely if they did not perform useful functions. Because these functions are central to the democratic process, they deserve consideration.

Figure 8—1. PRESSURE GROUPS AND PARTIES: HOW THEY DIFFER

1. Pressure groups are chiefly interested in influencing government policies.	1. Parties are chiefly interested in electing government officials.
2. Pressure groups may aid any candidate or party that promotes their goals.	2. Parties select their own candidates, help conduct campaigns, and staff government.
3. Citizens may support several pressure groups.	3. Citizens usually support one party or are independent.
4. Pressure groups are not accountable for actions to the general public.	4. Parties are accountable for actions to the general public at elections.
5. Pressure groups represent minority factions concerned with specific policies or a few interests.	5. Parties seek majorities comprised of coalitions which must achieve broad compromises related to many interests.
6. Pressure groups often devise and publicize new policy proposals.	6. Parties advocate or carry out policies which are usually already popular.
7. Pressure group organization is subject to few democratic legal controls.	7. Party organization is subject to many democratic legal controls.
8. Pressure group unity is usually based on shared interests and characteristics within population segments (women, factory workers, etc.).	8. Party unity is usually based on shared ambitions and broad attitudes within geographic areas (districts, states, etc.).
9. Pressure groups operate by many techniques including lobbying and demonstrations.	9. Parties operate almost entirely by seeking election victories.

Candidate Recruitment

Government is no better than the people who run it. Thus good government depends on the recruitment and nomination of good candidates by the major political parties. Parties have selected candidates during most of our history, but the methods used have changed considerably. Originally, candidates were chosen by party committees or by caucuses consisting of party members already in office. On the national level, congressional caucuses picked the party presidential candidates. Later, nominations were made by party conventions. These involved more people but still tended to be controlled by a small elite of party leaders. Finally, direct primary elections came into use. These permitted all voters who favored a particular party to help in selecting its candidates.

Before the introduction of the direct primary, a party was able to recruit candidates who were committed to the party's stand on major issues. Primary elections, however, make it possible for a popular or well-financed candidate to get nominated even though he or she may be opposed to the views held by most party leaders. Yet such a nominee might have a difficult time because the endorsement and support of organized party workers is probably still the surest method of getting both nominated and elected.

By their nominations, parties reduce the number of candidates finally facing one another in the general election. This, of course, simplifies the choices confronting the voters. At best, then, parties act as political talent scouts, nominating the most qualified people available. In the process, they have often provided ethnic and racial minorities greater opportunities for advancement in politics than have been available in private business or other social institutions.

Campaign Conduct

Parties not only nominate candidates for office but also help get them elected. They raise much of the money for campaign advertising, offer ready-made organizational support, provide many campaign workers, and advise on campaign strategy. By coordinating the efforts of their candidates for various offices, parties can save time, effort, and money. Precinct workers, for example, can distribute the literature of several candidates at the same time. A headquarters office can provide facilities for the entire party ticket. Campaign competition between the two parties makes democracy exciting and thereby generates public interest in political affairs. The heat of the campaign sheds at least some light on the major issues confronting the nation.

Policy Alternatives and Peaceful Change

One major problem confronting every political system is how to change government policies or personnel without resorting to rebellion. When free elections permit a choice between two or more political parties, that problem may be largely solved. This is especially true if the parties present genuine policy alternatives. American voters, for example, elected Lyndon Johnson rather than Barry Goldwater in 1964. In doing so, they chose civil rights legislation, Medicare, federal aid to education, and (they were told) nonintervention in Vietnam. Goldwater, by contrast, voted against most of the domestic legislation proposed by Johnson and urged heavy bombing of North Vietnam. Thus party competition at the polling booths permits the voters a peaceful choice among policies as well as personalities. It makes possible a peaceful transfer of power.

Sometimes in the U.S., however, both major parties pursue such a narrow middle of the road course that their policy proposals come out almost identical. The parties do this because they believe that the majority of voters favor a moderate position. They also do it to avoid extremes and to agree on a compromise satisfactory to most citizens.

In any event, the existence of competing parties keeps each of them fairly alert and responsive to the needs of large segments of the population. Each party watches the other, perhaps less like a hawk than a vulture hoping to capitalize on any mistake. The result is a system of political checks and balances which is just as important as the constitutional one.

Policy Coordination

The separation of powers among various agencies of the national as well as the state governments can cause friction and rivalry. But if several governmental branches or levels are in the hands of the same party, that party can help bridge the gaps among them. It can help coordinate government activities on behalf of similar policies. On the other hand, if different parties dominate different parts of the government, competition among them may result in a political deadlock. This is part of what happened when President Nixon tried to get welfare reform and the reorganization of executive departments through the Democratic-controlled Congress. Vigorous action, therefore, usually requires that the legislative and executive branches be under the control of the same party. Such a situation existed during the Kennedy and Johnson administrations, making possible many innovative New Frontier and Great Society programs.

Citizen Involvement

Political parties provide a link between the voters and the government. Their committees and conventions include both public officials and private citizens. Thus parties, like pressure groups, give people some direct and personal access to government power holders. At the same time, they provide officials additional opportunities to gauge public opinion and strengthen their popular support. Parties also make it easier for government officials to be held accountable to the citizens.

Other Functions

Finally, some less apparent functions of parties are important. Parties define the issues and shape the views of voters who identify with them. They also provide helpful contacts for people seeking government services, jobs, or contracts. This is because party leaders usually have greater influence on government officials than ordinary citizens.

The Number of Parties

Much can be learned about the nature of a political system by the number of parties which operate within it. We can distinguish three variations.

One-Party Politics

Some nations, such as the U.S.S.R. and Spain, have only one major party because it is illegal to form another one. Obviously, there is very little voter choice and free political activity in such nations. Occasionally, however, one party will dominate a government in spite of the existence of several other weak parties. This is the case in Mexico, India, and parts of the U.S.

Two-Party Politics

Taken as a whole, America has a two-party system. But this does not mean that there are only two parties. Nor does it mean that such a situation prevails to an equal degree everywhere in the nation. Rather it means that only the two major parties have a realistic chance of obtaining majorities in Congress or electing a president.

How did this system come about? In the first place, an example of a two-party system existed in Great Britain even before the Revolution. Secondly, congressmen and most state legislators are elected by simple pluralities (meaning the most votes) rather than by majorities (more than fifty percent of the votes) from *single-member* districts rather than from large *multimember* ones. This means that there is only one seat from each district and only one candidate—the one with the most votes—can win it. As a result, candidates who finish second or third get nothing. Such a winner-take-all system tends to discourage vigorous campaigns by small third parties. By contrast, in some Western European nations three or four candidates are elected from each large, multimember district. Small parties thus have a chance to elect a candidate who finishes third or fourth to one of the seats. Another closely related factor supporting the two-party system is found in the Constitution. It requires that the president be elected by a majority vote in the electoral college which has also evolved into a winner-take-all system. The candidate with the most votes in each state gets all of that state's electoral votes. This again discourages third parties from running presidential candidates.

Two additional factors may have contributed to the two-party system as well. First, federalism, dividing power between the national and state governments, also tends to divide voters into one broad group preferring action by the national government and another preferring state action. Those who vote Democratic usually favor national solutions, while those who vote Republican often favor state power. Finally, state election laws, passed by Republican and Democratic dominated legislatures, sometimes impose tough requirements on minor parties which try to get on the ballot.[1]

Once established, our two-party system was sustained both by the habits of the people and by practical political realities. Most voters are Republicans or Democrats largely because their parents were. The relative strength of the two leading parties varies widely from place to place. In about half the states they compete on a relatively equal basis.[2] Moreover, recent trends seem to indicate considerable Democratic strength in such hitherto Republican strongholds as Maine and Vermont. Meanwhile, Republicans have occasionally cracked the traditionally Democratic "solid South." Nevertheless, a survey of party affiliations in 1973 revealed that many states are still close to the one-party system. The Republicans, for example, dominated the North Dakota state legislature 120 to 33. And if the South is no longer solid, it remains under remarkably firm Democratic control. In the Alabama legislature Democrats had a margin of 139 to 2, and in Arkansas the margin was 133 to 2.[3] In presidential races, however, neither party can now take the South for granted.

Most congressional districts also reveal a lack of real competition. Two leading scholars have estimated that from 75 to 80 percent of all seats in the House of Representatives are "safe" for one party or the other.[4] Yet the central fact remains that the two-party system has dominated national politics during nearly all of our history. As state and local issues such as race relations and economic conditions become more similar in all sections of the country, chances are good that stiff two-party competition will also spread.

Multiparty Politics

Since there is a wide variety of possible opinions on political issues, many free nations have three or more relatively strong parties. Multiparty systems have a major disadvantage, however: they make political compromise more difficult, and an unstable situation often results in which no single party has a legislative majority. Several parties must then form an uneasy coalition in order to pass laws or support the executive branch effectively. In some parliamentary systems, such as Italy, this has caused frequent changes in government.

The Types of Parties

Aside from sheer habit, why do voters support a particular party? A partial answer is found in the three major types of parties, each with a distinctive voter appeal.

Charismatic Parties

Some political parties are formed largely to support a popular and magnetic candidate. This type of leader is said to have "charisma." Charisma is an intangible quality which inspires confidence and enthusiastic devotion among many people. It is hard to define but, like sex appeal, most people know it when they see it.

Few American parties have been primarily charismatic. Those that have come closest to it, such as Theodore Roosevelt's short-lived Progressive party in 1912, have been unable to get their leaders elected. Nevertheless, there is no doubt that both Franklin D. Roosevelt in the 1930s and John F. Kennedy in the 1960s possessed some charismatic appeal. Charisma may be more important in the future than in the past because of the vividness with which television projects the personalities of leading candidates into millions of living rooms. This poses a danger, however, for charismatic leadership, like romantic love, can obscure real issues and divert attention from hard problems.

Doctrinaire Parties

While only a few parties have rested on charismatic leadership, many outside the U.S. have been based on a political principle, doctrine, or ideology. The German Nazi party was founded on the doctrine of anti-Semitic racial supremacy. Communist parties rest on anticapitalist Marxism. And socialist parties believe that certain industries should be nationalized (owned and operated by the government).

The major political parties in the United States are not doctrinaire. Both parties include widely diverse points of view. Nonetheless, the Democrats, except for many in the South, tend to be liberal. They favor a larger role for the government in overcoming poverty or prejudice, or both. Yet large numbers of Democrats are conservative on such issues as abortion and drugs. Republicans are more generally conservative. They stress the importance of individual responsibility rather than government action in overcoming social problems. Since most Americans are moderates, if either party becomes too doctrinaire, the other party will probably win. This happened when Barry Goldwater preached a rigidly conservative brand of Republicanism in 1964. Similarly, many attributed George McGovern's defeat in 1972 to his overly liberal image.

Broker Parties

If American parties are primarily neither charismatic nor doctrinaire, what are they? The answer can be worded in different ways. They are pragmatic, interested in winning elections. They are consensus-oriented. That is, both parties attempt to gain enough agreement on as few issues among as many groups as is required to get a majority of the votes. They are flexible, bending their positions with the changing winds of public opinion.

In other words, American parties are broker parties. A broker is a middleman, one who helps people get together for a mutually beneficial deal on which he too can make a profit. In this sense, both parties are political brokers, compromising diverse and often conflicting demands. The Democratic coalition welded together in the 1930s is a classic example of broker politics. It included blacks, Southerners, unions, urban ethnic groups, and big city political "bosses." Each party tries to assemble a combination of voters from various geographic sections, from different ethnic and religious groups, and from diverse occupational, age, and income categories that will add up to a majority on election day. To do this, they put together as attractive a "package" as they can. They want as charismatic a candidate as possible and as many new programs as necessary without binding themselves to doctrinaire principles.

A number of important results stem from the broker nature of our two major parties:

1. Since both Republicans and Democrats usually appeal to a wide variety of groups, they tend to unify the country, rather than to divide it as Washington and Madison had feared.
2. In their search for a majority of votes, the two parties often appeal to the same groups (especially small businessmen, farmers, and skilled workers). Thus the party programs may sound very much alike. This has often led third parties to argue, with some justification but little success, that they provide the only real alternatives.

3. On the other hand, the similarities between the Republicans and Democrats have persuaded many pressure groups that they can work reasonably well with either party. Therefore they need not form a party of their own.
4. Whenever a new third party has increased rapidly in popularity, especially when it has received more votes than had been expected, at least one of the two major parties shifts its position. It moves closer to the position of the new party, thereby thwarting its growth.
5. The most frequent criticism of broker parties is that they make it more difficult to hold the government responsible to the people. Because responsibility is essential in a democracy, this charge deserves careful analysis.

Democracy, Responsibility, and Parties

By definition, a democracy should provide a government responsible to a majority of the people. But the word "responsible" has a double meaning. It means that the people should be able to hold government officials *accountable* for their conduct. They may reelect them if they deserve it or "turn the rascals out" if they don't. It also means that government officials should be *reliable* in the sense that they do what the people expected them to do when they were elected. But genuine responsibility, in terms of either accountability or reliability, is hard to come by in American government.

Accountability
The principal difficulty in holding elected officials accountable is that there are simply too many of them. In the 1974 general election, this author was confronted with a ballot listing thirty-four candidates running for eleven national and state offices, plus fifteen more seeking judgeships. Such a situation is typical of the whole country. Unfortunately, most voters lack the time, the information, or the desire to hold all public officials accountable.

Reliability
The failure of public officials to be reliable may be caused by unrealistic voter demands or by conflicting pressures on them. For instance, the voters may expect more government programs and also a tax cut. Or a newly elected congressman may discover that a tax cut will endanger important government activities. If the congressman votes for a tax cut anyway, such a bill can be defeated in either the House or the Senate or vetoed by the president. Even if the taxes imposed by the national government were reduced, this could be more than offset by increases in state taxes. The point is that power is so widely dispersed among so many officials in American government that no one of them (with the possible exception of the president in the area of foreign affairs) can usually be charged with unreliability for not doing what he or she promised.

Party Responsibility

In light of these difficulties, many argue that the political parties should be responsible for government action. If particular officials are not fully responsible for what finally happens, why not hold the winning party at the last election responsible? Although voters may know little of the individual candidates for whom they vote, at least the ballot usually indicates the party to which those candidates belong.

But complete party responsibility would require that all candidates of the same party favor the same government policies. For this to happen, there needs to be some method of party discipline to persuade all party members to vote the same way on important bills. In the British and other parliamentary systems, such discipline is exercised by the threat of dissolving Parliament. That is, the prime minister can call a new election whenever members of his majority party do not support him on major issues.

For broker parties, by definition loose coalitions of widely divergent views, this situation simply does not exist. In 1967, for instance, a conservative coalition of Republicans and southern Democrats in the House repeatedly defeated Democratic President Johnson on many of his key proposals. This occurred in spite of a sixty-one member Democratic majority in that chamber. Although southern Democrats were most notable in their defections, eight northern Democrats also voted with the Republicans on at least 54 percent of the crucial roll calls.[5]

Yet to emphasize legislators who vote against their party's majority tends to distort the picture. The fact remains that most Democrats are liberal and most Republicans are conservative. One major survey shows this distinction to be considerably more marked among party leaders than among the rank and file party members.[6] However, when in the same election the voters choose a Republican president and a Democratic-controlled Congress — as they did in 1956, 1968, and 1972 — a responsible party system is almost impossible.

PARTIES IN AMERICA

As we have seen, two major parties have been dominant in America during most of its history. We shall now examine their evolution and organization.

Party Origins: The Major Parties

The first important parties in the U.S. were the Federalists and the anti-Federalists or the Democratic-Republicans. The former were led by Alexander Hamilton and John Adams, while the latter were headed by Thomas Jefferson and James Madison. The Federalists favored a strong national government, drew support from commercial interests, and were pro-English. The Democratic-Republicans favored state power, were supported by farmers, and were pro-French.

By the 1820s, these early party loyalties had faded, however. This was largely because of a split among the Federalists over the War of 1812. During the next decade the supporters of Andrew Jackson became known as the Democratic party. His opponents formed the Whig party. As the Civil War approached, the issue of whether to permit slavery in the western territories killed the Whigs who were badly divided on the matter. The northern ex-Whigs were chiefly responsible for the present-day Republican party. And so the situation remains, more than a century later. In 1975 only two of the 535 members of Congress were neither Democrats nor Republicans.

Between 1861 and 1933, the Republicans occupied the White House for 56 years and the Democrats for only 16. Between 1933 and 1976, however, Democratic presidents have held office for 28 years and Republicans for 16. Democrats boast of guiding the nation through two world wars and the Great Depression. They take credit for laws providing for union recognition, pensions and Medicare through social security, and enforcement of black voting rights. The "Grand Old Party" (GOP), as the younger Republican party is inappropriately called, claims credit for ending slavery, acquiring Alaska, Hawaii, and Puerto Rico, and passing pure food and conservation laws. They also boast of ending the Korean conflict and of withdrawing troops from Vietnam.

Yet neither party has remained entirely loyal to the principles for which it initially stood. Broker parties, if they are to survive, cannot afford that moral luxury. They must be flexible, often in the face of strong challenges from third parties.

Winning Causes and Losing Candidates:
Minor Parties

I would rather vote for what I want, and not get it, than vote for what I don't want, and get it.

Eugene V. Debs

Third parties have influenced our politics in a number of significant ways. Most importantly, they have been among the first to champion new causes. Many of these causes were later adopted by the Republicans and Democrats—once their popularity was apparent. The People's (or Populist) party, perhaps the most significant minor party in our history, provides the best example. Formed in 1892, the Populists were among the first to advocate the popular election of U.S. senators, women's suffrage, a flexible expansion of currency, and other liberal reforms. They won three governorships and elected half a dozen congressmen, mostly at the expense of the Democrats. But in 1896 the Democratic National Convention nominated William Jennings Bryan, a Populist hero, for the presidency and adopted a platform that advocated many Populist ideas.

The Socialist party also has had an effect on the policies of the larger parties. Organized in 1901, it was years ahead of them in its call for a graduated income tax, unemployment compensation, and old-age pensions. Such reforms would surely have come about anyway. But the process was probably hastened by the 900,000 votes cast for Eugene V. Debs, the Socialist presidential candidate in 1912 and again in 1920. Four years later, the Socialists joined various farm groups, the AFL, and the independent railroad brotherhoods to support the newly created Progressive party. This party was led by Senator Robert M. ("Fighting Bob") La Follette, a liberal Republican from Wisconsin. The party urged government support for agriculture, collective bargaining for labor unions, and other proposals, which became part of the Democratic New Deal in the next decade. The Progressive presidential ticket won 16.6 percent of the popular vote in 1924—a figure not since surpassed by a third party.

Minor parties also help determine what ideas are considered politically extreme. When Alabama Governor George Wallace ran for president, for instance, he took "extreme" positions on school desegregation and law and order. His positions made the policies of the Republicans in these areas seem quite moderate by comparison. In fact, by shifting the center of the political spectrum to the right in 1968, Governor Wallace forced both the Democrats and Republicans to advocate more conservative policies. He also led both major parties, in their fear of losing votes to him, to focus their campaigns on the issues (mostly law and order) which he was emphasizing.

It is probably safe to assume that any time a third party threatens to get over 5 percent of the vote, and Wallace received 13.5 percent, it will have considerable impact on the two major contenders. One does not necessarily throw away one's vote, therefore, if it is cast for minor party candidates. They cannot win, but their ideas may prevail.

One other effect of third parties must be noted. If most of their votes are taken away from one major party, they may well guarantee victory for the other. In 1912, for example, angry Republicans formed a Progressive party to support the candidacy of Theodore Roosevelt, who had failed in his attempt to get the GOP nomination. As a result, the Democratic presidential candidate, Woodrow Wilson, was elected.

Party Organization

I don't belong to an organized political party. I'm a Democrat.
                                                    Will Rogers

Parties in the United States, at least in comparison with those in England and Western Europe, are highly decentralized. National party organizations have small staffs with little control over state parties. State parties, in turn, have little control over the organizations at the county or city level. Yet the national parties are major cogs in the machinery of American politics.

George Wallace, a strong contender in both the 1972 and 1976 presidential races, makes a political speech.

National Conventions: The People's Choice?
The national parties' most visible activity is the staging of national conventions. Every four years some five thousand delegates to the Republican and Democratic national conventions nominate the two presidential candidates between whom more than seventy million voters make a choice. To do this, the delegates congregate in a colorfully noisy atmosphere, arranged in part for maximum television impact. Often the scene resembles a carnival more than a convention.

How these delegates are chosen is clearly a matter of basic importance. It is also one of great complexity, since no two states select convention delegates in exactly the same way. In some states, the procedure is determined by state law. In others it is decided upon by the state committee of each party. There are even about ten states in which Republican delegates are chosen differently from Democratic delegates. With a few exceptions, however, two general methods are used: National convention delegates are either elected by the voters in presidential primaries or they are chosen by party conventions at the state or district levels.

Even among the twenty-some states that have presidential primaries, there are wide variations in procedure. The election of convention delegates may be accompanied by a presidential preference ballot in which voters can indicate their personal choice for their party's nomination. In New Jersey and West Virginia, for example, the result of the preference ballot is not binding on the state's delegates. But in Indiana and Oregon it is. The extent to which the delegates elected to the national convention are pledged in advance to vote for a particular presidential candidate is also important. New York does not even permit the presidential preference of the prospective delegate to appear on the ballot. In Florida, those seeking to become delegates may list themselves as favoring a certain presidential contender. But if elected to the convention, they may vote for someone else. Delegates from New Hampshire are elected as either pledged to a particular candidate, favoring a candidate, or expressing no preference. In Wisconsin and most other states, only the names of the presidential candidates appear on the ballot and delegates supporting the winner are pledged to vote for him at the convention. Most presidential primaries select at least a few of the delegates from districts into which the states are divided. Some elect delegates favoring various presidential candidates in the same proportion as the people voting for those candidates.

Among states in which district or state conventions select the delegates there is also little uniformity of procedure. Some, such as Colorado and Texas, allow wide voter participation. But Kansas and a few other states have been far less democratic. Illinois selects some of its delegates by state convention and some by primary. A few other states also use a similar combination of methods.

Complicating matters still more is the fact that many states often change their delegate selection methods. For the first time in 1976, Nevada, Kentucky, and Georgia will join the growing number of states which have abandoned state party conventions for selecting delegates in favor of primary elections.[7] In 1972, about one-third of the delegates to the Democratic National Convention were still chosen by state conventions. But this fraction is sure to grow smaller in the future.[8]

The number of delegates to which each state is entitled at a national convention is not governed by law. Rather it is determined by each party. Thus, the Republicans and Democrats differ in their apportionment of convention delegates. But both use formulas based on state population. And both reward those states where they have enjoyed recent election victories with extra bonus delegates.

At each party's national convention a candidate must receive a majority of the delegates' votes in order to win the nomination. Balloting is conducted by a roll call of the states. This allows the chairman of each state delegation to announce dramatically how many votes the state casts for each candidate. If none of the contenders receives a majority on the first ballot, additional votes are taken until someone clears the magic hurdle of 50 percent plus one. Not since 1952, when the Democrats nominated Adlai E. Stevenson on the third ballot, has it taken more than one roll call, however.

Nonetheless, one always finds an air of uncertainty at a national convention. There are several reasons for this. In the first place, many of the delegates are not legally pledged to vote for any particular candidate. Even those informally committed may be persuaded by some last-minute break (say, a new public opinion poll) to change their minds. Furthermore, there are usually half a dozen or more candidates seeking the nomination, making a clear majority difficult to obtain. Some of these candidates may hope, too, for a situation in which the front-runners will be deadlocked. Then the convention, after three or four ballots, might have to turn to them as a compromise or "dark horse" candidate. This doesn't happen often. But an obscure Ohio senator named Warren G. Harding was nominated on the tenth ballot at the 1920 Republican convention. He then went all the way to the White House.

Recent Reforms
Few political institutions in America have received more criticism than the national party conventions. Although polls reveal that they usually nominate the candidate favored by most members of their party, conventions have been indicted as unrepresentative elite groups with most of their delegates chosen by undemocratic methods. In 1968, for example, only 41 percent of the delegates to the Democratic National Convention were chosen in presidential primaries. At that convention, Hubert Humphrey captured the nomination without campaigning in a single primary. As a result, the demands for reform could not be contained even by the Chicago police force. In 1969 the chairman of the Democratic National Committee appointed George McGovern to head a reform commission. This commission was to devise guidelines for the selection of future convention delegates. The result was a requirement that delegate selection take place the same year as the convention and involve a maximum number of Democratic voters. More important, the reform commission imposed a modified quota system on the selection of delegates. This was to insure that young people, women, and some ethnic minorities would have convention representation in rough proportion to their total numbers in the Democratic party.[9]

Although these guidelines were not uniformly enforced, they greatly altered the power structure of the Democratic party. They also made a vital contribution to the nomination of Senator McGovern. Between the 1968 and 1972 Democratic National Conventions, the percentage of delegates under thirty years old jumped from 4 to about 20. The percentage of women grew from 13 to 40, and of blacks, Chicanos, and Indians from less than 8 to 35.[10] Not surprisingly, these were the very groups to which McGovern had appealed most strongly. To make room for the newcomers, however, quite a few delegates to past Democratic conventions were unable to crack the one in 1972. They included a number of big city "bosses" such as Mayor Daley of

Shirley Chisholm supporters stage a demonstration at the 1972 Democratic National Convention.

Chicago and some union officials. Since these old party leaders were resentful about their diminished power, they used McGovern's crushing defeat to justify demands that the quota system be abandoned in picking delegates to future conventions.

The Democratic Charter Convention
A party's national convention is its highest source of authority. Rules governing the selection of its delegates, therefore, determine who controls the party. That was the issue at stake in Kansas City, Missouri on December 6, 1974. There the Democrats met to adopt a party charter, as authorized by the 1972 convention. Both the meeting and its purpose were unique. It was the first time that a major party had met in a national convention (or mini-convention, as it was called by the media) between presidential election years. It was also the first time either the Republicans or Democrats had approved a charter or party constitution.

The Kansas City convention was a fairly harmonious one. The new charter contained compromises that commanded wide support from both the "new politics" reformers and the old-time party regulars. Only some union leaders seemed dissatisfied. Even though 190 of the 1700 mini-convention delegates were from organized labor, a few believed that their influence had been reduced to benefit blacks and other minorities.

The charter requires state party organizations to take "affirmative action" to insure that women, youth, and racial minorities are adequately represented in all Democratic national conventions from 1980 on. But it specifically prohibits numerical quota requirements for any of these groups. Moreover, "winner-take-all" presidential primaries in which the candidate with the most votes in a state gets all of that state's convention delegates are prohibited. So, too, is the "unit rule" which requires all of a state's delegates to vote the way a majority wishes them to. Taken together, these charter provisions make it less likely that any presidential candidate will be able to muster a majority nominating vote on the first ballot.

Of course, the winds of change do not blow selectively. The Republicans, too, felt a breeze. A special committee created by the GOP convention in 1968 made nonbinding recommendations for revised methods of delegate selection. As a result, the percentage of delegates under thirty years old at the 1972 Republican convention rose from 1 to nearly 10. The percentage of women rose from 17 to about 30, and of racial minorities from less than 3 to approximately 6.[11] A "Rule 29 Committee" created by the 1972 Republican convention was to recommend other changes in delegate selection to the 1976 convention.

Although the convention system remains imperfect as a method of nominating presidential candidates, it must be judged against the available alternatives. It is surely more democratic than nomination by caucuses, which are meetings of members of the same party in Congress. This was the method used prior to the first major party convention in 1832. Similarly, a nominating convention has at least one advantage over a nationwide presidential primary, which is the alternative most frequently recommended. A national primary would give an increased edge to the most well-financed candidates. This is because all-out campaigns throughout the country would then be necessary. Now such massive drives need only be launched in the presidential primary states, and usually only in some of these. Obviously, this is much cheaper, which makes the presidency accessible to more candidates.

Besides nominating a presidential candidate, a national party convention performs other functions. It elects members of the national committee. But in reality this simply confirms the persons already nominated by each of the state delegations. It also adopts a platform, which sometimes sparks a convention's most exciting controversies. The platform sets forth party policies, usually in a series of vaguely worded planks. But the platform is not binding on the candidates.

Another important convention task is choosing a vice-presidential running mate. By tradition, the national convention follows the recommendation of its presidential nominee in making this choice. But both campaign politics and the convention agenda require that the vice-presidential selection be made so quickly that it often cannot be made very wisely. Proof of this came in 1968 when Richard Nixon picked Spiro Agnew, later convicted of income-tax evasion. And in 1972 George McGovern chose Senator Thomas Eagleton, later revealed to have a history of emotional problems.

Two alternative methods of choosing running mates have been proposed. One would require each candidate for the presidential nomination to disclose his vice-presidential choice well in advance of the convention. The other would bypass the convention altogether for the vice-presidential selection. Rather, it would require the presidential nominee to submit his choice for approval by the national committee within 30 days after the convention adjourned. Either method would allow far more time to select the best possible vice-president. But as the 1976 conventions approached, it seemed that there would be no change whatsoever in the old procedures used by both parties.

No matter what selection process is used, the politically ideal vice-president is hard to find. He or she must be different enough from the presidential "running mate" to balance the ticket by winning votes otherwise likely to be lost. On the other hand, he or she must be similar enough to the head of the ticket to avoid conflict and assure continuity in government in case of the president's death.

National Committees: Prestige Without Power
The national committee of each party is chosen for a four-year term. It is the highest party authority between conventions. Traditionally, both the Republican and the Democratic committees have been chosen by the various

state delegations to the national conventions. They have usually consisted of a man and a woman from each state. But both parties have enlarged their national committees in recent years. Both national committees also elect a chairperson. This is usually done on the recommendation of the party's presidential candidate for whom the chairperson acts as a major campaign coordinator and advisor. When Jean Westwood was selected to head the Democratic National Committee in 1972, it was the first time either party had chosen a woman. Westwood did not remain in that capacity very long. But Mary Louise Smith shortly thereafter became the first woman ever to head the Republican National Committee.

The national committees of both parties have three major responsibilities: (1) They raise money to finance the national campaign and assist in campaign research, management, and strategy planning. (2) They try to promote cooperation among party organizations in the various states. (3) They plan their party's next national convention. This means that they select the city where it is held, appoint necessary convention officers and committees, and draw up the agenda. They also make all necessary arrangements for the housing and transportation of delegates and arrange for TV and other media coverage. In 1972 the Democratic National Committee was required to perform a fourth function when vice-presidential candidate Thomas Eagleton withdrew from the race. When a nominee for either president or vice-president dies or resigns, the rules of both parties state that a new candidate be selected by the national committee.

The national committees of both parties received much publicity as a result of the Watergate affair. Many Republicans all over the country stress that the use of campaign funds to burglarize the Democratic National Committee headquarters at the Watergate was not approved by the GOP National Committee. Instead, they say it involved politically inexperienced amateurs working for Richard Nixon's own campaign organization known as CREEP (Committee to Reelect the President). But if this group had not assumed many of the functions of the national committee, the events that led to the nation's first presidential resignation might never have occurred. To prevent a repetition in 1976, a group of influential Republicans recommended that no expenditure in excess of $1000 be permitted for the presidential campaign without the approval of the head of the national committee.[12]

State and Local Organization: Politics as Patronage
Although the national committees still have little control over state and local party organizations, the latter are not as powerful as they once were. At one time, party strength was most apparent in the politics of city and county government. The boss-controlled "machines" such as those of Ed Crump in Memphis, Tom Pendergast in Kansas City, and "Boss" Tweed in New York may have been greased with corruption but they ran exceedingly well on election day. All were examples of local organizations on which the state and national parties depended for many votes.

The declining influence of political machines in the past thirty years is due to several factors. As more government jobs were awarded on the basis of civil service exams, fewer were available as patronage plums. In other words, fewer jobs could be given out by machine bosses as rewards for loyal service and dedicated precinct work in bringing out the vote for the winning party. In addition to this decline in patronage jobs, machine influence has been weakened because more cities are electing officials on a nonpartisan basis. Moreover, many cities are substituting primary elections for local party caucuses as a means of selecting candidates. The availability of welfare benefits has also had an effect on machine power. Such benefits have lessened the dependence of poor people on payoffs from precinct captains and ward heelers. This has weakened the parties at the local level even more.[13] It is also possible that the increasing effectiveness of the mass media has substituted for door-to-door precinct work. Although it used to be characteristic of traditional party organization especially in the cities, the door-to-door approach is clearly less important than it once was.

But here one must be wary of generalizations. The youthful supporters of Senator McGovern created a very successful campaign organization before the primary elections based partly on person-to-person contacts. In local politics, Albany, New Haven, and Chicago still have highly efficient machine organizations, while Los Angeles, Detroit, and Seattle do not. At the city and county levels, moreover, we still find examples of the widespread use of patronage, such as in Centre County, Pennsylvania.[14]

Some of the same factors that have weakened the parties at the local level are also present on a statewide scale. Yet many state party organizations are still held together by throngs of workers and campaign contributors. These people are often motivated less by a firm belief in the party platform than by a desire for government contracts or jobs.

Although state party organizations differ greatly, they usually consist of city and/or county committees which generally choose district and/or state central committees. State party conventions are still common. Before the advent of the direct primary, they nominated candidates for governor and other state offices. This was the practice in New York until 1968.

Volunteer Groups: Politics as Principle
As many party organizations declined in vigor, a political void developed. Candidates had to look elsewhere for support. Those with enough money often turned to professional public relations firms and to greater television exposure. Some relied more heavily upon pressure group support. More idealistic candidates were delighted to find that new political volunteer groups were springing up around the country. The volunteers were more interested in policy than in patronage. They were eager to support candidates genuinely committed to the principles in which they believed.

Although these volunteer groups differ, their members tend to be disillusioned with established party organizations. Most are relatively young and well educated, but some are politically naive.[15] They also tend to be further to the left (or right) than most party supporters. This is not difficult to explain, since moderates do not work very hard in any volunteer group (unless motivated by personal gain) because they usually don't see too much wrong with society. But those who are more dissatisfied will work harder for change and for candidates who support change.

The Future of American Parties

The party system in America has been a crucial force which has molded and oriented the political beliefs of the people. Yet the strength of the Republicans and Democrats is slipping. We may be entering an age of party decline or realignment. Ticket splitting, for example, has reached epidemic proportions. In the 1974 off-year elections there were twenty-five states in which both U.S. senators and governors were elected. In eleven of them the voters chose a senator of one party and a governor of the other. Moreover, the number of independents has also increased steadily, as shown in Figure 8–2. In 1974 James Longley, one independent, made political history by defeating both the Republican and Democratic candidates for governor of Maine.

The major reasons for the disintegration of traditional party loyalties can be summarized briefly:

1. Television has enhanced the importance of personal charm and charismatic leadership at the expense of party loyalty.
2. Public relations and professional campaign management firms have assumed some of the functions of party organizations.
3. The emotional impact of social issues such as crime, abortion, and school busing, along with the growing importance of foreign policy, has eroded the economic foundations (rich Republicans versus poor Democrats) of party preference. This was especially apparent in the refusal of the AFL-CIO, for the first time in twenty years, to endorse the Democratic presidential candidate in 1972. Many individual unions, however, remained securely in the Democratic fold.

Figure 8–2. PARTY AFFILIATIONS OF THE PEOPLE

	Republican	Democrat	Independent
1974	24%	42%	34%
1968	27	46	27
1960	30	47	23
1950	33	45	22
1940	38	42	20

Source: Reprinted by permission of the American Institute of Public Opinion (The Gallup Poll).

4. The growth of civil service systems has deprived the parties of much patronage.
5. Nonpartisan elections and direct primaries have lessened the influence of party leaders in choosing the candidates for public office.
6. The increasing speed of social change makes it more difficult for parents to transmit old party loyalties to their children.
7. Increased disillusionment with politics springing from Watergate and related scandals has lowered public respect for the parties. A public opinion poll commissioned by the GOP National Committee found that Republicans were thought to be untrustworthy by 38 percent of the people and Democrats by 13 percent.[16]
8. Parties seem to have grown weaker in those states where pressure groups are strongest. This is because of the continuing availability of campaign contributions from generous lobbyists. Such contributions have permitted more financial independence from both major parties among candidates for office.
9. Both Republican and Democratic candidates have provided fewer new ideas or policy innovations than either pressure groups or minor parties. Thus, voters may view the major parties as somewhat irrelevant to the solution of current problems.

It would be misleading, however, to conclude that funeral arrangements should be made for the two-party, broker-oriented politics of the United States. Old habits die hard. Yet it is difficult to escape the feeling that both the Republican and the Democratic parties are confronted with a difficult challenge: Although still strong and seldom attacked, will they be increasingly ignored?

POLITICAL PARTIES AND POWER

The people have only two kinds of institutions—pressure groups and political parties—available to influence government policy. When one of these is weakened, as political parties surely have been, the people's power is also diminished. One could even argue that pressure groups represent people only as organized minorities. Thus it may be political parties alone that can put together the electoral and legislative majorities on which democracy rests.

There are some indications, however, that the once great parties are regaining some of their former strength. First of all, much power that used to belong to the parties was seized or at least redirected by recent presidents. A former Democratic campaign official has observed that a president "can be a serious impediment to building strong *party* institutions."[17] Indeed, this seems to have been the case with the Nixon reelection committee which undermined some of the traditional functions of the Republican National

Committee. And perhaps it was because there was no Democratic president in 1974 and 1975 that the Democrats were able to take advantage of that power void within their own party to institute two major reforms. As we have seen, they held a midterm convention to draft the first party charter. And, as we shall discuss in Chapter 10, they used the party caucus in the House of Representatives to increase party influence over congressional committee chairmen. Finally, the demand for "opening up" the selection of convention delegates to greater participation by women, youth, and minorities may invigorate the whole party machinery. Certainly, it will challenge the elite control over party affairs by the old-time "power brokers." It will also tend to strengthen the traditional links that parties have formed between elected public officials and the rank-and-file citizen. It seems obvious that as long as many people continue to vote for candidates *because* they are Republicans or Democrats, then the party machinery must continue to be strengthened if the power of the people is to be increased.

Notes

1. David Lindsay, "The Monopoly of Choice: Independents on the Ballot," *National Civic Review,* November 1971, pp. 548–53.
2. V. O. Key, Jr., *Politics, Parties, and Pressure Groups,* 5th ed. (New York: Thomas Y. Crowell Co., 1964), pp. 284–87.
3. *Book of the States: 1974–75* (Lexington, Ky.: The Council of State Governments, 1974), p. 68.
4. William J. Keefe and Morris S. Ogul, *The American Legislative Process: Congress and the States* (Englewood Cliffs, N.J.: Prentice-Hall, 1968), pp. 109–14.
5. *Congressional Quarterly Guide to Current American Government* (Spring 1968), pp. 88 and 91.
6. Herbert McClosky et al., "Issue Conflict and Consensus Among Party Leaders and Followers," *American Political Science Review* 54 (June 1960): 406–27.
7. Richard J. Carlson, "Election Legislation," *Book of the States: 1974–75,* p. 29.
8. Dennis G. Sullivan et al., *The Politics of Representation* (New York: St. Martin's Press, 1974), p. 19.
9. Commission on Party Structure and Delegate Selection, *Mandate for Reform* (Washington, D.C.: Democratic National Committee, 1970).
10. Ibid., pp. 26–28.
11. *Los Angeles Times,* July 28, 1972, pp. 14–15.
12. Ibid., Dec. 8, 1974, p. 18.
13. Fred I. Greenstein, *The American Party System and the American People,* 2nd ed. (Englewood Cliffs, N.J.: Prentice-Hall, 1970), pp. 47–54.
14. Frank J. Sorauf, "State Patronage in a Rural County," *The American Political Science Review* 50 (December 1956): 1046–56. The situation described may be fairly typical of the entire state of Pennsylvania, where the state civil service system covers only about 20 percent of its employees.
15. Greenstein, pp. 57–59.
16. *Los Angeles Times,* January 26, 1975, p. 7.
17. John G. Stewart, *One Last Chance* (New York: Praeger Publishers, 1974), p. 157.

9 THE PRICE OF DEMOCRACY:
Campaigns and elections

Politics is the gentle art of getting votes from the poor and campaign funds from the rich, by promising to protect each from the other.

Oscar Ameringer

A political campaign is the dramatic climax of the democratic political process. It magnifies everything we have examined in the last two chapters: Public opinion becomes more intense. Pressure groups grow more active. Party candidates either shine or wither under the spotlight of the mass media. In many ways each campaign is a unique event. It is a peculiar combination of people, issues, moods, and unpredictable developments. No two states or districts are identical. Looking back at the 1968 campaign, marked by the assassination of Robert Kennedy, and the 1972 race characterized by break-ins, wire-taps, and illegal contributions, Americans should be grateful that each campaign is indeed different from any other. But campaigns also display some similarities, and it is with these that we are primarily concerned in this chapter.

POLITICAL CAMPAIGNS

In many campaigns, the outcome is never in real doubt. This is because district boundaries have been gerrymandered to benefit one party over the other. In some campaigns, however, who wins depends to a considerable extent on the candidates chosen in the primaries. It also hinges on the money and other resources that the candidates have at their disposal, and on the skill with which they wage their campaigns.

The Primary Process

There are several ways for parties to choose their nominees, as indicated in the last chapter. During our early history, small groups of party leaders, known as caucuses, picked their party's candidates. In Andrew Jackson's time, in the 1830s, larger groups of party members began meeting in conventions for the same purpose. But full democracy eventually demanded that *all* voters be permitted to select the candidates of their party.

Primaries first appeared in Crawford County, Pennsylvania. There Democrats were allowed to vote for their party nominees as early as 1842.[1] The idea didn't catch on until 1903 when Wisconsin required that candidates be chosen by a direct vote of the people.[2] Since then, these preliminary elections, or primaries, have spread throughout the nation.

All states have their general elections on the first Tuesday after the first Monday in November. But the primaries at which voters nominate party candidates for senator, member of Congress, governor, and other state offices range from mid-March in Illinois to mid-September in Washington. Seeking to shorten the length of campaigns, Ohio and Texas both moved their primaries closer to the general election in the early 1970s.[3]

Each state uses some form of primary, but in 14 of them party conventions may still be used for nominating certain candidates. In Indiana, conventions nominate candidates for statewide office, while candidates chosen from legislative districts are nominated in primaries. In Iowa and South Dakota, party conventions pick candidates only if none get over 35 percent of the votes in the primary. But the reverse is true in Delaware, Connecticut, Utah, and Colorado. In these states, primary voters choose the candidates if none get more than a certain percentage in party conventions.[4]

Primary elections are a peculiarly American institution. They have not been used in any other major nation. Yet even though they were started quite early here, their effects have not been very well understood. People nominated by state party conventions normally have to impress a few hundred delegates with their charm or intelligence. But primary winners may need only enough money to buy billboard space and television time. In addition, convention nominees probably have to persuade party leaders that they feel obligations to them as well as loyalty to the party platform on major issues. By contrast, candidates coming out of primaries have greater obligations to their campaign contributors. They also tend to support policies that are popular with the voters, regardless of positions taken in the party platform. In brief, primaries involve more people and in that sense may be more democratic than conventions. But conventions tend to reduce the influence of pressure groups and other campaign contributors on the nominees. At the same time, they put a premium on party responsibility and support for the party's program.

Closed Primaries
Most states have laws that permit only persons who are registered as

members of a certain party to vote in that party's primary. Thus, the primary is closed to people outside the party. In the North, the closed primary tends to produce relatively clear-cut policy differences between the nominees of the two parties. This is because candidates for the Democratic nomination will have to appeal to more liberal voters, while those seeking the Republican nomination must have a more conservative appeal.

Generally, in a primary, the candidate who gets the most votes (a plurality) wins the party's nomination even though he or she may not have a majority (over 50 percent). In the South, however, the situation is somewhat different. Since the candidate who gets the Democratic nomination is almost certain to be elected there, he or she is required to get a majority of the primary votes. If no one does, there is a second, or *runoff,* primary between the two leading candidates. For many years, this reduced the chance that blacks would be nominated. In the end, it is quite possible that an elected official in a southern state has gone through three elections: the primary, the runoff primary, and the general election.

Open Primaries

Ten states now have open primaries in which the voter can help select either Republican or Democratic nominees, regardless of his or her own party preference.[5] This situation often produces many *crossovers.* Assume, for instance, that a Democrat is running for reelection to the U.S. Senate with no opposition in the Democratic primary. In this case, many Democrats may *cross* party lines and ask for the Republican primary ballot. They may then vote for the most liberal of the candidates seeking the Republican Senate nomination. Or they may vote for the Republican Senate candidate that they believe would be easiest to defeat in the general election. They will, however, only be able to vote for Republican choices for all other offices involved in the primary once they have asked for a Republican ballot.

Such open primaries can produce nominees who have appealed to voters of all parties, and who thus display relatively few policy differences. In the general election, voters would then be faced with a hazy choice between two moderate candidates.

Nonpartisan Primaries

In races for many local offices, and in the nonpartisan election of the state legislatures in Nebraska and Minnesota, candidates are chosen in primaries in which their party affiliations are not indicated on the ballots. Usually, if no candidate receives a majority of the total votes cast, there is a runoff election between the two front-runners, regardless of party.

Entering a Primary

What must a person do if he or she wishes to enter a primary and run for public office? Requirements vary from state to state, but normally the process is rather simple. This is true whether the candidate is seeking the nomination of a political party or is running for a nonpartisan job. All he or she has to do is get a nominating petition signed by a certain percentage of voters. In some states, there is also a small filing fee to pay. If a person wishes to run as an independent, or to organize a new party, election laws require a far higher number of signatures on the appropriate petition. Although ballots normally permit voters to write in the names of persons not printed there, write-in candidates almost never win. This is because voters have the habit of deciding among names already printed on the ballot. Also any technical error, such as misspelling a name, will invalidate a write-in vote.

Campaign Resources

A far greater number of registered voters for one party than for the other, a very popular incumbent, or some overwhelming issue can make the outcome of certain campaigns a foregone conclusion. Let us assume, however, that a campaign will make the difference between victory and defeat—as is often the case. What will be needed to win?

The Candidate

The first ingredient in the victory recipe is a good candidate. This means one with the following characteristics:

1. Intelligence. Americans admire common sense but are suspicious of too much scholarship. Depending on the district, the fact that a candidate has "been an Oxford scholar may be a help or something to be hidden."[6] The voters want someone with whom they can identify. They want someone who mirrors them at their best.
2. A wide acquaintance. Colonel Jacob M. Arvey, a longtime Democratic party leader in Chicago, once remarked, "It's tough to vote against a man you know—especially if you like him."[7] This may be less true at the congressional district or state level. But it is certainly important in a race for the local school board or city council, where many political careers begin. The ideal candidate, therefore, is or has been a joiner, since the more organizations one belongs to the more people one knows. Belonging to many groups also develops skill in interpersonal relations and in the use of parliamentary procedures.
3. A concern for people. The successful politician is usually one who finds pleasure in handshaking, backslapping, and small talk. He is also one who has an understanding of people, especially when they have a problem— no matter how minor. The demands of a campaign require candidates to compromise ideals less often than emotions. Unless a candidate genuinely likes people, he or she will find it difficult to appear interested when bored or helpful when indifferent.

4. Fluency. A candidate who is glib, who can talk easily and quickly, has an immense advantage. This is especially important when answering unexpected questions from an audience, or in face-to-face exchanges with an opponent or with news reporters.

5. Determination. What the "killer instinct" is to a boxer, determination is to a candidate. He must *want* to win with utmost persistence. As a former candidate for the Indiana senate put it: "You put all your personality into a campaign. You give it your time, your effort, your money, your heart, and your soul. . . ."[8]

6. Good health and family support. The strains of a campaign can be physically and emotionally exhausting. The candidate gets endless opportunities to eat and drink, but too little chance to sleep. Unfortunately, a disrupted family life or even divorce are also among the occupational hazards of the chronic campaigner.[9]

Money

It was Jess Unruh, a prominent Democratic leader in California, who said "money is the mother's milk of politics." Although he may have regretted it, his observation is essentially correct. The cost of political campaigns has skyrocketed even more rapidly than the cost of living. The presidential race in 1964 probably cost about $38 million, or approximately fifty-four cents per vote.[10] In 1968 national campaign spending climbed to over $62 million, or eighty-five cents per vote.[11] And in 1972, Nixon and McGovern spent a total $94 million, or a little more than $1.20 per vote.[12] Indeed, had Nixon fund raisers not been so successful in extracting more than $60 million from contributors, there might have been no Watergate. With less money in the total campaign budget, little would have been available to pay the $250,000 approved for political spying or the $450,000 "hush money" allegedly used to buy the silence of Watergate defendants. Any serious presidential campaign, however, will require at least $25 million. A race for governor or U.S. senator in a large state will cost well over one million.

Campaigns for the House of Representatives are less expensive. But they still range from a low of $15,000 to a high of more than $300,000.[13] This wide range results from the fact that some districts are safe for the majority party incumbent. But in others, where there are close contests, both parties often believe that a few more dollars will convert defeat into victory. In races for the state legislature, the spread in possible campaign costs is, for the same reason, equally great. From $1000 to $50,000 would cover most campaigns.

Where does all this money come from? Apparently, not from the average citizen because polls indicate that from 65 to 90 percent of adult Americans have never contributed anything to a political campaign.[14] Indeed, it appears that fewer than 1 percent of the voters usually contribute at least 25 percent of total campaign funds.[15] Reports show that six persons contributed $300,000 or more to the 1972 Nixon campaign. The leading donors were

W. Clement Stone, a Chicago insurance executive who gave $2.1 million, and Richard Mellon Scaife whose oil, banking, and aluminum interests allowed him to give $1 million.[16]

Not content with these gigantic but legal contributions, Nixon campaign finance officials solicited illegal ones as well. The Corrupt Practices Act passed by Congress in 1925 prohibits the donation of corporation funds to a political campaign for federal office. This restriction, however, was ignored. Nixon received contributions of $100,000 from Gulf Oil Corporation, $55,000 from American Airlines, and $40,000 from Goodyear Tire & Rubber Company.[17] Moreover, Democrats alleged in 1972 that the International Telephone and Telegraph Company (ITT) offered to pay part of the costs of the Republican National Convention in return for government leniency in an antitrust case. They also charged that dairy producers made contributions to insure higher milk price supports. Equally questionable, although far from unusual, was the relationship between campaign contributions and appointment to ambassadorships around the world.

Most campaign funds, however, are not obtained by illegal means. There are many legal ways to raise political money. The fund-raising dinner is an old standby. It entails appearances by prominent politicians and popular entertainers. The costs may range from a few dollars to $500 per plate, and the menu—from box lunches to filet mignon—varies accordingly. On the eve of the 1972 Democratic convention, a telethon featuring dozens of show business, sports, and political celebrities netted over two million dollars. Both parties seem to assume public endorsements by such stars can be translated into votes and money. At the local level, rummage sales, wine-tasting parties, benefit theater performances, and raffle tickets have all been used to fatten campaign coffers. The inventiveness with which money is raised can delight the imagination or—as we have seen—shock the conscience.

Campaign Finance After Watergate
Even before the 1972 campaign, it was obvious that restrictions on campaign finance were necessary. Some were already in effect, such as the prohibition on contributions from corporations or from union membership dues. In addition, earlier legislation restricted the political activity of employees of the federal government, and attempted to limit, very ineffectively, the amounts of money that could be raised and spent by political committees. In April of 1972 a new law took effect which limited most spending in federal campaigns to 10 cents per potential voter. It also required the disclosure of all contributions of $100 or more. President Nixon signed the new law and said enthusiastically: "By giving the American public full access to the facts of political financing, this legislation will guard against campaign abuses and will work to build public confidence in the integrity of the electoral process."[18]

Never had a president's own campaign staff made his words so ironically wrong. After the 1974 elections, Congress tried again to produce sweeping campaign reform, and passed a law with five major provisions.

1. Presidential races will receive some public financing, on a matching basis, from a fund accumulated through the voluntary income tax checkoff. This allows each taxpayer to donate annually $1.00 of tax money to political campaigns.
2. Total spending limits are imposed on races for the U.S. Senate, House of Representatives, and the presidency.
3. Individual contributors are limited to $3000 per candidate and a $25,000 total per campaign year.
4. Pressure groups are limited to $5000 per candidate, with no restriction on total contributions.
5. A six-member Federal Election Commission is established to administer these provisions. Two members each are to be appointed by the president, the Speaker of the House of Representatives, and the president pro tem of the Senate.

This new legislation has been criticized on the grounds that the limitations tend to favor incumbents. Challengers, it is argued, are less well known, and must spend substantially more than incumbents if they are to have any chance of winning. A campaign reform measure passed by California voters in 1974 recognized this argument by limiting incumbent candidates for state offices to 10 percent less spending than their opponents were permitted. The abuses of recent campaigns—funds "laundered" to conceal the names of the donors, the use of cash rather than checks, and illegal contributions from corporations—led nine states to pass campaign reform laws in 1973 and at least 21 others in 1974. Typically, these state laws require the reporting of contributions in excess of $100, and put limitations on total campaign expenditures. In Florida, for example, candidates for governor may spend only $250,000 in each primary race and $350,000 in each general election.[19]

The 1976 campaigns will provide the first significant test of whether these new laws—national and state—can effectively stop the misuse of money in American politics. If democracy is possible in modern society, it will require that elections be won, not bought.

The Organization

In addition to a good candidate and an adequate amount of money, an effective campaign organization is essential to most successful races. For partisan contests in states where there are strong parties, the organization may be ready-made and eager to support the party nominee. But in nonpartisan races, in states with weak parties, and in primary fights for the party nomination, a new organization may have to be developed from scratch. In either case, it is here that the average citizen becomes most involved in the political process. The blueprint for a good campaign organization should include the following basic components:

1. Precinct workers who will go door-to-door to generate support for their candidate. They will register new voters and distribute literature (thereby saving on mailing costs). Sometimes they will solicit campaign contributions, and get persons to the polls on election day.
2. A headquarters staff that maintains a well-run office. They give out stickers, and campaign brochures. They stuff and address envelopes for campaign literature, and make phone calls soliciting support and reminding people to vote. In addition, the office staff organizes and directs precinct workers. There is usually some building contractor, realtor, or other landlord who will donate a vacant store that can be used as a campaign headquarters for a few months.
3. A squad of people, often teen-agers, to help the precinct workers and office staff. They may put up campaign posters along major streets, drive people to the polls on election day, distribute literature at shopping centers, and baby-sit for other campaign workers and voters.
4. A finance committee to raise money from the "fat cats," the potentially large contributors. Small contributors may also be important at the local, grass-roots level.
5. Occupational or special-interest committees that appeal to specific groups for votes and other campaign support. This is usually done by writing letters to groups such as lawyers, teachers, veterans, farmers, ethnic organizations, and clergymen.
6. Public relations people to design billboards, newspaper ads, and campaign brochures, as well as to write stories for newspaper release.
7. Researchers who can provide the candidate with information and statistics on major issues, as well as data about positions taken by opponents.[20]
8. A campaign manager who can pull all these together and free the candidate from personal concern with too many details. The manager usually arranges for appearances and speeches by the candidate, deciding where his or her time is best spent. The manager also arranges advance work, making sure that a sufficient audience will be on hand, that there will be press coverage, etc. In general, he or she helps plan and execute the entire campaign strategy.

Just what is such an effective campaign organization worth? One of the few studies on precinct work, for example, found that it can be decisive. The study showed that in a midwestern industrial city "the increment to a party from the best, as compared with the worst, precinct workers amounted to about 5 percent in the 1956 presidential election."[21] Such a figure could make a difference in many a close contest. Yet the above question, like so many others in social science research, really requires the exasperating answer: It all depends. Of the three factors—candidate, money, and organization—the candidate may be most important in the smaller electoral districts where he or she can be widely known. At the other extreme, in state or national contests, there is evidence that money counts most. *The U.S. News & World Report* stated in 1968 that "eight times out of ten, the man who spends the most money is the winner."[22] It is probable that organization is most important at the intermediate level, in the election of state legislators or U.S. representatives. But effective organization means the recruitment of campaign workers. It is one of the ironies of politics that legislators, to whom workers may be most important, have the fewest government jobs with which to reward them.

Campaign Strategy: How to Win

The hardest thing about any political campaign is how to win without proving you are unworthy of winning.

Adlai E. Stevenson

Campaign strategy should combine candidate, money, and organization in the most skillful way possible. Despite the impression created by Watergate, such strategy is almost always restricted by moral as well as legal considerations.

Dirty Tricks

Dick Tuck, widely regarded as a Democratic "prankster" in the 1960s, is sometimes blamed for triggering the Republican "dirty tricks" revenge of the 1970s. Tuck, dressed as a railroad trainman, once signaled a train to pull out just before a Republican candidate was to make a speech from its rear platform. On another occasion, at a "Chinatown" campaign appearance, he stuffed the fortune cookies with questions embarrassing to the candidate.

When Richard Nixon, the prime target of this mischief, was running for reelection in 1972, the Republicans hired Donald Segretti to strike back. Segretti was convicted for sending out a letter over the phony signature of Senator Henry Jackson (D–Wash.). The letter falsely accused two other candidates, Senators Hubert Humphrey (D–Minn.) and Edmund Muskie (D–Maine), of extramarital sexual activity. More significantly, E. Howard Hunt and G. Gordon Liddy organized the burglary at the Watergate headquarters of the Democratic National Committee. The burglary was supposedly to determine whether any relationship existed between the Democratic candidates and foreign agents.

Although the 1972 campaign revealed shocking attempts to control the electoral system through fraud and force, lesser examples of such activities have characterized American politics for many years. But to accept them as permissible campaign practices is to assure victory for the most crooked candidates rather than the most competent ones.

Getting Around

Even if a large amount of money is available, it must be budgeted carefully. One of the biggest expenses in a national or statewide race is apt to be the cost of flying the candidate, a few of his staff, and dozens of reporters from one place to another. Buses and trains are still used occasionally, but they too require money.

TV or Not TV?

Television has had a greater impact on campaign budgets than any other factor in recent history. In the course of the 1964 presidential campaign, $4.1 million was spent for time on the three national television networks. By 1968 this figure had spiraled to $8.9 million.[23] In addition to the television time itself, political commercials cost a lot of money to produce. Joseph Napolitan, former campaign manager of Pennsylvania's Governor Milton Shapp, has strong feelings on this subject: "When some candidates have, say $100,000 for television, they put maybe $5,000 into production so they can spend more on time. I'd rather spend $30,000 on production and only $70,000 on time. . . . [Y]ou just can't make good cheap films."[24]

The campaign reform law that took effect in 1972 limited the amount of money which could be spent on broadcasting. As a result, the totals for that year dropped accordingly for candidates for federal office. State candidates, however, not restricted by the legislation, spent more money than ever on television and radio.

But increasingly high costs mean that broadcasting must come in small doses. For example, there are spot announcements as short as twenty seconds that are over before the viewer has time to switch channels. In the early 1970s, thirty seconds on a network TV station in Chicago cost $2,330 during prime viewing time. A half hour on a nationwide network sold for $75,000. A 30-second radio spot, by contrast, cost only about $80.[25]

Is television worth the price? Most of the experts seem to think so, and can provide at least a few examples to help prove it. In 1966 the first Republican ever elected to Congress from a district in Houston put 80 percent of his campaign budget into advertising. Of this amount 59 percent went for television and only 3 percent went to newspapers.[26] In 1970, however, Governor Dale Bumpers of Arkansas and Senators Lawton Chiles of Florida and Adlai Stevenson of Illinois all defeated candidates who outspent them for media time.[27] Yet the cost of television to the American political process may be more than monetary. Its critics say that it substitutes images for ideas, personality for principle, glamour for wisdom.

The Price of Polls

Public opinion polls serve many purposes in a political campaign. Initially they can be used to determine whether the potential candidate has any chance of winning. They can also indicate what his strength is in various geographic regions, and what issues the voters are most worried about.

Along with air travel and TV, polls have greatly increased the costs of modern campaigning. Louis Harris, whose fame was first established as John F. Kennedy's private pollster, estimates that no more than $75,000 was spent for polls in the 1946 and 1948 campaigns combined. By 1960 the figure had probably reached $1.5 million. It is not hard to spend that much nationally when in a single congressional district the minimum cost for a public opinion poll is $2000.[28] According to one estimate, three-fourths of the candidates for governor, two-thirds of the candidates for the U.S. Senate, and one-tenth of the candidates for the House of Representatives used polls in 1962.[29] "A candidate," writes a man who was one, "now pays less attention to district leaders than to opinion polls."[30]

Professionalized Campaigns

The use of professional campaign consultants began in San Francisco in the late 1930s, with the public relations firm of Whitaker and Baxter, a husband-and-wife team. In 1952 a New York company — Batten, Barton, Durstine and Osborn — became the first involved in a national race, that of Dwight D. Eisenhower.[31] It is no coincidence that this was the year when "[t]elevision and the airplane came of age as campaign agencies."[32] Yet the desirability of this advertising approach to politics was not accepted by everyone. One of those who questioned it was Adlai E. Stevenson, the man Eisenhower defeated twice for president. He said that the "idea that you can merchandise candidates for high office like breakfast cereal . . . is the ultimate indignity to the democratic process."[33]

Nevertheless, the entrance of professional public relations and advertising firms into the campaign management field has provided candidates with help in four areas:

1. They perform many functions which in the past were usually the responsibility of party organizations. These include the issuance of press releases, recruitment of campaign workers, fund raising, and research on issues. Political parties still assist their candidates with all these, but they are no longer capable of doing what they once did. Professional management firms have rushed to fill the void.
2. They plan and execute much of the media campaign. They know about television technicalities, such as editing or staging, about voice control, and about the ideal content of broadcast messages. These are subjects about which the old-fashioned party leader has little expertise.
3. Similarly, they have the knowledge required for public opinion polling. This involves sampling techniques, the phrasing of questions, population comparisons, computer processing, and statistical interpretation. Here, again, the average politician has little competence.
4. They have the budgeting skills necessary to get the most votes for each advertising dollar. This requires careful choices among newspapers, radio, billboards, and other means of reaching people. As Leonard Hall,

former chairman of the Republican National Committee, put it, "You sell your candidates and your programs the way a business sells its products."[34]

Today advertising and public relations firms are the well-paid allies of both major parties. In fact, Madison Avenue, the New York address of many such firms, now symbolizes the professional approach to politics. A 1972 survey revealed ninety-six persons classifying themselves as full-time professional political consultants.[35] The impact of professional advertising on American politics reached a new peak after the election of Richard Nixon to the presidency. Two employees of the J. Walter Thompson advertising agency who had worked in Nixon's campaign, H. R. Haldeman and Ron Ziegler, became White House Chief of Staff and presidential press secretary respectively.

Choosing the Issues: An Adventure in Prophecy
The road to victory does not always lead down Madison Avenue. Most candidates for a city council or state legislature do not need and cannot afford the services of professional consultants. Those seeking the bottom rungs of the political ladder must usually rely on their own popularity and their ability to correctly assess the issues that most concern the voters.

Sometimes major issues arise that are beyond the control of candidates for even the highest offices. The Depression in 1932 and the communist offensive in Vietnam in 1967–68 are cases in point. But sometimes candidates can make their own issues. In 1961 Sam Yorty was elected mayor of Los Angeles in part because he promised to end the rule that bottles and cans be separated from other garbage for trash collection purposes. In 1958 many Republicans decided to support "right-to-work" proposals which prohibited union membership as a requirement for holding a job. These proposals were bitterly condemned by labor unions. Supporting them was believed to have contributed to the loss of thirteen Republican seats in the U.S. Senate, forty-nine in the House, and control of seventeen state legislative chambers.[36] More recently, issues such as changes in land zoning and school busing have affected the outcome of many local elections. At the state and national levels, Republican losses in 1970 were partly attributed to too much emphasis on the law and order "social issue" and too little stress on economic problems.[37]

Although public opinion polls can help identify the problems that most concern people, the selection of effective campaign issues is still a challenge even to the best prophets. There is some evidence that the closeness of a campaign influences the choice of issues. In a lopsided race where the outcome is a foregone conclusion, the issues may be sharply drawn. The probable winner attempts to "educate" the voters while the opponent is not afraid to speak out, even if it means taking controversial stands. In a close contest, however, candidates have a tendency to moderate their views. They

James H. Pickerell

Congressman John M. Ashbrook of Johnstown, Ohio speaks to a small group who have gathered in a home.

tend to emphasize only those relatively safe issues designed to win the crucial but undecided vote.[38]

The Best Time and the Proper Place

Some candidates, notably Richard Nixon, believe that a campaign should begin slowly, gradually pick up speed, and finally peak on election day. Others believe in what has been called a "scrambling" technique in which an all-out effort is made for the entire duration of the campaign. Regardless of which approach is used, the closing date of registration is often nearly as important a deadline as election day. Campaign organizations must make sure that every neighborhood whose residents are likely to vote "right" has been covered by a door-to-door registration drive. Registration laws vary in each state, but voters must usually be registered about 30 days before the election.

There is also the question of where the candidate should concentrate the most effort. As a general rule, the probable winner is well advised to cultivate the greenest fields—those counties, towns, or neighborhoods in which he or she is strongest. The reason for this is simple: large numbers of supporters do no good if they stay home on election day. The candidate who is trailing, on the other hand, must be spread a bit more thinly. He or she should not only campaign where popularity is greatest in order to get out the committed vote, but must also reach out into opposition territory to try to get new votes.

The Campaign Budget

Another decision confronting every campaign organization is how to spend the limited amount of money available. Television and travel expenses have already been mentioned. There may also be newspaper ads. These vary in cost from $300 per page in small town dailies to as high as $5000 per page in big city papers.[39] While newspaper ads may be optional, a basic leaflet describing the candidate and his stands is considered essential in any campaign. It can be distributed in door-to-door precinct work, at factory gates and shopping centers, or used in direct mailings.

A recent innovation in campaign technology is the use of computerized letters which appear to be directed to each voter personally. If such material is mailed, it is worth the money to send it first class, so it will not be thrown out with the junk mail. That can cost $60 or $70 per 1000 voters. In comparison, a spot radio announcement—although not as selective as mail in its coverage—costs only a dollar or two per 1000 listeners.[40] Billboards are a lot more expensive, but many observers feel that a few of them are necessary. They are especially helpful if the candidate is not well known and needs to establish name recognition as a major contender. Billboards average about $55 per month, but those along major highways rent for far more.

There are literally dozens of other items that can gobble up a campaign budget. These include cards, matchbooks, straw hats, plastic bags, etc., all bearing the candidate's name. In the 1968 campaign the Nixon forces, for example, ordered over half a million balloons, over twenty million buttons, and nine million bumper stickers. The latter, at a little more than three cents each, cost $300,000.[41] For some of these items, their cost may be exceeded only by their uselessness. Fifty coffee hours during which candidates appear briefly in private homes to talk with ten or twenty neighbors may be worth all the campaign buttons ever pinned to a lapel. This assumes, of course, that the candidate speaks well, looks good, and avoids taking stands on controversial issues that are bound to lose votes.

The Incumbency Factor

In 1974 nearly 80 percent of the 435 members of the House of Representatives won reelection. In part, this shows the campaign advantage held by incumbents (those already in office). As public officials, they command more publicity than the private citizens who may run against them. They know personally many of the lobbyists working for influential pressure groups. Often their names appear first on the ballot. Moreover, the boundaries of their districts may have been drawn to help them win.

Incumbents can also stress what they have done, rather than what they promise to do. They can claim that their constituents would benefit by their experience and the power which seniority often brings. These are formidable assets, indeed. But what can the challenger do to offset them? He must be aggressive in attacking the weakest aspects of the incumbent's record. And he can pray for a landslide on behalf of his party.

ELECTIONS

We . . . regard the man who takes no part in public affairs, not as one who minds his own business, but as good for nothing.

Pericles, 430 B.C.

Voting Behavior

Many influences converge upon the voters on election day. They have been subjected to the political attitudes of family, friends, and schools.They have absorbed (or ignored) political information from the mass media. They have been surveyed and categorized by census statisticians, poll takers, and political candidates. Their support has been sought by pressure groups and they have been courted strenuously by political parties. The result of all this lavish attention is what the voters do when they cast their ballots. At that moment, they reign supreme.

How, then, do they vote? That is perhaps the central question in a democracy. Many don't vote at all. In the last half century the percentage of the voting-age population that cast ballots in presidential elections has varied between 43.5 (in 1920) and 64.0 (in 1960).[42] In 1972, the 55.7 percent voter turnout was the lowest in a presidential election in 24 years. The 39 percent showing in the 1974 elections, reflecting disgust with Watergate-style politics, was worse than in any congressional elections since 1946.[43]

Of those who do vote, what influences their choices when they finally stand alone in the voting booth? In varying degrees and combinations, at least three obvious factors are involved: the candidates (especially for the major offices), party preference, and campaign issues.

Voting for the Man

Many people say that they vote for the man, and not for the party. Perhaps they do, but only if they know something about the people who are running. Yet in 1973 only 46 percent of the voters knew the name of their representative in Congress.[44] Only about a fifth of them knew how he or she voted on any major bill. Although most people are aware of the candidates for major offices, chances are they "know" them in the sense that they have a "feel" for their personalities as projected by TV. But they probably do not know much about their intelligence, executive ability, or even their stand on important issues.

Voters seem to sense the limitations of the information available to them. Since they know less about candidates for Congress than for president, the voter turnout in off-year congressional elections has been from 13 to 23 percent less than in presidential election years.[45] Moreover, in voting for congressional and state legislative candidates, who are generally less well known, voters seem to rely primarily on party affiliation in making up their minds. The Democratic vote in presidential elections dropped 19 percent between 1964 and 1968. But the Democrats lost only 1 percent of the seats in the House of Representatives. And they lost only two-tenths of 1 percent of all state legislative seats as a result of the 1968 balloting.[46] It seems that when voters know nothing about the candidates — in spite of what they may say — they vote their party preference. In other words, they do the best they can.

The Primacy of Party

As is shown in Figure 9–1, there are more Democrats than Republicans in the nation. This is reflected in public opinion polls and in the long-standing Democratic majority in Congress. The importance of such a numerical edge is somewhat offset, however, by a lower voter turnout among Democrats and independents than among Republicans. The key reason for this is probably related to less education among many Democrats which in turn is related to a lack of knowledge or interest in political matters. Even considering lower Democratic turnout, however, the influence of party affiliation is very predictable in most congressional or state legislative races. If a district is about 52 percent Republican or 58 percent Democratic in voter registration, it is assumed to be safe for the majority-party candidate.

Figure 9–1. PARTY IDENTIFICATIONS AMONG VARIOUS GROUPS

	Republican	Democratic	Independent	Other or Don't Know
National Totals	24%	49%	24%	3%
Sex				
Male	23	49	26	2
Female	25	50	22	3
Age				
21–29	19	47	31	3
30–49	20	52	25	3
50 and over	31	48	19	2
Education				
Grade school	20	58	18	4
High school	22	50	26	2
College	38	34	26	2
Income				
Under $5,000	21	55	21	3
$5,000–$9,999	22	50	26	2
$10,000 and over	39	34	25	2

Class Identification				
Propertied	54	22	23	1
Middle	33	38	26	3
Working	16	62	21	1
Occupation				
Professional, business	34	37	26	3
White-collar workers	25	45	29	1
Farmers	28	44	28	under .5
Blue-collar workers	17	57	24	2
Union Member				
Yes	15	60	23	2
No	27	46	24	3
Religion				
Protestant	29	45	24	2
Catholic	12	63	22	3
Jewish	9	65	22	4
Ethnic Groups				
English	35	36	27	2
German	33	38	28	1
Scandinavian	31	37	30	2
Irish (Catholic)	14	59	26	1
Italian	14	63	22	1
Eastern or Central European	15	63	20	2
Race				
White	27	45	26	2
Negro	3	87	6	4
Ideological Spectrum[1]				
Liberal, completely or predominantly	8	66	25	1
Middle-of-road	16	60	21	3
Conservative, predominantly	30	42	25	3
Conservative, completely	40	30	28	2

[1]An explanation of President Nixon's 1972 victory lies in the results of a Gallup poll taken three months before the election: 41 percent of the voters view themselves as conservative, 30 percent middle-of-the-road, and 24 percent liberal, with 5 percent holding no opinion. At the same time, Nixon was viewed as substantially more conservative than Senator McGovern, his Democratic opponent. *Los Angeles Times*, August 27, 1972, p. 7.

Source: "Party Identification by Voter Characteristics" from *The Political Beliefs of Americans, A Study of Public Opinion*, by Lloyd A. Free and Hadley Cantril, Rutgers University Press, New Brunswick, New Jersey, 1968. Reprinted by permission.

Campaign Issues

Hardest to interpret is the effect of actual issues on voting behavior. To understand this factor, we must know what issues the voter thinks are important and what the candidates' positions are on these issues. We must also know the degree to which the voter correctly perceives the candidates' positions. This last element is quite difficult to measure.

Yet the issues stressed by candidates may not always be the key to voter decisions. In the 1960 campaign, for example, there was much debate by the candidates over the so-called missile gap between the United States and Russia. But John F. Kennedy's Catholicism, which received less comment by the candidates, was a more important issue to most voters. We should also be aware that the "real" issues may be neither those that candidates talk about nor those that the voters think about. During the 1972 campaigns, for instance, the most important issue confronting the nation *may* have been environmental pollution. Meanwhile, many candidates stressed school busing and tax loopholes, and many voters fretted most about inflation and welfare.

The distinction between economic and social issues can be important here too. A great many blue-collar workers, for example, are liberal on such economic matters as national health insurance and minimum wages. But they are conservative on social questions such as marijuana and abortion. How they vote, therefore, may depend on which kind of issue they believe to be most important in a particular campaign.

Voting Qualifications

The history of American voting laws is marked by two long-term trends. The first is the gradual elimination of requirements based on religion, property ownership, tax payments, race, sex, and literacy. The second is the transfer of considerable authority over voting regulations from the states to the national government.

When the Constitution went into effect, states were free to set up whatever voting restrictions they wished with one exception. Article I, Section 2 allowed anyone to vote for members of the U.S. House of Representatives who was permitted to vote for members of the lower house of the state legislature. In the next half century, most of the states, having long since abandoned religious voting requirements, also repealed laws requiring the ownership of property. In 1870 the Fifteenth Amendment stated that no citizen could be prohibited from voting because of race. It took ninety-five years, until the passage of the Voting Rights Act of 1965, before this amendment was uniformly enforced. At that time, as we saw in Chapter 6, racial justice was finally brought to polling booths throughout the nation.

Shortly before the 1920 presidential election, Amendment Nineteen banned voter qualifications based on sex. Women's suffrage, granted earlier in a few states, had become a demand the nation could no longer deny. Amendment Twenty-four, added in 1964, eliminated the payment of a poll tax, or any other tax, as a voting qualification. While once a barrier to voting by the poor in many states, all but four had voluntarily abandoned the poll tax before this amendment was adopted. Finally, in 1971, the Twenty-sixth Amendment lowered the nationwide voting age to eighteen, following the examples set by Georgia in 1944 and Kentucky in 1955. The result was to enfranchise over eleven million young people who otherwise would have been unable to vote in the 1972 elections.

The preceding developments have greatly expanded the franchise (the right to vote). But they have also limited the states severely in the voting requirements they can set up. Yet four areas remain where the states still have some control.

1. Citizenship. Aliens were once permitted to vote in some areas, usually because local machine bosses benefited by their votes. But today citizenship is a requirement in all states.
2. Residency. All states once had minimum residency requirements. These ranged from two years in Mississippi to sixty days in West Virginia. The 1970 Voting Rights Act, however, set a thirty-day maximum as sufficient for voting for president and vice-president. Court decisions have since ruled this to be adequate for the election of all officials.
3. Registration. A minimum period of residency is implied in state laws that make voters register before the first election in which they wish to vote. Registration is relatively new as voting requirements go. It emerged toward the end of the last century to guarantee honest voting, especially in large northern cities where fraud ran rampant: There, people ineligible to vote were urged (and sometimes paid) to do so, using fictitious names and addresses. "Vote early and vote often" seemed to be the motto of the corrupt politician. To obtain a reliable list of persons eligible to vote, most states now use a system of permanent registration. It requires people to reregister only if they have moved, changed their name, or failed to vote in the last general election. North Dakota is the only state that permits people to vote without any prior registration at all.
4. Literacy. About fifteen states have some sort of literacy requirement. Rather ironically, the practice was first used in the 1850s by Connecticut and Massachusetts to deal with immigrants. But it has been most frequently employed in the southern states to disenfranchise blacks. Literacy may mean anything from the simple ability to read and write to the capacity to "interpret" a complex provision of the state constitution. New York, for example, required a fifth-grade educational level. To prevent literacy tests from being used to conceal racial discrimination, the Voting Rights Act of 1965 suspended them in counties in which less than 50 percent of the adults were registered to vote.

At the root of this and most other disputes about voting qualifications is a fundamental dilemma: Legally, voting is a privilege, but in democratic theory, it is a right. Should only the wise, the informed, or the successful be allowed to vote? That group, depending on its definition, might be very small. Or on the other hand, should everyone affected by government policy be permitted to vote for government officials? Consider the implications.

Balloting

What happens on election day is influenced to some extent by the voting procedures and ballot forms prescribed in the election laws of each of the fifty states.

Voting Procedures
Prior to 1880, incredible as it may seem to the modern citizen, it was relatively easy to find out how someone else voted. This was because the

ballots were printed by individual candidates or parties and varied in size or color. But today the Australian or *secret ballot* is used throughout the country. It has almost eliminated the possibility that one person—a spouse, employer, or creditor—can dictate the voting choices of another.

All ballots were printed on paper and marked by hand until Lockport, New York introduced the use of voting machines in 1892. Over two-thirds of the states now authorize their use, but the decision is often left to individual counties. There is little doubt that voting machines, or a system of computerized punch-card ballots, help to prevent deliberate fraud or unintentional mistakes in the counting of votes. The chief objections to the use of voting machines center upon their expense and the possibility that they can be "fixed."

Ballot Forms
There are two basic distinctions involved in an analysis of ballot forms. One has to do with the way in which candidates' names are arranged and the other with the ballot's total length. About thirty states use the Indiana, or *party-column ballot.* It has all the candidates running for all the offices from the same party listed in the one column. Opposite is another column for all the candidates running for the same offices from the other party. With this kind of ballot, the voter may easily make one mark, or pull a voting machine lever, to vote a straight ticket for all the candidates of one party. The remaining states use the Massachusetts, or *office-block ballot.* On it candidates' names are grouped according to the offices for which they are running. Although party affiliations are listed, the voter must vote for each office individually. Thus, with this type of ballot it is just as time-consuming to vote a straight ticket as a split ticket.

Campaign strategy, as one might expect, is influenced by these facts. Especially in states with party-column type ballots, many lesser candidates can sweep into office on the coattails of a popular candidate for president, governor, or U.S. senator at the top of the party list. In order to vote for them, people will just pull the straight ticket lever at the top of the column and all the candidates for minor offices in the same party column will get their votes as well. In the final analysis, the party-column ballot encourages party loyalty while the office-block ballot shifts attention to the qualifications of individual candidates. When Ohio changed to the latter form in 1950, the late Senator Taft estimated that he gained at least 100,000 votes.[47]

Partisan elections using the office-block ballot, like nonpartisan elections, present a special problem: How is the order in which names appear on the ballot to be determined? It is an important question, since many politicians believe that the top spot is worth as much as 5 percent of the vote. But state laws answer this question in a variety of ways. In some places the incumbents' names are listed first, while in others the arrangement is alphabetical. It can also be based on drawing straws, or rotated so that all candidates have their names in top position on an equal number of ballots.

The question of ballot length is likewise important. As indicated earlier, the average voter has neither the inclination nor the information needed to make intelligent decisions on a long list of choices. The long ballot may contain state constitutional amendments which require a yes or no vote by the electorate, as well as initiative or referendum measures. The initiative, provided for in twenty-one states, permits the voters to propose new laws by obtaining a certain number of signatures on a petition. The referendum, authorized in twenty-three states, allows the voters to uphold or repeal certain actions of the state legislature. In addition, of course, the long ballot contains the names of candidates for numerous local, state, and national offices ranging from county coroner to president.

The remedy for this is simply a short ballot. The movement in that direction has concentrated on two specific reforms. The first is making many state and local offices appointive rather than elective. The second is scheduling local elections at different times of the year from state and national ones. The latter reform, which means that voters can decide on local issues separately, has been more successful.

Yet fewer people vote for local offices than for president or governor regardless of which system is used. On long, consolidated ballots there is ordinarily a drop-off of about 25 to 30 percent between the number of people who vote for the major candidates at the top of the ballot and those who bother to choose among local candidates at the bottom.[48] If local elections are separated from state and national ones, the total turnout is often less than one-quarter of those eligible to vote.

INTELLIGENT VOTING AND POWER

Much has been written about the citizen's obligation to vote. Some argue that it makes no difference for whom you vote—just so you vote. This is patently absurd. It makes a great deal of difference if the majority votes for a crook for state treasurer or a fool for president. If one knows or cares only about a few candidates, one should vote only in the races in which they are involved—and then go home. Otherwise, the vote becomes a menace to good government.

Increasing numbers of people, however, have decided not to vote at all even though they do have some familiarity with the candidates, parties, or issues on the ballot. For various reasons, those who have the least political power of other kinds—less money, prestige, experience, or expertise—are also the ones who are least likely to vote. While 39 percent of the total voting-age population went to the polls in 1974, only 21 percent of those 18 to 21 years of age voted, along with 22 percent of those of Spanish origin and 24 percent of blacks.[49] Ironically, to repeat, those who suffer from the greatest inequality in other political resources often fail to use the vote, which is the political resource distributed most equally.

A possible reason for not voting is the belief that to vote intelligently one must spend long hours of study and attend many political meetings. But it just isn't that hard. An intelligent voter is simply one who takes about a day every year or two to assess the nation and his or her place in it. Some voters with years of experience make wise voting decisions with little systematic deliberation. Others find that they can vote more confidently if they systematically take such factors as the following into consideration:

1. Their own general degree of satisfaction with existing conditions, especially with those affected by government action. Favorable conditions give the edge to the incumbent party, unfavorable ones to the challengers.
2. Their own opinion of the major economic and social problems and the party that they feel is best equipped to handle them.
3. The major economic and social problems in the opinion of the candidates. Usually one should vote for the candidate who emphasizes the same problems as you do.
4. The party affiliation of the candidates, and whether their views generally coincide with the liberal or conservative ones associated with their party. In voting for candidates for Congress and the state legislature, except in primary elections, this may be all the voter who is a strong Democrat or Republican needs to know before entering the polling booth.
5. In voting for president, governor, mayor, and other executive jobs, the amount of administrative experience the candidates have had, and the leadership potential that can be sensed from their personalities.

If one knows too little about issues or candidates, it is not necessarily stupid to vote a straight ticket for the party of one's considered choice. This increases that party's chances of controlling both the executive and the legislative branches. As we have noted, such a situation can promote cooperation between the two branches and allow the party to gain more legislative committee chairmanships.

Of course, a citizen doesn't have to do the job of intelligent voting without any help. If one trusts one's union or the editorial policy of a newspaper, for example, there is nothing wrong with voting for the candidates they endorse. If one wishes to know how a congressman or state legislator voted on a particular issue, pressure groups such as the Chamber of Commerce probably know. If one wants to see brief biographies of the candidates and short statements of their major views, the League of Women Voters often compiles them. But before following others' recommendations, one should consider the interests and biases of those who make them.

After going to the trouble to cast an intelligent vote, one may still ask, will it do any good? In the end, we are guaranteed as little in politics as in business, love, or any other area of human life. But it is well to remember that fewer than a dozen votes separated the candidates for the U.S. Senate in New Hampshire in 1974. Those votes had incredible power and may, sooner or later, determine congressional action on a tax increase, a draft law, or an impeachment.

Yet even if a single vote makes no obvious, tangible difference as is usually the case, it has an intangible significance for many citizens. It acknowledges their *interdependence* with the community in which they live as well as their *independence* to make a potentially important decision on their own. As such, voting is the most solemn ritual of democratic politics—a symbol of our common faith in ourselves and in a majority of our fellow citizens.

Notes

1. Hugh A. Bone and Austin Ranney, *Politics and Voters* (New York: McGraw-Hill, 1963), p. 111.
2. Howard R. Penniman, *The American Political Process* (New York: Van Nostrand Reinhold Co., 1962), p. 83.
3. Richard J. Carlson, "Election Legislation," *Book of the States 1974–75* (Lexington, Ky.: The Council of State Governments, 1974), p. 29.
4. Ibid., p. 31.
5. The states with open primaries are Alaska, Michigan, Minnesota, Montana, New Jersey, North Dakota, Utah, Vermont, Washington, and Wisconsin.
6. Stimson Bullitt, *To Be a Politician* (Garden City, N.Y.: Anchor Books, Doubleday & Co., 1961), p. 82.
7. Quoted in Michael J. Kirwan, *How to Succeed in Politics* (New York: Macfadden-Bartell Corp., 1964), p. 33.
8. James B. Kessler, "Running for State Political Office," in *Practical Politics in the United States,* ed. Cornelius P. Cotter (Boston: Allyn & Bacon, 1969), p. 141.
9. *Time,* July 3, 1972, pp. 44–47.
10. *Politics in America, 1945–1966,* 2nd ed. (Washington, D.C.: Congressional Quarterly, Inc., 1967), p. 88.
11. U.S. Bureau of the Census, *Statistical Abstract of the United States, 1971* (Washington, D.C.: U.S. Government Printing Office, 1972), p. 367.
12. Computed from General Accounting Office figures reported in the *Los Angeles Times,* March 24, 1974, p. 12. The figures represent only those expenditures made after April 7, 1972 when a new campaign reporting law took effect.
13. The 1972 average was about $45,000. *Los Angeles Times,* September 14, 1973, p. 23.
14. Harris poll, 1973, reported in n.a., *Confidence and Concern: Citizens View American Government* (Cleveland: Regal Books/King's Court Communications, 1974), p. 22. Also see Herbert E. Alexander, *Political Financing* (Minneapolis: Burgess Publishing Co., 1972), p. 33.
15. Herbert E. Alexander, "The Cost of Presidential Elections," Cotter, op. cit., pp. 281–82.
16. *Los Angeles Times,* September 30, 1973, p. 5.
17. Ibid., October 8, 1973, p. 15.
18. *Los Angeles Times,* February 8, 1972, p. 6.
19. Carlson, pp. 28–29; and *Los Angeles Times,* June 10, 1974, p. 8.
20. Some of this material is discussed in more detail in Paul P. Van Riper, *Handbook of Practical Politics,* 3rd ed. (New York: Harper & Row, 1967), pp. 45–63. I am also indebted to Dorothy Le Conte, a campaign manager with few peers, who taught me much of what is reflected in the material of this chapter.
21. Philips Cutright and Peter H. Rossi, "Grass Roots Politicians and the Vote," *American Sociological Review* 23 (April 1958).
22. Quoted in *We the People* (n.p.: California State Chamber of Commerce, 1970), p. 45. This Chamber of Commerce election pamphlet asserts that "One of every five United States Senators is a millionaire."
23. *The New York Times Encyclopedic Almanac, 1970* (New York: New York Times Publishing Co., 1969), p. 155.

24. Quoted in Herbert M. Baus and William B. Ross, *Politics Battle Plan* (New York: The Macmillan Co., 1968), pp. 331–32.

25. Robert Agranoff, *The New Style in Election Campaigns* (Boston: Holbrook Press, 1972), pp. 31–32.

26. Joe McGinniss, *The Selling of the President, 1968* (New York: Pocket Books, 1970), pp. 37–40.

27. *Newsweek,* November 16, 1970, p. 77.

28. Van Riper, p. 130.

29. Kirwan, p. 30.

30. Bullitt, p. 65.

31. By the mid-1950s, Whitaker and Baxter had managed seventy-five campaigns and won seventy of them. For a brief account of some of their successes, along with the importance of BBD&O, see Vance Packard, *The Hidden Persuaders* (New York: Pocket Books, 1958), pp. 155–63.

32. Jasper B. Shannon, *Money and Politics* (New York: Random House, 1959), p. 61.

33. Quoted in Packard, op. cit., p. 172.

34. Quoted in McGinniss, p. 21.

35. *Los Angeles Times,* February 23, 1973, p. 18.

36. Kirwan, p. 136.

37. *Los Angeles Times,* November 7, 1970, p. 10.

38. John W. Kingdon, *Candidates for Office* (New York: Random House, 1966), p. 133.

39. Agranoff, p. 32.

40. Van Riper, pp. 185–87.

41. Dale E. Wagner, "The Relationship Between Party Campaign Finance and Campaign Materials," unpublished paper delivered at the 1970 Annual Meeting of the American Political Science Association in Los Angeles, September 11, 1970.

42. *Statistical Abstract 1970,* p. 368.

43. *Christian Science Monitor,* April 21, 1973, p. 14; and *Los Angeles Times,* November 7, 1974, p. 35.

44. *Confidence and Concern,* p. 18; and Fred I. Greenstein, *The American Party System and the American People,* 2nd ed. (Englewood Cliffs, N.J.: Prentice-Hall, Inc., 1970), pp. 13–14.

45. Greenstein, op. cit., p. 10.

46. Philip E. Converse et al., "Continuity and Change in American Politics: Parties and Issues in the 1968 Election," *American Political Science Review* 63 (December 1969): 1084–85.

47. V. O. Key, Jr., *Politics, Parties, and Pressure Groups,* 5th ed. (New York: Thomas Y. Crowell Co., 1964), pp. 641–44, has been very helpful for this section. A study of the 1952 and 1956 elections showed that 18 percent fewer voters who classified themselves as independents voted a straight ticket on office-block ballots than on party-column ballots. Angus E. Campbell and Warren E. Miller, "The Motivational Basis of Straight and Split Ticket Voting," *American Political Science Review* 51 (June 1957): 307.

48. Key, p. 646.

49. *Los Angeles Times,* January 27, 1975, p. 4.

Bibliography

CHAPTER SEVEN   THE PEOPLE'S INFLUENCE

Cirino, Robert. *Don't Blame the People.* Los Angeles: University Press, 1971.
Congressional Quarterly Service. *Legislators and the Lobbyists,* 2nd ed. Washington,
   D.C.: Congressional Quarterly, Inc., 1968.
Dawson, Richard E., and Prewitt, Kenneth. *Political Socialization.* Boston: Little,
   Brown and Co., 1969.
Graham, Hugh Davis, and Gurr, Ted Robert. *Violence in America.* New York: A
   Signet Book, New American Library, 1969.
Greenstein, Fred I. *Children and Politics.* New Haven: Yale University Press, 1965.
Lakoff, Sanford A., ed. *Private Government.* Glenview, Ill.: Scott, Foresman and
   Company, 1973.
N.A. *Report of the National Advisory Commission on Civil Disorders.* New York:
   Bantam Books, 1968.
N.A. *Confidence and Concern: Citizens View American Government.* Cleveland:
   Regal Books/King's Court Communications, 1974.
Skolnick, Jerome H. *The Politics of Protest.* New York: Ballantine Books, 1969.
Truman, David. *The Governmental Process,* 2nd ed. New York: Alfred A. Knopf, 1971.

CHAPTER EIGHT   GOVERNMENT BY THE PEOPLE

American Political Science Association, Committee on Political Parties. *Toward a
   More Responsible Two-Party System.* New York: Holt, Rinehart & Winston, 1950.
Bone, Hugh A., and Ranney, Austin. *Politics and Voters.* New York: McGraw-Hill,
   1963.
Campbell, Angus, et al. *The American Voter.* New York: John Wiley & Sons, 1960.
Goldman, Ralph M. *The Democratic Party in American Politics.* New York: The
   Macmillan Co., 1966.
James, Judson L. *American Political Parties.* New York: Pegasus, 1969.
Jones, Charles O. *The Republican Party in American Politics.* New York: The
   Macmillan Co., 1965.
Key, V. O., Jr. *Politics, Parties, & Pressure Groups,* 5th ed. New York: Thomas Y.
   Crowell Co., 1964.

CHAPTER NINE   THE PRICE OF DEMOCRACY

Agranoff, Robert, ed. *The New Style in Election Campaigns.* Boston: Holbrook Press,
   Inc., 1972.
Bullitt, Stimson. *To Be a Politician,* rev. ed. Garden City, N.Y.: Anchor Books,
   Doubleday & Co., 1961.
Cotter, Cornelius P., ed. *Practical Politics in the United States.* Boston: Allyn &
   Bacon, 1969.
Lane, Robert. *Political Life.* Glencoe, Ill.: The Free Press, 1959.
McGinniss, Joe. *The Selling of the President, 1968.* New York: Pocket Books, 1970.
Van Riper, Paul P. *Handbook of Practical Politics,* 3rd ed. New York: Harper & Row,
   1967.

PART FOUR

THE PEOPLE'S GOVERNMENTS

[An] accumulation of all powers, legislative, executive, and judiciary, in the same hands, . . . may justly be pronounced the very definition of tyranny.

James Madison

The separation of powers among the legislative, executive, and judicial branches underlies the entire structure of our government. The three branches are constitutionally equal. The system of checks and balances operating among them usually makes the cooperation of all three essential. In practice, however, it is obvious that the three branches are not always equally effective. The growth of executive power has caused particular concern in recent years, especially as a result of Vietnam and Watergate. Yet this problem is not a new one. The role of the president as commander in chief of the armed forces has always expanded executive power in time of war. But, when the fighting draws to a close, Congress has reasserted its power with retaliatory vigor. It would be a mistake, however, to assume that a more vigorous Congress will produce any significant reduction in the size of the executive branch. All that can be expected is that Congress will regulate its performance more closely.

While the scales of power have tilted back and forth between the president and Congress, the Supreme Court has guaranteed the continued vitality of the judicial branch as well. Its decisions on racial segregation and the rights of suspects in the 1950s and early 1960s, and its 1974 decision requiring the release of presidential tapes, may have had a more profound effect upon the nation than the actions of the other two branches combined.

In the long run, the relative power of the three branches has shifted frequently. Yet no branch has succeeded in completely dominating the other two. This would have pleased the Founding Fathers. Each branch is examined individually in Chapters 10, 11, and 12.

10 THE LEGISLATIVE BRANCH:
Congress and the legislative process

Of all the powers with which the people have invested the Government, that of legislation is undoubtedly chief.

Select Committee of the House
of Representatives, 1816

According to almost every diagnosis, Congress was in bad shape as 1972 drew to a close. Even its own members sounded pessimistic. Senator Charles Mathias, a Republican from Maryland, said that "Congress today has become a third- or fourth-class power, a separate and thoroughly unequal branch of our national government."[1] Senator Hubert Humphrey, the veteran Democratic leader from Minnesota, agreed. "We're outmoded," he said. "We're out of step. We're outdated."[2] Rep. Donald W. Riegle, Jr., of Michigan endorsed the views of his colleague, Rep. Richard Bolling of Missouri. Bolling observed that "the primary failures of political leadership . . . are found in the United States Congress."[3]

Outside Congress, opinions were equally critical. *Time* magazine found that Congress was a branch of government "bent and in danger of snapping."[4] Meanwhile a public opinion poll showed that confidence in both the Senate and House of Representatives was lower than confidence in either the executive or judicial branches.[5]

By 1975, however, four dramatic developments had not only improved the public image of Congress but had also strengthened its power relative to the executive branch. Legislative action forced the resignation of the president, restricted his war-making powers, established more effective control over government expenditures, and modified the role of seniority in choosing congressional committee heads. Congress once again seemed capable of playing its historic role as an equal branch of our government.

LEGISLATIVE FUNCTIONS

Within the separation of powers established by the Constitution, Congress has four principal functions: (1) establishing public policy by passing laws, (2) controlling finance, (3) revising the Constitution, and (4) checking the other two branches of government.

Policy Making

In passing laws, often called statutes, Congress is performing its best-known and probably its most important function. By this means it establishes official policy and the general methods by which such policy is to be implemented. The lawmaking authority of Congress is defined by the first article of the Constitution. It is broadly interpreted by the courts. As a result, the powers *enumerated* in Article I, Section 8 have given rise to a vast array of *implied* powers deemed "necessary and proper" to carry them into effect. On many occasions, Congress exercises its powers directly, as when it creates national parks or prohibits racial discrimination in hiring workers. Sometimes, however, Congress delegates substantial policy-making power to the executive branch. It did this when it authorized the president to allocate fuel supplies and the Food and Drug Administration to prohibit the sale of products which are hazardous to health.

Controlling the Purse Strings

It does little good to pass a law without money to administer it. Congress controls the purse strings through appropriation bills. These bills allocate funds to all agencies of the national government for their operating expenses. Naturally, the legislature cannot appropriate money unless it raises it in some fashion. This can be either by taxes or by borrowing funds through the sale of government bonds. Chief Justice John Marshall long ago acknowledged the scope of this type of authority when he wrote that the power to tax is the power to destroy. Although the president and his advisors make detailed budget recommendations, Congress finally determines both where the money comes from and where it goes. In effect, it takes from some what it gives to others, a process that can involve the redistribution of wealth.

In two-house legislatures, the lower house is often the most important in exercising financial controls. In Congress, the House of Representatives has exclusive authority, under Article I, Section 7, to initiate bills to raise revenue. It has similar power, though only by tradition, to introduce bills which spend money. Nevertheless, the Senate usually has a considerable impact on money bills. They are all subject to amendment and final approval by each house before they are sent on to the chief executive for his signature.

There are actually two steps in the process by which Congress spends money. The first is the passage of legislation *authorizing* the expenditure of funds for a stated purpose. The second is the enactment of a bill actually *appropriating* the money. Sometimes the amount appropriated is smaller than that authorized. In most cases, the final figure is a compromise between the amounts approved by the Senate and by the normally more frugal House of Representatives. Too often, however, many separate appropriations have been voted without regard either for total expenditures or for the probable tax revenues available. The Budget Reform Act of 1974 was passed to remedy such situations.

Constitutional Revision

It is generally the task of a legislature to propose whatever changes it thinks necessary in the state or national constitutions. In order for Congress to amend the United States Constitution, the proposed change must be passed by a two-thirds vote of both houses. It must then be approved, or ratified, by three-quarters of the state legislatures. Other methods of amendment are also provided for by the Constitution.

Checking the Other Branches

In the system of checks and balances, legislative bodies have several ways to influence the other two branches.

Confirmation

One of the checks on the executive branch is the power of the Senate to approve appointments made by the president. All top officials in the executive departments and agencies, plus all judges, are chosen by the president subject to the "advice and consent" of a Senate majority. In practice, most presidential appointments are confirmed without much trouble, although there have been some notable exceptions. President Eisenhower, for example, appointed Lewis Strauss, former chairman of the Atomic Energy Commission, to be Secretary of Commerce. But the Senate refused to confirm him. Rather than even risk Senate rejection, President Lyndon Johnson withdrew his nomination of Abe Fortas as Chief Justice of the Supreme Court. More recently, the Senate rejected two of President Nixon's appointees to the U.S. Supreme Court. Clearly, more careful scrutiny and sometimes rejection of presidential appointments is one of the ways that Congress is reasserting its power to check the executive branch.

Under the Twenty-fifth Amendment, the president also has the authority to appoint someone to fill a vacancy in the vice-presidency. Here too, the executive power is not unlimited. Confirmation is required by a majority vote in the House of Representatives as well as in the Senate. In this way, of course, Gerald Ford took a giant step closer to the White House. After he became president, Congress again reasserted the importance of its confirmation power. This time it conducted a long and thorough investigation of Ford's appointment of Nelson Rockefeller before approving him as the new vice-president.

Senatorial Courtesy

There are close to a thousand posts in the national government requiring Senate confirmation. In addition to top department heads, these include U.S. district attorneys, judges, ambassadors, tax collectors at various ports, and many postmasters. The president cannot possibly make so many selections on the basis of his own personal evaluations. Customarily, therefore, he appoints people who have been recommended by senators of his own party from the states where the job vacancies exist. If he does not, his choices will be rejected by the Senate as a result of the custom known as senatorial courtesy. This was illustrated when President Truman appointed two men to U.S. district court judgeships in Illinois, neither of whom had been recommended by Illinois Senator Paul Douglas, a fellow Democrat. The Senate refused to confirm Truman's appointees. The practical effect of such senatorial courtesy is to give U.S. senators who belong to the president's party a certain amount of patronage.

Impeachment

The most important check Congress ever exerted on a president occurred when Richard Nixon resigned rather than face the even greater humiliation of constitutional removal. As a result, the congressional power of impeachment, seldom discussed and totally unused in nearly 40 years, rose from the dusty pages of the Constitution. It suddenly became a vital and realistic method of replacing government leaders. How did it all happen? The full Nixon story is best left to future biographies, but the role of impeachment in that saga is significant here. First, how does impeachment work?

The impeachment process is the only method the Constitution provides for removing judges or executive officials from office. It is a two-step procedure. Impeachment itself is technically a formal accusation made by a majority vote of the House of Representatives. The Senate then acts as a sort of trial jury in which a two-thirds vote is necessary to convict the impeached official and thereby remove him or her from office. When the Senate is sitting in an impeachment trial involving the president, the Chief Justice of the Supreme Court presides over it.

President Nixon's slow and agonizing downfall began in the summer of 1973. At that time, impeachment resolutions were introduced by Rep. Robert F. Drinan, a Massachusetts Democrat, and a number of other House members. These were referred to the House Judiciary Committee which assembled a special staff to investigate the charges against the president. Moving with painstaking thoroughness, the committee chaired by Rep. Peter Rodino (D–N.J.) began hearing evidence on May 9, 1974. After seven weeks of testimony, the eyes of the nation followed the closing stages of its proceedings on television. Finally, the Judiciary Committee recommended to the entire House of Representatives that three "Articles of Impeachment" be leveled against President Nixon. The date of the last committee vote was July 30, 1974 – 364 days after Rep. Drinan had first introduced an impeachment resolution.

From that date on, events moved swiftly. Impeachment debate by the entire House was scheduled for August 19. White House aides began counting probable House votes for impeachment and Senate votes for conviction. On August 5, tape-recorded evidence released by Supreme Court order prompted key supporters of the president to desert him. On August 9, 1974, he became the first president in history to resign from office. He said, "I no longer have a strong enough political base in the Congress . . . ." But he meant, "I'll be impeached by the House and convicted by the Senate."

Mr. Nixon's resignation left at least two unanswered questions about the impeachment process. The first is: Can an official be impeached for something other than a criminal act? While the Constitution, in Article II, Section 4, lists the grounds of impeachment as "Treason, Bribery, or other High Crimes and Misdemeanors," there is disagreement regarding the definition of the last of these. In other words, is failure to fulfill one's constitutional obligations a sufficiently grave "misdemeanor" to warrant impeachment, even though no crime punishable by a court has been committed? The matter of just what a judge can be impeached for is also partially unanswered. President Ford, when a member of the House of Representatives, once argued that since Article III states that federal judges shall hold office "during good behavior," they could be impeached for whatever reason the House wished. A second unresolved question is: Can an official facing impeachment be held accountable for the actions of those responsible to him? There was little doubt that President Nixon's most important aides were involved in illegal acts. But many insisted that he could not be impeached unless "the smoking gun" was held in his very own hands. Indeed, the recorded conversations finally proved that it had been.

After the Nixon resignation, Andrew Johnson remained as the only president ever to have been impeached. He was acquitted in the Senate in 1868 by a margin of just one vote. Yet the House Judiciary Committee voted that their decision to impeach Nixon (if he had not resigned first) be recorded in the official House proceedings even though it was not acted upon formally by the whole House. In our entire history the House has impeached only twelve officials. Of these only four – all lower-court judges – were convicted by the Senate.[6]

Treaty Approval

To some extent, the president's control over foreign policy is checked by the requirement that treaties with other nations be approved by a two-thirds vote of the Senate. This, along with its authority to confirm appointments, gives the Senate a larger role in limiting executive power than is possessed by the House.

The Expansion of Government Machinery

Legislative power over the other branches also includes the authority to create and fund government agencies. The increasing demands on modern governments have resulted in the steady expansion of executive departments and commissions. For example, Congress created the Department of Housing and Urban Development (HUD) in 1965 and the Consumer Product Safety Commission in 1972. These new government agencies are usually answerable to the president. Similarly, Congress has the power to create new federal courts but the decisions of such courts can be appealed to the Supreme Court.

Declaring War

As commanders in chief, presidents have plunged American military forces into prolonged conflict in Korea in 1950 and Vietnam in 1965. In order to check this power, and to reaffirm its own constitutional authority to declare war, which requires a majority vote of both houses, Congress cut off funds for Cambodian bombing in 1973. More importantly, it passed the War Powers Act of 1973 which, among other restrictions, placed a 60-day time limit on the president's power to keep American troops in foreign battle without congressional approval. To pass this act, Congress had to override a Nixon veto. It was clearly determined to reassert its authority in this area and to check excessive executive power. When Cambodia seized the merchant ship *Mayaguez* in April 1975, President Ford informed Congress of the use of armed forces to gain the ship's release. This was required by the War Powers Act and was the first time that law was actually used.

Legislative Oversight

After a law is passed, lawmakers have the right, perhaps even the duty, to see how effectively it is being administered. This involves the process of overseeing executive agencies, a process which is carried on by various legislative committees. Usually it is done by the same standing committees (or their subcommittees) that originally considered the legislation. Sometimes, however, special investigating committees are set up to oversee a certain department or agency, or section thereof. In any event, such inquiries enable Congress not only to check up on the executive branch but also to compete with it in getting public attention.

Committees carry out their function of oversight by holding hearings. They ask or sometimes compel witnesses, mainly executive branch officials, to testify on whatever is being investigated. Such witnesses may bring along a lawyer to advise them. They may also invoke the Fifth Amendment protection against compulsory self-incrimination. Members of Congress, however, are protected by *congressional immunity* from being sued for what they say on the Senate or House floor or in committee hearings.

Ken Regan, Camera 5

Senators Kennedy and Tunney listen to testimony at the Indian Subcommittee hearing in California.

Although some investigations can be considered "muckraking," most constitute a healthy examination of important problem areas in public policy. In June 1972, for example, various congressional committees held hearings on the trans-Alaska oil pipeline, health and accident insurance, the abuse of barbiturate drugs, and pesticide control. As usual, the leading witnesses were lobbyists, executive officials, and interested legislators. It is important to note that such investigations serve the dual purposes of uncovering information that may lead to new laws as well as showing how efficiently those already on the books are being administered. Unfortunately, the appeal of proposing new legislation is much greater than that of checking the enforcement of old laws. As a result, one of the chief criticisms of Congress has been its ineffectiveness in exercising proper oversight of such powerful executive agencies as the F.B.I. and the C.I.A. In 1975, however, there seemed to be a new desire by Congress to perform the oversight function more effectively.

In conducting their investigations, legislative committees have been limited by a number of factors. These include inadequate staffs and a reluctance of lawmakers to embarrass the heads of agencies whom they agree with in principle and like personally. Tradition, moreover, along with the principle of separation of powers, has usually excused presidents from testifying before congressional committees. This tradition was weakened in 1974 when Gerald Ford made a public appearance before a congressional committee. His purpose was to explain and defend to a House Judiciary subcommittee his pardon of ex-President Nixon.

A final restriction on the power of legislative investigations is that questions put to witnesses must have some relationship to subjects over which there is power to pass laws. The investigating process, in other words, cannot be used for the sole purpose of accusing or harassing witnesses. As former Chief Justice Earl Warren said in the case of *Watkins* v. *U.S.,* "there is no Congressional power to expose for the sake of exposure."[7]

Checks on the Courts

In addition to confirming court appointments or impeaching judges, there are two other legislative checks on the judicial branch. One is the power of Congress to change the number of judges serving on any federal court. The size of the Supreme Court has varied between five and ten, although it has remained at nine ever since 1869.

A second check on the Supreme Court is the authority of Congress to determine its appellate jurisdiction or the kinds of cases that it can hear on appeal from lower courts. If the lawmakers don't like the decision of the Court in a certain kind of case, they can alter its appellate jurisdiction to prevent similar cases from reaching the high court in the future. This has not been done for more than a century. But unpopular decisions involving school prayers, unequally apportioned legislative districts, and compulsory school busing gave rise to threats of doing so in recent years.

STRUCTURE AND MEMBERSHIP

Congress (and all but the Nebraska state legislature) are two-house, or bicameral, bodies. Members of the lower houses represent constituencies rather different from those represented by members of the upper houses. Moreover, the way in which a state is apportioned into congressional districts makes a big difference in who gets elected to the House of Representatives.

Bicameralism

There were many reasons for the establishment of bicameral legislatures in the United States. They include the example of the English Parliament and the fact that two houses helped win the support of both large and small states for the Constitution. But the survival of bicameralism indicates that it has some inherent advantages. The fact that a bill must pass two houses should theoretically produce better legislation. The mistakes, passions, or prejudices of one chamber can be corrected by the other. Some critics charge, however, that bicameralism confers too much power on *conference committees* that must somehow reconcile the differences when the two chambers pass different versions of the same bill. We will discuss this further in "The Legislative Process."

The Allocation of Legislative Seats

Congressional Apportionment

No characteristic of a legislative body is more important than the way in which seats are allocated among the people to be represented. The Founding Fathers viewed the decision to grant each state two seats in the Senate as immensely significant. This was the only provision in the Constitution which they made impossible to amend. They also provided that membership in the U.S. House of Representatives would be reapportioned among the states every ten years on the basis of an official population census, with each state having at least one seat.

As the original thirteen states grew in population, and as new ones were gradually admitted to the Union, the total size of the House went from 65 members to 435 after the 1910 census. Congress then decided that the House would soon be too large to function efficiently. As a result, a law was passed freezing its size at 435. Now when a state gains additional seats because its population has grown faster than the national average, states with slower population growth must lose seats. After the 1970 census, California gained five additional members of the House and Florida three. New York and Pennsylvania lost two each. Ten other states gained or lost one seat.

Following every census, each state is informed of the number of seats to which it will be entitled for the next ten years. The state legislatures then determine the boundaries of the districts from which their representatives will be elected. The inevitable result is a bitter redistricting fight.

State Legislative Apportionment

As indicated in Chapter 6, state legislatures draw both their own and congressional districts so that they have approximately equal population. In other words, today all states elect almost all legislators, except for U.S. senators, on a one-man, one-vote basis. Reapportionments are mandatory after each census.

The Politics of Gerrymandering

Whenever reapportionment is necessary, nearly every conceivable interest group attempts to influence the reshaping of district boundaries to its own advantage. This process is known as *gerrymandering*.

The most influential groups concerned with redistricting are the political parties. The majority party in a state legislature can usually draw boundaries that will improve the reelection chances of most of its candidates. They can do this by making a careful analysis of past election results in every part of the state. Assume that in Figure 10–1 each letter represents an equal number of voters. *R* stands for areas predominantly Republican, while *D* stands for areas predominantly Democratic. If the Republicans have a majority in the state legislature, they might draw boundaries so that they could win easily in three of the four districts. But if there is a Democratic majority in the state capitol, the same region might be arranged to elect only one Republican and three Democrats, as shown in Figure 10–2. Compromise boundaries, favoring two Republicans and two Democrats, might be worked out as shown in Figure 10–3.

Party considerations are not the only ones important in apportionment, however. Racial groups, for example, also have a stake in the matter. Given various boundaries, black candidates may be elected in no districts, in one, or in two, as illustrated in Figure 10–4.

The interplay of personal ambitions is also a major factor. Members of the lower house of a state legislature may wish to have district boundaries drawn to help get them elected to the upper house or to Congress. At a minimum, they would like to guarantee their own reelection.[8] Thus one of the most predictable results of gerrymandering is the creation of many safe districts where incumbent legislators can hardly lose.

Figure 10–1. REPUBLICAN-CONTROLLED GERRYMANDER

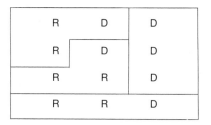

Figure 10–2. DEMOCRATIC-CONTROLLED GERRYMANDER

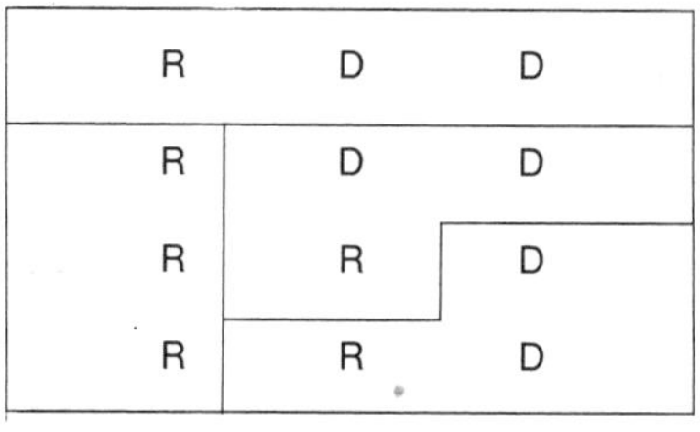

Figure 10–3. COMPROMISE

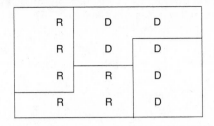

Figure 10–4. RACIAL GERRYMANDER

Possibility A

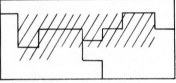

Probable winners: 3 whites, 0 blacks

Possibility B

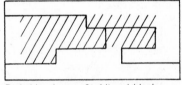

Probable winners: 2 whites, 1 black

Possibility C

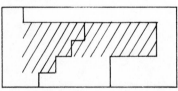

Probable winners: 1 white, 2 blacks

Racial and ethnic minorities have contended that the boundaries of congressional and state legislative districts are gerrymandered so as to make it very difficult for their candidates to get elected. These three examples indicate how district boundaries might be drawn to increase the likelihood that no blacks would be elected (Possibility A), that one would be elected (Possibility B), or that two would be elected (Possibility C). In all three examples, each square represents the same number of people, and the population of the three districts is equal.

◨ blacks

☐ no blacks

City and county officials feel that they too have an interest in state legislative and congressional apportionment. In general, they believe that if units of local government are split by district boundaries a sense of unity may be lost and community interests poorly represented.[9] The late Justice Frankfurter summed up the importance of the whole issue. The "practical significance of apportionment," he wrote, "is that the next election results may differ because of it."[10] So too may the kinds of legislation enacted.

The Members of Congress

In Congress, all 435 members of the House of Representatives are elected every two years. The 100 senators are elected for six-year terms, with a third of the members facing reelection every two years. Congress convenes each January, as required by the Constitution, and usually remains in session until the following autumn. Members of both houses received annual salaries of $42,500 in 1975, plus considerable expense money, and the franking privilege which permits them to send postage-free mail.

If Congress is to accurately represent the interests of the people, some have argued that the characteristics of its members must be similar to those of the total population. In fact, however, lawmakers are a rather special breed, unlike their fellow citizens in certain key respects.

Sex and Race
Women, to cite the most extreme example, constituted a little more than half the total population but only 3.4 percent of Congress in 1975 (19 out of 535). Blacks, comprising more than 11 percent of the population, held only 18 seats, about the same percentage as women.

Religion
Jews and Catholics, as we have noted, are traditionally more Democratic than the general population. Thus it is not surprising that the sweeping Democratic victory in the 1974 congressional elections boosted Jewish representation from 14 to 24. And the number of Catholic members grew from 115 to 123, the most they have had in our history. The strength of both groups in Congress now closely approximates their ratio in the total population. Winning candidates in 1974 also included 85 Methodists, 66 Episcopalians, 65 Presbyterians, and 57 Baptists.[11] For Baptists, the largest Protestant denomination, this constitutes substantial underrepresentation. A partial explanation for this may lie in their relatively low average income.

Occupational Background
An analysis of the 1972 Congress discloses additional information about the types of people most likely to win election. Of the 535 members, 462 had previous experience in public office, mostly state and local, while 387 were military veterans.[12] Occupationally, lawyers make up fewer than 1 percent of American workers, but well over half of all members of Congress. Other well-represented occupations on Capitol Hill were business and banking, 173 members; teaching, 72; farming, 47; and journalism, 36.[13] It is wise, if one wishes to run for legislative office, to have a secure occupation to which to return if one loses.

Since service in many state legislatures (unlike service in Congress) is not a full-time occupation, it usually holds little promise of providing a satisfying career. As a result, there is a much higher turnover in the membership of state legislatures than in Congress. In elections held in 1971 and 1972, about 40 percent of all state legislators were replaced. Yet in the 1974 congressional elections, with a greater turnover than at any time in recent history, newcomers accounted for only 21 percent of the winners.[14]

Age
Practical considerations prohibit young people from gaining their proportionate share of legislative seats. One can seldom hope to accumulate the acquaintances, money, or prestige necessary for a successful campaign before reaching middle age. In 1973, when the median age for all Americans was 28, the median age for all congressmen was in the 50s. For the 38 chairmen of the standing committees it was 63.[15]

The Unrepresentative Representatives
Out of this array of statistics, an overriding conclusion emerges: Legislative representatives are not very representative. Those who make our laws are generally male, white, professionally trained, business-oriented, and middle-aged. With inevitable exceptions, this means that legislators are rarely inclined to favor major changes in the society in which they have attained high status.

INTERNAL ORGANIZATION

Within any legislature, some members have more power than others. Generally, maximum influence is exerted by presiding officers, committee chairmen, and party leaders.

Presiding Officers

The presiding officers have the authority to recognize speakers, interpret the rules of procedure, and decide on the committee to which each bill will be sent.

The Vice-President
The Constitution authorizes the vice-president to preside over the U.S. Senate. But he is not considered a member of that body and cannot participate in legislative debate. He can vote on bills only in case of a tie. If the vice-president is absent, the presiding officer is the president pro tem. He is a senator elected to this position by his colleagues and is usually the member of the majority party with longest Senate service. Each legislative chamber adopts its own rules of procedure. Since those in the Senate are relatively few and informal, the vice-president or president pro tem must rarely render significant interpretations. Moreover, since Senate rules provide for unlimited debate, it often makes little difference who the presiding officer recognizes to speak at any particular time. Each senator will have a chance sooner or later anyway.

The Speaker of the House

The House of Representatives elects its own presiding officer on a straight party-line vote. Thus, the Speaker is recognized as the most popular member of the majority party in the House and probably also the most powerful person in Congress. When Speakers were at the peak of their power, prior to certain reforms in House rules enacted in 1910, they ruled the chamber in a nearly dictatorial fashion. Even now a strong Speaker, like the late Rep. Sam Rayburn of Texas, is second only to the president of the U.S. in general political influence. Constitutionally, he is third in line to become president in the event of death or resignation.

The sources of the Speaker's vast power are numerous. Because rules of procedure are far more intricate in the House than in the Senate, his authority to interpret them is more significant. Similarly, his power to recognize members to speak is more important. This is because severe time limits on House debate prevent many representatives from speaking at all. The Speaker also appoints members to certain special committees (as distinct from standing committees, discussed below), assigns bills to committees, and performs personal but meaningful services for House members, such as the allocation of office space. Moreover, if the president belongs to his party, the Speaker plays a major role in gaining congressional approval of administration proposals.

Standing Committees

Congress in session is Congress on public exhibition, whilst Congress in its committee rooms is Congress at work.

Woodrow Wilson

Most of the work of modern legislative bodies is done in their standing committees. These provide for a division of labor which enables each lawmaker to specialize in a particular area of public policy. Every legislator is assigned to at least one standing committee which considers all bills dealing with its specialized field. Before he was elected president, Woodrow Wilson called the standing committees of Congress "little legislatures" with the power to bury a bill in "dim dungeons of silence whence it will never return."[16] In this respect, things haven't changed much.

Committee Assignments and the Seniority System

In both houses, there is nothing more important to the average legislator than his or her committee assignments. A congressperson's preference for a certain committee will be dictated by three main considerations: first, the major concerns of the home district, second, his or her own background and interests, and third, the influence and publicity to be derived from membership on a particular committee.

However, for freshmen congresspersons there may be a wide gulf between the committee posts they would like and those they actually get. They can blame two factors for this: the party-ratio tradition and, at least in the Senate, the seniority system. On most of the standing committees, the ratio of Republicans to Democrats is roughly the same as in the whole chamber. Thus, if there are sixty Democrats and forty Republicans in the Senate, a ten-member standing committee would probably consist of about six Democrats and four Republicans. The seniority system is a bigger obstacle to a desired committee assignment. It usually means that legislators are given their choice of committees in order of their length of continuous service in the Senate or House. That is, those who have been in Congress the longest will get their first choices.

Earthquake in the House
Since 1910 in the House and since the 1840s in the Senate, the seniority system has been used to determine committee chairmanships. More precisely, this meant that the chairperson of each standing (permanent) committee was the member of the majority party who had served the longest on that particular committee. The most obvious result of this seniority system was that it produced committee chairpersons of long experience, advanced age, and—sometimes—questionable competence. More important, perhaps, was that the legislators who accumulated enough seniority to become chairpersons often were able to do so because they came from areas where the two parties did not compete on an equal basis. Such noncompetitive, one-party regions, often in the South, tended to reflect social change and shifting opinion very slowly. Hence the chairpersons, with few exceptions, were more conservative than most members of Congress.

The seniority system has been among the most widely criticized of congressional procedures. Thus Rep. Les Aspin (D–Wis.) called it "an earthquake" when seniority was disregarded in the selection of four committee chairpersons in the House of Representatives in 1975. No doubt it had been weakened by years of growing dissatisfaction, but the seniority system cracked chiefly as a result of pressures brought to bear by 75 newly elected Democrats. This was combined with the shock caused by the recently publicized relationship of an ill committee chairman, Wilbur Mills of Arkansas, with an Argentine stripteaser. Like Rep. Mills of the powerful Ways and Means Committee, the three other chairmen who were unseated were also from the South. They were Reps. F. Edward Hebert of the Armed Services Committee, from Louisiana; W. R. Poage of the Agriculture Committee, from Texas; and Wright Patman of the Banking Committee, also from Texas. While the old power structure was thereby jolted in the House, there were at least some tremors which indicated possible after-shocks in the Senate as well.

The Power of the Chairperson
The seniority system would be less important if the committee chairpersons

were less powerful. They determine the agendas of committee meetings, when to have hearings, and who will testify at them. They also decide what subcommittees to create, and whether to refer a particular bill to one of them. Frequently, chairpersons prevent bills from reaching the floor at all by pigeonholing them (refusing to schedule them for committee consideration). If a bill is not discussed in committee, or if the committee refuses to report it out to the floor, it is almost certainly dead. It can be revived only by a discharge petition or motion. This requires the approval of a majority of the entire membership of either chamber, and is rarely used.

Rounding out their authority, committee chairpersons play prominent roles in floor debate on those bills reported out from their committees. They also participate in conference committees to iron out differences between the two houses. In addition, they hire most of the professional staff members who assist committees in their work. As the late Rep. Clem Miller once observed, "There are all sorts of ways to get things done in Congress. The best way is to live long enough to get to be a committee chairman."[17] But the length of human life is not yet determined by majority vote. Thus it is easy to see why reformers worked for several decades to obtain a more democratic method than the seniority system for selecting committee chairpersons.

Committees in the U.S. Senate

There are eighteen standing committees in the Senate. Their members are chosen by party committees, which in turn are selected by the Democratic floor leader and the chairperson of the Republican Senate Conference. As we have seen, seniority carries great weight, although personal and political factors are also involved. When former President Johnson was the leader of the Senate Democrats in 1953, he broke with previous tradition by persuading his party's Committee on Committees to award each new Democrat one major committee assignment.[18] In 1975, this nineteen-member Democratic steering committee ignored seniority in filling an important post on the Judiciary Committee. Seniority, however, still determined all Senate committee chairmanships.

Two Senate committees have unique importance because they deal with matters beyond the scope of any committees in the House. One is the Foreign Relations Committee. Because treaties with foreign nations must be approved only by the Senate, this is the only committee that has an opportunity to review them before they are put to a vote. Similarly, the Senate Judiciary Committee reviews presidential appointments to the federal courts. This again is a matter over which the House of Representatives has no control. But the Judiciary Committees in both houses consider most civil rights bills and proposed constitutional amendments.

Committees in the House of Representatives

There are twenty-one standing committees in the House. Republicans are

Figure 10–5. SENATE STANDING COMMITTEES, 1974 (MEMBERSHIP IN PARENTHESES)

Aeronautical and Space Sciences (13)	Foreign Relations (17)
Agriculture and Forestry (13)	Government Operations (16)
Appropriations (26)	Interior and Insular Affairs (13)
Armed Services (15)	Judiciary (16)
Banking, Housing, and Urban Affairs (16)	Labor and Public Welfare (16)
Budget (15)	Post Office and Civil Service (9)
Commerce (18)	Public Works (14)
District of Columbia (7)	Rules and Administration (9)
Finance (17)	Veterans' Affairs (9)

Source: Ann Golenpaul, ed., *Information Please Almanac, 1975* (New York: Dan Golenpaul Associates, 1974), p. 46.

assigned to them by a Committee on Committees consisting of one GOP congressperson from each state. For House Democrats, committee assignments are made by their Policy and Steering Committee. This consists of 12 members elected by the whole Democratic caucus from geographic regions and 12 others comprised of party leaders in the House and persons appointed by them. It was this group, voting on each committee chairmanship by secret ballot instead of merely "rubber-stamping" the senior incumbents, that broke the seniority tradition in 1975. But seniority still determined the election of the vast majority of chairpersons. And it is still a factor, along with popularity, the recommendations of party leaders, and geographic balance, in the selection of all committee members.

The most desired committee posts in the House are on the Rules, Ways and Means, and Appropriations Committees. The Rules Committee is extremely powerful because it determines when and for how long bills approved by other standing committees will be debated on the House floor. It also decides whether floor amendments may be offered on bills. The rules issued by this committee are supposed to speed up action on pending legislation. But sometimes the committee's power is used to prevent any floor action at all if a bill is opposed by the committee chairperson or a majority of its members. The result of this whole process is that most bills must get through two committees before they reach the floor of the House, but only one to receive consideration in the Senate. The vast power of the Rules Committee is defended on the basis of the far larger number of bills introduced in the House than in the Senate. But its abuse of authority has made it, along with the Senate filibuster and the seniority system, one of the most undemocratic of congressional characteristics.

The Ways and Means Committee derives its special influence from that provision of the Constitution (Article I, Section 7) which states that "all bills for raising revenue shall originate in the House of Representatives. . . ." Most such measures are tax bills and all are referred to this committee. All expenditure bills are also traditionally introduced first in the House. Thus its

Figure 10–6. STANDING COMMITTEES OF THE HOUSE OF REPRESENTATIVES, 1974 (MEMBERSHIP IN PARENTHESES)

Agriculture (36)	Interstate and Foreign Commerce (43)
Appropriations (55)	Judiciary (38)
Armed Services (43)	Merchant Marine and Fisheries (39)
Banking and Currency (39)	Post Office and Civil Service (26)
Budget (23)	Public Works (39)
District of Columbia (25)	Rules (15)
Education and Labor (38)	Science and Astronautics (30)
International Relations (40)	Standards of Official Conduct (12)
Government Operations (40)	Veterans' Affairs (26)
House Administration (26)	Ways and Means (25)
Interior and Insular Affairs (41)	

Source: *Information Please Almanac, 1975*, p. 46.
Note: On a few matters, notably atomic energy and defense production, there are joint standing committees consisting of both senators and representatives, rather than separate ones in each chamber.

Appropriations Committee has an advantage comparable to that of Ways and Means. No committees receive more attention from the president interested in getting his proposed programs approved, or from interest groups interested in obtaining subsidies or avoiding taxes.

The number of standing committees in Congress is changed from time to time, either by law or as each house sees fit. In 1974 the Budget Reform Act created new budget committees in both houses to help coordinate and limit total government expenditures more effectively. In 1975, the House abolished its Internal Security Committee. Formerly known as the Un-American Activities Committee, this panel had frequently been criticized for irresponsible accusations against the patriotism of controversial citizens. It was this committee on which Rep. Richard Nixon served in the late 1940s when he first gained national prominence as a staunch anti-Communist.

Select Committees

In addition to the standing committees just discussed, either house of Congress may establish temporary select committees to investigate special problems. One of these was the so-called Watergate Committee, created by the Senate in 1973 to investigate illegal campaign practices. This committee was chaired by Senator Sam Ervin (D–N.C.) who became an overnight folk hero to many who saw the committee's televised hearings. These hearings produced the first testimony involving President Nixon himself in illegal acts and they led to the discovery that presidential conversations in the White House had been taped. In 1975, the Senate established another select committee, headed by Sen. Frank Church (D–Idaho), to investigate charges that the Central Intelligence Agency had illegally spied on American citizens and been involved in plans to assassinate foreign leaders.

Party Leadership

In addition to the presiding officers of each house provided for by the Constitution, there are several other very important congressional leaders whose roles, like those of committee chairpersons, have evolved through custom. These are the party leaders of each house who are in charge of the organization and procedures of the majority and minority parties.

Floor Leaders in the U.S. Senate

The *majority leader,* or floor leader of the majority party, in the U.S. Senate is the most powerful member of that body. His strength stems from several sources. First, he has great influence over committee assignments. Second, he controls the order in which the Senate debates bills reported out of the various committees. Third, by tradition, the majority leader will be recognized by the presiding officer whenever he wishes to speak. Finally, he derives power from his close relations with the White House—especially if the president belongs to the same party. In a sense, the Senate majority leader has no comparable counterpart in the House of Representatives, since he combines some of the powers of the Speaker, the House majority leader, and the Rules Committee chairperson—all rolled into one. Yet because each individual senator is more important than each representative, the overall power of the Senate majority leader is probably not as great as that of the Speaker of the House.

The minority leader, who heads the smaller party in the Senate, has somewhat less power. He helps to determine committee appointments for his party. He is consulted by the majority leader on the agenda for Senate debate. And if the president belongs to *his* party, he may act as the semiofficial spokesperson for the administration on pending bills.

Both the majority and minority leaders are elected by a vote of all senators from their party, meeting in what are known as party *caucuses* or (more recently) *conferences.* Although seniority may exert some influence, factors such as personality, ideology, legislative skill, and the accumulation of political debts play major roles in the final choices.

The Democratic conference gives its floor leader more power than the Republicans give theirs. Both conferences also elect an assistant leader, known as the majority or minority *whip.* The whips assist the leaders in making sure party members are on the Senate floor when important matters come up for a vote. Whip positions are often a stepping-stone to bigger things. Sen. Mike Mansfield (D–Mont.), the present majority leader, was previously the majority whip. Sen. Hubert Humphrey (D–Minn.), rose from whip to vice-president.

Party Organization in the House

Here, as in the Senate, members of Congress meet in party caucuses (conferences) to elect majority and minority leaders and whips. In a sense, they play the same roles as their Senate counterparts, but with two major differences. One is that the most important member of the majority party in the House is elected Speaker, with the majority leader ranking second, and the majority whip third. The majority leader is often considered the heir apparent to the Speaker. Both Rep. John W. McCormack (D–Mass.) and Rep. Carl Albert (D–Okla.) made this rather natural transition in 1962 and 1971, respectively. Similarly, the minority leader has a good chance of becoming Speaker if congressional elections shift control of the House from one party to the other. This, it is said, is all Minority Leader Gerald R. Ford had hoped for until he was appointed to the vice-presidency.

A second major difference in the influence of House and Senate party organizations is that—as noted earlier—the order of business in the House is determined by the Rules Committee rather than by the party leadership. But the importance of party organization in the House soared spectacularly in 1975 when the Democratic Caucus replaced seniority with secret ballot elections in determining committee chairpersons. As the Democratic Caucus became more powerful, so too did its chairperson, the youthful Rep. Phillip Burton of California. Many "Congress-watchers," in fact, believe him to be even more influential than the majority leader, Rep. Thomas (Tip) O'Neill of Massachusetts.

Informal Power

Informal power is less easy to describe, but no less real than formal authority. Almost every legislative body has informal alliances that may include the official leadership, may sometimes challenge it, or may simply exist as alternative centers of power.

In the House of Representatives, for example, over a hundred liberal Democrats belong to the Democratic Study Group. This group raises campaign funds for its supporters, employs a small staff, and works to gain support for bills important to its interests. It played a major role, along with pressure from Common Cause and League of Women Voters lobbyists, in successfully challenging the seniority system.

The Wednesday Club is a somewhat similar group consisting of moderate and liberal Republicans. In addition, there is a Black Caucus in the House which seeks to promote black interests. Sectional and economic groupings in Congress are much older, but less organized. There is, for example, a "farm bloc," a narrower "cotton bloc," an "oil bloc," and so on. Each bloc consists of congresspersons from states where one of these is a major product.

In the Senate, smaller and more intimate than the House, a kind of inner "club" has developed across party lines. It has no formal membership, but seems to consist of personal friends with considerable seniority. It subtly enforces Senate traditions and behavior norms among younger members, and has considerable influence. There is also a group of conservative

Republican senators, calling itself the "Steering Committee," which meets periodically.

Of all the informal groups in Congress, probably the most important has been a loose coalition of Republicans and conservative southern Democrats. This coalition has controlled most major committees and often has had an operating majority in Congress since World War II. In both houses, it has worked against the passage of civil rights bills and other liberal reforms.

The sum total of formal and informal organization in Congress is a considerable fragmentation of power. This creates numerous points of access for lobbyists, many obstacles to the passage of a bill, and hence a frustrating slowness in the legislative process as we shall see below.

THE LEGISLATIVE PROCESS

As President Kennedy observed in 1962: "It is very easy to defeat a bill in the Congress. It is much more difficult to pass one."[19] He was neither the first nor the last president to be frustrated by that painful legislative truth. It is necessary, therefore, to understand the obstacle course that confronts bills in Congress—and in most of the state legislatures as well. In the following sketch of a bill's passage in Congress, we see in sequence some of the factors mentioned earlier.

Introduction of a Bill

Although a bill must be introduced by either a senator or a representative, it may be suggested or even written by others. The president's staff, departmental officials, lobbyists, or influential constituents may draft proposed legislation. (Tax, or other revenue bills, it will be remembered, must be introduced first in the House.) Occasionally, identical bills are introduced at the same time by a senator and a representative. Usually, however, a bill is considered by one house only after it is passed, or nearly passed, by the other house. Once introduced, each bill is given an identifying number and is referred by the presiding officer to the appropriate standing committee.

The types of bills that each committee considers are spelled out quite clearly in House and Senate rules. Thus there is usually not much choice in a bill's committee assignment. Once in a while, however, as with the Civil Rights Act of 1964, a presiding officer will not send a bill to certain burial in the committee which would normally have jurisdiction over it. Instead it will be referred to a committee known to be more favorable toward it.

Committee Consideration

Ordinarily, the committee has the power of life or death over bills referred to it, and most receive the death sentence. That is, the committee chairperson may decide never to consider a bill (pigeonhole it). In 1963–64, for example, less than 12 percent of all bills were reported out by the committee to which they were sent.[20]

If committee chairpersons decide not to pigeonhole a bill, they may refer it to a subcommittee which they can create and whose members they usually appoint. Committee or subcommittee chairpersons may then schedule open public hearings. They decide which lobbyists and officials from the executive branch will testify at these hearings regarding the bill's merits or defects. After public hearings have been concluded, the committee meets privately to "markup" the bill and add whatever amendments it wishes. The relatively few bills that win a majority vote in committee (and sometimes in a subcommittee before that) usually have been subjected to grueling controversy and numerous amendments.

Floor Action, Filibusters, and Conference Committees

[It] is not debate that is a hindrance to action, but rather not to be instructed by debate before the time comes for action.

Pericles

In the House most important bills go from a standing committee to the Rules Committee. This committee determines if and when the bill will arrive on the floor of the entire House. It is not uncommon for as many as thirty bills a year to die in the Rules Committee. For those bills that it does not kill, the Rules Committee normally gives them "rules" limiting debate by the entire House of Representatives to one or two hours per bill. Occasionally it prohibits amendments from being proposed from the floor. The chairperson and other members of the committee or subcommittee that considered the bill usually dominate floor debate. Other congresspersons generally follow their recommendations and most bills are passed in more or less the same form as they are reported out by the considering committee. In the House, a quorum of 100 members called the Committee of the Whole can act on and amend bills. But their decisions must be approved, and every bill must be passed, by a majority of 218 House members.

In the Senate, any bill that gets out of committee may be brought to the floor by any senator. The Senate Rules Committee cannot interfere, but bills are usually scheduled by the majority leader. While it is easier to get a bill before the Senate than the House, the absence of time limits on debate make it harder to bring a bill to a vote. In other words, unlimited debate in the Senate means that each senator can normally talk as long and as often as he or she wishes on any bill before it can be brought to a vote.

Unlimited debate permits a leisurely and thoughtful consideration of a bill. But it also permits a small minority of the Senate to defeat a bill favored by a clear majority. This is accomplished by a *filibuster*. A filibuster is a series of marathon speeches that can tie up the Senate for weeks and prohibit it from considering any other pending legislation. Finally, the pressures of pending business force the majority to give in to the minority of filibustering senators and agree to kill the bill that they oppose. While talking a bill to death, a senator may speak about anything and may even read—as Senator Huey Long of Louisiana once did—the Bible, the Constitution, and the Sears Roebuck catalogue.

Before 1917 there was no way to end a filibuster. In that year, however, Senate Rule 22 provided for the termination of debate through a procedure known as *cloture.* Sixteen senators must first sign a petition requesting that a filibuster be ended and then sixty votes are required to stop debate. Ending a filibuster was even harder before the success of a liberal reform in 1975. It then took a two-thirds vote of those present (67 senators if there were no absences) to stop further oratory. This reform as well as others was opposed for a long time by the informal coalition of Republicans and conservative, mostly southern Democrats mentioned earlier. It was only with the election of more liberal senators in the 94th Congress that it was finally passed.

Most senators are proud of their tradition of unlimited debate, but when it is abused and leads to filibustering it is a barrier to majority rule. There have been fifty-three cloture votes since 1917, but only eight have succeeded in shutting off debate. Yet for all this talk, Senator Carter Glass of Virginia said that after more than thirty years in Congress he had never seen a single mind changed by speeches from the floor.[21]

Nevertheless, when the Senate is not abusing the privilege of unlimited debate, things go fairly smoothly. Debate is often limited by unanimous consent of all senators brought about by an agreement between the majority and minority leaders. The Senate then votes, first on amendments and then on the bill itself. A majority of those senators present is needed for passage.

After a bill has passed one house of Congress, it is sent to the other where the procedure begins anew with referral to a standing committee. If the second house passes the bill in the same form as the first, it is sent to the president for his signature. But if new amendments are added, the revised bill must be returned to the originating chamber for approval of the changes. Should it refuse to approve, which happens about one-tenth of the time, both the Senate and House versions of the bill are sent to a conference committee.

A conference committee consists of about a dozen senators and representatives, usually chosen by the presiding officers from the two standing committees in each chamber that considered the bill earlier. The task of this committee is to come up with a compromise version of the bill. Sometimes entirely new provisions are added at this stage. The conference committee is an ideal place for pressure groups to attempt to influence the final form of the bill. Moreover, whatever changes the conference committee agrees upon must be accepted on an all-or-nothing basis by each house. If they are not accepted, the bill is dead. Thus members of both houses usually decide that the revised bill is better than none at all in this situation, and the conference committee version becomes law.

Presidential Action

By the time an important bill reaches the president's desk, it may bear little resemblance to any bill he initially requested. Or it may indeed be a bill he never wanted at all. The president's options are discussed in the following chapter, but should he choose to veto any bill, a two-thirds vote is then required in both houses of Congress before it can become law. This is called a vote to *override* a presidential veto.

LEGISLATIVE DILEMMAS

No man can represent another man, and no man's will can be treated as a substitute for, or representative of, the wills of others.

G. D. H. Cole

The Representative Function

As we all know, legislators are supposed to *represent* the people. But after several centuries of representative government, there is still little agreement on what this means. In one sense, it means that a representative "acts for" the people, doing what they instruct him or her to do.[22] Yet in another sense it means that the legislator is trusted by them to use his or her own good judgment in making decisions which serve them and the country.

The Legislator as Errand Boy
The first view of the legislator's role frequently makes him seem something like an errand boy. The representative serves as a link between the government and the people and spends many hours helping constituents deal with various government agencies. When the average citizen wants a visa for a relative in a foreign country, a change in a proposed highway route, or reconsideration of an unemployment claim, the first impulse is often to write to his or her congressperson or state legislator. As a member of the House of Representatives in Washington, D.C. remarked: "[W]e spend too much time on errand boy activities. . . . But the real question is how we can avoid doing that. I think that . . . we cannot."[23] A 1965 study found that the average congressperson spends 28 percent of his or her time (and 41 percent of staff's time) servicing constituents. In comparison, 26 percent of working time is spent on the floor of the Senate or House.[24]

Two recommendations have been made to lessen the errand-boy burdens of lawmakers. One is to provide them with larger office staffs to do some of these chores. This was accomplished in 1975 when members of the House were permitted to increase their staffs from 16 to 18 persons. Senators may hire more staff members because they have larger constituencies and more tasks. The office of Sen. John V. Tunney (D–Calif.), for example, must cope with about 6000 letters per week. The second recommendation, broader in scope, is for the legislature to appoint an ombudsman to help solve citizen problems with executive agencies. The office of ombudsman was created in Sweden over a century ago. It has proved so effective in cutting bureaucratic red tape and righting administrative wrongs that it has spread to several other nations and to the state governments of Hawaii, Nebraska, Iowa, and Oregon.

The Legislator as Representative

But the representative function is much more complex than being an errand boy. A legislator is supposed to be in tune with those he or she represents. Does this mean that only teen-agers or machinists or blacks can faithfully represent teen-agers or machinists or blacks? A legislator may also be expected to respond so automatically to constituents' wants and needs that the people—through him—rule themselves. But does this mean that he should reflect only home district views, even at the expense of the rest of the nation? Does it mean ignoring his or her own judgment, even when the constituents may be wrong on a certain matter?

Conscience or Conformity?

Such questions lead us to another way of looking at the dilemma facing every legislator. As a "good" representative, does he vote his own conscience or conform to constituents' wishes when there is a conflict between these two courses of action? Two schools of thought provide alternative answers.

The Agency Theory

One view is that the legislator's job is to do what the people who elected him or her would do themselves, if they had the chance. This is sometimes called the agency theory of representation. According to it the official is the agent of the voters and obligated to do their bidding. Often, of course, this is the best way to get reelected. But those who expound the agency theory generally believe that it imposes a moral obligation. As John Tyler, later to become president, put it in his maiden speech to the House of Representatives:

Is the servant to disobey the wishes of his master? How can he be regarded as representing the people when he speaks, not their language, but his own? He ceases to be their representative when he does so, and represents himself alone.[25]

The Trustee Theory
Another view of the representative's role is as a trustee to whom the voters have delegated the authority to act in their behalf in whatever way he or she sees fit. The classic statement of this doctrine was made by Edmund Burke, the great English scholar-politician, in 1774:

[Your representative's] unbiased opinion, his mature judgement, his enlightened conscience, he ought not to sacrifice to . . . any set of men. . . . Your representative owes you not his industry only, but his judgement; and he betrays, instead of serving you, if he sacrifices it to your opinion.[26]

Legislators might well note that in the next election Burke was defeated. Nevertheless, more than a century and a half later, a survey of congresspersons found that 54 percent agreed with Burke while 37 percent believed they should vote with the consensus in their constituencies.[27] More recently, a study of four state legislatures revealed that the trustee conception was embraced by 81 percent of Tennessee lawmakers, 61 percent of those in New Jersey, 56 percent in Ohio, and 55 percent in California.[28]

There are certain conditions, however, which make it easier for legislators to act as trustees and to vote their own judgment on controversial bills. In other words, legislators are more likely to disregard conflicting constituency opinion (1) if they have a few years (as in the case of U.S. senators) before their next bid for reelection, (2) if they were last reelected by a big margin from a safe, noncompetitive district, or (3) if their judgment is strongly supported by the party or by pressure groups likely to contribute to the next campaign.

Conflicting Demands

The actual behavior of a lawmaker is, of course, the product of many influences. In addition to their general orientation (prolabor or probusiness, liberal or conservative), lawmakers must consider many cross-pressures. Constituents back home, the party leadership, powerful lobbyists, and trusted colleagues all may be clamoring for their vote.

Constituency Opinion: The Elusive Butterfly
The lawmaker knows exactly what vote each of these groups want with one exception: Seldom is it known for sure what a majority of the voters (the only group that controls his or her whole career) want on any given piece of legislation. Neither mail nor public opinion surveys done by congressional staffs will usually reflect opinion accurately. One study showed an amazingly low relationship between what congresspersons thought their constituents favored on certain issues and what their views really were.[29] Moreover, it is not known what percentage of the voters are even aware of a particular issue. Yet congresspersons seem to believe that their voting records have a

greater effect upon their chances of winning another term than is probably the case. They seem to maintain this belief even in the face of evidence that less than half of the people know anything about either candidate in most races for the House of Representatives.

The importance of constituency pressure, then, lies partly in the fact that legislators are acutely conscious of it, no matter how inaccurately they may perceive it. It also lies partly in the characteristics of the districts from which lawmakers are elected. It is usually assumed, for example, that the U.S. Senate is more liberal than the House of Representatives because senators have larger constituencies. The state-wide districts from which they are elected almost always include some traditionally liberal voters such as blacks or union members. Many representatives, however, are chosen from small districts with very few liberal voters.

Lobbyists, Leaders, and Likable Colleagues
It is difficult to generalize about the impact of lobbyists upon legislative votes. This is largely due to the subtle nature of lobbying and the lack of statistics. Some legislators are "resistors" who don't believe in pressure group lobbying, while others are "facilitators" who believe it beneficial.[30] Similarly, with respect to political parties, some lawmakers think of themselves as "loyalists" who place a high premium on support of party leaders, while others are proud to be "mavericks." In spite of many exceptions, however, it is generally agreed that in Congress, party affiliation is the best single indicator of how lawmakers will vote. In the 1973–74 session, a majority of Republicans opposed a majority of Democrats on 39 percent of all roll-call votes. This was up 6 percent over the figure for the 1969–70 session.[31]

The influence of a lawmaker's colleagues also weighs heavily on the decision-making scales. Although the average legislator is primarily concerned with the needs of his or her own district, the welfare of the entire state or nation is sometimes stressed by legislators from other areas. Chances are that most legislators have grown to like their colleagues. They come to realize, moreover, that unless they vote the way their colleagues wish upon occasion, they cannot expect to receive the same treatment. This kind of vote trading therefore is not merely practical, but is also an indication of mutual respect.[32]

All government—indeed every human benefit and enjoyment, every virtue and every prudent act—is founded on compromise and barter.

Edmund Burke

The Legislature as Institutionalized Compromise
In conclusion, a legislative body, if truly representative, will consist of many lawmakers advancing as many conflicting interests as are found in the entire society. About the best a legislator can do for constituents, therefore, is to

fight as hard as he or she can for what they would like and then strike as good a bargain as possible for what they can actually get. This, of course, requires compromise among the competing interests – labor versus business, city versus suburb, and so forth. It is a process for which a legislative body is uniquely suited.

The Need for Reform

The first congressional reform law in twenty-four years was passed in 1970. It required that all roll-call votes taken in committee be made public, and that committee procedures be made slightly more democratic. It also required that more votes on the House floor be recorded. In 1975, as we have seen, further changes improved budget procedures, made it somewhat easier to stop filibusters in the Senate, and modified the seniority system for selecting committee chairmen in the House. But more remains to be done, especially in reducing the power of the House Rules Committee to determine what can be considered by the entire membership. On the whole, however, significant progress has been made in redistributing congressional power more evenly among the members and in limiting the capacity of a minority of Congress to thwart majority action.

LEGISLATIVE POWER

The President proposes, Congress disposes.
Unknown

Each of the three branches of government possesses all three kinds of power described in Chapter 1 – force, influence, and authority. Each branch, however, is uniquely equipped to exercise one particular kind of power more effectively. The legislative branch exerts most of its power through the use of influence.

Congressional influence is especially apparent in its power over the budget. By appropriating or refusing to appropriate money for the vast variety of government programs, Congress exerts a potent check on the other two branches. It also has an enormous impact on the distribution of wealth among the people. By the way in which they allocate tax funds, lawmakers help establish the priorities of the government. They decide among competing demands for better health care, greater national security, more effective pollution control, and many other goals.

Power is more diffuse in the legislature than in the other branches of government. As a result, this is the branch on which the people and their pressure groups can exert the greatest influence. The fact that there are 435 members of the House of Representatives in itself makes Congress particularly accessible to those seeking government action. Moreover, because the whole House and a third of the Senate are elected every two years, Congress can be held accountable to the people more frequently than officials in the other two branches.

Yet just as the concentration of executive power in the hands of a president or governor tends to increase that power, so also does the dispersion of legislative power among committee chairpersons, presiding officers, and party leaders tend to reduce it. As presidential power expanded during most of this century, congressional power contracted. In the last decade, two things — presidential errors and internal legislative reorganization — have started to reverse these trends.

President Johnson's tragic miscalculations regarding American victory in Vietnam and President Nixon's unscrupulous misconduct were serious errors which drove both men from office. These errors and the accompanying loss of presidential prestige created a kind of power vacuum which the lawmakers had long wished to fill. In 1973–74, the Ninety-third Congress (they are numbered after each election every two years) rose to the occasion by passing some extremely important laws. It guaranteed pension rights for many workers in private industry, imposed tough restrictions on campaign finance, increased social security benefits, and approved construction of the trans-Alaska oil pipeline. It also subsidized health maintenance organizations (HMOs), altered budget procedures, limited the use of American troops abroad, and authorized mandatory fuel allocations. Moreover, the Ninety-third Congress investigated Watergate, gathered evidence to impeach President Nixon, and confirmed the first two vice-presidential appointments in history.

The Ninety-fourth Congress, inspired by its predecessor's impressive record, moved quickly in 1975 to establish its own niche in history. It did so by reforming congressional machinery so that committee chairpersons could be elected on the basis of their views on government policy rather than on how long they had been around. This defiance of the seniority system altered power relationships within the House in at least four ways.

1. It reduced the power of the South since the lack of a strong two-party system in that section of the country had given most southerners more seniority than representatives from other regions.
2. It gave the majority party caucus control over committee chairpersons.
3. It increased the power of liberals since they constitute a larger majority among all congressional Democrats than those with the longest service.
4. Just as importantly, the change also represented a triumph for the democratic principle of majority rule over a system that conferred power automatically, with little regard for either merit or popularity.

In the Senate, too, reformers were on the march, but without such an important victory. Nevertheless, like a seesaw, as the White House at one end of Pennsylvania Avenue moved down in public esteem and political power, Congress, at the other end, was moving up.

Notes

1. *Christian Science Monitor,* December 7, 1972, p. 1.
2. *Los Angeles Times,* December 26, 1972, p. 15.
3. *Congressional Record,* December 29, 1969, p. E11023.
4. *Time,* January 15, 1973, p. 12.
5. Results of a Louis Harris poll in n.a., *Confidence and Concern: Citizens View American Government* (Cleveland: Regal Books/King's Court Communications, 1974), p. 7.
6. Henry J. Abraham, *The Judicial Process* (New York: Oxford University Press, 1962), p. 42.
7. 354 U.S. 178 (1957).
8. Leroy C. Hardy and Charles P. Sohner, "Constitutional Challenge and Political Response: California Reapportionment, 1965," *Western Political Quarterly* 23 (December 1970): 733–51.
9. For a staunch defense of the community as an important and almost mystical basis of representation, see Alfred de Grazia, *Apportionment and Representative Government* (New York: Praeger Publishers, 1963).
10. *Baker* v. *Carr,* 369 U.S. 186 (1962).
11. These figures were compiled by the magazine *Christianity Today* and reported in the *Los Angeles Times,* December 2, 1974, Part II, p. 1.
12. *The New York Times Encyclopedic Almanac 1972* (New York: New York Times Publishing Co., 1971), p. 108.
13. Ibid.
14. Computed from *The World Almanac & Book of Facts 1975* (New York: Newspaper Enterprise Association, 1974), pp. 44–47.
15. *New York Times Encyclopedic Almanac 1972,* p. 108.
16. Quoted by Bertram M. Gross, *The Legislative Struggle* (New York: McGraw-Hill, 1953), p. 266.
17. Clem Miller, *Member of the House* (New York: Charles Scribner's Sons, 1962), p. 39.
18. Daniel M. Berman, *In Congress Assembled* (New York: The Macmillan Co., 1964), pp. 144–50.
19. See Robert Sherrill, *Why They Call It Politics* (New York: Harcourt Brace Jovanovich, 1972), p. 101.
20. Lewis A. Froman, Jr., *The Congressional Process* (Boston: Little, Brown and Co., 1967), p. 36.
21. Mark J. Green, James M. Fallows, and David R. Zwick, *Who Runs Congress?* (New York: A Bantam/Grossman Book, 1972), p. 67 and 205–06.
22. Joseph Tussman, *Obligation and the Body Politic* (New York: Oxford University Press, 1960), p. 61.
23. Quoted in Charles L. Clapp, *The Congressman: His Work as He Sees It* (Garden City, N.Y.: Anchor Books, Doubleday & Co., 1963), p. 118.
24. Green, Fallows, and Zwick, pp. 199 and 205.
25. Quoted in John F. Kennedy, *Profiles in Courage* (New York: Pocket Books, 1957), p. 13.
26. Quoted in Hanna Fenichal Pitkin, ed., *Representation* (New York: Atherton Press, 1969), pp. 174–75.

27. Alfred de Grazia, *Public and Republic* (New York: Alfred A. Knopf, 1951), p. 158.
28. John C. Wahlke, Heinz Eulau, William Buchanan, and Leroy C. Ferguson, *The Legislative System* (New York: John Wiley & Sons, 1962), p. 281.
29. Warren E. Miller and Donald Stokes, "Constituency Influences in Congress," *American Political Science Review* 57 (March 1963): 45–57.
30. Wahlke et al., pp. 502–3 and passim.
31. David S. Broder, "A Widening Split on Domestic Issues," *Los Angeles Times,* February 12, 1975, Part II, p. 7.
32. Donald R. Matthews, *United States Senators and Their World* (Chapel Hill: University of North Carolina Press, 1960). For an interesting analysis of "deviant senatorial behavior" see Ralph K. Huitt, "The Outsider in the Senate: An Alternative Role," *American Political Science Review* 55 (September 1961): 566–75.

11 THE EXECUTIVE BRANCH:
The president and the bureaucracy

. . . [I]f the President is possessed of ambition, he has the power . . . to ruin his country.

George Clinton, 1787

Richard M. Nixon has acted in a manner contrary to his trust as President and subversive of constitutional government, . . . to the manifest injury of the people of the United States.

Judiciary Committee
of the House of
Representatives, 1974

As the nation moved toward its two-hundredth anniversary, the American people felt a profound distrust of executive power. Such distrust was perhaps deeper than any since that felt toward King George III at the time of the Revolution. This time, however, the feelings of distrust were mixed with a sense of betrayal. Americans did not choose George III to rule them. But in November 1972 they elected the Nixon-Agnew ticket by the widest popular vote margin in history. Yet eleven months later, Vice-President Spiro Agnew was found guilty of income tax evasion and resigned from office. Ten months after that, President Richard Nixon, confronted with the most damaging charges ever facing an American president, also resigned. Suddenly, for the first time since the days of British rule, Americans found themselves governed by chief executives whom they did not elect.

THE PRESIDENT

Power corrupts and absolute power corrupts absolutely.
Lord Acton

After the Agnew and Nixon resignations, many people seemed to believe that either crooks were attracted to executive power or that executive power made men crooks. Yet, whether some American presidents have wanted absolute power or not, our whole structure of government is designed to prevent them from getting it. The rights and freedoms of the people limit presidential authority. So does federalism, with its guarantee of reserved powers to the state governments. So also does the separation of powers among three somewhat independent branches of government.

In fact, the events which forced Nixon's resignation produced a clearer understanding of the separation of powers than had previously existed. President Nixon, in refusing to turn over tape-recorded conversations to be examined as possible criminal evidence, defended his position by a doctrine called "executive privilege." What he meant by that doctrine was explained by his lawyers in arguments before the Supreme Court. It is an executive privilege, the president contended, to carry on White House conversations in privacy. If what the president or his advisors say in these conversations must be revealed either to judges or to members of Congress, then such discussions will no longer have the frankness necessary for a full analysis of problems. Moreover, if either of the other two branches can force the disclosure of such conversations, then the principle of separation of powers is destroyed and the executive branch can be dominated by the courts or Congress. But on July 24, 1974, the Supreme Court unanimously ruled that the president must submit the tapes in question. They were necessary, the Court said, to the "fundamental demands of due process of law in the fair administration of criminal justice." In passing, however, the Court acknowledged that in noncriminal matters, the concept of executive privilege does give protection to the confidentiality of presidential conversations.[1]

The Pomp and the Power

The scope and variety of executive power is so great that the president must play many roles or—as some say—wear many hats. Of course, all of his functions overlap to some extent and each affects all of the others.

Head of State
The first executive "hat" is almost crownlike. The president is the head of state who plays a patriotic role much like that of a royal monarch. He symbolizes the ties that bind us together, the links between a proud past and a perilous future. As the head of state, he may lay the cornerstone for a new government building, award medals of honor to heroic servicemen, entertain foreign officials, or throw out the first baseball of the season.

Many nations—England, West Germany, Japan, and others—have both a chief of state and a chief executive. The former performs ceremonial functions, while the latter runs the government. In the United States, the president does both. A skillful leader exploits the prestige and the publicity of the first role to enhance his power in performing the second. Thus, when a president issues a Labor Day proclamation, he is not only acting as chief of state. He also hopes to gain additional political support from union members that will strengthen his position as head of the government.

But the ceremonial role can pose a hazard. People sometimes confuse the chief executive's policies with his role as a symbol of the nation. It may be useful for a president to encourage this confusion so as to minimize policy criticism. But most people have learned to cherish the role of the president as head of state, while often criticizing his performance as head of government.

Chief Politician

A chief executive must be, by definition, one of the most skillful politicians in the country. He has, usually, blended the ingredients of power—nomination by a major party, money, personal popularity, and all the rest—into a successful victory formula.

After his election, a president does not cease to be a politician. This entails the skillful use of power—the ability to alter people's behavior in socially significant ways. If the leader is unable or unwilling to use the full range of his power—to threaten vetoes, to promise appointments, or to deploy troops, progress toward his goals will be slow indeed. On the other hand, to squander power resources on trivial objectives is to risk their depletion when really needed.

Among the power resources available to a president is his position as leader of his own political party. As noted earlier, tradition permits the president to choose his vice-presidential running mate and the chairman of his party's national committee. Through his influence with that committee he can affect the allocation of campaign funds to his party's candidates. Through speeches at fund-raising dinners he can attract campaign contributions. He can personally endorse the candidates he favors, as President Ford did in 1974 by campaigning for Republican congressional nominees in twenty states. In addition, he can often see to it that government contracts are awarded within the districts of favored congressmen. Finally, by judicious use of his vast patronage powers he can reward the party faithful with prestigious appointments. Or he can punish the party heretics by ignoring their existence. Republican Senator Charles Goodell, for example, lost his seat in 1970 largely because he had opposed President Nixon who later made sure he got no support from the Republican party.

But why should a president bother himself with such petty partisan politics? The answer is that if he wishes his legislative program passed, his vetoes upheld, his appointments confirmed, and his treaties approved, he needs congressional support. Since he can expect relatively little from members of the opposition party, he must secure as much as possible from his own. Besides, he may wish to seek reelection, and for that the full support of his party's machinery is essential.

Manager of the Economy

As each level of government has expanded, so too has its impact upon the economy. Governments now are major employers, landowners, purchasers, stockpilers, awarders of contracts, and producers of electric power and nuclear weapons. All these functions are authorized by legislatures but directed and implemented by the executive bureaucracy.

Executive influence on the economy was greatly strengthened in 1921 when Congress gave to the president the responsibility of submitting a unified budget proposing specific expenditures for every agency in the national government. All states except Arkansas have also adopted this so-called executive budget. But most state governors possess a power that even the president lacks. They have an *item veto* on appropriation bills. This enables them to veto expenditures for certain purposes while signing the rest of a budget bill into law.[2] Thus while legislative bodies still vote the money for government programs, they rely upon the executive not only for initial overall planning but also for control through the veto power. President Nixon attempted to compensate for his lack of an item veto by simply refusing to spend, or "impounding," some appropriated money. The Budget Reform Act of 1974, however, gave Congress the authority to override such impoundments, and also provided stricter legislative controls on the initial appropriations process.

In addition to his budgeting responsibility, the president has other obligations in the economic arena which were stated in the Employment Act of 1946. This act created the Council of Economic Advisers and required the president to send an annual economic message to Congress. In the message, the president is expected to recommend measures needed to move the nation closer to full employment.

One of the more dramatic examples of presidential influence on the economy came in 1962. President John F. Kennedy was faced with an announced price increase by the nation's leading steel companies. Kennedy was certain that such an increase would be dangerously inflationary. Thus he denounced the steel executives on television, threatened to transfer government contracts, and instigated antitrust investigations. Within a week, the steel corporations revoked the price boost.[3] President Nixon also exercised his economic power rather dramatically. When he decided to impose direct wage and price controls, a power which Congress had given him a year earlier, it was a startling reversal of his administration's policy. He knew, certainly, that his success as a candidate in 1972 might well depend on his success as a manager of the economy in 1971. President Ford, like his predecessors, also seemed determined to use his economic power to maximum advantage. Early in 1975 he announced an increase in the tariff on foreign oil imports. This was an attempt to raise the price of petroleum products and thereby decrease the amounts purchased by American consumers.

The Chief Diplomat

The president determines the official attitude of the United States toward every nation on earth. Constitutionally, he signs treaties with other countries, recognizes and exchanges diplomatic representatives with other governments, and appoints American ambassadors abroad. He also enters into executive agreements with other nations. Unlike treaties, these do not require Senate approval. They involve such matters as the establishment of foreign military bases, the reduction of tariffs, and other subjects over which the president has been given legal authority by Congress. Although American treaty commitments like membership in the United Nations and limitations on nuclear tests are usually better publicized, executive agreements are far more numerous and nearly as significant. Finally, through his control of various agencies in the executive branch, the president directs American espionage and propaganda abroad.

In a very real sense, the prospects for survival in a nuclear world may depend on the wisdom of presidential foreign policy. Future historians, for example, may view President Nixon's involvement in the Watergate crimes as less important than the changes he initiated in American relations with communist countries. Aided by the diplomatic skills of Secretary of State Henry Kissinger, his foreign travels launched new cooperative endeavors with the Soviet Union. Even more importantly, Nixon resumed diplomatic contact, for the first time in twenty years, with the government of the Chinese mainland. A policy of cold war hostility with the People's Republic of China was thereby modified by one of détente. This new policy acknowledged at least the possibility of peaceful rivalry and diplomatic accommodation.

Commander in Chief

The opening words of Article II, Section 2 of the U.S. Constitution provide that "The President shall be commander in chief of the army and navy . . . and of the militia of the several states, when called into the actual service of the United States." In effect, this means that he can order troops anywhere, anytime, to fire on any foe. It is one of the most controversial provisions of the Constitution because its utilization undermines the clause in Article I, Section 8 which gives Congress the "power to . . . declare war."

The growth of the president's role as commander in chief, ignoring the constitutional authority of Congress, has been a gradual one. But full-scale "presidential wars" made their debut in 1950 when Harry S. Truman ordered U.S. forces to resist aggression against South Korea. The result was a period of hostilities lasting three years and killing more than thirty thousand Americans. These losses exceeded those in the Mexican and Spanish-American Wars combined, both of which were declared by Congress. When President Johnson sent combat forces to Vietnam in 1965, he entered a conflict which claimed more than fifty thousand American lives and lasted longer than any in our history.

It is probable that the Founding Fathers never intended to authorize the president to send troops into battle without either a congressional declaration of war or an enemy attack on American soil. Instead, it seems likely that they made the president commander in chief to insure civilian supremacy over career military officials. This principle is a vital one, for if government policy yields to the generals armed with bombers and tanks, it cannot be directed by those armed only with votes.

In an era of hostile power blocs, there is no doubt that the president must have the capacity to respond rapidly and reasonably to military provocations. But Congress gradually realized that presidential authority as commander in chief came dangerously close to dictatorship in military matters. This prompted passage of the War Powers Act of 1973, a very significant reassertion of legislative power. The act limits presidentially ordered foreign combat to 60 days without congressional approval and requires that the president notify Congress as soon as he sends troops into action.

Checking the Other Branches

In addition to the president's power as head of the executive branch, the constitutional system of checks and balances gives him influence over the other two branches as well.

The Legislative Initiative

Rather oddly, the executive branch has become the source of most major legislative proposals. Article II, Section 3 directs that the president shall "from time to time give to the Congress Information of the State of the Union, and recommend to their Consideration such Measures as he shall judge necessary and expedient . . . ." This process has now become rather ritualized, with an annual State of the Union message usually delivered in person each January. In that message, the president spends less time describing what the state of the union is than what he would like it to be. He uses it to outline very broadly the kind of new legislation he would like to see Congress pass. The State of the Union address is followed closely by his budget and economic messages, mentioned earlier. In the months that follow, the president also dispatches special messages to Congress. These are prepared by various executive agencies to request the passage of specific bills outlined in great detail. All presidential legislation is then introduced by sympathetic members of Congress. Since 1953 no president has sent fewer than 170 legislative proposals to Congress in a single year. It has been observed that in "the last two decades, roughly 80 percent of the major laws passed have started in the executive branch."[4]

As a result, much recent legislation is often described in such terms as "Johnson's war on poverty," or "Ford's energy program."

A Variety of Vetoes

Other checks by the president on the legislative branch are his power to call special sessions, to adjourn the legislature if the two houses cannot agree on an adjournment date, and to veto legislation. Of these, the last is by far the most important.

When the president receives a bill, he can sign it, thereby completing its enactment into law. Or he can veto it by returning it to the House where it was introduced along with a veto message explaining his reasons for not signing the bill. He is given ten days in which to make up his mind, and if he chooses a veto, the decision is usually fatal for the bill. It takes two-thirds of those voting in both houses of Congress to enact a bill by overriding a president's veto.

Should the president neither sign a bill nor veto it within the ten days, the bill normally becomes law automatically. But if Congress has adjourned and gone home before the time limit has expired, the president can exercise his *pocket veto.* He simply takes no action on the bill which kills it without formally vetoing it. The number of bills passed and vetoed in a recent twenty-year-period are shown in Figure 11 – 1.

Executive Clemency

We already noted that the president appoints all federal judges with Senate approval. In addition, he has another check on the judicial process. This is the power of executive clemency which permits him to show leniency toward those accused of federal crimes. Until the 1970s, this power was important mainly to released prisoners, their families, and friends. Since then, however, it has produced public controversy on four occasions. First, and least explosive, President Nixon pardoned James R. Hoffa, former president of the Teamsters Union. The pardon came shortly before that union endorsed Nixon for reelection, but any relationship between the two events is still unproved. Second, and of greater significance, was Nixon's discussion of possible clemency for the Watergate defendants in return for their silence on their ties with the White House. When such a discussion was revealed on the White House tapes, it contributed to the growing demands for the president's removal from office.

On September 8, 1974, one day less than a month after he took office, President Ford pardoned ex-President Nixon of any crimes that he "committed or may have committed or taken part in" while he was president.

Figure 11–1. CONGRESSIONAL BILLS AND PRESIDENTIAL VETOES, 1961–1974

Bills Passed	Regular Vetoes	Pocket Vetoes	Overridden Vetoes
7,361	73	54	9

Source: U.S. Bureau of the Census, *Statistical Abstract of the United States: 1975*, pp. 444.

The negative reaction to the pardon included the resignation of J. F. terHorst as White House Press Secretary, and the inevitable suspicion that the pardon had been part of a secret deal involving the Nixon resignation. Although there was no doubt of its constitutionality, the pardon was unusual in that it was granted before any conviction or even indictment. Since pardons must be accepted in order to be legally valid, most observers agreed that the Nixon acceptance constituted an admission of guilt. Nevertheless, Nixon's statement acknowledged only "regret" for his "mistakes."

Eight days after pardoning the former president, Vietnam draft resisters and military deserters were offered a conditional amnesty by President Ford. An amnesty is a group pardon, given in this case to those persons willing to accept up to two years of work in public service jobs. To administer the program, the president established a nine-member clemency board headed by Charles E. Goodell, the former U.S. senator from New York who had been a leading Republican critic of American policy in Vietnam. The amnesty program was assailed from the right by those opposed to any leniency. It was also criticized from the left by those who favored an unconditional amnesty. Only a small percentage of the people eligible actually accepted Ford's offer. It should be noted that the power of executive clemency extends not only to pardons, but also to commutations which reduce criminal sentences, and to reprieves which postpone them.

THE MAKING AND MAINTENANCE OF CHIEF EXECUTIVES

Americans once took great pride in both the quality of their leaders and in the way power was transferred, orderly and peacefully, from one to another. Only five times in twenty-eight years, for example, did an incumbent president fail to top the most-admired man-of-the-year survey done by the Gallup Poll.[5] When a president dies in office, thereby upsetting the usual succession, it was reported that substantial numbers of citizens displayed symptoms of physical illness.[6] Yet in 1974 Americans found that their leaders were less admirable than they had been accustomed to expect. Moreover, they found that a transfer of power from one president to another had occurred in a new and unprecedented way. The method by which we choose our chief executives, therefore, became a subject of intensified concern.

Room at the Top—for Whom?

The office of chief executive is the highest rung on the ladder of political success. What are the characteristics of those who have occupied it?

Qualifications for Office
The president and vice-president must meet constitutional standards set forth

in Article II, Section 1. They must be citizens by birth, at least thirty-five years old, and must have resided in the United States for fourteen years or more. It seems doubtful that many political careers have been thwarted by these requirements.

[Lyndon] Johnson was born with the instinct of power, and long before he reached the White House he knew exactly where it rested [and] how to obtain it. . . .
Rowland Evans and Robert Novak

Characteristics of Chief Executives

The characteristics of the thirty-seven persons who have become president could be a guide to the kinds of people who have the best chance to attain that office in the future. A composite description reveals that the "average" president is a male Caucasian, in his fifties, of English or Scotch-Irish descent, and Christian in religion. He is most often a lawyer who has previously served as a governor or U.S. senator.

The youngest ever to serve as president were Theodore Roosevelt at forty-two and John F. Kennedy at forty-three. The oldest were William Henry Harrison at sixty-eight and Dwight D. Eisenhower at seventy. There have been no non-Christians and only one Roman Catholic (Kennedy), although four presidents had no formal religious affiliation. Methodists and Baptists, most numerous among Protestant denominations in the general population, have each sent only two to the White House. Episcopalians can claim nine presidents and Presbyterians seven.

U.S. senators who speak out on national and international issues are considered particularly likely presidential possibilities. Ideologically, a moderate image is an enormous asset. The "log cabin" tradition, moreover, occupies a special place in American political lore. It assumes that any boy could grow up to be president, and that a poor boy who made good has an even better chance. Recent history indicates that humble origins are neither a help nor a hindrance, as long as one can raise $25 million or so for a presidential campaign. Nevertheless, it is possible that officials drawn from the ranks of the relatively well-to-do may have difficulty understanding the problems and the attitudes of those less favored than themselves. Conversely, groups such as the poor, ethnic minorities, young people, and women may become increasingly alienated from a society that passes them by so frequently in recruiting its top leadership.

However, one cannot be sure of the future significance of these presidential characteristics, nor of the very similar ones shared by most members of Congress and judges. Times are changing. Former Vice-President Spiro Agnew is of Greek extraction and his opponent in 1968, Senator Edmund Muskie, is of Polish parentage. In the future, the most important characteristic of presidential candidates may well be the intensity with which they want the office, rather than socioeconomic factors. Campaigns are long, exhausting, expensive, and sometimes destructive of family relationships. Yet by February of 1975 six men had already announced their candidacy for the 1976 election. Another hopeful, Senator Walter Mondale (D – Minn.) decided that it wasn't worth the sacrifice.

The Election Process

The procedures by which the president is chosen are complex and often controversial.

The Electoral College

At the constitutional convention, a major controversy raged over who should elect the president. The compromise finally agreed upon provided that he be chosen by an electoral college. But each state was entitled to select its electoral college members in whatever way it wished. It was further agreed that each state would have the same number of electoral college votes as it had members of Congress. Thus, its total number of electors would equal two senators plus as many representatives as its population warranted.

Initially, the Constitution had each elector cast two votes. The person receiving the most votes would be president. The person placing second would be vice-president. If no candidate received a majority, the election of the president was transferred to the House of Representatives, where each state was given a single vote. If the person finishing second lacked a majority, then the U.S. Senate would elect the vice-president.

This procedure, outlined in Article II, Section 1, worked smoothly until 1800. At that time, a tied vote in the electoral college between Thomas Jefferson and Aaron Burr (who belonged to the same party) threw the election into a long and bitter fight in the House of Representatives. This crisis prompted the passage of the Twelfth Amendment. It provided that each member of the electoral college would cast one vote for president and a second, separate vote for vice-president.

But this change did not alter the fact that the electors were chosen in a very undemocratic manner. Until the ninth presidential election in 1824, members of the electoral college in most states were chosen by the state legislatures. The system worked like this.

Gradually, however, state laws were changed to eliminate the state legislatures from this process. The voters were permitted to elect members of the electoral college directly, as they do today in every state.

A second major change has democratized the process still more. Candidates for the electoral college are now nominated on political party tickets. They are pledged in advance to vote for the presidential nominee of their party. It was the rise of political parties, therefore, that transformed the role of the individual elector. Instead of being a free agent voting for whom he pleased, the elector became a political mirror reflecting the voters' preference for his party's candidate. Indeed, in most states ballots contain only the names of the presidential and vice-presidential nominees. The names of the candidates for the electoral college who are committed to vote for these nominees do not even appear on the ballot.

Political parties have had another effect on the process of electing the president. As a result of the two-party system, one of the major party candidates is almost certain to get a majority in the electoral college. This minimizes the possibility that a presidential election will be thrown into the House of Representatives. Only twice in our history, in 1800 and again in 1824, has there been a third candidate sufficiently popular to prevent an electoral college majority. It could, of course, happen again. Some observers see the third-party candidacy of George Wallace as being the most threatening.

Electoral College Reform

There are two major criticisms of the present electoral system. One is that nothing can prevent a member of the electoral college from voting for someone other than the candidate of his party. Occasionally this has happened, but it has never altered the outcome of a presidential election. However, to avoid the possibility, President Lyndon B. Johnson proposed that individual electors be eliminated. Instead electoral votes would automatically be awarded to the candidate with the most popular votes in each state.

The second, and more serious, accusation against the electoral college is that it permits the election of a president whose opponent received more popular votes. This objection cannot be dismissed lightly, for it actually occurred after the elections of 1824, 1876, and 1888. In those cases, the voters' second choice became president. The reason for this disregard of majority rule is that members of the electoral college are elected at large in each state. As a result, if a candidate carries a state by just one vote, he wins all of that state's electoral votes. Such a situation greatly affects presidential campaign strategy. It enhances the importance of urban areas in presidential elections, since it is the states with big cities that have many electoral votes.

Let us see how the electoral college might work in any presidential election. Assume that two candidates are running neck and neck throughout the nation as a whole, both in popular and electoral votes. Assume further that the result will depend on the outcome of races in California and North Dakota. In California, each voter is voting for forty-five members of the electoral college, and in North Dakota for three members. Finally, the vote count is completed, and the results are announced, as shown in Figure 11–2.

Given such a distribution of votes, the Democratic candidate would win in the electoral college, even though his Republican opponent was favored by more people. Such an injustice can occur whenever one candidate carries

Figure 11–2. HOW A MAJORITY CAN LOSE

| | Popular Vote | | Electoral Vote | |
	Republican	Democratic	Republican	Democratic
North Dakota	160,000	80,000	3	0
California	3,390,000	3,400,000	0	45
Total	3,550,000	3,480,000	3	45

the large urbanized states (e.g., California) by even a few votes, while losing the small rural states (e.g., North Dakota) by a wide margin.

Several reforms have been suggested to eliminate this possibility. The Lodge-Gossett plan would split a state's electoral vote in the same proportion as the division of the popular vote. Former Senator Karl Mundt (R–S.D.) proposed that the people elect one member of the electoral college from each congressional district and choose only two at large from every state. A final plan, once proposed as a constitutional amendment, would abolish the electoral college completely in favor of a direct vote by the people. If no candidate receives at least 40 percent of the popular vote, a runoff election would be held between the two candidates with the most votes.

Those who favor the electoral college argue that its abolition would undermine the importance of the states and encourage the formation of minor parties. Some also suggest that since small states are overrepresented in the U.S. Senate, the electoral college should be kept because it balances this by giving more power to the big states. People who want a direct popular vote for president rest their case chiefly on the grounds that it conforms most closely to the democratic theory of majority rule.

Service and Succession

When Spiro Agnew resigned, it was only the second vice-presidential resignation in history, the first since 1832, and the first under charges of criminal misconduct. Less than a year later, Richard Nixon became the only person ever to resign the presidency. Gerald Ford then became the first nonelected vice-president to become president. When Nelson Rockefeller assumed the vice-presidency late in 1974 he became the third person to occupy that office in just fifteen months.

These were unsettling experiences for a nation justly proud of the political stability which comes from fixed terms of office. We have come to accept death in high office—eight presidents and seven vice-presidents died before their terms had expired. But resignations prompted by impeachment threats and criminal convictions were something new. Under such circumstances, the smoothness of the leadership transition paid tribute to the maturity of our people and the flexibility of the Constitution. How did it all happen?

A worker at the Helena Post Office Building carries President Nixon's portrait to storage after Nixon formally left office, August 9, 1974.

Succession

The Constitution (Article II, Section 1) provides that the vice-president shall assume the powers and duties of the president in the event of his removal, death, resignation, or inability. It gives Congress the power to provide for succession if both the president and vice-president are disqualified. The Speaker of the House of Representatives is now next in the line of succession. He is followed by the president pro tem of the Senate and then by the cabinet officials, beginning with the Secretary of State. Thus far, only vice-presidents have been summoned to fill a vacant presidency, and the torch has always been passed peacefully.

The possibility of a prolonged vice-presidential vacancy, such as occurred after the assassination of John F. Kennedy, was eliminated by the Twenty-fifth Amendment in 1967. This requires the president to appoint a vice-president, should there be none, subject to the confirmation of a majority vote in the House and Senate.

The process was first used when Gerald Ford was appointed to succeed Spiro Agnew. It was used again when Ford, after becoming president, appointed Nelson Rockefeller as vice-president. This improbable series of events created a situation that some said was inconsistent with democracy: The nation had a president and vice-president who were both appointed. As Senator John O. Pastore (D–R.I.) put it in calling for a better system, the vice-president is "the appointee of an appointee."[7] While admitting that the system works, Senator Pastore argues that it would be more democratic and more desirable to call a special election for president if the office becomes vacant with more than 12 months of a term remaining. He has proposed a constitutional amendment to that effect.

The Problem of Disability

The Constitution authorizes the vice-president to take over when the president is unable to discharge his powers and duties. But it does not say what constitutes inability or who should determine whether it exists. As a result, no vice-president, no matter how sick or incapacitated the president has been, ever dared to displace him. President Garfield lay more than two months in a coma, and Presidents Cleveland, Wilson, and Eisenhower all experienced prolonged illnesses. In each case, the ship of state drifted without its captain (although fortunately in placid waters).

The Twenty-fifth Amendment, in addition to providing a way to fill vice-presidential vacancies, establishes methods to cope with presidential disability. It permits the president to declare himself disabled. If he does not or cannot, it allows the vice-president and a majority of either the cabinet, or of some other body designated by Congress, to declare him disabled. Should the president object, the matter is submitted to Congress, with a two-thirds vote of both houses needed to overrule him.

Terms and Salaries

Originally, no limit was placed on the number of four-year terms a president might serve. The examples of Washington, Jefferson, Madison, Monroe, and Jackson soon established a two-term tradition, however. It was not until Franklin D. Roosevelt was elected to a third term in 1940 and a fourth in 1944 that this precedent was broken. Amendment Twenty-two was designed to prevent a repetition of the Roosevelt example. It limited the president to two terms or, if he had served a portion of his predecessor's term, no more than ten years in office. President Ford, for example, would be ineligible to run in 1980 if he wins in 1976, because he served more than two years of the term began by President Nixon.

Among the many aspects of our political system which the Watergate scandals subjected to critical reexamination was the president's term of office. Some argued that it was too long, or that it was too difficult to remove the president by the impeachment process before the term expired. Others contended that the chief problem was the temptation of an incumbent to abuse presidential powers to insure his own reelection. Mike Mansfield (D–Mont.), the Senate Majority Leader, has introduced a constitutional amendment that would limit the president to a single six-year term. This arrangement seems to work well in Mexico, and favorably impressed both Presidents Johnson and Nixon. Still others favor the repeal of the Twenty-second Amendment. They argue that during his second term the president is treated as a "lame duck" with badly diminished power, unless he is eligible for another term. Lame duck or not, the president now receives a salary of $200.000 for each year that he is in office.

The Vice-Presidency

John Adams, our first vice-president, complained that his was "the most insignificant office that ever the invention of man contrived or his imagination conceived." The vice-presidency has never quite recovered from that assessment. Theodore Roosevelt was put in the post to get rid of him as governor of New York. John Garner, a salty old Texan who had the job for eight years, advised Lyndon Johnson not to take it because he believed the vice-presidency wasn't "worth a bucket of warm spit."

Yet, eight vice-presidents (including Theodore Roosevelt and Lyndon Johnson) have assumed the presidency because of the deaths of their predecessors, and one because of his resignation. The office obviously has great potential. But it is also important in itself.

In addition to presiding over the Senate and "checking the president's health," vice-presidents have been given increased responsibilities in the last quarter of a century. Perhaps the most powerful was Vice-President Richard M. Nixon. President Eisenhower authorized him to call cabinet meetings and oversee the administration while he was recuperating from his several illnesses. Mr. Nixon also assumed many campaign responsibilities for the president and represented him at a variety of ceremonial functions. The vice-president has become a world traveler as well. He is often asked by the president to make various goodwill or fact-finding tours. He is also now a member of the influential National Security Council.

The point is not that the vice-president is inherently powerful, but that he may become as important as the president wishes. His office is a largely untapped resource, yet one that has come into the public eye much more in recent years. Vice-President Rockefeller, for example, was thoroughly investigated by the Senate Rules Committee and the House Judiciary Committee before they recommended that Congress confirm his appointment. Shortly after Rockefeller took office, moreover, President Ford chose him as chairman of a special commission to investigate well-publicized charges that the C.I.A. had engaged in illegal spying. The most important evidence of the growing stature of the vice-presidency is its increasing use as a springboard to a presidential nomination. This was demonstrated by both Nixon in 1960 and Hubert Humphrey in 1968.

THE POWER OF THE PRESIDENCY — AN OVERVIEW

The power of the presidency, both as man and institution, somehow exceeds the sum of its parts. The president's unique power is best explained, perhaps, in terms of two interrelated considerations. First, his authority is concentrated. He personally embodies most of the power of the executive branch. By contrast, legislative authority is dispersed among 535 members of Congress and judicial authority among 512 judges on the federal level alone. Even final judicial power is distributed among nine Supreme Court justices. The fact that Congress and the courts consist of so many people naturally disperses the pressures brought to bear on them by corporations, columnists, litigants, lobbyists, union leaders, and ordinary citizens around the country. To influence national executive action, however, the ultimate target must be the man in the White House. He is the focus for all the demands, desires, and fears of our diverse society.[8]

This concentration of executive power gives the president at least two tremendous advantages. In the first place, he can act much more quickly than the other two branches. The speed of jet-age change makes this increasingly important. Secondly, the mass media can focus more effectively and dramatically on single individuals than on large institutions. Thus the actions of the president command more public recognition than those of the other two branches. Only he can command nationwide television time on a few hours notice. Only members of his family can compete with Elizabeth Taylor for coverage in movie magazines or gossip columns. In short, the power of the president is more personalized, more intimate, somehow more *human* than that wielded by other officials. As a result, he has the unique ability to focus the attention of the entire nation on a particular problem. He can mobilize support for whatever solution he proposes. To an unexcelled degree, he has the power to persuade.

The other unique factor involved in presidential power is that the chief executive's constituencies, the groups which may affect his political future, are as varied as they are numerous. Most obviously, the president is the only public official (discounting the vice-president) who is chosen by voters throughout the entire nation. This national constitutency looks to him for moral leadership, as they have since the time of Washington. Only the president can transcend our infinite diversity to define our national purpose and attain our common goals. In addition, the president's international constituency has become very important, especially since World War II. It pressures him for the military assistance, trade concessions, or financial aid sometimes necessary for survival. Also significant are two specific domestic constituencies. One is the partisan coalition which supported his candidacy (campaign workers, party leaders, financial contributors, and so forth). The other consists of members of Congress and administrative officials—the bureaucracy—without whose help presidential efforts are doomed to failure.[9]

Taken together, these multiple constituencies impose on the president the obligation to meet a vast array of sometimes contradictory expectations. His enormous power is challenged by the enormous demands made upon it. Yet the very immensity of the challenge holds out a promise of greatness.

However, there is a paradox, a kind of contradiction, regarding presidential power. On the one hand, the president is widely believed to be the most powerful person in the world. On the other hand, he heads only one of three equal branches of government. He can send thousands of American troops to their deaths and probably plunge the world into war. Yet the courts, as we have seen, can require him to produce word-for-word records of his private conversations and congressional impeachment hearings can compel his resignation.

These contradictions create an enigma, a fascinating mystery, about the office of the presidency. Of course, the limits upon presidential power are determined largely by the Constitution. But for the actual scope and breadth of presidential power we must look beyond the Constitution. We must look to the man, his personal as well as institutional authority and prestige, and to the way he handles his roles and his constituencies.

THE ADMINISTRATIVE BUREAUCRACY

Not I, but ten thousand clerks rule Russia.
                    Czar Nicholas I

Executives get their name from the fact that it has been their historic function, in the words of Article II, Section 3, "to Take Care that the Laws be faithfully executed . . . ." In other words, they administer, enforce, and thus carry out the laws. With thousands of laws on the books, huge administrative bureaucracies have been created to help the executives. These bureaucracies include the departments, commissions, and other agencies which are part of the executive branch.

National Executive Organization

When I woke up this morning, the first thing I saw was a headline . . . that our Navy was going to spend two billion dollars on a shipbuilding program. Here I am, the Commander in Chief of the Navy having to read about that for the first time in the press. Do you know what I said to that? . . . I said: "Jesus Chr-rist!"

President Franklin D. Roosevelt

If the president spent just one hour a week supervising each of the agencies directly responsible to him he would have about a seventy-hour work week. He would have to sign or veto bills, plan new legislative programs, make appointments, and perform all the rest of his functions in what little time was left. Confronted with such overwhelming tasks, he does the best he can. The president appoints people he trusts to head the various executive agencies. He usually intervenes personally only when troubles arise. Yet the president knows that the ultimate responsibility is his.

Most of the agencies reporting to the president may be grouped into four categories: (1) the departments headed by cabinet members, (2) agencies in the Executive Office of the President, (3) regulatory commissions, and (4) government corporations. Only the most important of these can be discussed here.

The Departments

The eleven departments now in the executive branch have been created by Congress over many years. These departments are generally well known to the public. Their heads, usually called secretaries, are included in the president's cabinet. Traditionally, four departments (State, Defense, Treasury, and Justice) have been considered more important than the others. But expanded welfare programs and increased concern with environmental pollution have focused much attention on the Department of Health, Education and Welfare and the Department of the Interior. The relative influence of all the departments depends, in part, on the people who head them, and their relationships to the president. A structural diagram of the whole national government is shown in Figure 11–3. A list of the departments, with their major functions, appears in Figure 11–4.

The Executive Office of the President

The Executive Office is actually a collection of more than a dozen agencies. They provide the president with specialized advice, assistance, and coordinated effort in various fields. Among the more important agencies in the Executive Office are the four whose descriptions follow.

The National Security Council (NSC) integrates foreign policy and often

Figure 11–3. THE STRUCTURE OF THE NATIONAL GOVERNMENT

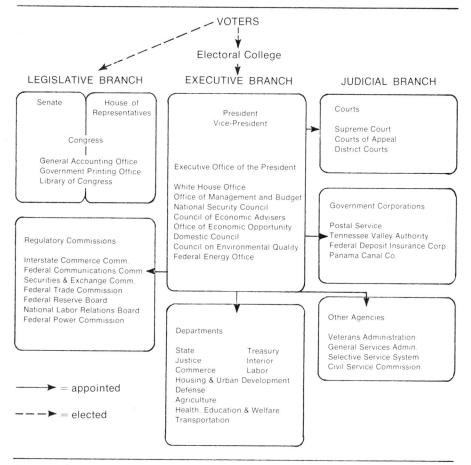

Note: Many agencies are not shown.
Source: U.S. Bureau of the Census. *Statistical Abstract of the United States: 1971*, p. 371.

Figure 11–4. EXECUTIVE DEPARTMENTS IN THE NATIONAL GOVERNMENT

Department and Date Established	Number of Employees, 1974[1]	Major Functions
State, 1789	33,296	Supervises diplomatic personnel; advises on foreign policy; administers foreign aid.
Defense, 1947[2]	1,042,090	Coordinates budgeting, logistics, and general administration of armed services; supervises Joint Chiefs of Staff; awards military contracts.

Treasury, 1789	126,260	Collects taxes; coins money; sells bonds; in charge of the Secret Service to enforce laws in this area and protect government leaders.
Justice, 1870[3]	49,285	Administers F.B.I. to enforce acts of Congress; prosecutes court cases for U.S. government; maintains federal prisons; investigates violations of federal antitrust and civil rights laws; gives legal advice to government; supervises immigration.
Health, Education and Welfare, 1953[4]	139,024	Administers social security pension and Medicare programs, federal aid to education, pure food and drug laws, and public health research and assistance.
Interior, 1849	69,024	Administers Bureau of Indian Affairs, mine safety laws, conservation of mineral resources, national parks, overseas territories, some hydroelectric power facilities.
Agriculture, 1862	103,621	Guarantees minimum prices on certain crops; stores food surpluses; provides crop insurance; administers national forests; helps finance farm services.
Commerce, 1903	35,359	Awards patents; promotes exports of U.S. products; administers Bureau of the Census and the National Weather Service.
Labor, 1913[5]	13,572	Enforces minimum wage and occupational safety laws; administers unemployment compensation; compiles cost-of-living statistics.
Housing and Urban Development, 1965	16,769	Directs urban renewal financial grants, government-guaranteed home purchase loans, and public housing assistance.
Transportation, 1966	70,552	Administers interstate highway programs, air safety standards, automotive safety laws, the Alaska railroad, and the Coast Guard.

[1]U.S. Bureau of the Census, *Statistical Abstract of the United States: 1974,* p. 236.
[2]The Defense Department replaced the War Department, in charge of army affairs, and the Navy Department, both established in 1789. The employment figure includes civilians only.
[3]The office of Attorney General was created in 1789 but he was given no departmental responsibility until 1870.
[4]The national government performed functions in these fields through separate agencies long before the department was created.
[5]The Labor Department was once a part of a Department of Commerce and Labor.

deliberates on action to be taken in cases of national emergency. Sometimes it eclipses the functions of the State Department to a certain extent. The NSC consists of the president, the vice-president, the Secretaries of State and Defense, and other close advisers whom the president may wish to include. The Central Intelligence Agency, which gathers and interprets vital information on security matters, reports to the NSC.

The White House Office is an organizational extension of the president himself. It helps to manage his time, fill his brain, publicize his thoughts, and execute his commands. More than any other agency, it is a monument to the institutionalization of the presidency. The nation's highest office, in a sense, has outgrown the man who holds it. It has expanded to deal with each new problem facing the nation.

To some degree, the White House Office is molded by the personal preferences of each president. Individual titles vary, but the functions of the White House staff have become rather standardized. There are always a few speech writers and a press secretary in charge of press releases and news conferences. Usually included are a chief adviser for national security matters and a congressional liaison man, who acts as the president's chief lobbyist. There are also several special advisers who have major policy-making responsibilities. These men are closest to the president. They accompany him on his weekend retreats and are his most trusted political confidantes. If one wanted to understand President Ford's view of the world in 1975, one would need to inquire into the vistas opened to him by such members of the White House staff as Donald Rumsfeld, Ron Nessen, Robert Hartman, and Philip Buchen.

The growth of the White House Office was particularly rapid during the Nixon administration. It went from 311 employees in 1970 to 527 in 1974.[10] But its arrogant and irresponsible use of power attracted more criticism than its growth. Leading figures of the Nixon White House Office included H. R. Haldeman, John Ehrlichman, Dwight Chapin, Charles Colson, and John Dean—all found guilty of Watergate crimes. But even before that, members of Congress and cabinet officials complained that these men constituted a kind of "palace guard" which isolated the president from those whose views they opposed. More and more, it seems that the White House staff, who do not require Senate confirmation, are exercising greater influence on policy decisions than Cabinet members whose appointments do require Senate approval. This is seen by some as an indication that our government is run by an unelected and somewhat unapproachable elite rather than by the people's representatives.

Such a criticism is now less valid when applied to a third essential agency in the Executive Office, the Office of Management and Budget (OMB). The OMB is very powerful because it prepares the president's proposed budget. Recommending allocations of money to Congress is perhaps the most important tool available to a president in establishing national priorities. All government agencies must submit their estimates of desired expenditures

President Ford meets with his advisers.

to the OMB. Then this office undertakes the complicated process of coordinating, evaluating, and making specific recommendations for spending the taxpayers' dollars. The importance of having this job be subject to some kind of democratic control was recognized in 1974 when Congress passed a law requiring Senate confirmation of the director of the OMB.

The Council of Economic Advisers is another vital part of the Executive Office. Its members, usually prominent economists, are supposed to provide the president with the best economic advice. They focus their efforts on how to curb inflation and unemployment, while increasing both the living standard and the gross national product.

Regulatory Commissions

There are also many "independent" agencies of the national government which are not included in the eleven departments of the Executive Office. Several are commissions charged with protecting the public by regulating various phases of private business activity. In this area, a distinction should be made between two kinds of industries. There are those in which laws approve monopolistic control by a single corporation, and those in which the government has encouraged free and vigorous competition among many firms.

Monopoly is most common in the public utility industries whose services are vital to the entire population. If two electricity, natural gas, railroad, or telephone companies were competing in the same area, for example, there would be duplicate pipes, rails, and wires. This might increase costs, cut the profits of each corporation, and possibly result in higher rates for the consumer. In the radio and television industries, it is essential to grant each station a monopoly on a particular wave length. Yet if consumer choice is limited by monopolistic control in such industries who is to protect the public from the abuses that may result—exorbitant rates, sloppy service, or poor programming?

The protectors, presumably, are the regulatory commissions of the national and state governments which grant franchises, set up rate limitations, and establish minimum standards. Some of these commissions impose certain controls upon competitive industries as well. The functions of the major ones are shown in Figure 11–5.

Figure 11–5. REGULATORY COMMISSIONS IN THE NATIONAL GOVERNMENT

Commission and Date Established	Number of Members	Terms	Functions
Interstate Commerce Commission, 1887	11	7 yrs.	Licenses and fixes rates for railroads, trucks, buses, and domestic shipping.
Federal Reserve Board, 1913	7	14 yrs.	Controls supply of currency and certain banking policies.
Federal Trade Commission, 1914	5	7 yrs.	Assists in enforcing antitrust laws and prohibits false advertising.
Federal Power Commission, 1920	5	5 yrs.	Regulates prices and services in electric power and natural gas industries.
Federal Communications Commission, 1934	7	7 yrs.	Grants radio and television licenses and fixes rates for telegraph and telephone services.
Securities and Exchange Commission, 1934	5	5 yrs.	Licenses stock and bond brokers and protects market investors.
National Labor Relations Board, 1935	5	5 yrs.	Holds elections to determine union collective bargaining rights and forbids unfair labor practices.

Civil Aeronautics Board, 1938	5	6 yrs.	Assigns airline routes and regulates rates and services.
Federal Maritime Commission, 1961	5	5 yrs.	Regulates dock charges and foreign routes for American merchant ships.
Equal Employment Opportunities Commission, 1965	5	5 yrs.	Prohibits employment discrimination by race or sex.
Consumer Product Safety Commission, 1972	5	5 yrs.	Establishes product safety standards and bans unsafe products.

Regulatory commissions differ from most other executive agencies in four respects. First, they have what is sometimes called quasi-legislative and quasi-judicial powers. This simply means that they function a little like lawmaking bodies in formulating rules for the corporations they regulate, and somewhat like courts in holding hearings relative to those rules. Second, they are multiheaded agencies whose decisions are made by all their commissioners or board members rather than by single administrators. Third, they are bipartisan in membership to encourage diverse viewpoints. Finally, they are largely independent of the president. This insures—among other things—that he cannot force them to grant preferred treatment to corporations in which his friends own stock. Members of these commissions, moreover, are appointed for specific terms of office and cannot be fired (except for demonstrated cause) until their terms have expired. In fact, these agencies are so independent that they are sometimes viewed as a fourth branch of the government.[11]

The major criticism levied against the regulatory commissions is that they are business-oriented. Their relative independence from overall government control has allowed them to fall under the influence of industry interests from whose ranks their members are often chosen. Corporation wolves, it is argued, are sent to guard the defenseless chickens, i.e. the consumers. As *Newsweek* magazine summed up the charge, "the [regulatory] agencies seem more concerned with serving the industries they are supposed to regulate than with protecting the public."[12] By 1973, however, such criticism was weakened with respect to at least one of these agencies. The Federal Trade Commission was rapidly emerging as an increasingly effective barrier to fraudulent advertising.[13]

Government Corporations
There are about twenty government-owned corporations in the national government. They were created to sell some form of services that will defray all or a large part of their operating costs. The newest of these, the U.S.

Postal Service created in 1970, is also by far the largest. Before 1970, the post office was operated as a government department whose 727,645 employees made it second only to the Defense Department among the largest government employers.[14]

Previously, the Tennessee Valley Authority, providing hydroelectric power, flood control, and recreation facilities in seven southeastern states, was the largest government corporation.[15] The Federal Deposit Insurance Corporation, guaranteeing private bank deposits up to $20,000, and the Panama Canal Company are also important. Even more than the regulatory commissions, government corporations are largely independent of presidential control. They are also favorite targets of right-wing attacks upon socialistic programs.

Miscellaneous Agencies
There are many other agencies in the executive branch that cannot be squeezed into neat pigeonholes. One of these, the Veterans Administration, is next only to the Defense Department and Postal Service in number of employees. It dispenses G.I. college benefits, administers veterans' hospitals, and allocates funds for pensions.

The General Services Administration is also important. It employs over 38,000 people, yet is engaged in activities that command little attention. It is responsible for the purchasing of supplies and the management of property for many other government agencies. It tries to reduce the waste of tax money and the duplication of government activities. The Environmental Protection Agency, the National Aeronautics and Space Administration, and the U.S. Information Agency which is in charge of American public relations programs overseas, are of considerable significance as well.

From Spoils to Merit: The Civil Service
During most of our early history, the victorious presidential candidate appointed his friends and supporters to public jobs. This *spoils* or *patronage* system is associated with President Andrew Jackson who justified it by the principle of rotation in office. He argued that the potential corruption of government employees could be checked by replacing them frequently. He insisted, moreover, that almost any man had enough common sense to hold almost any job. Thus it was democratic to give as many people as possible an opportunity to work for the government.

However worthy Jackson's intentions may have been, the spoils system deprived the government of experienced workers and often resulted in the appointment of poorly qualified people. But it was not until 1883 that Congress passed the Pendleton Act creating a Civil Service Commission. The commission was to supervise the selection of government employees on the basis of merit demonstrated in competitive exams. Initially less than 15 percent of all jobs were covered. Over the years, the merit system has gradually expanded to include more than 90 percent of the civilian employees of the U.S. government.

Figure 11–6. SOME CHARACTERISTICS OF CIVILIAN EMPLOYEES OF THE UNITED STATES GOVERNMENT

(by percent of total)

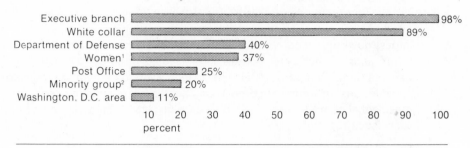

[1] In the highest job classifications, 8% are women.
[2] About 77 percent are blacks. Of government employees with the highest job classifications (GS 12–GS 18) 14 percent are members of minority groups.
Source: U.S. Bureau of the Census. *Statistical Abstract of the United States: 1974*, pp. 235–39

The Civil Service Commission consists of three persons appointed by the president, only two of whom may belong to the same party. From offices in ten cities, it coordinates employment, promotion, and dismissal procedures for most agencies in the executive branch.

In 1974 there were 2,835,000 civilians employed by the national government, nearly three times the number employed in 1940. These federal employees possessed a range of occupations almost as diverse as the entire economy. They included, for example, about 149,000 engineers and architects as well as about 11,000 painters and paperhangers. Their salaries ranged from $4798 to $36,000 per year in 1973.[16] Related information about the federal civil service is found in Figure 11–6.

The overwhelming majority of government employees must pass a civil service exam. They are then given job classifications in one of the General Schedule (GS) grades, numbered from 1 to 18. The hiring officer in each bureau must fill any vacancy by employing one of the three persons scoring highest on the civil service exam. However, disabled veterans, their wives, or widows are given a ten-point bonus on their exam scores. Any veteran receives a five-point bonus. Once employed and retained during a probationary period, civil service employees cannot be fired without a public hearing. Under certain circumstances, they may appeal to the Civil Service Commission itself.

The Problem of Bureaucratic Responsibility

He'll sit here . . . and he'll say 'Do this! Do that!' *And nothing will happen.* Poor Ike (Dwight D. Eisenhower) — it won't be a bit like the Army. He'll find it very frustrating.

Harry S. Truman

The central problem posed by administrative bureaucracies is how to make them accountable to the people — or to officials elected by the people. There is a widespread feeling that bureaucracies mean rule-bound, delay-filled indifference to the citizen. Moreover, many people believe that they are high in both operating costs and in project failures. For example, the Federal Housing Administration has been criticized for granting mortgage insurance on "almost totally defective" homes.[17] All too often, the bureaucracy seems to be a self-serving entity — too important to abolish and too complex to control.

Such charges are important because government directly touches most people's lives through the executive bureaucracies. Somewhere in an administrative office many decisions are made affecting the ordinary citizen's life. They may grant or deny one's right to practice a profession. They may determine how safe one's food will be, what textbooks one's children will read, or where roads will be constructed. Thus, in applying general laws to concrete cases, administrators in effect have a policy-making role of great consequence.

There is no easy way for either voters or their elected officials to compel a vast bureaucracy to carry out its role in the public's interest. Random checks may be made and flagrant abuses may be investigated. But still the system is too large and too complex to be placed under constant watch. Thus we must rely to a great extent on the positive influence of our political culture. Its stress on the rule of law, on the importance of fair treatment, and on procedures for redress of grievances provides one method of checking the bureaucracy.

Another means is to make bureaucracies more efficient by reorganizing the executive branch. This was done in the early 1950s at the national level as a result of recommendations made by a commission headed by former President Herbert Hoover. Many agencies that had previously reported directly to the White House were combined. In this way the president's administrative tasks were lightened. But twenty years passed and new agencies were created. President Nixon decided that reorganization was again required. He created a Domestic Council within the Executive Office of the President to provide better coordination among various agencies. He also asked Congress for the legislation necessary to combine eight existing departments into four new ones. But Congress would not go along with his request, perhaps because the departmental bureaucracies were too entrenched and had too much support from the pressure groups interested in their operation.

True responsibility, however, means more than efficiency. Executive agencies are filled with thousands of experts who are inherently irresponsible because their jobs are so specialized. Neither the president nor the voters can usually understand what they are doing. When scientists testify that they need X number of new employees or dollars to develop a harmless pesticide or a mass transit system, few have the knowledge to verify or dispute their claim. Secrecy, too, prevents an intelligent assessment of bureaucracies. If the voters, or even Congress, cannot be told what the C.I.A. is doing, how can they know if it is being done well, or even if it should be done at all?

A final barrier to the effective control of bureaucracy is its sheer size. In response to the demand for increased government services, the number of employees on the public payroll has forged steadily upward. The number of state government employees increased by 70 percent between 1963 and 1973 to a total of 3 million. During the same period, local governments expanded their work force by 54 percent, to reach a peak of more than 8 million. However, the number of civilians employed by the national government remained relatively stable at a little under 3 million. But the combined employees of federal, state, and local governments accounted for about 1 out of every 6 workers in 1974, up from 1 out of 9 in the early 1950s. With their growing numbers, government employees naturally gained more political influence. To further increase their strength, more of them joined unions and showed far less reluctance to go out on strike, whether legal or not, than in the past.

The problem of holding bureaucrats responsible for their performance and accountable to elected officials is thus increasingly difficult. Sheer size, specialized expertise, and secrecy may be as big a threat to genuinely democratic government as any we now face. However, if Congress continues to reassert itself and to carry out its function of oversight with renewed vigor, there will be at least one weighty balance on the scale of bureaucratic accountability.

EXECUTIVE POWER

The President is at liberty, both in law and in conscience, to be as big a man as he can.
Woodrow Wilson

The executive branch has a virtual monopoly of governmental force. The armed forces, national guard units, the F.B.I., the secret service, and federal prisons are all executive agencies. Because force is the ultimate form of power, the executive is the most dangerous branch. Its power is further expanded by its control over secret investigations of individuals and private groups. Such government spying gives the executive branch immense influence by enabling it to deprive persons of their privacy and perhaps their jobs and reputations as well. According to charges made in 1975, the F.B.I. bugged the bedroom of Martin Luther King, Jr., in the 1960s. It also spied on a number of congressmen, including one subject to blackmail for homosexual conduct. President Lyndon Johnson had access to these F.B.I. materials, we are told, and on occasion used that fact to exert influence on "vulnerable congressmen."[18]

Executive branches are not only the most dangerous to personal rights, but by far the biggest in both budgets and numbers of employees. As a result, their bureaucracies have developed another form of influence—specialized knowledge about hundreds of subjects—on which the legislative branch must often depend.

This staggering accumulation of executive powers is concentrated largely in the hands of the president—sometimes on a totalitarian scale. In 1973, a special Senate Committee on Emergency Powers found that no fewer than 470 laws gave the president extraordinary authority during periods of national emergency. The most shocking was the power to declare any part of the nation a military zone during an emergency, thereby subjecting anyone in it to up to a year in prison. Moreover, it was startling to learn that four national emergencies had been declared by various presidents since 1933 and that all were still in effect,[19] although the emergency powers were not actually being used. By 1975, legislation was pending to end these national emergencies, terminate future ones after six months unless continued by Congress, and require the president to account for significant actions taken under emergency powers.

Perhaps presidential power would not have been checked had it not first been disgraced by the Watergate crimes. In the last few years, four major developments have placed executive power under tighter control:

1. Congressional limitation on the continuation of foreign military combat (War Powers Act, 1973).
2. Congressional limitation on the impoundment of funds (Budget Act, 1974).
3. Demonstration by the House of Representatives that impeachment procedures are capable of working.
4. Limitation by the Supreme Court of the "executive privilege" to withhold White House evidence from criminal prosecutors.

In addition, President Ford has strengthened the prestige of the more accountable federal departments, and thereby weakened to some extent the power of the White House office. He has done this by appointing cabinet members more distinguished than their Nixon-named predecessors. John Dunlop, a Harvard professor, was appointed Secretary of Labor. William Coleman, a prominent attorney and the second black cabinet member in history, was named Secretary of Transportation. Edward Levi, president of the University of Chicago, was chosen as Attorney General. The appointment of Carla A. Hills to be Secretary of Housing and Urban Development brought to the cabinet the third woman in history, as well as a respected attorney and experienced government administrator. These Ford appointees have all been praised for their competence and balanced judgment.

But if praise is being given for pruning the executive branch of its excessive power, most of it belongs outside the structure of government. It was the press which tore away the Watergate cover-up and television which vividly displayed its weird intrigue. When President Nixon fired the special

Watergate prosecutor, it was the people themselves, in a "firestorm" of furious letters and telegrams, who demanded that somehow the presidency must be tamed; it must be purged of the arrogant corruption which had dishonored it. The days of the "imperial presidency," as historian Arthur Schlesinger, Jr., called it, were numbered.[20]

Notes

1. Nos. 73–1766 and 73–1834. Chief Justice Burger writing for the Court.
2. Clyde F. Snider, *American State and Local Government,* 2nd ed. (New York: Appleton-Century-Crofts, 1965), pp. 261, 694.
3. Louis W. Koenig, "Kennedy and Steel: The Great Price Dispute," in *The Centers of Power,* ed. by Alan F. Westin (New York: Harcourt Brace Jovanovich, 1964), pp. 1–52.
4. Mark J. Green, James M. Fallows, and David R. Zwick, *Who Runs Congress?* (New York: A Bantam/Grossman Book, 1972), p. 94.
5. *Los Angeles Times,* December 29, 1974, p. 4.
6. Fred I. Greenstein, "Popular Images of the President," *American Journal of Psychiatry,* November 1965, p. 524.
7. *Los Angeles Times,* November 17, 1974, Part VIII, p. 5.
8. James MacGregor Burns, *Congress on Trial* (New York: Harper & Bros., 1949), pp. 181–92.
9. Richard E. Neustadt, "The Presidency at Mid-Century," *Law and Contemporary Problems* 21 (Autumn 1956): 609–45.
10. U.S. Bureau of the Census, *Statistical Abstract of the United States: 1974,* (Washington, D.C., U.S. Government Printing Office, 1975), p. 236.
11. A mammoth collection of court decisions, official documents, and enlightened commentary on the regulatory commissions may be found in *Separation of Powers and the Independent Agencies: Cases and Selected Readings* (Washington, D.C.: U.S. Government Printing Office, 1970).
12. *Newsweek,* Aug. 24, 1970, p. 45.
13. *Los Angeles Times,* Sept. 12, 1973, p. 1.
14. *Statistical Abstract: 1970,* pp. 396–97.
15. A favorable account of the TVA, often condemned as America's most socialistic enterprise, is found in David E. Lilienthal, *TVA: Democracy on the March* (Chicago: Quadrangle Books, 1944).
16. *Statistical Abstract: 1974,* p. 240.
17. *Congressional Quarterly Weekly Report,* June 24, 1972, p. 1538. For many other examples of allegedly wasted tax money, see *Los Angeles Times,* December 26, 1974, p. 1.
18. *Newsweek,* Feb. 17, 1975, p. 21.
19. *Los Angeles Times,* March 18, 1974, p. 1.
20. Arthur Schlesinger, Jr., *The Imperial Presidency* (New York: Houghton Mifflin, 1973).

12 THE JUDICIAL BRANCH:
Courts and judges

Under our constitutional system, courts stand against any winds that blow as havens of refuge for those who might otherwise suffer because they are helpless, weak, outnumbered, or because they are non-conforming victims of prejudice and public excitement. . . .

Justice Hugo L. Black

Every government must pass laws and carry them out. These are the functions of legislative and executive branches. They are sometimes called the political branches of government because they are most subject to group pressures and public opinion. But for a people who value justice, there must be a third branch, somewhat independent of the other two. It is the branch which applies the law to specific disputes and alleged crimes in a humane and impartial fashion. This is the work of the courts, the presumably nonpolitical judicial branch of the government.

COURT JURISDICTION AND PROCEDURE

The federal division of power between the national and state governments requires a dual system of courts—one national and one state. Each, as we shall see, has the authority to hear certain kinds of cases. Each set of courts, in other words, has its own jurisdiction. There are, of course, certain nonjusticiable matters over which no court has power. Many of these are subjects which involve the legislative and executive branches.

The Reach of the Judicial Arm

It is emphatically the province and duty of the judicial department to say what the law is.

Chief Justice John Marshall

Judges have authority over two types of cases. They settle disputes between citizens, and they deal with violations of the law. The first type of controversy is a civil case. The second, far less common, is a criminal one.

Civil Cases

In judicial controversies between two private parties, the government merely provides the courtroom, judge, and perhaps the jury to settle the dispute impartially. The government stands above the battle. Decisions are often rendered on the basis of judge-made common law decided in similar cases in the past.

Such civil cases are of two types: (1) Contract cases in which the opposing sides have some legally binding relationship with one another, such as an employment contract, marriage, mortgage, lease, or will. Divorce is by far the most common type of contract case. (2) Tort cases in which there is personal injury or property damage but no legal relationship between the parties. Most of these cases result from car accidents, which take up as much as 17 percent of the time of American judges.[1] Beginning with Massachusetts in 1970, ten states have instituted "no-fault" auto insurance to reduce the number of such cases.[2]

In civil cases, a plaintiff sues a defendant. Traditionally, the law requires that each side assume equal responsibility for justifying its position and that the decision favor the one with the most evidence. The Seventh Amendment to the U.S. Constitution guarantees the right to trial by jury in civil cases involving over $20. It is applicable only in federal courts although even there the defendant usually waives this right and prefers to let the judge render the verdict.[3] As Amendment Seven does not apply in state courts, they show an even higher ratio of civil cases decided by judges rather than by juries. Still, much time is spent in both the national and state court systems trying to select juries for civil cases. When juries are used, a two-thirds vote is usually sufficient to reach a verdict.

Criminal Cases

Although there are cases in which governments sue or are sued in civil cases, their direct courtroom involvement is most important in criminal cases. These pit the government, as the prosecution, against the accused defendant.

Criminal cases involve alleged violations of law and are of two broad varieties. These are felonies (major crimes), usually punishable by at least a year in prison, and misdemeanors (minor crimes), entailing less severe sentences. In all criminal cases the burden of proof falls exclusively on the prosecution. The government must prove the defendant's guilt beyond a reasonable doubt. A slight edge in evidence, therefore, is not sufficient for a conviction. The defendant is presumed innocent until *proven* guilty.

The Constitution guarantees the right of trial by jury in criminal cases in state as well as federal courts. Until the Supreme Court ruled otherwise in 1972, the common law required a unanimous verdict in criminal jury trials.

Even now it appears that a vote of 8 to 4 would be too narrow a margin to reach a decision. If the jurors cannot agree, there occurs a mistrial, or hung jury. The prosecution then has the option of either dropping the charges or beginning the trial again with a new jury.

Amendment Six of the Constitution requires a speedy trial in criminal cases. Thus they take precedence over civil cases, with the result that it may be years before a civil suit gets into court. Also, the constitutional guarantee of the right to legal counsel is limited only to criminal cases.

Crisis in the Courts

While Americans may have been considered a notoriously lawless people, they seem to have a reverence for the law as a potential solution for every problem. "There oughta be a law . . . ," cries a massive chorus every time the public sees a potential threat to its safety or even to its feelings. The result is many laws, many lawbreakers, and a staggering number of cases brought before the courts. Too many cases and too few judges have produced a serious judicial crisis.

One of the more dramatic examples of this crisis occurred in New York City in October 1970. There prisoners staged a five-day jail riot and seized thirty-two guards as hostages in protesting overcrowded conditions and delays of up to a year before trial. Manhattan Criminal Court was so overburdened that some judges heard nearly three hundred cases a day. "The result," as one reporter noted, "is turnstile justice in a subway rush-hour atmosphere."[4]

In the federal courts, too, the work load has increased dramatically. As already noted, one of the reasons for this is our reliance on the courts to settle an excessive variety of problems. Chief Justice Burger has expressed doubts about "whether such things as divorce, child custody, adoptions . . .

Figure 12–1. NUMBER OF CASES IN FEDERAL COURTS

Courts	1950	1960	1973
U.S. District Courts			
Civil trials	5663	6002	10896
Nonjury	3648	3161	7289
Jury	2015	2841	3607
Criminal trials	2314	3040	8571
Nonjury	825	943	2927
Jury	1489	2097	5644
Total	7977	9042	19467
U.S. Supreme Court			
Total cases filed	1181	1940	4640[1]

[1]This figure is for 1972.
Source: U.S. Bureau of the Census, *Statistical Abstract of the United States: 1974*, p. 160.

belong in the courts at all. . . . [T]he chronic alcoholic, the narcotic addict, the serious mental patient—there's a . . . question whether they should be dealt with in the judicial framework."[5]

Burger suggested that such problems, in addition to car accident cases, might be handled instead by administrative agencies. Others have urged that the private use of marijuana and homosexual activity by consenting adults be legalized. This would free the police, prison officials, and judges for the more pressing business of protecting life and property. Drunkenness, for example, accounts for one-third of all persons arrested in the U.S.[6] Marijuana charges produced one-tenth of all criminal cases that came before the federal District Courts in 1973.[7] Many people believe that such "victimless crimes" should not be crimes at all. It has been estimated that "one-half of the cases in American courtrooms are due to behavior in which no one was injured. . . ."[8]

Besides removing certain matters from the jurisdiction of the courts, judicial burdens might be eased by an increase in the number of judges. Another suggestion is "the appointment of para-judges to deal with the enormous mass of pretrial hearings, motions, and administration of court calendars, all of which take up a major portion of a judge's time."[9] A few schools have started to train students as court executives using modern management methods.[10] Forty-two states have offices of court administrators, six of them established in 1972 and 1973.[11]

The Road to Justice

Original and Appellate Jurisdiction
Original jurisdiction is the authority to decide either criminal or civil cases that have never been tried in court before. The lowest of the state courts and the federal district courts, at the bottom of the judicial ladder in the national system, have original jurisdiction only. Appellate jurisdiction is the authority of higher courts to hear cases on appeal that have been tried before in a lower court.

The Adversary System: Legal Warfare
The American people love a good fight. That may explain the popularity of plays, television series, and novels based upon courtroom drama. For the Anglo-American legal tradition conceives of a trial as essentially an honest battle between two adversaries, out of which the truth will somehow emerge and the best man will finally win. A leading authority has described it well:

[T]he judge will question a witness only to avert grave injustice, not to advance the case for either side. He is not in any sense an active elicitor of truth regarding the testimony presented. . . . [H]e is an independent arbiter. . . . This is a concept basic to the common law adversary proceeding . . . that "sets the parties fighting."[12]

There is reason to believe that this adversary system is well suited to criminal cases where a defendant is simply innocent or guilty. But it might be inappropriate for settling more complex civil disputes, such as divorce or accident liability cases, where both parties may be at fault. If no one is committed to the active, impartial search for truth, truth may not be found.

Thus it is encouraging to find that there is a growing use of pretrial conferences in many of these cases. Such conferences permit the opposing attorneys to try to agree on as many facts as possible, thereby limiting the issues in dispute. A somewhat similar purpose is served by the procedure of discovery. It permits each lawyer to learn what evidence is possessed by the opposition in advance of the trial. In addition, many disputes are settled by informal negotiations between the opposing attorneys. In civil cases, for example, a compromise financial settlement may be hammered out in the judge's private chambers. Such out-of-court solutions no doubt fall short of perfect justice, but they represent more or less voluntary agreements which reduce court time.

The Plea Bargaining Debate

In criminal cases, informal negotiations often involve *plea bargaining* in which the defendant pleads guilty to a charge less serious than that for which he was initially arrested. Plea bargaining, however, may provide society with too little protection from hardened criminals. Or it might induce innocent defendants to plead guilty to avoid a long prison sentence based on circumstantial evidence. Surely justice should not be sacrificed in the interest of convenience.

The controversy over plea bargaining seems certain to get more bitter. A committee of the American Bar Association recommended its abolition by 1978. This prompted a sharp and unanimous reaction by a task force of the National District Attorney's Association. They defended plea bargaining as "not only necessary . . . but also effective."[13] Its importance is underscored by the fact that about 90 percent of all criminal convictions are obtained by guilty pleas, many of which are the result of plea bargaining. The process goes on at every level. An unemployed dishwasher arrested on a burglary charge may plead guilty to "unlawful entry" in order to get a lighter sentence. Vice-President Agnew may have made no defense against an income tax evasion charge in order to avoid prosecution for bribery or extortion. Leonard Downie, Jr., an outspoken critic of plea bargaining, is equally outraged by another common practice. Prosecuting attorneys, attempting to relieve the burden of the courts as well as their own work loads, often drop charges altogether against many defendants.[14]

COURT STRUCTURE AND PERSONNEL

In the long run, there is no guarantee of justice except the personality of the judge.
Justice Benjamin Cardozo

National Courts

Article III of the Constitution provides for a U.S. Supreme Court and whatever lower courts Congress may wish to establish. The resulting judicial system is relatively simple.

Federal District Courts

In 1789, the first year Congress met, it created the U.S. district courts. There are now over four hundred judges serving on ninety-three district courts with at least one in each state and territory. In criminal cases, these courts have original jurisdiction over all acts — felonies and misdemeanors alike — prohibited by Congress. In addition, they have jurisdiction over most civil cases to which the U.S. government is a party. They may also hear cases involving citizens of different states in which more than $10,000 is at stake. In most instances, only one judge hears each case, and the defendant may claim the right to trial by jury. Sometimes these judges exert historic

Figure 12–2. THE JUDICIAL BRANCH

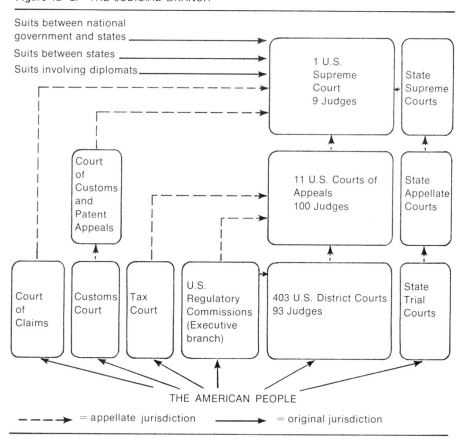

Suits between national government and states

Suits between states

Suits involving diplomats

1 U.S. Supreme Court 9 Judges

State Supreme Courts

Court of Customs and Patent Appeals

11 U.S. Courts of Appeals 100 Judges

State Appellate Courts

Court of Claims

Customs Court

Tax Court

U.S. Regulatory Commissions (Executive branch)

403 U.S. District Courts 93 Judges

State Trial Courts

THE AMERICAN PEOPLE

- - - → = appellate jurisdiction ——→ = original jurisdiction influence. U.S. District Court Judge John Sirica did so by making the final sentences of the Watergate burglars conditional upon their cooperation in finding out who ordered the break-in. This helped crack the case—and the Nixon presidency as well.

In a February 1975 address, Chief Justice of the Supreme Court Warren Burger urged Congress to create more than fifty new federal district judgeships. This was necessary, he argued, to avert a possible crisis caused by the Speedy Trial Act which was scheduled to take effect later. The new law provided that criminal trials must begin within 100 days of the defendant's indictment. In addition, Burger called for a 20 percent pay raise for all federal judges in order to retain superior jurists. Judges had received no salary increase in more than five years and five of them resigned in 1974, in part because of economic factors.[15]

Courts of Appeals

In 1891, Congress created the courts of appeals. Standing between the district courts and the U.S. Supreme Court, they have appellate jurisdiction in both criminal and civil cases. There are now about one hundred judges distributed among eleven courts of appeals. Three judges usually hear each appealed case. The vast majority of cases reaching these courts come from the U.S. district courts. A few arrive from other sources such as the regulatory commissions in the executive branch.

The Supreme Court

The highest court in America is the U.S. Supreme Court. Here, at the judicial summit, nine judges (a number determined by Congress) exercise authority equaling that of the president or Congress. The Supreme Court has both original and appellate jurisdiction. Article III of the Constitution, as altered by the Eleventh Amendment, establishes original jurisdiction for the Supreme Court over suits involving foreign diplomats, those between states, or those between the national government and a state. All in all, the Court has heard an average of less than five cases a year under its original jurisdiction. These mainly involve interstate disputes. The most notable in recent times have been those between Maryland and Virginia over oyster fishing and between California and Arizona concerning water from the Colorado River.[16] In 1947 a major dispute involving national versus state ownership of offshore (or tidelands) oil resources also reached the Supreme Court under its original jurisdiction.[17]

The vast majority of cases reaching the Supreme Court are heard on appeal. They consist of cases heard earlier by the federal courts of appeals or by the state courts. Some cases involving important constitutional issues may arrive directly from the federal district courts. The only circumstance under which a case can be appealed from a state court is one in which a state or local government has been charged with violating the U.S. Constitution or a federal law or treaty. Such cases go directly from the highest state court to which it may be appealed to the U.S. Supreme Court.

Most cases reach the Supreme Court on *writs of certiorari,* which are court orders granting appeals from lower courts. These writs are usually issued when four Supreme Court justices feel a case to be of great enough importance. Of more than 4000 cases presented to it each year, the Court renders decisions on only three or four hundred. Less than half of these are given full written opinions. In order to lighten the burden of Supreme Court justices, Chief Justice Burger has endorsed a proposal to create a "national court of appeals." This would screen out the less important cases coming from the eleven courts of appeals to the Supreme Court.

Other Federal Courts

Various specialized courts complete the federal judicial branch. One is the Court of Claims in which citizens may bring civil suits against the national government for damages of one kind or another. A second is the U.S. Customs Court which reviews administrative decisions involving taxes on imported goods. Third, there is the Court of Customs and Patent Appeals which hears appeals from the Customs Court, the Patent Office in the Commerce Department, and the Tariff Commission.

State Courts

Since a substantial number of the cases reaching the U.S. Supreme Court begin in the state courts, some attention needs to be paid to these as well. State court structures are similar to the federal one, but usually are organized in four or five levels.

Justices of the Peace

Justice courts, at the bottom of the judicial structure and often charged with dishonesty, are being replaced in most states. In these courts, the justices of the peace (J.P.'s) are often part-time judges, without legal training, paid only from fines and costs they themselves impose. In order to encourage more civil suits and improve their business, J.P.'s have a notorious reputation for ruling for the plaintiff. The jurisdiction of these petty officials is confined to civil cases involving no more than a few hundred dollars and the most minor of misdemeanors. They often pick up a few extra dollars by performing marriage ceremonies, collecting police fines, etc.

Other Trial Courts

In many states, the functions of the J.P.'s are usually exercised by full-time, salaried, professionally qualified judges. They serve on municipal courts, or similar tribunals with different names, which have original jurisdiction only. In addition, every state has higher trial courts (generally known as county, superior, district, or circuit courts) with authority over all major cases. At this level a million-dollar damage suit or a murder case, for example, will be brought to trial. Supplementing this original jurisdiction is appellate jurisdiction over cases heard first by J.P.'s or municipal court judges.

At the trial court level, there is either a variety of specialized courts handling particular kinds of cases, or general trial courts organized in specialized divisions. Both systems permit judges to gain considerable experience and expertise in a certain field of law and presumably raise their level of competence. For example, judges may specialize in juvenile cases, probate matters, or domestic relations.

Reform at the lower court levels has been sorely needed in many states. It serves not only to root out corruption and gross incompetence, but also to reorganize courts with confusing and overlapping jurisdictions. It is heartening to note progress in that direction. Courts were reorganized in Colorado, Idaho, and Oklahoma (where J.P.'s and county courts were abolished) in 1969. Significant court integration recently took place in Ohio, Pennsylvania, Rhode Island, Alabama, and South Carolina as well.[18] More than a dozen states now have unified state court systems, following the lead of New Jersey in 1948.

Although more and more decisions by trial court judges are being reviewed by appellate courts, the fact that most of them are not gives trial judges awesome powers. As we saw in Chapter 5, they have enormous discretion in determining the sentences of guilty defendants. They can put them on probation rather than send them to prison, or perhaps sentence them to one year or perhaps five years. As a noted expert in the field has observed, "Some judges are harsh to certain kinds of offenders while their colleagues are lenient. Some judges consistently mete out the same penalty for particular crimes: others are less predictable."[19]

The Appellate Courts

All states have a supreme court to hear cases appealed from their trial courts. In addition, twenty-four states have intermediate appellate courts to help screen out and reduce the work load of the highest state court.[20] The number of state supreme court judges ranges from three (in Delaware) to nine (in seven states).

The Selection of Judges

Judicial Appointment

All federal judges are appointed by the president subject to confirmation by a majority vote of the U.S. Senate. But the situation at the state level is both different and far more complex. State supreme court judges are appointed by the governor in sixteen states.[21] They are appointed by the legislature from nominations submitted by the governor in Connecticut, and elected by the legislature in Rhode Island, South Carolina, Vermont, and Virginia. They are elected by the voters in the remaining twenty-nine states. Most lower court judges are also elected, although some are chosen by higher courts, city councils, or other local governing bodies.[22]

The case for appointing judges rather than electing them rests primarily on two arguments: (1) The voters know too little about prospective judges to be able to elect them intelligently. (2) To force a judge to seek office in an election campaign compromises the independence and integrity he needs to act impartially.

Judicial Election

Among the states in which supreme court judges are chosen by the voters, in fifteen they are elected on a partisan basis. That is, the judicial candidates are nominated by the opposing political parties.[23] In fourteen they are elected on a nonpartisan ballot, with the party affiliation of the candidates unlisted.[24]

The election of judges is often justified on the grounds that judges frequently decide cases in ways which reflect their own values. The whole common law tradition, in fact, allows each judge to establish some legal principles whenever statutes and precedents seem inapplicable. Hence, it is argued, democratic theory requires that judges, like all important policy-makers, be selected by the people. The policy choices available to judges is indicated by a study of 298 national and state supreme court justices. It disclosed that in at least nine kinds of cases the decisions of Republican and Democratic judges differed significantly. This finding may suggest that people should be permitted to elect judges whose views are most similar to their own.

Yet the same study also revealed that the decisions of judges who were appointed reflected party affiliation much less often than those of judges who were elected.[25] People who value a politically independent judiciary may cite this evidence to support the case for appointed judges. But there is another argument for elective judgeships. They prevent chief executives from using judicial appointments as a form of patronage to reward their supporters. Among federal judges, it is worth noting that President Lyndon Johnson appointed 155 Democrats and 12 Republicans. President Nixon chose 220 Republicans and 18 Democrats.[26]

The Care and Characteristics of Judges

Our judges are as honest as other men, and not more so. They have . . . the same passions for party, . . . power, and . . . privilege. . . .
                                                                Thomas Jefferson

Few jobs in our society carry the prestige and honor of a judgeship, especially on a higher court. Let us examine some of the factors affecting the judicial life-style, as well as the characteristics of the men and women who enjoy its rewards.

Judicial Tenure and Salaries

Judges in the federal court system have lifetime jobs, subject only to their unlikely removal on impeachment charges. At the state level, however, few are so lucky. The vast majority of the state higher court judges have terms ranging from six to twelve years. Terms on state trial courts range from two to six years. However, most elected judges have little difficulty getting reelected. The voters in many states, distracted by better publicized races for other offices, tend to vote for incumbent judges almost automatically.[27]

The Chief Justice of the U.S. Supreme Court receives an annual salary of $62,500. The eight associate justices get $60,000, court of appeals judges $42,500, and district court judges $40,000. At the state level, supreme court judges receive from a low of $22,500 in Montana to a high of $63,143 in New York. Major trial judges earn from $14,175 in Oklahoma, to $43,317 in New York. While judges hardly go hungry on such salaries, they earn far less than thousands of lawyers. Why, then, would one want to become a judge? There are perhaps as many reasons as there are judges. Among them are the prestige and relative security of judicial office, its usefulness as a springboard to higher office, and a desire for public service. In addition, there are fringe benefits. Most judges do not have to pay for their office space, secretarial help, or other professional necessities.

Characteristics of Judges

Except for justices of the peace, nearly all jurists are lawyers. Oddly enough, this is true in the federal system only as a result of tradition, common sense, and the political influence of bar associations. Although the U.S. Constitution prescribes rather detailed requirements for legislative and executive officials, it imposes none on judges. In many states, however, admission to the bar is now a constitutional requirement for judges. One effect of the attorneys' monopoly over the judicial branches is that judges have a higher socioeconomic background than the average American.

The courts are not only dominated by lawyers, but by male lawyers. No woman has ever served on the U.S. Supreme Court. A survey of the names of state supreme court justices reveals only five women in all the fifty states.[28] It is probable that this situation is the result of institutionalized sexism within the legal profession. In 1970 only 9000 of 315,000 lawyers in America were females.[29]

THE SUPREME COURT AND JUDICIAL REVIEW

Scarcely any political question arises in the United States that is not resolved, sooner or later, into a judicial question.

Alexis de Tocqueville

Courts in all countries have the job of settling disputes, acquitting the innocent, and punishing the guilty. But American courts have the unique additional power of judicial review. This means that they can declare legislative and executive acts unconstitutional and therefore invalid.

In the hands of state courts, judicial review becomes a sort of two-edged sword, cutting down government actions which violate either the state or federal constitutions. But whenever any action is declared contrary to the federal Constitution, it will almost always result in an appeal to the U.S. Supreme Court.

The Court of Last Resort

The Supreme Court is well named. It is the final interpreter of the law, the ultimate watchdog of the whole governmental process, the court of last resort. It is the final arbiter of what the Constitution permits and what it prohibits. If one dislikes a Supreme Court decision, one has but three choices: defy it, wait patiently in the hope the Court will reverse itself later, or seek a constitutional amendment nullifying its ruling.

The Politics of Judicial Selection

Many factors influence a president's nomination of Supreme Court judges. One is party loyalty. Another is general political philosophy. In either case, a president may be disappointed to find his appointee voting against his expectations. Once cloaked with black-robed independence, prestige, and life tenure, Supreme Court justices have often used their authority in ways the president has not liked. President Theodore Roosevelt was quickly angered by Justice Oliver Wendell Holmes, shortly after he appointed him. President Eisenhower was thought to regret his selection of Chief Justice Earl Warren. But President Nixon apparently made his appointments more carefully. During the 1968 campaign, he stated his intention to choose justices with a preference for a "strict construction" or narrow interpretation of the Constitution. Seldom has a campaign promise been kept so well. Before he left office, Nixon had the rare opportunity to make four Supreme Court selections. His choices justified his confidence, with the ironic exception of the presidential-tapes decision which led to his resignation 16 days later. Nevertheless, as a result of the men he appointed, conservative court decisions in the areas of police power, freedom of the press, and race relations may have altered the interpretation of the Constitution for decades to come.

Emphasis is sometimes placed on the maintenance of a geographic and religious balance on the Supreme Court. But balance is a relative concept and each president has his own idea of what it means. Less than a quarter of all Supreme Court justices have come from west of the Mississippi River. New York, Ohio, and Massachusetts have produced nearly a third of the total number.[30] President Nixon tried to appoint three persons from the South, on the grounds that this section was underrepresented on the Court. But only one of them won Senate confirmation.

The concept of a religious balance has traditionally meant seven Protestants, a Catholic, and a Jew. But this tradition is a relatively recent one.

It has produced only six Catholics and five Jews out of the one hundred justices who have served on the Court. President Nixon repudiated religion as a factor in judicial recruitment. As a result, our highest court is now without a Jew (with Justice William Brennan as the lone Catholic) for the first time since 1916. President Lyndon B. Johnson broadened the ideal of a balanced Court by selecting the first black, Justice Thurgood Marshall, to sit on that body.

In making his Supreme Court choices, the president relies in large part upon the recommendations of his attorney general. He, in turn, has usually sounded out the Committee on the Federal Judiciary of the American Bar Association.[31] Naturally, the likelihood of Senate opposition must also be considered, as well as pressures brought to bear by influential interest groups. The rejection of two Nixon appointees reflects the close scrutiny the Senate, and especialiy its Judiciary Committee, gives to Supreme Court nominations. It also indicates the influence of the labor and civil rights lobbies, both strongly opposed to the president's choices. Another factor involved in Supreme Court appointments is prior judicial experience. Over a third of the justices throughout our history had never held a judgeship before. These have included such notable ones as Chief Justices John Marshall, Roger Taney, and Earl Warren. All justices, however, have had legal experience or training. These and other considerations can be brought together in a composite picture of the "typical" Supreme Court justice. He is

probably Protestant; of Anglo-Saxon stock . . . ; a background of upper-level social status; reared in an urban environment; a member of an economically comfortable, civic-minded, politically active family; with B.A. and LL.B. degrees; experienced in some public or civic office.[32]

A final factor, not mentioned in the composite picture, is age. In 1975, seven of the nine justices were over sixty years of age. Justice William O. Douglas, for example, was 78 years old and had served 36 years on the Court. Throughout our history, ten Supreme Court justices have held their posts for more than 30 years.

The Mystique of Court Procedure
The Supreme Court is big on ceremony, both public and private. Its many rituals lend a certain mystique to its procedures. Opposing attorneys in each case present written briefs to the Court. But at least eight days a month are devoted to oral arguments. Each side of every case is usually permitted an hour to emphasize its most persuasive contentions. Such sessions begin with an ancient cry: "Oyez, oyez, oyez! All persons having business before the Honorable Supreme Court of the United States are admonished to draw near . . . ." The chief justice takes the middle chair, and the eight associate justices arrange themselves, in order of seniority, on either side of him. Each of the nine justices may direct questions, sometimes sharp, to the opposing

lawyers. Occasionally, to the delight of the press and public present, the justices exchange verbal barbs with one another.

Then, on Friday, the Court meets in secret conference, each justice first shaking hands with each of his judicial brethren. The chief justice presides and summarizes the cases on the agenda. Each of the associates, in order of seniority, makes additional comments. Then voting begins, in reverse order, with the most recently appointed associate voting first and the chief justice last.

A (dissenting opinion) in a court of last resort is an appeal to the brooding spirit of the law, to the intelligence of a future day.

Charles Evans Hughes

The Assignment of Opinions

When the votes are counted, the chief justice assigns the responsibility of writing the majority opinion of the Court. This explains the case briefly, describes the issues it presents, and justifies the Court's decision. The majority opinion provides guidance to lower courts in deciding similar cases. It also attempts to persuade the nation of its correctness. Just as the Constitution is the heart of American law, Supreme Court opinions are its lifeblood. They apply constitutional principles to the gravest disputes in the nation.

If the chief justice has voted with the minority, the task of assigning the majority opinion falls to the senior associate justice who voted with the majority. Once written, the opinion is circulated among other members of the majority. If any justice disagrees with its reasoning, he may write a concurring opinion giving his own reasons for reaching the same conclusion as the majority. Similarly, any justice who voted with the minority may write a dissenting opinion in which he states why he believes the majority was wrong. Often, the dissenting opinion of one justice will be endorsed by all members of the Court minority. Such minority opinions are sometimes as influential as those of the majority. They can fan a spark of doubt about the majority's wisdom that may lead the Court on some future occasion to reverse its earlier decision. This has happened about a hundred times since the adoption of the Constitution.

The Nature of Judicial Review

Judicial review has been controversial since the doctrine was first used in the case of *Marbury* v. *Madison*. Yet it has now become deeply entrenched in our constitutional system. Judicial review is used to declare government acts unconstitutional primarily under three circumstances. They are: if one level of government (national or state) exercises power properly belonging only to the other, if one branch of the government exercises power properly belonging only to either of the other two, or if any government agency or official exercises power that violates the constitutional rights of an individual. But two quite different interpretations of judicial review have staunch supporters on the Supreme Court.

Judicial Self-Restraint

One group of judges, now led by Chief Justice Burger, contends that the power of judicial review should be used with great restraint. It should only be applied against laws or actions that are blatantly unconstitutional. Burger and others complain that too often judges interpret the Constitution to reflect their own views. Thus they invalidate government acts simply because they don't like them. President Nixon clearly advocated this doctrine of judicial self-restraint when he asserted his intention to appoint judges who

would be strict constructionists who saw their duty as interpreting law not making law. They would see themselves as caretakers of the Constitution and servants of the people, not superlegislators with a free hand to impose their social and political viewpoints upon the American people.[33]

Perhaps the essence of judicial self-restraint was best captured in a remark made by Justice Oliver Wendell Holmes to Justice Harlan Fiske Stone:

Young man, about 75 years ago I learned that I was not God. And so, when the people . . . want to do something I can't find anything in the Constitution expressly forbidding them to do, I say, whether I like it or not, "Goddamit, let 'em do it."[34]

This spirit has taken the form of specific rules that the Court has imposed upon itself to minimize the use of judicial review. Mr. Justice Brandeis summarized them in a concurring opinion in the case of *Ashwander v. Tennessee Valley Authority* in 1935:

1) The Court will not pass upon the constitutionality of legislation in a friendly, non-adversary, proceeding. . . .
2) The Court will not anticipate a question of constitutional law in advance of the necessity of deciding it. . . .
3) The Court will not formulate a rule of constitutional law broader than is required by the precise facts to which it is to be applied. . . .
4) The Court will not pass upon a constitutional question . . . if there is also present some other ground upon which the case may be disposed of. . . .
5) The Court will not pass upon the validity of a statute upon complaint of one who fails to show that he is injured by its operation. . . .
6) The Court will not pass upon the constitutionality of a statute at the instance of one who has availed himself of its benefits.
7) When the validity of an act of the Congress is drawn in question, and even if a serious doubt of constitutionality is raised, it is a cardinal principle that this Court will first ascertain whether a construction of the statute is fairly possible by which the question may be avoided.[35]

To these so-called Ashwander rules, two others must be added that also serve to limit the number of acts declared unconstitutional: First, the Court will not decide "political questions" that are within the proper domains of the other two branches (although what these domains are is sometimes disputed). Second, the burden of proof rests on those claiming that a particular act is unconstitutional. Yet in spite of these rules, the Supreme Court has declared 106 acts of Congress and about 800 state laws unconstitutional between 1789 and 1973.

Judicial Activism

A somewhat different interpretation of judicial review is held by those sometimes called judicial activists, or loose constructionists. This group now includes Justices William J. Brennan and William O. Douglas. They contend that it is difficult to construe "strictly" such "loose" constitutional phrases as *"unreasonable searches and seizures," "cruel and unusual punishments,"* and *"due process of law."* The broad language of the Constitution, they argue, requires broad latitude for the Court in interpreting it and enforcing its provisions. Activists stress the importance of judicial review in protecting individual rights. They see it as a refuge for minorities from oppressive government action.

Here it is important to note two quite different kinds of provisions in the Constitution. First, there are those that *grant* power to government officials. For example, the "necessary and proper" clause grants congressional authority, and the "commander in chief" clause confers presidential power. To interpret these provisions broadly or loosely would *increase* governmental power and result in fewer acts declared unconstitutional.

But, secondly, there are the constitutional provisions, such as the Bill of Rights, that *limit* the power of government in the interests of protecting individual liberties. To interpret these broadly would *diminish* governmental power and result in more acts declared unconstitutional. Thus judicial activism, implying a readiness to exercise judicial review, involves *a strict construction of power grants and a loose construction of power limitations.* Few judges are entirely consistent on this matter, although it is generally agreed that judicial activism reached its peak during the era of Chief Justice Earl Warren (1953–69). It is equally clear that the Burger Court, under the influence of the Nixon appointees, shows a strong preference for judicial self-restraint.

Judicial Politics

Whether the courts pursue policies of activism or restraint, it seems clear that their decisions will have a greater political impact than has previously been assumed. The Warren Court rendered important policy decisions by interpreting the Constitution to ban prayer in the public schools, to require that criminal suspects be informed of certain rights, and to prohibit the election of lawmakers from unequally populated districts.

Although such decisions have represented triumphs of judicial activism, they have also revealed profound political splits among the justices. In 1957, for example, activist Justices William O. Douglas and Hugo Black voted together in 89 percent of the cases on which the Court was divided. They sided with Justice John M. Harlan, noted for his self-restraint, in only 29 and 33 percent of the cases, respectively.[36] In 1974 the four Nixon appointees, Burger, Blackmun, Powell, and Rehnquist, voted together 75 percent of the time.[37]

The truth is that judges could not stay out of politics, even if they wanted to, because politics involves making decisions about government policy. The higher the court, the more frequent and important are the policy decisions it is required to make. For example, when judges exercise their power of judicial review, they pass judgment on the constitutionality of a law or executive procedure which is already established. If they uphold the challenged action, they are *perpetuating existing political policy.* If they declare the action unconstitutional, they are *changing existing political policy.* A fundamental issue between activism and restraint, therefore, may not be whether or not the courts should intervene in the actions of the other branches of government, but on whose side. It is also important to note that some laws are worded so broadly that their enforcement requires the courts to decide precisely what they mean. In such situations, there is little doubt that judges become policy-making officials.

Even when a case involves no question of constitutionality, it may reflect some of the enduring conflicts in our society: employers versus employees, manufacturers versus consumers, whites versus blacks, prudes versus pornographers. When the courts render a decision, they lock into public policy a legal preference favoring the interests of one group over another. That is a policy decision which is profoundly political in nature.

Finally, judges are trapped in the web of politics woven around them by external political pressures. Interest groups exert influence for and against the appointment of particular judges. Their lawyers intervene in specific cases through the submission of *amicus curiae* briefs on behalf of one side or the other. Presidents and governors use judicial appointments to reward the party faithful or to perpetuate their own political attitudes. Courts must also be sensitive to public opinion, puzzling as it often is. They have no armies, few jobs, and little money to help them gain compliance with their decisions. Devoid of force and influence, the power of judges stems from authority rooted in the faith and confidence of the people.

JUDICIAL POWER

The Constitution is what the judges say it is.
Charles Evans Hughes

The judicial branch must rely almost exclusively on authority. It depends especially on the Constitution, that supreme source of authority which pledges equality of legal protection. If the courts are unable to gain voluntary compliance with their orders, only the executive has the power to enforce them. If that branch refuses, races will remain segregated, contracts will be violated, alimony will be unpaid, and suspects will be forced to confess. The law will be washed away in a sea of anarchy, with only the strongest or richest remaining afloat.

Endless debate still rages about whether modern-day legislators or presidents are better or worse than in the "good old days." But virtually every informed observer would agree that today's judges are the finest the nation has ever seen. This has nothing to do with how one may feel about their decisions. Rather it is related to their training and relative independence. Of course, judges were always expected to embody justice. They should be less swayed than politicians by mass emotion, sympathy with particular pressure groups, or dedication to a specific political ideology. While these ideals may be unattainable in total, they are useful measuring sticks for judicial performance.

Obeying the Court

That performance can be partially evaluated by the extent to which there is compliance with judicial rulings. Supreme Court decisions have often dealt with the most personal parts of daily life and have stirred up "gut level" emotions. Where our children go to school, whether they can pray in class, when abortions are permissible — these are issues decided by the Court about which few people feel indifferent. But it does no good to establish a legal doctrine if it is widely ignored. This would indicate a serious lack of power for the judicial branch. To what extent has this been the fate of Supreme Court decisions?

On most matters, there has been substantial compliance. To cite two major examples, legislatures have been reapportioned into equally populated districts and, although it has taken two decades, there is widespread school integration in the South. But the record is not uniformly good. Some trial court judges stubbornly resist or carelessly disregard the rules of law established by higher courts.[38] Wisconsin district attorneys displayed little knowledge of Supreme Court obscenity rulings. Selective Service personnel sometimes proceeded in violation of Court decisions on conscientious objection. Much of this can be explained, according to two leading observers, by the means lower courts can use to evade higher court rulings. They can, for example, emphasize the way in which the facts of one case differ from those on which an earlier ruling was based. Or they can distort the meaning of words used in appellate court decisions to fit their own biases.[39] Thus lower court judges have a great deal of political power which can be used to defy the orders of our highest court. But the highest court too has tremendous power, much of which is embodied in the doctrine of judicial review.

Judicial Review, Democracy, and Freedom

The chief attack on judicial review is that it is undemocratic because it gives too much power to nine appointed justices. And so it seems to be, if democracy means majority rule. It is difficult to imagine anything less democratic, in fact, than a law passed by an overwhelming majority of elected legislators, enthusiastically signed by an elected president, and then declared unconstitutional by a 5 to 4 vote of the appointed Supreme Court.

Yet the American political system is dedicated to individual freedom as well as to democracy. In defense of this freedom judicial review can make its greatest contribution. Since most legislative and executive officials are elected by majorities, they are compelled both by moral obligation and by their own political interests to do what the majority wishes. The protection of minority rights against a prejudiced and hostile majority is, therefore, the responsibility of an independent court system. Armed with judicial review and staffed by judges neither selected by majorities nor in danger of removal by them, the court system is able to provide such protection. The U.S. Constitution is basically an experiment in the limitation and control of power—whether exercised by a majority or a minority—through the rule of law. Without the protection of judicial review, it is doubtful whether that great experiment can succeed. If it does not, both majority rule and minority rights will perish with it.

Notes

1. Jeremy Main, "Only Radical Reform Can Save the Courts," *Fortune,* August 1970, pp. 110–14.
2. Charles G. Whitmire, "Transportation," *Book of the States, 1974–1975* (Lexington, Ky.: *The Council of State Governments,* 1974), pp. 352–53.
3. In U.S. district courts in 1973, civil cases outnumbered criminal ones by an almost 3 to 2 margin. Of the civil cases, over 3000 were decided by a jury and about 7000 without one.
4. *Los Angeles Times,* Dec. 7, 1970, p. 1.
5. *U.S. News and World Report,* Dec. 14, 1970, p. 35.
6. Main, pp. 110–14.
7. U.S. Bureau of the Census, *Statistical Abstract of the U.S.: 1974* (Washington, D.C.: U.S. Government Printing Office, 1975), p. 161.
8. Alan V. Sokolow, "The State of the Judiciary," *Book of the States, 1974–1975,* p. 119.
9. *Los Angeles Times,* Nov. 15, 1970, Sec. F, p. 3. Suggestion made by Judge Irving R. Kaufman, U.S. Court of Appeals, 2nd Circuit.
10. *U.S. News and World Report,* Dec. 14, 1970, pp. 32–33.
11. Sokolow, *Book of the States, 1974–1975,* p. 119.
12. Henry J. Abraham, *The Judicial Process* (New York: Oxford University Press, 1962), p. 94.
13. *Los Angeles Times,* Feb. 8, 1975, p. 19.
14. Leonard Downie, Jr., *Justice Denied* (New York: Praeger Publishers, Inc., 1971), pp. 18–33.
15. Abraham, pp. 157–58.
16. *United States* v. *California,* 332, U.S. 19 (1947).
17. *Los Angeles Times,* February 24, 1975, p. 4.
18. William L. Frederick, "State Judicial Systems," *Book of the States, 1970–1971,* pp. 117–18, and Sokolow, *Book of the States, 1974–1975,* pp. 115–16.
19. Herbert Jacob, *Justice in America,* 2nd ed. (Boston: Little, Brown and Co., 1972), p. 177.
20. *Book of the States, 1974–1975,* p. 121.
21. Alaska, California, Colorado, Delaware, Hawaii, Iowa, Kansas, Maine, Maryland, Massachusetts, Missouri, Nebraska, New Hampshire, New Jersey, Oklahoma, and Utah.
22. *Book of the States, 1974–1975,* pp. 130–32.
23. Alabama, Arkansas, Florida, Georgia, Illinois, Indiana, Louisiana, Mississippi, New Mexico, New York, North Carolina, Pennsylvania, Tennessee, Texas, and West Virginia.
24. Arizona, Idaho, Kentucky, Michigan, Minnesota, Montana, Nevada, North Dakota, Ohio, Oregon, South Dakota, Washington, Wisconsin, and Wyoming.
25. Stuart S. Nagel, "Political Party Affiliation and Judges' Decisions," *American Political Science Review* 55 (December 1961): 843–50.
26. Henry J. Abraham, *The Judiciary,* 3rd ed. (Boston: Allyn and Bacon, 1973), p. 123, and *Los Angeles Times,* April 23, 1975, p. 1.

27. In Kansas, for example, of the 309 district court judges seeking reelection between 1930 and 1956, less than 40 percent were opposed and fewer than 8 percent defeated. Duane Lockard, *The Politics of State and Local Government,* 2nd ed. (New York: The Macmillan Co., 1969), p. 451.

28. *Book of the States, 1974–1975,* pp. 538–87.

29. *Statistical Abstract of the U.S., 1974,* p. 159.

30. Much of the material in this section, somewhat updated, has come from Abraham, pp. 47–81.

31. John R. Schmidhauser, *The Supreme Court* (New York: Holt, Rinehart & Winston, 1961), pp. 77–91.

32. Henry J. Abraham, *The Judiciary* (Boston: Allyn and Bacon, 1965), p. 96.

33. *Los Angeles Times,* April 19, 1970, Sec. E, p. 3.

34. Charles P. Curtis, *Lions Under the Throne* (Boston: Houghton Mifflin Co., 1947), p. 281.

35. 297 U.S. 288 (1935).

36. Glendon A. Schubert, *Constitutional Politics* (New York: Holt, Rinehart & Winston, 1960), p. 159.

37. *Los Angeles Times,* Aug. 4, 1974, p. 20.

38. For a few concrete examples, see Jethro K. Lieberman, *How the Government Breaks the Law* (Baltimore: Penguin Books, 1973), pp. 57–66.

39. James P. Levine and Theodore L. Becker, "Toward and Beyond a Theory of Supreme Court Impact," *American Behavioral Scientist* 13:4 (March/April 1970), pp. 561–73.

Bibliography

CHAPTER TEN   THE LEGISLATIVE BRANCH

Burns, John. *The Sometime Governments: A Critical Study of the 50 American State Legislatures.* New York: Bantam Books, 1971.
Clapp, Charles L. *The Congressman: His Work as He Sees It.* Garden City, N.Y.: Anchor Books, Doubleday & Co., 1963.
Crane, Wilder, Jr., and **Watts, Meredith W., Jr.,** *State Legislative Systems.* Englewood Cliffs, N.J.: Prentice-Hall, 1968.
Davidson, Roger H. *The Role of the Congressman.* New York: Pegasus, The Bobbs-Merrill Co., 1969.
Froman, Lewis A., Jr. *The Congressional Process: Strategies, Rules, and Procedures.* Boston: Little, Brown and Co., 1967.
Green, Mark J., et al. *Who Runs Congress?* New York: Bantam Books, 1972.
Keefe, William J., and **Ogul, Morris S.** *The American Legislative Process: Congress and the States,* 2nd ed. Englewood Cliffs, N.J.; Prentice-Hall, 1968.
Wahlke, John C. et al. *The Legislative System.* New York: John Wiley & Sons, 1962.

CHAPTER ELEVEN   THE EXECUTIVE BRANCH

Corwin, Edward S. *The President: Office and Powers,* 4th ed. New York: New York University Press, 1957.
Koenig, Louis W. *The Chief Executive,* rev. ed. New York: Harcourt Brace Jovanovich, 1968.
N.A. *Book of the States.* Lexington, Ky.: Council of State Governments. Published biennially.
N.A. *U.S. Government Manual.* Washington, D.C.: U.S. Government Printing Office. Published biennially.
Neustadt, Richard E. *Presidential Power.* New York: John Wiley & Sons, 1960.
The Staff. *The New York Times. The End of a Presidency.* Toronto: Bantam Books, 1974.
Rossiter, Clinton. *The American Presidency,* rev. ed. New York: Harcourt Brace Jovanovich, 1960.
Sorensen, Theodore C. *Decision-Making in the White House.* New York: Columbia University Press, 1963.
Woll, Peter. *American Bureaucracy.* New York: W. W. Norton & Co., 1963.

CHAPTER TWELVE   THE JUDICIAL BRANCH

Abraham, Henry J. *The Judicial Process,* 2nd ed. New York: Oxford University Press, 1968.
Friedman, Leon, and **Israel, Fred L.,** eds. *The Justices of the United States Supreme Court 1789 – 1969.* New York: R. R. Bowker Co., 1969.

Jackson, Robert H. *The Supreme Court in the American System of Government.* New York: Harper & Row, 1955.

Jacob, Herbert. *Justice in America: Courts, Lawyers, and the Judicial Process,* 2nd ed. Boston: Little, Brown and Co., 1972.

Jacob, Herbert, ed. *Law, Politics, and the Federal Courts.* Boston: Little, Brown and Co., 1967.

Roche, John P., and **Levy, Leonard W.,** eds. *The Judiciary.* New York: Harcourt Brace Jovanovich, 1964.

Schmidhauser, John R. *The Supreme Court.* New York: Holt, Rinehart & Winston, 1961.

PART FIVE

THE PEOPLE
AND PUBLIC POLICY

Politics: Who Gets What, When, How
Harold Lasswell

The final payoffs, the ultimate outputs of the entire political system, are the policies made and enforced by government bodies. These policies profoundly affect the quality of our lives. They are the only really persuasive reasons for studying politics at all. No one book, let alone a single chapter, can describe or evaluate all such policies. What follows, therefore, is a brief analysis of the policy-making process and three illustrations of the kinds of government programs that have resulted from it. Specifically, we shall discuss "victimless crimes," labor-management relations, and the Central Intelligence Agency. Along the way, there is an examination of taxation policy, without which most other public policies would be impossible.

13 POWER, PEOPLE, AND POLICIES

The final end of Government is not to exert restraint but to do good.

Rufus Choate

At the beginning of this exploration of American politics, power was defined as the ability to change socially significant behavior. The government, examined in Part Four, possesses more of this power than any other institution. It exercises its power through decisions which help some groups get more of the good things in life—money, education, health, safety, etc.— than others. Such decisions, influenced by the pressure groups, political parties, and election processes described in Part Three, constitute public policy. In fact, an enormous range of behavior is encompassed by public policy. It includes supplying food stamps, fighting wars, running schools, building roads, prosecuting criminals, collecting taxes, and financing medical care for the elderly. Before looking at a few examples of such public policy, we will first examine some of the ways in which it can be studied and, perhaps, understood.

THE POLICY-MAKING PROCESS

Political scientists with different interests look at government, or public, policy in different ways. As we noted in Chapter 1, some are elitists who believe that most policies are controlled by the same small, educated, well-to-do elite. Others feel that policy-making is pluralistic, with different groups determining different policies and many programs resulting from compromise among several groups with conflicting preferences. Those who contend that a single elite group determines all public policy seem to underestimate two important considerations. One is the decentralization of government power in a federal system operating over an immense continent. The second is that public policy ranges over such a variety of subjects that a specialization of interests is probable and a specialization of knowledge is inevitable. An elite group of insurance executives, for example, may influence policy regarding no-fault auto insurance and medicare. But it will have relatively little information about, or concern with, policy on oil imports or drug abuse.

How Is Policy Made?

Another perspective focuses not so much on who has the greatest influence on policy, but on the factors that are taken into account when making it. Robert Dahl, a distinguished political scientist, has suggested five such considerations: (1) available choices or alternatives, (2) the consequences or effects of each alternative, (3) the importance or value of the effects of each choice, (4) the probability that such effects will actually take place, and (5) the willingness of the persons making the decision to risk taking a chance when the effects are uncertain.[1]

These considerations, for example, might be applied to a decision regarding the problem of inflation in the following way: (1) Among the various choices available to a member of Congress are the establishment of price controls, a cut in government expenditures to reduce the amount of money that people can spend, or no action of any kind. (2) The consequences of price controls might include the loss of some campaign contributions from business interests at the next election, as well as an illegal black market. A cut in expenditures might result in increased unemployment and weakened national defense due to the cancellation of government contracts. No action might result in even worse inflation and the loss of votes at the next election. (3) The relative importance of each of these effects will depend on each lawmaker's political and personal values and goals. Is government already meddling too much in the economy? Is it important that "we keep ahead of the Russians" in the number of submarines or tanks? Is getting reelected more important than voting one's convictions? (4) In estimating the likelihood that any of the possible consequences might take place, the senator or representative is engaging in uncertain prophecy. He may think it somewhat unlikely that a vote for price controls will cost him many campaign contributions, for example. But he may believe it highly probable that a cut in government spending would throw thousands of people out of work. (5) He may well make a choice on the basis of his psychological tendency to take a gamble. Price controls may seem to him to involve the least undesirable risks, while at the same time offering the best chance of curbing inflation. Although this brief analysis of inflation omits more than it includes, it indicates the enormous complexities involved in the decision-making process.

What Are the Goals of Public Policy?

Decisions regarding specific policies frequently entail means, not ends. They are merely methods by which certain broad objectives or goals may—with luck—be attained. These goals, in turn, are affected by broad ethical standards regarding what is "good" or "just." They are also affected by personal priorities identifying the values that are most important to the individual. Usually, of course, the values that one loves most are the same as those one believes to be ethically best.

Harold Lasswell, who has probably influenced political science as much as anyone alive, has classified values into eight categories. For Lasswell and many other political scientists, the process by which the government distributes these values among the people is what politics is all about. These values are listed below, with just a few of the public policies corresponding to them.

1. *Power* (decisions involving prison sentences, military service, wars, government jobs, licenses, and permits).
2. *Respect* (decisions involving civil rights laws, patriotic customs, proclamations, and awards).
3. *Rectitude* (decisions involving moral issues such as gambling, abortion, the death penalty, and famine relief).
4. *Affection* (decisions involving marriage, adoption, and child custody laws).
5. *Wealth* (unemployment benefits, social security pensions, government contracts, and taxation).
6. *Well-being* (medicare, military defense, product safety laws, and police protection).
7. *Enlightenment* (regulation of radio and television and public colleges).
8. *Skill* (vocational education, man-power training programs, and public schools).[2]

Since people differ about the relative importance of these values, political conflict occurs when government decisions are made regarding them. This is especially true when there is not enough money to satisfy everyone. Should more funds be appropriated for old-age pensions, the armed forces, or energy development? These are hard choices and require some agreement on the priorities assigned to each of them.

One way to find out what values a society cherishes most is to look at where the government spends its money. Budgets, in other words, are a means of establishing the relative importance of various goals. Figure 13–1 provides the most comprehensive evidence available on American budget priorities. Certainly, total government spending is a major factor in distributing the things people want among the entire population. In sending his 1976 budget proposals to Congress, President Ford noted that all government expenditure "now makes up a third of our national output."[3] Federal spending alone accounts for 22 percent.

Figure 13-1. TOTAL NATIONAL, STATE, AND LOCAL GOVERNMENTAL EXPENDITURES, 1972

Rank	Function	Amount[1]
1	Armed Forces	$75.2
2	Education	70.0
3	Old-age pensions, survivors and disability benefits, and health insurance (medicare)	46.9
4	Public welfare	23.6
5	Interest on general debt	23.1
6	Highways	19.4
7	Natural resources	14.2
8	Hospitals	12.6
9	Postal service	9.4
10	Government employee retirement benefits	8.6
11	Veterans' services	6.9
12	Police protection	6.5
13	Housing and urban renewal	5.4
14	Unemployment compensation	4.9
15	Sanitation and sewerage	4.7
16	Health	4.4
17	Space research and technology	3.4
18	Local fire protection	2.6
19	Local parks and recreation	2.3
20	Other	49.2
	Total	$397.4

[1] In billions of dollars
Source: U.S. Bureau of the Census, *The Statistical Abstract of the United States: 1974*, pp. 223 and 246.

Taxation: Who Pays the Bill?

To carry out public policy imposes a heavy tax burden on the American people. Because it is heavier for some than for others, tax policy as well as government expenditure tends to redistribute one important value—wealth— among the people. The distinction between progressive and regressive taxes is a crucial one in this regard.

Progressive Taxes

A progressive tax takes a higher and higher percentage of earnings as income increases. It thereby reduces income differences. The graduated income tax is the most widely used progressive tax. It produces more revenue for the national government than any other source. In addition, it is imposed by all but ten states. The federal income tax rates are steeply progressive, ranging from 14 percent for a taxable income of less than $2000 to 70 percent for an income of over $100,000.[4] A 1972 poll found that people believed it to be the fairest of all taxes.[5]

Figure 13–2. PRINCIPAL SOURCES OF NATIONAL GOVERNMENT TAX REVENUE

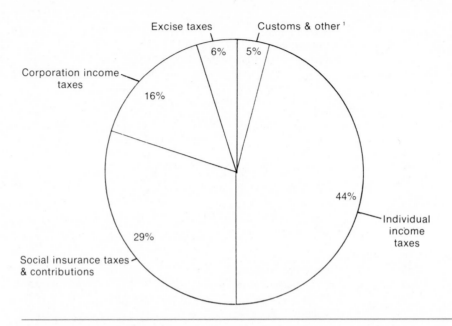

1974 Est.

Excise taxes — 6%
Customs & other[1] — 5%
Corporation income taxes — 16%
44% — Individual income taxes
29% — Social insurance taxes & contributions

[1]Other includes estate and gift taxes and other receipts.
Source: U.S. Bureau of the Census. Data from U.S. Office of Management and Budget. *Statistical Abstract of the United States: 1974*, p. 220.

Yet the income tax structure is far less progressive than it looks because of loopholes. These provide tax exemptions and tax the income from certain kinds of investments less heavily than income from wages. Amidst revelations that 156 Americans who earned over $200,000 a year had paid no income taxes in 1967, Congress passed a tax reform act in 1969.[6] In spite of the new changes, the next year, 56 of the 1203 persons who had adjusted gross incomes of more than $1 million still paid no federal income taxes.[7] According to a former Assistant Secretary of the Treasury, the income tax rate actually paid by all those with incomes exceeding $1 million averages 33 percent.[8]

Among the most important deductions providing tax shelters or loopholes are interest on municipal bonds, exemptions for business entertainment expenses, and most capital-gains income derived from profits on the sale of stock or real estate. If income from capital gains alone were taxed at the same rate as wages, it would produce $14 billion of additional revenue.[9]

Regressive Taxes
A regressive tax is just the opposite of a progressive one. It takes a higher

percentage of low incomes than of high ones. The chief example is the sales tax. This revenue source provides more money for state governments than any other, and is imposed by all but five states.[10] Such taxes require a person making $4000 a year to pay as much as one earning $400,000 each time he buys a gallon of gas or a bar of soap. Put differently, a truly progressive tax is based on ability to pay. A regressive tax is not.

Another example of a regressive tax is the excise tax. This is a specialized sales tax levied by both national and state governments on such items as liquor, cigarettes, gasoline, and cosmetics. Payroll tax deductions for social security benefits are also regressive. When hospital and nursing home care for senior citizens was added to social security coverage and retirement pensions were increased, the taxes needed to meet the cost of these programs tripled in just ten years. In 1975, social security taxes were levied at a rate of 5.85 percent of a worker's salary, matched by an identical tax on the employer, on the first $14,100 earned. Above that amount, no matter how much more an employee might earn each year, the social security tax bite would remain the same. Some economists are concerned not only about the regressive nature of these taxes, but also about the lower birth rate and growing unemployment rate. They are fearful that these might result in too few workers to produce the taxes necessary to pay benefits for those already retired. A few have suggested that the program might be better financed, at least in part, from general tax revenue.

Figure 13–3. PRINCIPAL SOURCES OF STATE AND LOCAL GOVERNMENT REVENUE. 1972

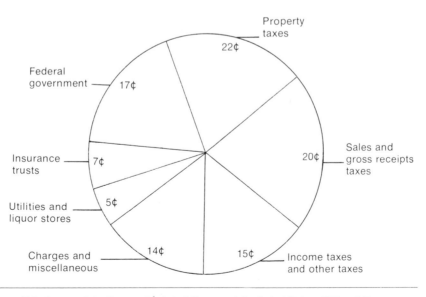

Property taxes 22¢

Federal government — 17¢

Insurance trusts — 7¢

Utilities and liquor stores — 5¢

Charges and miscellaneous — 14¢

Income taxes and other taxes 15¢

Sales and gross receipts taxes 20¢

Source: U.S. Bureau of the Census. *Statistical Abstract of the United States: 1974*, p. 243.

Just as the national government relies primarily on the income tax and state governments on the sales tax, so the financial pillar for cities and counties is the property tax. It too is regressively applied. Among all taxes, the property tax was voted "least fair" by a landslide margin in a government-authorized public opinion poll.[11]

The principle of taxation based on ability to pay is violated not only by· regressive taxes, but also by the differing tax burdens imposed in various parts of the nation. The amount of state and local taxes paid on each $1000 of personal income recently ranged from a low of $97.83 in Alaska and $100.71 in Ohio to a high of $155.51 in Wisconsin and $157.88 in New York.[12]

Tax Reform

From city halls to the corridors of Congress, demands for tax reform reached a peak in the early 1970s. There are three explanations for this outcry. In the first place, the combined taxes of all levels of government nearly doubled between 1960 and 1970. They rose from $711 per person to $1348.[13] About two-thirds of this went to the U.S. Treasury and the remainder to state and local governments. Second, it became increasingly apparent that the middle class, the great workhorse of the American economy, was saddled with the heaviest tax burden. The poor received government benefits far exceeding the taxes they paid. The rich were reaping most of the benefits of tax loopholes and exemptions. Thirdly, the need for reform gained greater public impact when it was revealed that President Nixon paid federal income taxes of only $878.03 in 1971 on an income exceeding $250,000. Certain deductions he had claimed, however, were later declared illegal, and he agreed to pay over $430,000 in back taxes and penalties.

Borrowing Money

President Ford proposed a 1976 budget in which the income of the national government was expected to fall nearly $52 billion short of expenditures. It was the largest deficit in peacetime history. Like people, governments can spend more money than they receive only by borrowing money. Governments do this by selling bonds. The cost of this debt is the interest that must be paid on these bonds. Some of the national government's debt is owed to the Federal Reserve System. However, most of its bonds are owned by corporations and private individuals. In one of its more futile gestures, Congress has placed a legal limit on the national debt, but raises the ceiling whenever the debt approaches it. Unlike federal deficit spending, state and local indebtedness must frequently be authorized by special procedures, such as a vote of the people.

SOCIAL POLICY: "VICTIMLESS" CRIMES

How small of all that human hearts endure,
That part which laws or kings can cause or cure!
                                        Samuel Johnson

As indicated in Chapter 12, an enormous amount of time is spent by prosecutors and judges at both the national and state levels on so-called victimless crimes. These are the crimes such as prostitution, marijuana possession, and illegal gambling that produce no complaints to the police by the people involved. Yet the laws relating to these crimes are among the most controversial public policies because enforcement of them not only overloads our criminal justice system but also touches off bitter disputes regarding personal morality. They bring government into the most intimate areas of human behavior and as a result they are among the most difficult laws to enforce. Moreover, while the crimes in question may have no victim, many argue that they victimize the entire society in ways suggested later. This applies also to the use of drugs such as cigarettes and alcohol which are not normally crimes but which may still victimize large numbers of people.

Although public policy in this area is subject primarily to state regulation, the national government has substantial authority over it. This is the case whenever such crime involves taxation, use of the mail, or interstate (and sometimes foreign) commerce. Most pertinent criminal statutes are passed by state legislatures, but in some states "local option" permits cities or counties to decide such matters for themselves.

The first important question involves the influences which determine public policy in the area of victimless crimes. Any answer must begin with the standards of rectitude or morality which are so important a value in the American political culture. These standards are largely derived from the religious doctrines of Puritanism which took a dim view of people who placed too much emphasis on personal pleasure. Sexual activity outside the marriage was viewed as especially sinful.

But traditional moral codes have undergone substantial change in recent times. As a result, there are many people who urge repeal of the victimless crime laws. These people tend to fall into three groups. First there are those, liberal and relatively young in most cases, who see nothing immoral in activities which involve no force or fraud and seem to harm no one else. The second group, which includes some conservatives, consists of people who fear tyranny from any government that attempts to interfere with personal behavior which they regard as their own business. Finally there are the pornography publishers, "pot" pushers, and would-be casino operators who wish to get rich. "You can't legislate morality" is their frequent battle cry.

We are dealing with social policies, therefore, which involve health, morality, money, and the proper scope of government power. That is why they generate such explosive controversy.

Drug Cultures

Nearly all societies, ancient as well as modern, have developed drugs to seek pleasure or escape pain. Many times governments have been called upon to regulate or prohibit their use. With changing tastes and technological advances, different people have come to prefer different drugs. In contemporary America, not surprisingly, those that appeal most to the old are legal, while some favored by the young are not.

Tobacco

The health hazards of tobacco were identified in the late 1850s. But no serious attempts to obtain governmental control were launched until this century. In 1964 the Surgeon General of the U.S. issued a report, *Smoking and Health,* which documented its dangers. In 1966 under the leadership of Senator Maurine Neuberger (D–Ore.), the national government required cigarette packs to bear the words, "Caution: Cigarette Smoking May Be Hazardous to Your Health." In 1971 this inscription was strengthened to read, "Warning: The Surgeon General Has Determined That Cigarette Smoking Is Dangerous to Your Health." Cigarette advertising was also banned on television, which had earned 8 percent of its revenue from this source. Many believe that it should be prohibited completely.

There is overwhelming evidence to justify such action. Abnormal lung cells have been identified in 93.2 percent of smokers and in only 1.2 percent of nonsmokers. Heart disease and respiratory ailments also seem related to cigarettes. Moreover, the total death rate "for male smokers between the ages of 45 and 64 is twice as high as that for nonsmokers."[14] But government attempts to discourage smoking have powerful enemies. These include the tobacco farmers, cigarette manufacturers, advertising companies, and the magazines which derive advertising revenue from them.

Among men, the proportion of cigarette smokers has dropped a little in recent years, to about 40 percent. Among women it has remained fairly constant at about 30 percent. But from 1968 to 1972 smoking among boys 12 to 17 years old increased from 11.5 to 12.8 percent and among girls of the same age it nearly doubled, from 6.2 to 11.3 percent.[15]

The smoking issue acquired a new dimension of both medical and political significance in 1972 when the U.S. Surgeon General reported that even nonsmokers might suffer ill effects if they were exposed to smoke in confined areas. The political response to this new evidence was the passage of laws in Arizona, Nebraska, Oregon, and Connecticut which prohibited smoking in elevators or certain public meetings. New York City; Wichita, Kansas; Charlotte, North Carolina; and Newton, Massachusetts enacted similar ordinances. Although the antismoking forces were clearly on the offensive, the new laws were generally not enforced every effectively.[16] Moreover, tobacco farmers demonstrated their political power in 1974 by gaining a guarantee of 100 percent of their gasoline needs from the Federal Energy Administrator, even though ambulances and police cars might have to settle for smaller allocations.[17]

Tobacco usage illuminates the difficult distinction between personal and social morality. If a nicotine addict with a dependent wife and several young children dies of lung cancer caused by smoking, is he not a social menace?

Does government have a responsibility to protect his family from his folly? Such questions strike at the heart of the politics of personal morality. They also involve a wide range of political decision-making because government policy with respect to smoking is affected by congressional legislation, state and federal taxes, labeling requirements by the Federal Trade Commission, scientific analysis by the Surgeon General in the Department of Health, Education and Welfare, advertising controls by the Federal Communications Commission, and—ironically—various kinds of assistance to tobacco farmers by the Department of Agriculture.

Alcohol

Beers, wines, and liquors are among the oldest beverages known to man. Their use is more widespread than tobacco, less addictive or habit-forming, but with far more serious social consequences. Alcoholism is a disease that plagues about four percent of the American population—a number exceeding the population of New York City. In 1973, the National Commission on Marijuana and Drug Abuse called it "without question . . . the most serious drug problem in the country today."[18] In 1974, a Gallup poll showed that 68 percent of all adults drink at least occasionally, up from a low of 55 percent in 1958. It was the highest figure recorded in 35 years of polling on the subject.[19] More alarming was the growing popularity of alcohol among juveniles. According to one study in Brookline, Mass., an "upper-middle-class Boston suburb," 14 percent of sixth-graders and 36 percent of eighth-graders said they have been drunk.[20]

Alcohol has attracted far more political attention than cigarettes. The prohibition movement, designed to outlaw the sale of alcoholic beverages, was led by Methodists and Baptists. It resulted in the ratification of the Eighteenth Amendment to the Constitution shortly after World War I. By 1933,

Figure 13–4. USE OF ALCOHOLIC BEVERAGES, 1974

Category	Percentage of Users	Category	Percentage of Users
Men	76	$20,000 and over	88
Women	61	$15,000–19,999	78
Under 30 years	79	$10,000–14,999	64
30–49 years	75	$7,000–9,999	58
50 years and older	54	$5,000–6,999	57
		Under $5,000	46
East	78		
Midwest	75	Protestants	61
South	51	Catholics	83
West	70		

Source: Gallup Poll, *Los Angeles Times*, June 9, 1974, p. 19.

however, the Twenty-first Amendment repealed the Eighteenth. Americans had participated in a classic example of a government's inability to administer public policy in the face of widespread public defiance. When a law loses too much authority, there is too little force to compel obedience to it. Prohibition, however, remained in effect in some states for many years. Even now many local governments have exercised the option to remain "dry."

While the old-time prohibition movement has lost most of its momentum, alcoholic beverages remain an important concern of government policy. Liquor advertisements are banned from radio and television. State laws fix licensing requirements for dealers or restrict retail distribution through state-owned liquor stores. Sales are limited to certain hours and in some areas forbidden entirely on Sundays and election days. All 50 states tax the sale of alcoholic beverages. This revenue, plus the tax on tobacco products, swells their treasuries by an annual total of $22 for every human being in the nation.[21]

Marijuana
Regardless of its other effects, "pot," "grass," or whatever else marijuana might be called, has provoked bitter controversies. Out of these disputes, however, one can extract a few broad areas of agreement.

1. Unlike tobacco and alcohol, its use is illegal. There is a trend, however, to reduce simple possession (in contrast to selling) from a felony to a misdemeanor. This was recommended by the American Medical Association in a reversal of its previous, more punitive stand.[22] In 1972, the National Commission on Marijuana and Drug Abuse recommended that laws prohibiting private possession for personal use be repealed. But President Nixon, who appointed most of the commission members, rejected that proposal. In 1973, the American Bar Association also passed a resolution urging "decriminalization" of simple marijuana possession. The same year Oregon became the first state to do just that. A new law there placed possession of up to one ounce a mere "violation," no more serious than a traffic offense, punishable by a maximum fine of $100.[23]
2. Marijuana may not be physically addictive and does not require increasingly greater amounts to feel its effect.[24]
3. "The principal danger is that one may become psychologically dependent on marijuana and, instead of coping with everyday problems, withdraw through frequent use of the drug."[25] In addition, there is some recent evidence that heavy usage by young males may cause sterility, and that heavy usage by pregnant women may endanger the fetus.
4. Use of marijuana is widespread. Estimates of the number of Americans who have "gone to pot" at least once range from 12 to 25 million. The number of arrests for drug offenses, mostly involving marijuana,

increased 291 percent between 1967 and 1972, a larger jump than for any other type of crime.[26] Gallup polls reveal that most Americans still oppose easing marijuana penalties. But the National Organization for the Reform of Marijuana Laws (NORML) has become a more effective pressure group in working toward that objective.

Several problems seem to complicate intelligent political action in this field. One is that early reports of the dangers of marijuana were undoubtedly exaggerated. This produced a "credibility gap" which led young people to disregard more accurate warnings against harder drugs. While pot is not a narcotic by scientific analysis, it is legally classified as such. Among the users themselves, however, few report any ill effects. A second problem stems from a comparison of marijuana with tobacco and alcohol. Young people feel that it is hypocritical to legalize the latter, while prohibiting the former. Some older persons, on the other hand, argue that although the dangers of pot are no greater than cigarettes and liquor, two wrongs don't make a right. Why compound the existing evils, they ask, by condoning still another?

The Hard Stuff

The new drug culture includes not only marijuana but also other, more dangerous drugs. Many of these are legally available only when prescribed by a licensed physician.

Amphetamines (stimulants) are a good example. They are pep pills or "uppers" and aid in the treatment of fatigue, obesity, and certain mental disorders. "Speed," or Methedrine, is a variety of upper often used to dangerous excess. Accumulated tolerance to these drugs seems to require increased dosages to obtain the desired effect. Excessive amounts can cause nervousness, insomnia, and delusions. Barbiturates are depressant drugs, or "downers," widely used as sleeping pills. They produce physical dependence and overdoses may be fatal. Hallucinogenic or psychedelic drugs are unavailable by prescription and are sometimes said to produce the wildest "turn on," the farthest "trip" of all. With the use of LSD, for example, vivid colors appear and sound and perspective are distorted. Most dangerously, acute feelings of fear may develop, along with severe mental illness.[27] Peyote and mescaline are milder varieties of hallucinogens. Some observers believe that cocaine was the addictive drug increasing in use most rapidly in 1975.

The nearly 100,000 narcotics addicts in the nation in 1973 represent more than a 120 percent increase since 1960.[28] The vast majority are hooked on heroin, an escalating and illegal habit costing upwards of $40 a day. Theft is usually necessary to support such a habit. In 1971 it was reported that in New York City's twenty-fourth police precinct nearly two-thirds of the crime was connected with drugs.[29] The commission on drug abuse, mentioned earlier, has recommended that persons arrested for heroin and other illegal drugs be offered medical treatment rather than jail,[30] although this proposal has been widely ignored.

The Politics of Drugs

Charges have been made that manufacturers of cigarettes and wine have opposed the legalization of marijuana in order to freeze out competition. Similarly, some argue that financial greed has led drug companies and physicians to advocate sedatives and appetite suppressants that aid only a fraction of those who use them. As Dr. Daniel X. Freedman, chairman of the University of Chicago psychiatry department, put it: "We have to learn that we can't always take a pill to take care of our pain."[31] The liquor store clerk, neighborhood druggist, and family doctor may be the most dangerous pushers of all.

The Sexual Evolution

The middle-aged American is often staggered by recent changes in sexual behavior. Some colleges have established coeducational dormitories. Many young people live together openly before marrying. Prostitution (legal only in certain Nevada counties) flourishes in some cities under the guise of massage parlors. What does it all mean? The answers range from moral decay to a new dawn of frankness and freedom.

Sex has many political implications. Divorce cases crowd court calendars. Illegitimacy places additional burdens on welfare programs. Prostitution crackdowns consume police resources as well as newspaper headlines. Venereal disease frequently requires treatment by public health facilities. In addition, the differences are widening between the law and many kinds of sex relations, both in and out of marriage. Yet public debate has focused more on pornography than on the matters just mentioned.

Pornography

The best evidence of changing sex standards is found in the increased frequency with which nudity and erotic material is openly available to the interested public. Topless bars and stag movies have appeared in large urban centers and total nudity has made its debut on the American stage. Much of this development has been described in Chapter 4 in terms of recent court decisions. As sex became more commercial, however, many Americans were quick to demand other kinds of government control. Leading the antipornography forces was a pressure group called the Citizens for Decent Literature. In 1967 Congress responded to the growing controversy by creating the Commission on Obscenity and Pornography to study the problem and to make appropriate recommendations.

When this commission's report was issued three years later, the Senate rejected it by a vote of 60 to 5 and President Nixon denounced it strongly. "So long as I am in the White House," he stated, "there will be no relaxation of the national effort to . . . eliminate smut from our national life. . . . Pornography can corrupt a society. . . . It should be outlawed in every state in the union."[32] Seldom had a legally authorized scientific study been so thoroughly and promptly condemned by political leaders.

What did the commission recommend to prompt such protest? First it urged "that a massive sex education effort be launched . . . aimed, as appropriate, to all segments of our society, adults as well as children." This effort, it said, "should be a joint function of several institutions . . . . : family, school, church, etc." Absorbing most of the attack was the commission's recommendation that "legislation prohibiting the sale, exhibition, or distribution of sexual materials to consenting adults should be repealed."[33] The breadth of this proposal is indicated by the fact that it would affect antipornography laws in 48 states as well as several congressional statutes. Extensive studies, the commission concluded, show no significant relationship between exposure to erotic materials and crime, delinquency, deviant behavior, or emotional disturbance.[34]

While a majority of the American people may still disapprove of pornography, their number is rapidly diminishing. The percentage objecting to nudes in magazines dropped from 73 to 55 between 1969 and 1973. In the same period, those offended by topless waitresses dropped nearly as much, from 76 to 59 percent.[35]

The struggle between those who wish to enjoy sexually oriented entertainment and those fighting it is not easy to compromise. In 1974 Boston officials launched a novel experiment, however, by zoning a two-block strip in the downtown area as an "adult entertainment district." They hoped, as a result, to confine strip-tease shows, X-rated theaters, and adult bookstores to that part of the city.[36]

The "New Morality" .

Attitudes about sexual behavior are changing as rapidly as those about pornography—and much more rapidly than the law. The percentage of people who believed sex relations before marriage were "wrong" dropped by 20 points, from 68 to 48, between 1969 and 1973.[37] Yet in 1974 an unmarried policeman in Coral Gables, Florida, was suspended from the force for living with a female friend. The police chief justified the punishment by citing a 106-year-old state law against "cohabitation."[38] At about the same time, a Newark, New Jersey judge imposed a $50 fine on a man convicted of violating a 1796 law prohibiting single persons from having sexual relations.[39] Similar laws are seldom enforced but remain on the books in 22 states, along with criminal statutes against adultery in 40 states.[40] While there is no longer a moral consensus to support the authority of laws regulating sexual behavior, there are no pressure groups influential enough to get them repealed. As a result, most sex behavior takes place in a power vacuum, penetrated only by the force of an occasional police officer or prosecuting attorney.

Homosexuality

Another important indicator of changing attitudes has been the recent insistence of homosexuals upon equal treatment. Homosexuals have included an impressive number of distinguished men and women. But their private lives have been subjected to criminal prosecution in most nations throughout most of recent history. By and large, they have accepted this with fearful timidity as the price they must pay for their sexual "orientation." In the last few years, however, many "gay" people are demanding that legal discrimination against them be abolished.

They have enjoyed some limited success. Early in 1975, the city council in Portland, Oregon passed an ordinance prohibiting discrimination on the basis of sexual orientation in hiring city employees. The same year, the California legislature legalized all private sexual relations between consenting adults. A church-dominated pressure group threatened to try to repeal the legislation by taking the issue to the voters in a referendum election. In Massachusetts bills were introduced, with the support of the governor, to ban discrimination against homosexuals in employment and housing, and to legalize homosexual intercourse. They were authored by Rep. Elaine Noble (D–Boston), the first admittedly gay state legislator in the nation.[41]

The movement for "gay liberation" gained influential support in 1974 when the American Psychiatric Association voted to remove homosexuality from its list of "mental disorders."[42] Effective organization through such pressure groups as the Daughters of Bilitis has also helped further the gay cause. Its major obstacle, however, remains the influence of overwhelmingly hostile public opinion upon vote-hungry lawmakers. A Roper Organization poll of 3000 women in 1974 discovered that while 48 percent would accept a daughter who lived with a male outside marriage, 70 percent would *not* accept a daughter's homosexual relationship.[43] Public policy in this area affects an estimated seven million homosexual Americans, two-thirds male and one-third female.

Gambling

The gambling issue has become increasingly controversial as more and more states, hard pressed for additional revenue, view it as a lucrative source of potential taxes. New Hampshire, New York, and New Jersey succumbed to the temptation by authorizing state-run lotteries in the 1960s and at least 7 other states have followed suit.[44] New York City legalized offtrack betting in 1971. Racetrack betting produces $500 million annually for the 28 states that allow it. In Nevada, the only state with legal casinos, gambling defrays 40 percent of state expenses.[45]

Illegal gambling is a major source of money for organized crime. It resulted in more than 60,000 arrests in 1972, down 14 percent from 1967. By contrast, there were about 20,000 fewer arrests for prostitution than for gambling.[46]

Advocates of legalized betting repeat the familiar argument that this is a crime without a victim. But here again, the persistent voice of morality raises some questions: Does gambling not tempt the poor to squander money they cannot afford? Are not the families of losing gamblers the victims? If those families apply for welfare benefits, are not all taxpayers the victims?

ECONOMIC POLICY: LABOR-MANAGEMENT RELATIONS

Most Americans make their living by working for someone else. Relations between employees and employers are therefore of prime importance to the welfare of individual workers as well as to the health of the entire economy. As indicated in Figure 13–5, 8 percent of all working Americans represent employers, as managers or administrators, 90 percent are nonmanagement employees, while only 2 percent work for themselves. Increasingly, labor-management relations affect both sexes. The percentage of women working outside the home has increased steadily from 31 in 1950 to 44 in 1973. Among married women living with their husbands, the 42 percent holding jobs is more than double the 1950 figure.[47]

The Role of Government

The demand for government intervention in labor-management relations came from reformers concerned about frequent, often violent strikes which disrupted production and about oppressive working conditions as well. In 1914, for example, a strike in the Colorado coal fields led to the notorious "Ludlow Massacre." This attack on a miner's camp resulted in the deaths of 16 men, women, and children. In 1917 the average work week in factories ranged from 54 to 60 hours.[48] There are endless other examples of both intolerable working conditions and strike-inspired violence.

State governments were the first to pass legislation to help correct these conditions. Their interest has continued. In 1972–73 the states, according to one authority, "broke all prior records both in the number of labor laws

Figure 13–5. CHARACTERISTICS OF THE AMERICAN LABOR FORCE

	Year	Millions	Percentage
Total employed	1974	87.4	100
Civilian	1974	85.2	97
Armed forces	1974	2.2	3
Agricultural	1974	3.4	4
Nonagricultural	1974	84.0	96
Managers & administrators (nonagricultural)	1973	8.6	10
Self-employed	1973	1.7	2
Non-self-employed	1973	6.9	8
Nonmanagers & administrators (nonagricultural)	1973	75.8	90
Public sector (government) employees	1973	14.1	17
Private sector	1973	70.3	83
Employed by 500 largest industrial corporations	1973	15.5	18
Union membership	1972	20.9	26

Source: Computed from U.S. Bureau of the Census, *Statistical Abstract of the United States: 1974,* pp. 235, 265, 336, 350, 351, 486.

adopted and in diversity of subject matter."[49] Among other things, such legislation regulates how often wages must be paid and what deductions may be made from them, places restrictions on private employment agencies, and reduces hiring discrimination against the handicapped. The most important state labor legislation concerns compensation to workers injured on the job and to those collecting unemployment insurance.

Since the 1930s, however, the national government has been the dominant influence in the field of labor-management relations, especially on such issues as the right to join unions and to go out on strike. At both the state and national levels, statutory labor law determines general policy. But legislatures have delegated substantial rule-making authority to various administrative bodies. The major example is the National Labor Relations Board whose five members are appointed by the president. It determines such matters as who is guilty of unfair labor practices and which groups of employees constitute appropriate "bargaining units" for union representation.

Public policy in this area is usually a compromise between organized labor on one side and corporate business on the other. There are no issues on which the two major political parties are more often in disagreement. Democrats, of course, usually champion the cause of unions and Republicans defend the business position. The political struggles in this arena are the best refutation of those who contend that all policy results from the decisions of a single power elite.

Many values are affected by labor-management relations. Since it deals with jobs and salaries, the distribution of wealth is the paramount value. What should be the minimum wage? Should overtime work receive higher pay? What should be the wage scale for government employees? Yet the stakes are high with respect to other values as well. In terms of power, for example, collective bargaining contracts determine layoff policy. Should layoffs be based on seniority, as unions usually insist, or is it a "management prerogative" to decide which workers to let go? In most states, such contracts may also require employees to join a union. A sense of well-being is involved here, too. The general public feels insecure if a transit strike makes it difficult to get to work. Employees worry about receiving adequate pension benefits. Underlying these other values is respect, as important as it is intangible. The primary goal of working people, whether they are accountants in plush offices or machinists in grimy factories, is the self-respect which comes from some influence over the conditions under which they work. This, too, is affected by collective bargaining agreements and by whether strikes and worker boycotts have legal protection.

Wages, Hours, and Employment

Eight hours work, eight hours play,
Eight hours sleep and an eight hour day.
                              Old union slogan

Labor Laws

Government assistance to workers is comparatively recent. Attempts to regulate child labor had begun by the mid-1800s, but not until 1938 was it largely prohibited. Unfortunately, the prohibition has not been totally effective. In 1970 the Labor Department uncovered 13,000 violations of the child labor law—ranging from a Detroit motel to the Oregon berry fields.[50] Concern for the welfare of children was followed by attempts to protect women from excessively long hours of sweatshop labor. In 1908 the Supreme Court upheld an Oregon law regulating hours for working women.

The struggle to afford workingmen some of the same protection was more difficult. In part this was because of opposition by the Supreme Court. Not until the 1930s was the goal of an eight-hour day finally attained. In addition to a shorter workday, the major objective of industrial workers was decent pay. Massachusetts adopted a minimum wage law for women in 1912. But the Supreme Court, clinging to a laissez-faire interpretation of the Constitution, invalidated such laws in 1923.[51]

Finally, one of the most significant bills ever enacted by Congress, the Fair Labor Standards Act of 1938, incorporated all three of labor's major objectives: Child labor was outlawed, payment of time-and-a-half for work over 40 hours a week was required, and a minimum hourly wage was established. The Supreme Court, under heavy public pressure, surrendered to the needs of the twentieth century and upheld the law three years later.[52] It was an important beginning which laid the basis for future legislation embracing more workers and increasing the minimum wage, in many stages, to $2.30 an hour on January 1, 1976.

Unemployment

Work is deeply ingrained in the American character. The early New England Puritans imputed to it a dignity, even a moral virtue, which has permeated the nation. People identify strongly with their jobs. One thinks of oneself as "a carpenter," "an engineer," or "a housewife." President Nixon stressed this "work ethic" in his acceptance speech at the Republican National Convention in 1972. "Here in America," he said, "a person should get what he works for, and work for what he gets."

It was an embarrassment, therefore, that unemployment climbed to more than 9 percent in 1975. This was an old problem, however. Government · action to combat it began rather modestly with the establishment of a number of state employment offices. In 1933 a heavily Democratic Congress, confronted with the worst depression in history, passed the Wagner-Peyser Act. This act authorized the U.S. Employment Service in the Department of Labor to establish employment offices where none existed and to assist the states in financing them. Two years later, with unemployment still high, Congress passed the Social Security Act. In addition to providing pensions and other benefits, it established a system of unemployment compensation. The system was supported by federal funds but financed largely by state unemployment insurance taxes levied on employers. Benefits vary widely from state to state, with minimums ranging from $10 to $25 per week in 1973.[53] Congress may extend the number of weeks for which benefits are payable, as it did in 1974.

Congress has also financed vocational training programs such as the Job Corps, established as part of President Johnson's much heralded "war on poverty" in 1964. Proposals that the federal government itself become an "employer of last resort" have been acted upon only in times of high unemployment. During the 1930s thousands of workers were employed by the federal Works Progress Administration (WPA). In 1974 Congress appropriated funds to enable states and cities to give public employment to some of the jobless. In doing so, it took a small step forward in fulfilling the commitment made in the Employment Act of 1946. That law acknowledged the responsibility of the national government to take all practical steps to insure maximum employment.

The Sick or Injured Worker

All states now require employers, usually through their insurance companies, to provide compensation for workers disabled or killed as a result of some work-related accident or illness. These benefits are normally paid regardless of whether the worker was at fault. But they are so small in some states that demands arose for congressional legislation establishing minimum nationwide standards for workers' compensation.

As a result of massive union lobbying activity, Congress did enact the Occupational Safety and Health Act (OSHA) of 1970. This law made it illegal for an employer to permit "recognized hazards" to safety at his place of business. It also authorized the Secretary of Labor to draft detailed standards prohibiting other dangerous conditions. State governments were permitted to enforce their own regulations if they were at least as strict as the national ones. About half the states had done so by 1974. OSHA also provided for government medical research in the area of occupational diseases. The need for some action was indicated by the nearly 8 million workers injured on the job in 1972.

Private Pension Plans

The first important legislation approved by President Ford, signed on Labor Day 1974, was a pension reform act covering 35 million workers. It did not require all employers to provide pension plans. But it protected retirement benefits for the employees of those who did. Specifically, it guaranteed a minimum pension for such employees if they worked for the company at least five years and it required that money be set aside by the employer for that purpose.

Strikes and Collective Bargaining

Since a strike is a work stoppage by a group of employees, it is clearly impossible unless those employees are organized, formally or informally, in some sort of labor union. Until 1842, however, strikes were considered criminal conspiracies. Long after that, they were often broken by viciously enforced court injunctions. To prohibit strikes was to deprive workers of their only influence—the ability to withhold their labor. This often subjected them to whatever terms their employers might dictate. As a result, union influence was weakened drastically as long as antistrike injunctions could be justified as necessary to protect corporation property or eliminate a "restraint of trade."

The Norris-La Guardia Act, passed by Congress in 1932, represented the first important protection for the union movement in America. It outlawed "yellow dog" job contracts, which denied workers their right to join a union. In addition, it prohibited the use of court injunctions in most strikes. Three years later, this law was reinforced by the passage of the Wagner Act (the National Labor Relations Act). It required that whenever a majority of the employees of a company wished to be represented by a labor union, the company had to bargain with that union regarding wages, hours, and working conditions. Unions were legally empowered to sign contracts for all the workers collectively. It is important to note that stockholders were bargaining collectively, through corporation management, well before workers balanced the industrial scales by bargaining collectively through unions.

The Wagner Act also created the National Labor Relations Board to prohibit unfair labor practices. The Board was also authorized to conduct elections to determine which union, if any, the workers wished to have as their bargaining agent. As a result of this legislation many contracts were signed that provided for a *union shop* in which workers were required to join the union within several months after they had been hired. Occasionally, contracts established a *closed shop* instead, requiring the employer to hire only those who were already union members.

After World War II, a wave of unpopular strikes led a Republican-controlled Congress to pass the Taft-Hartley Act over President Truman's veto. It authorized the president to obtain a court injunction to prevent workers from striking for 80 days if he felt a strike would create a national emergency. The law also made closed shop contracts unenforceable. It permitted the states (in its controversial Section 14b) to forbid union shop contracts as well. On the assumption that no one should be forced to join a union, 20 states exercised this option by banning the union shop through "right to work" laws. Opponents of these laws contend that union membership is not too much to require of those benefiting from union negotiations. The Taft-Hartley Act also prohibited contribution of union dues to political campaigns. In 1959, in the wake of publicity over labor-racketeering scandals, the Landrum-Griffin Act required unions to submit annual financial reports to the Department of Labor and to guarantee a secret ballot in the election of the union officers.

The Politics of Labor-Management Relations

Favorable congressional legislation is the major prize in the endless tug of war between labor and management. During the last 50 years of struggle labor has improved its position enormously. Its most notable victories have been the passage of the Norris-La Guardia Act, the Wagner Act, the Fair Labor Standards Act, and the Occupational Safety and Health Act.

Labor's chief political weapons include union campaign contributions and the effectiveness of union lobbying. The AFL-CIO has a staff of seven full-time lobbyists in Washington, D.C. It is headed by Andrew J. Biemiller, a former two-term congressman from Wisconsin who has become such a fixture in capitol politics that he is sometimes called "the 436th representative."[54]

Management's record, however, is far better than it at first appears. In addition to the passage of the Taft-Hartley and Landrum-Griffin Acts, it can claim major credit for the defeat of many bills favored by labor. These include measures that would have established a guaranteed annual income, a consumer protection agency, and national health insurance. Indeed, congressional procedures which make it so difficult to pass new laws are major assets skillfully used by business lobbyists to block reforms advocated by unions. Among the most influential of business lobbyists is Hilton Davis of the U.S. Chamber of Commerce. He heads a Washington staff which includes "three legislative counsels, about 45 issues managers and four professionals in the legislative action section."[55] The Chamber keeps business interests informed about pending legislation. It encourages letters to legislators through a weekly paper sent to 30,000 of its members.

The victory of either union or business lobbyists on a particular issue before Congress depends on many factors. Several of these are illustrated by labor's success in obtaining the passage of a bill increasing the minimum hourly wage from 75 cents to $1 in 1955, compared with its failure to prevent the passage of the Landrum-Griffin Act in 1959.[56] One of the most important factors in 1955 was the general political climate. In the 1954 elections, labor-endorsed candidates won an increased number of seats in Congress. Moreover, President Eisenhower had proposed a raise in the minimum wage to 90 cents an hour in his 1955 State of the Union message. Finally, prevailing public opinion was sympathetic to the union position as a result of recent increases in the cost of living.

By contrast, labor was confronted with an unfavorable political climate in 1959 when widely publicized reports of union corruption led to the passage of the Landrum-Griffin Act. Moreover, while union leadership was badly divided on legislative tactics in 1959, there was unified action on the 1955 minimum wage bill. It was spearheaded by the close cooperation of four unions in the textile industry. There was another important difference in the two situations. On the minimum wage, unions were willing to compromise on $1 an hour, less than the $1.25 they had advocated but more than the 90 cents the President had recommended. The Landrum-Griffin Act, however, was worse from the point of view of labor leaders than a more satisfactory bill that would probably have passed had several top union officials been more flexible.[57]

Two other factors were crucial in the minimum wage victory. One was an informal coalition with members of Congress from agricultural areas. Because of labor support for legislation favored by farmers, unions were able to win support from the farm bloc on the minimum wage increase. This is similar to a vote-trading process known as "logrolling." It is most frequently used in gaining the passage of "pork barrel" legislation which provides money for some government project that benefits a particular region or district rather than a larger area or the country as a whole. Members of Congress frequently trade votes to support each other's pork barrel measures, and lobbyists have also found this logrolling technique very effective.

The final factor which clinched labor's success was the choice of the right pressure-group strategy. Unions could have concentrated their lobbying activity on lawmakers who were undecided. This group included 23 senators whose votes were essential. Or they could have directed their influence toward all senators and representatives, as well as toward the president. They chose the latter course for a number of reasons. Legislators who favored the bill were contacted by union lobbyists so they could be prepared with better arguments to convince their undecided colleagues. Those who opposed the bill or were doubtful about its merits were bombarded with letters from workers. They could use such letters to explain a prounion vote to their more conservative constituents. Labor lobbyists had an additional reason for urging union members to write their senators and representatives. They wished to convert the minimum wage campaign, as one lobbyist put it, "into one great class in civics" for workers throughout the nation.[58] In addition, during the 1955 Easter recess, delegations from local unions called on members of Congress who had returned home from Washington. Top union officials met with President Eisenhower to gain widespread press coverage for the minimum wage bill. Lobbyists visited all congressional offices but placed particular emphasis on conversations with House Speaker Sam Rayburn, Senate Majority Leader Lyndon Johnson, and key committee members. The result of this massive lobbying effort, for which unions allocated about $20,000, was clearly worth the cost. When the bill was signed into law on August 12, 1955, another act had been written in the steadily evolving drama of American labor-management relations.

FOREIGN POLICY: THE ROLE OF THE C.I.A.

In dealing with certain aspects of social and economic policy, we have been concerned primarily with laws passed by state legislatures and by Congress. These are domestic matters in which the legislative branches have dominant authority. In the area of foreign policy, however, the Constitution gives primary power to the president. Because of the delicate nature of international relations, this power is often exercised secretly. As a result it is less subject to the influence of the people than is the case with domestic issues. If the secrecy of the process is challenged, it is defended as necessary for "national security."

In recent years, however, the veil of secrecy has been torn aside just enough to reveal that the Central Intelligence Agency (C.I.A.) has played an important and previously undisclosed role in world affairs. In this section, we will not be focusing primarily on the substance of American foreign policy. Rather, we are examining the impact of the C.I.A., a relatively small and elite group, on foreign policy formulation and execution.

Formation and Purpose

The C.I.A. was created by the National Security Act of 1947 as a successor to the Office of Strategic Services, a World War II espionage agency. It is responsible to the National Security Council headed by the president. Its chief function is to coordinate intelligence data gathered by all government agencies and collect additional information as well. Intelligence means information about any developments throughout the world that may affect American security. Intelligence can be overt, relying on newspapers and open observation. Or it can be covert, requiring acquisition of secret information, if necessary by spying.[59] Each of the armed services also maintains an intelligence unit. In mid-1970 their combined payrolls totaled over 136,000 persons and they spent $2.9 billion.[60] In addition, there is the Defense Department's National Security Agency and separate intelligence activity carried on by the State Department.

The first task of the C.I.A. is to gather information from these sources, as well as from journalists, businessmen traveling in foreign nations, and other private citizens. It supplements data from such contacts by its own espionage efforts. These include the use of aerial surveillance by U-2 planes like those which detected the installation of Russian offensive missiles in Cuba in 1962. Finally, the C.I.A.'s job is an interpretive one. It must decide, for example, the significance of a possible cut in the price of Soviet refrigerators. Does it mean that Russians are demanding more consumer goods? Is it a reflection of increased steel production? Are metals being diverted from military to nonmilitary production? The correct answers may hold the key to the future of Soviet-American relations.

It is important to note that the C.I.A. is legally prohibited from engaging in domestic spy activities. The official description of its functions, in fact, states that it "Has no police, subpoena, or law enforcement powers or internal security functions."[61] Such activity would interfere with, or at least duplicate, the tasks assigned to the Federal Bureau of Investigation and local police agencies.

The Growing Controversy

The use of espionage seems to be as old as recorded history, but the C.I.A. has evoked controversy principally because of its other activities. For example, the C.I.A. was responsible for planning the disastrous Bay of Pigs invasion of Cuba in 1962. It also organized the successful overthrow of President Jacob Arbenz Guzman of Guatemala in 1954.[62]

The role of the C.I.A. in opposing Chilean President Salvadore Allende prior to his assassination in 1973 is not known in precise detail. Its director, William Colby, reportedly testified before the House Foreign Affairs Committee that it had "penetrated" all major political parties in that nation and given "some assistance" to certain groups.[63] Since it is a matter of record that the agency has trained foreign invasion forces, overthrown foreign governments, and meddled in the internal politics of foreign countries, there was little skepticism when the press reported that it had also attempted the assassination of unnamed foreigners.[64] Premier Fidel Castro of Cuba was believed to be the most probable target.

Yet the nature of many C.I.A. operations remains a mystery. Influential members of Congress have bemoaned their lack of knowledge concerning the agency. Senator Stuart Symington, a member of the Armed Services Committee's subcommittee on C.I.A. oversight, regretted the secrecy surrounding the agency's role in the war in Laos. He charged that "Nobody knows the amounts the C.I.A. is spending. . . . When we ask about specific operations, they say they are top secret."[65] One thing is clear: the C.I.A. has moved beyond merely gathering information to a role which involves molding major events.

While the secret operations of the C.I.A. in other countries have been severely criticized, they did not create as much furor as revelations regarding activities within the U.S. In January 1975, former C.I.A. director Richard Helms reported to the Senate Armed Services Committee about such activities. His testimony seemed to contradict statements he had made less than two years earlier. He admitted that the C.I.A. had investigated some Vietnam war protestors as well as certain other Americans in the belief that they were inspired by foreign sources.[66] This confirmed the testimony which Colby, his successor, had given the preceding day. Colby reported that the C.I.A. had planted a dozen informers inside various Washington, D.C. protest organizations. They had also established files on 10,000 Americans, set up 21 domestic wire taps, and made 3 "surreptitious entries" of private property in the U.S.[67] Both men, however, denied any "massive domestic spying."

Whether massive or not, such incidents appeared to be in violation of legal restrictions upon the scope of C.I.A. authority. They raised a number of questions, not the least of which was who had authorized such actions. These questions were naturally directed to Secretary of State Henry Kissinger who doubles as executive director of the National Security Council which is supposed to supervise the C.I.A. A spokesman for Kissinger reported that

"The Secretary has never seen any survey of American citizens by the C.I.A. and he doesn't know if any such surveys exist."[68]

The public image of the C.I.A. was further disfigured by revelations that it equipped members of the White House "plumbers" who burglarized the office of Daniel Ellsberg's psychiatrist and that it cooperated to some extent in the cover-up of the Watergate burglary.[69] The result was a chorus of voices demanding a thorough investigation of C.I.A. activities, especially those of a domestic nature. Two responses came very quickly. President Ford appointed an 11-member commission headed by Vice-President Rockefeller, and the Senate established a Select Committee on Intelligence Activities chaired by Senator Frank Church (D–Idaho). Both pledged to ferret out the facts.

After a 5-month investigation, the Rockefeller Commission issued its report in June 1975. It confirmed and condemned a long list of C.I.A. activities which it said "were plainly unlawful and constituted improper invasions upon the rights of Americans." These included 32 wiretaps involving at least three newsmen. One of these was approved by Attorney General Robert F. Kennedy in 1962. In addition, the C.I.A. opened thousands of letters to American citizens from foreign countries with at least the knowledge of Postmasters General in the Eisenhower, Kennedy, and Nixon administrations. When told of this mail interception program in 1971, Attorney General John Mitchell replied that he had no "hang-ups" concerning it. The C.I.A. also engaged in 12 break-ins, mostly to check the reliability of its own past and present employees. It exceeded its authority in still another area during the Johnson and Nixon administrations as a result of "repeated presidential requests for additional information" about domestic protest groups. "Operation CHAOS" was created to infiltrate these groups and help obtain material for secret files on 7200 Americans.[70]

Nevertheless, the Rockefeller Commission concluded that "the great majority of the C.I.A.'s domestic activities comply with its statutory authority." Accompanying its report to President Ford, the commission submitted secret but admittedly inadequate findings regarding charges that the C.I.A. was involved in foreign assassination plots, possibly in cooperation with members of the Mafia. The president relayed this information to the Church committee of the Senate for more thorough investigation.[71] Whether political and/or national security considerations will permit public access to all of the facts remained to be seen.

The Problem of Control

The diversified projects carried out by the C.I.A. in a clandestine, or secret, fashion emphasizes the necessity of making such a powerful body responsible to elected officials. In theory, it is accountable to both the president as head of the National Security Council and to Congress which appropriates funds for it. In practice, however, the situation seems quite different. All secret operations are said to be approved by a 5-member group called, most recently, the "40 Committee." It consists of Kissinger as its chairman, the Director of the C.I.A., the Undersecretary of State for Political Affairs, the Deputy Secretary of Defense, and the Chairman of the Joint Chiefs of Staff—none of them elected to office. Other responsibilities leave several of these men little time to evaluate proposed operations and they tend to view the intelligence "experts" with considerable awe. According to one "inside" source, "Although the President either reviews or personally authorizes all . . . secret interventions in other countries' internal affairs, he never signs any documents to that effect."[72] Presumably, this enables him to deny any personal responsibility for what takes place.

Congressional oversight seems even more inadequate. Subcommittees of the Senate and House Armed Services and Appropriations Committees are authorized to perform this function. But several of their members have indicated that they prefer not to know precisely what the C.I.A. is doing.[73] Little budgetary control is exercised, since most of the money intended for the agency's use is appropriated to the Defense Department. In 1971, Senator Symington complained that the Senate was voting money for the C.I.A. with only five senators knowing what the amount was. One of those, Senator Allen Ellender, admitted that even he was unaware that previous appropriations had been used to finance a 36,000 man "secret" army in Laos. In 1967, the congressional appropriations subcommittees voted for the full $700 million requested by the C.I.A. without even a hearing on the subject.[74]

The revelation of past activities led to numerous demands in 1975 that Congress keep a tighter rein on C.I.A. operations. It was clear that behind its sometimes necessary cloak of secrecy, the C.I.A. had wielded irresponsible power without effective legislative control. Procedures are necessary to make sure that no agency pursues goals not publicly debated and legally approved. Equally important, the secret methods used to achieve those goals, must at least be authorized by elected officials accountable to the people. Although the Rockefeller Commission recommended minor changes, how this can be done is yet to be determined.

POWER AND PUBLIC POLICY

Government policy in the area of personal morality has probably been determined more by the authority of tradition and religious teachings than by any other form of power. Influence is exerted, of course, by church groups on one side. They are pitted against commercial gambling interests, the liquor industry, and pornography peddlers on the other. But the laws themselves often seem to be historic relics of past behavior codes. These are now severely threatened by changing social standards and a variety of life-styles. The challenge facing our society today is to develop a willingness to revise or perhaps repeal laws regulating many aspects of personal conduct. This must be done without entirely cutting the tie between morality and politics. It is that link alone which restrains power, maintains the authority of government, and brings nobility to the political profession. The challenge can be met by a reaffirmation of those few and fundamental values essential to our common democracy: respect for diversity, commitment to human dignity, and compassion for our fellow citizens. Many life-styles can be accommodated to these ideals.

Labor-management relations constitute the foremost example in domestic politics of a classic power struggle. Unions and corporations array enormous influence both against one another and upon government officials expected to referee the struggle. It is not always a fair fight, as illustrated by the use of force upon occasion by both sides. The political resource that constitutes much of labor's influence is sheer numbers—the voting power of American workers. When they are divided, their collective influence is nullified. This is what happened in 1972 when the Teamsters Union, largest in the nation, backed Nixon, the U.A.W., second largest, supported McGovern, and the AFL-CIO leadership sat out the presidential campaign. Management has a great deal of the political resource most capable of counteracting numbers: money. Labor and management have each developed effective leaders and considerable skill, which are also invaluable resources. But it may be significant that while business administration is a part of nearly every college curriculum, few schools offer courses in union organization or labor administration. Both sides occasionally appeal to basic values in our political culture to legitimize their goals and drape the mantle of authority around their demands. Unions do it by appeals for industrial democracy, and an emphasis on the brotherhood and solidarity which equality may entail. (Sometimes formally and sometimes sentimentally, union members call each other brother or sister.) Corporations invoke the authority of capitalism and glorify the American heritage of individualism. Politically, the two contestants are rather well matched. Economically, management's power to decide what to produce and whom to hire is usually a decisive advantage.

The C.I.A. presents the most fascinating opportunity of all for a power-oriented analysis. Since it operates secretly, it has no need for legitimacy or moral authority. Sometimes it displays little reliance on legal authority either. Indeed, its power would be puny if it required much authority of any kind, for it depends largely on stealth and deceit. These qualities have little overt support in our political culture, no matter how much they may characterize our behavior. The only source of authority even remotely related to intelligence-gathering, however, is an important one. Americanism, to the degree that it implies approval of any means, fair or foul, to protect the nation, has been sufficient to give the C.I.A. the respectability necessary for its survival. The agency has only a bit more influence than it has authority. This is true even though it does spend money to influence and support foreign political movements sympathetic to the U.S. Thus the C.I.A.'s major power resource is force, always more acceptable in international relations than in domestic politics. Perhaps the chief dilemma confronting American society is how to harness the use of force to carry out democratically determined policies when that force is used secretly. Democracy requires that those with power in any form be held accountable for its use. When the people cannot be told how power is used, they cannot hold its users accountable. Secrecy, to some extent, is necessary for national survival. To the same degree, it diminishes the possibility of democratic government.

Thus, in the final analysis, we come to the ultimate question for a democracy: Is the people's power sufficient to control public policy? In an age of rapid change, the answer to this question (like so many others) must always be tentative. Every year, every day, new issues emerge which demand that it be answered again. It has been common and even fashionable in academic circles to view the future of representative government with some skepticism. Moreover, the people themselves seem to have lost faith in their own power to influence official policy.

It is far too early, however, for the people to throw in the towel. There is little reason for them either to accept the loss of their power with resigned despair or to burn the system down. On the contrary, the survival of American political institutions for nearly two centuries displays resilience and flexibility. It reveals a capacity for change and regeneration too great to be abandoned now. If government is remote and secretive, callous to considerations of moral decency, or insensitive to the concerns of a troubled people, it is not because something is wrong with our basic political principles. Rather it is because we have permitted distortions in the process of applying them. Such distortions, however, can be corrected only if the people exercise their power resources more effectively than ever before.

Notes

1. Robert A. Dahl, *Modern Political Analysis*, 2nd ed. (Englewood Cliffs, N.J.: Prentice-Hall, 1970), pp. 100–103.
2. Lasswell discusses these values in many of his works, although he is not responsible for the public policy examples cited here. See *The Political Writings of Harold Lasswell* (New York: The Free Press, 1951).
3. *Los Angeles Times,* Feb. 4, 1975, p. 19.
4. U.S. Bureau of the Census, *Statistical Abstract of the United States: 1974* (Washington, D.C.: U.S. Government Printing Office, 1975), p. 226.
5. *Los Angeles Times,* May 20, 1972, p. 14.
6. *Labor Looks at Congress* (Washington, D.C.: AFL-CIO Legislative Report, 1971), p. 4.
7. The figure was reported by Rep. Henry S. Reuss (D–Wis.), now chairman of the House Banking Committee. *Los Angeles Times,* March 29, 1971, p. 1.
8. *Los Angeles Times,* Feb. 6, 1973, p. 18.
9. This is the estimate of tax expert Philip M. Stern. *Los Angeles Times,* May 10, 1973, Part VII, p. 1.
10. *Book of the States, 1974–75* (Lexington, Ky.: The Council of State Governments, 1974), p. 240. The five states without sales taxes are Alaska, Delaware, Montana, New Hampshire, and Oregon.
11. *Los Angeles Times,* May 20, 1972, p. 14.
12. *Book of the States,* p. 222.
13. *Time,* March 13, 1972, p. 66.
14. A. Lee Fritschler, *Smoking and Politics* (New York: Appleton-Century-Crofts, 1969), p. 17.
15. These are figures reported by Dr. Luther Terry, former Surgeon General. *Los Angeles Times,* April 25, 1973, Pt. IV, p. 11.
16. *Los Angeles Times,* Dec. 5, 1974, Part 1-B, p. 2.
17. Ibid., August 28, 1974, p. 1.
18. Quoted in *Los Angeles Times,* March 23, 1973, p. 1.
19. Ibid., June 9, 1974.
20. *Newsweek,* March 5, 1973, p. 68.
21. *Statistical Abstract of the U.S., 1974,* p. 260.
22. *Los Angeles Times,* Feb. 10, 1971, p. 5; and *Newsweek,* July 3, 1972, p. 50.
23. *Los Angeles Times,* August 12, 1973, p. 4.
24. *Newsweek,* Sept. 7, 1970, p. 22.
25. James L. Goddard, *Life,* Oct. 31, 1969, p. 34. Dr. Goddard was once the director of the U.S. Food and Drug Administration.
26. *Statistical Abstract of the U.S., 1974,* p. 153.
27. *Report of the President's Commission on Law Enforcement and the Administration of Justice* (Washington, D.C.: U.S. Government Printing Office, 1967), pp. 213–16.
28. *Information Please Almanac 1975,* p. 732.
29. *Newsweek,* Feb. 1, 1971, p. 76.
30. *Los Angeles Times,* March 23, 1973, p. 16.
31. Ibid., February 16, 1973, Part VI, pp. 6–7.
32. Ibid., Oct. 18, 1970, Sec. G., p. 4 and Oct. 25, 1970, pp. 1 and 10.

33. Earl Kemp, ed., *The Illustrated Presidential Report of the Commission on Obscenity and Pornography* (San Diego: Greenleaf Classics, 1970), pp. 52–53.
34. Ibid., pp. 53 and 212–17.
35. Gallup Poll reported in *San Francisco Chronicle,* Aug. 13, 1973, p. 1.
36. *Los Angeles Times,* June 8, 1974, p. 23.
37. *San Francisco Chronicle,* Aug. 13, 1973, p. 1.
38. *Playboy,* November 1974, p. 60.
39. *Los Angeles Times,* October 2, 1974, p. 9.
40. *Playboy,* August 1972, pp. 188–89.
41. *The Advocate,* January 15, 1975, pp. 1 and 5.
42. *Los Angeles Times,* April 9, 1974, p. 9.
43. Ibid., Oct. 6, 1974, Part IX, p. 14.
44. Rhode Island, Maryland, Michigan, Massachusetts, Pennsylvania, Connecticut, and Maine. *Los Angeles Times,* June 26, 1974, Part 1-A, p. 11.
45. *Newsweek,* April 10, 1972, pp. 46–52.
46. *Statistical Abstract of the U.S.: 1974,* p. 153.
47. *Statistical Abstract of the U.S.: 1974,* p. 340.
48. Joseph G. Rayback, *A History of American Labor* (New York: The Free Press, 1966), pp. 258–59.
49. *Book of the States,* p. 493.
50. Lloyd D. Musolf, *Government and the Economy* (Glenview, Ill.: Scott, Foresman and Co., 1965), p. 80; and *Newsweek,* April 12, 1971, p. 83.
51. *Adkins* v. *Children's Hospital,* 261 U.S. 525 (1923).
52. *U.S.* v. *Darby Lumber Co.,* 312 U.S. 100 (1941).
53. *Book of the States,* pp. 518–19.
54. *Los Angeles Times,* Feb. 25, 1973, Part VI, p. 5.
55. Loc. cit.
56. Gus Tyler, "A Legislative Campaign for a Federal Minimum Wage," Charles H. Rehmus and Doris B. McLaughlin, eds., *Labor and American Politics* (Ann Arbor: The University of Michigan Press, 1967), pp. 234–50.
57. Sar A. Levitan, "Union Lobbyists' Contribution to Tough Labor Legislation," ibid., pp. 250–57.
58. Tyler, op. cit., p. 240.
59. Allen W. Dulles, *The Craft of Intelligence* (New York: Harper & Row, 1963), p. 58. Mr. Dulles was once the director of the C.I.A.
60. *Los Angeles Times,* May 19, 1970, p. 8.
61. General Services Administration, *United States Government Manual 1973–74,* p. 83.
62. David Wise and Thomas B. Ross, *The Invisible Government* (New York: Bantam Books, 1965), pp. 6–77 and 177–96.
63. Victor Marchetti and John D. Marks. *The C.I.A. and the Cult of Intelligence* (New York: Dell Publishing Co., 1974), p. 42. Unless otherwise indicated, most of the material on the C.I.A. is from this source.
64. *Los Angeles Times,* March 5, 1975, p. 10.
65. *Congressional Quarterly Guide to Current American Government* (Spring 1972), p. 69.
66. *Los Angeles Times,* Jan. 17, 1975, pp. 1 and 6.
67. Ibid., Jan. 16, 1975, pp. 1 and 15–18.
68. Ibid., Jan. 12, 1975, Part VII, p. 5.
69. Marchetti and Marks, pp. 218 and 241.
70. *Newsweek,* June 23, 1975, pp. 16–27, and *Los Angeles Times,* June 11, 1975, pp. 1, 7–11, 14, 16–17, 21–28.
71. Ibid.
72. Marchetti and Marks, p. 311.
73. Ibid., p. 324.
74. Ibid., p. 327.

Bibliography

CHAPTER THIRTEEN **POWER, PEOPLE, AND POLICIES**

Cohen, Sanford. *Labor Law.* Columbus, Ohio: Charles E. Merrill Publishing Co., 1964.

Conway, M. Margaret, and Feigert, Frank B. *Political Analysis: An Introduction.* Boston: Allyn and Bacon, 1972.

Dulles, Allen W. *The Craft of Intelligence.* New York: Harper & Row, 1963.

Fritschler, A. Lee. *Smoking and Politics.* New York: Appleton-Century-Crofts, 1969.

Lasswell, Harold. *The Political Writings of Harold Lasswell.* New York: The Free Press, 1951.

Marchetti, Victor, and Marks, John D. *The C.I.A. and the Cult of Intelligence.* New York: Dell Publishing Co., 1974.

Monthly Labor Review. Washington, D.C.: Bureau of Labor Statistics, U.S. Department of Labor.

Packard, Vance. *The Sexual Wilderness.* New York: Pocket Books, 1970.

Report of the Commission on Obscenity and Pornography. Washington, D.C.: U.S. Government Printing Office, 1970.

Wise, David, and Ross, Thomas B. *The Invisible Government.* New York: Bantam Books, 1975.

Young, Oran R. *Systems of Political Science.* Englewood Cliffs, N.J.: Prentice-Hall, 1968.

The Constitution
of the United States

We the People of the United States, in Order to form a more perfect Union, establish Justice, insure domestic Tranquility, provide for the common defence, promote the general Welfare, and secure the Blessings of Liberty to ourselves and our Posterity, do ordain and establish this Constitution for the United States of America.

ARTICLE I

Section 1. All legislative Powers herein granted shall be vested in a Congress of the United States, which shall consist of a Senate and House of Representatives.

Section 2. The House of Representatives shall be composed of Members chosen every second Year by the People of the several States, and the Electors in each State shall have the Qualifications requisite for Electors of the most numerous Branch of the State Legislature.

No Person shall be a Representative who shall not have attained to the Age of twenty five Years, and been seven Years a Citizen of the United States, and who shall not, when elected, be an Inhabitant of that State in which he shall be chosen.

Representatives and direct Taxes shall be apportioned among the several States which may be included within this Union, according to their respective Numbers, which shall be determined by adding to the whole Number of free Persons, including those bound to Service for a Term of Years, and excluding Indians not taxed, three fifths of all other Persons. The actual Enumeration shall be made within three Years after the first Meeting of the Congress of the United States, and within every subsequent Term of ten Years, in such Manner as they shall by Law direct. The Number of Representatives shall not exceed one for every thirty Thousand, but each State shall have at Least one Representative; and until such enumeration shall be made, the State of New Hampshire shall be entitled to chuse three, Massachusetts eight, Rhode-Island and Providence Plantations one, Connecticut five, New-York six, New Jersey four, Pennsylvania eight, Delaware one, Maryland six, Virginia ten, North Carolina five, South Carolina five, and Georgia three.

When vacancies happen in the Representation from any State, the Executive Authority thereof shall issue Writs of Election to fill such Vacancies.

The House of Representatives shall chuse their speaker and other Officers; and shall have the sole Power of Impeachment.

Section 3. The Senate of the United States shall be composed of two Senators from each State, chosen by the Legislature thereof, for six Years; and each Senator shall have one Vote.

Immediately after they shall be aseembled in Consequence of the first Election, they shall be divided as equally as may be into three Classes. The Seats of the Senators of the first Class shall be vacated at the Expiration of the second Year, of the second Class at the Expiration of the fourth Year, and of the third Class at the Expiration of the sixth Year, so that one third may be chosen every second Year; and if Vacancies happen by Resignation, or otherwise, during the Recess of the Legislature of any State, the Executive thereof may make temporary Appointments until the next Meeting of the Legislature, which shall then fill such Vacancies.

No Person shall be a Senator who shall not have attained to the Age of thirty Years, and been nine Years a Citizen of the United States, and who shall not, when elected, be an Inhabitant of that State for which he shall be chosen.

The Vice President of the United States shall be President of the Senate, but shall have no Vote, unless they be equally divided.

The Senate shall chuse their other Officers,

and also a President pro tempore, in the Absence of the Vice President, or when he shall exercise the Office of President of the United States.

The Senate shall have the sole Power to try all Impeachments. When sitting for that Purpose, they shall be on Oath or Affirmation. When the President of the United States is tried, the Chief Justice shall preside: And no Person shall be convicted without the Concurrence of two thirds of the Members present.

Judgment in Cases of Impeachment shall not extend further than to removal from Office, and disqualification to hold and enjoy any Office of honor, Trust or Profit under the United States: but the Party convicted shall nevertheless be liable and subject to Indictment, Trial, Judgment and Punishment, according to law.

Section 4. The Times, Places and Manner of holding Elections for Senators and Representatives, shall be prescribed in each State by the Legislature thereof; but the Congress may at any time by Law make or alter such Regulations, except as to the Places of chusing Senators.

The Congress shall assemble at least once in every Year, and such Meeting shall be on the first Monday in December, unless they shall by Law appoint a different Day.

Section 5. Each House shall be the Judge of the Elections, Returns and Qualifications of its own Members, and a Majority of each shall constitute a Quorum to do Business; but a smaller Number may adjourn from day to day, and may be authorized to compel the Attendance of absent Members, in such Manner, and under such Penalties as each House may provide.

Each House may determine the Rules of its Proceedings, punish its Members for disorderly Behaviour, and, with the Concurrence of two thirds, expel a Member.

Each House shall keep a Journal of its Proceedings, and from time to time publish the same, excepting such Parts as may in their Judgment require Secrecy; and the Yeas and Nays of the Members of either House on any question shall, at the Desire of one fifth of those Present, be entered on the Journal.

Neither House, during the Session of Congress, shall, without the Consent of the other, adjourn for more than three days, nor to any other Place than that in which the two Houses shall be sitting.

Section 6. The Senators and Representatives shall receive a Compensation for their Services, to be ascertained by Law, and paid out of the Treasury of the United States. They shall in all Cases, except Treason, Felony and Breach of the Peace, be privileged from Arrest during their Attendance at the Session of their respective Houses, and in going to and returning from the same; and for any Speech or Debate in either House, they shall not be questioned in any other Place.

No Senator or Representative shall, during the Time for which he was elected, be appointed to any civil Office under the Authority of the United States, which shall have been created, or the Emoluments whereof shall have been encreased during such time; and no Person holding any Office under the United States, shall be a Member of either House during his Continuance in Office.

Section 7. All Bills for raising Revenue shall originate in the House of Representatives; but the Senate may propose or concur with Amendments as on other Bills.

Every Bill which shall have passed the House of Representatives and the Senate, shall, before it become a Law, be presented to the President of the United States; If he approve he shall sign it, but if not he shall return it, with his Objections to that House in which it shall have originated, who shall enter the Objections at large on their Journal, and proceed to reconsider it. If after such Reconsideration two thirds of that House shall agree to pass the Bill, it shall be sent, together with the Objections, to the other House, by which it shall likewise be reconsidered, and if approved by two thirds of that House, it shall become a Law. But in all such Cases the Votes of both Houses shall be determined by Yeas and Nays, and the Names of the Persons voting for and against the Bill shall be entered on the Journal of each House respectively. If any Bill shall not be returned by the President within ten Days (Sundays excepted) after it shall have been presented to him, the Same shall be a Law, in like Manner as if he had signed it, unless the Congress by their Adjournment prevent its Return, in which Case it shall not be a Law.

Every Order, Resolution, or Vote to which the Concurrence of the Senate and House of Representatives may be necessary (except on a question of Adjournment) shall be presented to the President of the United States; and before the Same shall take Effect, shall be approved by him, or being disapproved by him, shall be repassed by two thirds of the Senate and House of Representatives, according to the Rules and Limitations prescribed in the Case of a Bill.

Section 8. The Congress shall have Power To lay and collect Taxes, Duties, Imposts and Excises, to pay the Debts and provide for the common Defence and general Welfare of the United States; but all Duties, Imposts and Excises shall be uniform throughout the United States;

To borrow Money on the Credit of the United States;

To regulate Commerce with foreign Nations, and among the several States, and with the Indian Tribes;

To establish an uniform Rule of Naturalization, and uniform Laws on the subject of Bankruptcies throughout the United States;

To coin Money, regulate the Value thereof,

and of foreign Coin, and fix the Standard of Weights and Measures;

To provide for the Punishment of counterfeiting the Securities and current Coin of the United States;

To establish Post Offices and post Roads;

To promote the Progress of Science and useful Arts, by securing for limited Times to Authors and Inventors the exclusive Right to their respective Writings and Discoveries;

To constitute Tribunals inferior to the supreme Court;

To define and punish Piracies and Felonies committed on the high Seas, and Offences against the Law of Nations;

To declare War, grant Letters of Marque and Reprisal, and make Rules concerning Captures on Land and Water;

To raise and support Armies, but no Appropriation of Money to that Use shall be for a longer Term than two Years;

To provide and maintain a Navy;

To make Rules for the Government and Regulation of the land and naval Forces;

To provide for calling forth the Militia to execute the Laws of the Union, suppress Insurrections and repel Invasions;

To provide for organizing, arming, and disciplining, the Militia, and for governing such Part of them as may be employed in the Service of the United States, reserving to the States respectively, the Appointment of the Officers, and the Authority of training the Militia according to the discipline prescribed by Congress;

To exercise exclusive Legislation in all Cases whatsoever, over such District (not exceeding ten Miles square) as may, by Cession of particular States, and the Acceptance of Congress, become the Seat of the Government of the United States, and to exercise like Authority over all Places purchased by the Consent of the Legislature of the State in which the Same shall be for the Erection of Forts, Magazines, Arsenals, dock-Yards, and other needful Buildings;—And

To make all Laws which shall be necessary and proper for carrying into Execution the foregoing Powers, and all other Powers vested by this Constitution in the Government of the United States, or in any Department or Officer thereof.

Section 9. The Migration or Importation of such Persons as any of the States now existing shall think proper to admit, shall not be prohibited by the Congress prior to the Year one thousand eight hundred and eight, but a Tax or duty may be imposed on such Importation, not exceeding ten dollars for each Person.

The Privilege of the Writ of Habeas Corpus shall not be suspended, unless when in Cases of Rebellion or Invasion the public Safety may require it.

No Bill of Attainder or ex post facto Law shall be passed.

No Capitation, or other direct, Tax shall be laid, unless in Proportion to the Census or Enumeration herein before directed to be taken.

No Tax or Duty shall be laid on Articles exported from any State.

No Preference shall be given by any Regulation of Commerce or Revenue to the Ports of one State over those of another: nor shall Vessels bound to, or from, one State, be obliged to enter, clear, or pay Duties in another.

No Money shall be drawn from the Treasury, but in Consequence of Appropriations made by Law; and a regular Statement and Account of the Receipts and Expenditures of all public Money shall be published from time to time.

No Title of Nobility shall be granted by the United States: And no Person holding any Office of Profit or Trust under them, shall, without the Consent of the Congress, accept of any present, Emolument, Office, or Title, of any kind whatever, from any King, Prince, or foreign State.

Section 10. No State shall enter into any Treaty, Alliance, or Confederation; grant Letters of Marque and Reprisal; coin Money; emit Bills of Credit; make any Thing but gold and silver Coin a Tender in Payment of Debts; pass any Bill of Attainder, ex post facto Law, or Law impairing the Obligation of Contracts, or grant any Title of Nobility.

No State shall, without the Consent of the Congress, lay any Imposts or Duties on Imports or Exports, except what may be absolutely necessary for executing its inspection Laws: and the net Produce of all Duties and Imposts, laid by any State on Imports or Exports, shall be for the Use of the Treasury of the United States; and all such Laws shall be subject to the Revision and Controul of the Congress.

No State shall, without the Consent of Congress, lay any Duty of Tonnage, keep Troops, or Ships of War in time of Peace, enter into any Agreement or Compact with another State, or with a foreign Power, or engage in War, unless actually invaded, or in such imminent Danger as will not admit of delay.

ARTICLE II

Section 1. The executive Power shall be vested in a President of the United States of America. He shall hold his Office during the Term of four Years, and, together with the Vice President, chosen for the same term, be elected, as follows

Each State shall appoint, in such Manner as the Legislature thereof may direct, a Number of Electors, equal to the whole Number of Senators and Representatives to which the State may be entitled in the Congress: but no Senator or Representative, or Person holding an Office of Trust or Profit under the United States, shall be appointed an Elector.

The Electors shall meet in their respective States, and vote by Ballot for two Persons, of whom one at least shall not be an Inhabitant of the same State with themselves. And they shall make a List of all the Persons voted for, and of the Number of Votes for each; which List they shall sign and certify, and transmit sealed to the Seat of the Government of the United States, directed to the President of the Senate. The President of the Senate shall, in the Presence of the Senate and House of Representatives, open all the Certificates, and the Votes shall then be counted. The Person having the greatest Number of Votes shall be the President, if such Number be a Majority of the whole Number of Electors appointed; and if there be more than one who have such Majority, and have an equal Number of Votes, then the House of Representatives shall immediately chuse by Ballot one of them for President: and if no Person have a Majority, then from the five highest on the List the said House shall in like Manner chuse the President. But in chusing the President, the Votes shall be taken by States, the Representation from each State having one Vote; A quorum for this Purpose shall consist of a Member or Members from two thirds of the States, and a Majority of all the States shall be necessary to a Choice. In every Case, after the Choice of the President, the Person having the greatest Number of Votes of the Electors shall be the Vice President. But if there should remain two or more who have equal Votes, the Senate shall chuse from them by Ballot the Vice President.

The Congress may determine the Time of chusing the Electors, and the Day on which they shall give their Votes; which Day shall be the same throughout the United States.

No Person except a natural born Citizen, or a Citizen of the United States, at the time of the Adoption of this Constitution, shall be eligible to the Office of President; neither shall any Person be eligible to that Office who shall not have attained to the Age of thirty Five Years, and been fourteen Years a Resident within the United States.

In Case of the Removal of the President from Office, or of his Death, Resignation, or Inability to discharge the Powers and Duties of the said Office, the Same shall devolve on the Vice President, and the Congress may by Law provide for the Case of Removal, Death, Resignation or Inability, both of the President and Vice President, declaring what Officer shall then act as President, and such Officer shall act accordingly, until the Disability be removed, or a President shall be elected.

The President shall, at stated Times, receive for his Services a Compensation, which shall neither be encreased nor diminished during the Period for which he shall have been elected, and he shall not receive within that Period any other Emolument from the United States, or any of them.

Before he enter on the Execution of his Office, he shall take the following Oath or Affirmation:—"I do solemnly swear (or affirm) that I will faithfully execute the Office of President of the United States, and will to the best of my Ability, preserve, protect and defend the Constitution of the United States."

Section 2. The President shall be Commander in Chief of the Army and Navy of the United States, and of the Militia of the several States, when called into the actual Service of the United States; he may require the Opinion, in writing, of the principal Officer in each of the executive Departments, upon any Subject relating to the Duties of their respective Offices, and he shall have Power to grant Reprieves and Pardons for Offences against the United States, except in Cases of Impeachment.

He shall have Power, by and with the Advice and Consent of the Senate, to make Treaties, provided two thirds of the Senators present concur; and he shall nominate, and by and with the Advice and Consent of the Senate, shall appoint Ambassadors, other public Ministers and Consuls, Judges of the supreme Court, and all other Officers of the United States, whose Appointments are not herein otherwise provided for, and which shall be established by Law; but the Congress may by Law vest the Appointment of such inferior Officers, as they think proper, in the President alone, in the Courts of Law, or in the Heads of Departments.

The President shall have Power to fill up all Vacancies that may happen during the Recess of the Senate, by granting Commissions which shall expire at the End of their next Session.

Section 3. He shall from time to time give to the Congress Information of the State of the Union, and recommend to their Consideration such Measures as he shall judge necessary and expedient; he may, on extraordinary Occasions, convene both Houses, or either of them, and in Case of Disagreement between them, with Respect to the Time of Adjournment, he may adjourn them to such Time as he shall think proper; he shall receive Ambassadors and other public Ministers; he shall take Care that the Laws be faithfully executed, and shall Commission all the Officers of the United States.

Section 4. The President, Vice President and all civil Officers of the United States, shall be removed from Office on Impeachment for, and Conviction of, Treason, Bribery, or other High Crimes and Misdemeanors.

ARTICLE III

Section 1. The judicial Power of the United States, shall be vested in one supreme Court, and in such inferior Courts as the Congress may from time to time ordain and establish. The Judges, both of the supreme and inferior Courts, shall hold their Offices during good Behaviour, and shall, at stated Times, receive for their Services, a Compensation, which shall not be diminished during their Continuance in Office.

Section 2. The judicial Power shall extend to all Cases, in Law and Equity, arising under this Constitution, the Laws of the United States, and Treaties made, or which shall be made, under their Authority;—to all Cases affecting Ambassadors, other public Ministers and Consuls;—to all Cases of admiralty and maritime Jurisdiction;—to Controversies to which the United States shall be a Party;—to Controversies between two or more States; between a State and Citizens of another State;—between Citizens of different States;—between Citizens of the same State claiming Lands under Grants of different States, and between a State, or the Citizens thereof, and foreign States, Citizens or Subjects.

In all Cases affecting Ambassadors, other public Ministers and Consuls, and those in which a State shall be Party, the supreme Court shall have original Jurisdiction. In all the other Cases before mentioned, the supreme Court shall have appellate Jurisdiction, both as to Law and Fact, with such Exceptions, and under such Regulations as the Congress shall make.

The Trial of all Crimes, except in Cases of Impeachment, shall be by Jury; and such Trial shall be held in the State where the said Crimes shall have been committed; but when not committed within any State, the Trial shall be at such Place or Places as the Congress may by Law have directed.

Section 3. Treason against the United States, shall consist only in levying War against them, or in adhering to their Enemies, giving them Aid and Comfort. No Person shall be convicted of Treason unless on the Testimony of two Witnesses to the same overt Act, or on Confession in open Court.

The Congress shall have Power to declare the Punishment of Treason, but no Attainder of Treason shall work Corruption of Blood, or Forfeiture except during the Life of the Person attainted.

ARTICLE IV

Section 1. Full Faith and Credit shall be given in each State to the public Acts, Records, and judicial Proceedings of every other State. And the Congress may by general Laws prescribe the Manner in which such Acts, Records and Proceedings shall be proved, and the Effect thereof.

Section 2. The Citizens of each State shall be entitled to all Privileges and Immunities of Citizens in the several States.

A Person charged in any State with Treason, Felony, or other Crime, who shall flee from Justice, and be found in another State, shall on Demand of the executive Authority of the State from which he fled, be delivered up, to be removed to the State having Jurisdiction of the Crime.

No Person held to Service or Labour in one State, under the Laws thereof, escaping into another, shall, in Consequence of any Law or Regulation therein, be discharged from such service or Labour, but shall be delivered up on Claim of the Party to whom such Service or Labour may be due.

Section 3. New States may be admitted by the Congress into this Union; but no new State shall be formed or erected within the Jurisdiction of any other State; nor any State be formed by the Junction of two or more States, or Parts of States, without the Consent of the Legislatures of the States concerned as well as of the Congress.

The Congress shall have Power to dispose of and make all needful Rules and Regulations respecting the Territory or other Property belonging to the United States; and nothing in this Constitution shall be so construed as to Prejudice any Claims of the United States, or of any particular State.

Section 4. The United States shall guarantee to every State in this Union a Republican Form of Government, and shall protect each of them against Invasion; and on Application of the Legislature, or of the Executive (when the Legislature cannot be convened) against domestic Violence.

ARTICLE V

The Congress, whenever two thirds of both Houses shall deem it necessary, shall propose Amendments to this Constitution, or, on the Application of the Legislatures of two thirds of the several States, shall call a Convention for Proposing Amendments, which, in either Case, shall be valid to all Intents and Purposes, as Part of this Constitution, when ratified by the Legislatures of three fourths of the several States, or by Conventions in three fourths thereof, as the one or the other Mode of Ratification may be proposed by the Congress; Provided that no Amendment which may be made prior to the Year One thousand eight hundred and eight shall in any Manner affect the first and fourth Clauses in the Ninth Section of the first Article; and that no State, without its Consent, shall be deprived of its equal Suffrage in the Senate.

ARTICLE VI

All Debts contracted and Engagements entered into, before the Adoption of this Constitution, shall be as valid against the United States under this Constitution, as under the Confederation.

This Constitution, and the Laws of the United States which shall be made in Pursuance thereof; and all Treaties made, or which shall be made, under the Authority of the United States, shall be the supreme Law of the Land; and the Judges in every State shall be bound thereby, any Thing in the Constitution or Laws of any State to the Contrary notwithstanding.

The Senators and Representatives before mentioned, and the Members of the several State Legislatures, and all executive and judicial Officers, both of the United States and of the several States, shall be bound by Oath or Affirmation, to support this Constitution; but no religious Test shall ever be required as a Qualification to any Office or public Trust under the United States.

ARTICLE VII

The Ratification of the Conventions of nine States, shall be sufficient for the Establishment of this Constitution between the States so ratifying the Same.

Done in Convention by the Unanimous Consent of the States present the Seventeenth Day of September in the Year of our Lord one thousand seven hundred and eighty seven and of the Independence of the United States of America the twelfth. In witness whereof We have hereunto subscribed our Names.

(The first 10 Amendments were ratified December 15, 1791, and form what is known as the "Bill of Rights.")

AMENDMENT 1

Congress shall make no law respecting an establishment of religion, or prohibiting the free exercise thereof; or abridging the freedom of speech, or of the press; or the right of the people peaceably to assemble, and to petition the Government for a redress of grievances.

AMENDMENT 2

A well regulated Militia, being necessary to the security of a free State, the right of the people to keep and bear Arms, shall not be infringed.

AMENDMENT 3

No Soldier shall, in time of peace be quartered in any house, without the consent of the Owner, nor in time of war, but in a manner to be prescribed by law.

AMENDMENT 4

The right of the people to be secure in their persons, houses, papers, and effects, against unreasonable searches and seizures, shall not be violated, and no Warrants shall issue, but upon probable cause, supported by Oath or affirmation, and particularly describing the place to be searched, and the persons or things to be seized.

AMENDMENT 5

No person shall be held to answer for a capital, or otherwise infamous crime, unless on a presentment or indictment of a Grand Jury, except in cases arising in the land or naval forces, or in the Militia, when in actual service in time of War or public danger; nor shall any person be subject for the same offence to be twice put in jeopardy of life or limb; nor shall be compelled in any criminal case to be a witness against himself, nor be deprived of life, liberty, or property, without due process of law; nor shall private property be taken for public use, without just compensation.

AMENDMENT 6

In all criminal prosecutions, the accused shall enjoy the right to a speedy and public trial, by an impartial jury of the State and district wherein the crime shall have been committed, which district shall have been previously ascertained by law, and to be informed of the nature and cause of the accusation; to be confronted with the witnesses against him; to have compulsory process for obtaining witnesses in his favor, and to have the Assistance of Counsel for his defence.

AMENDMENT 7

In Suits at common law, where the value in controversy shall exceed twenty dollars, the right of trial by jury shall be preserved, and no fact tried by a jury, shall be otherwise reexamined in any Court of the United States, than according to the rules of the common law.

AMENDMENT 8

Excessive bail shall not be required, nor excessive fines imposed, nor cruel and unusual punishments inflicted.

AMENDMENT 9

The enumeration in the Constitution, of certain rights, shall not be construed to deny or disparage others retained by the people.

AMENDMENT 10

The powers not delegated to the United States by the Constitution, nor prohibited by it to the States, are reserved to the States respectively, or to the people.

AMENDMENT 11
[RATIFIED FEBRUARY 7, 1795]

The Judicial power of the United States shall not be construed to extend to any suit in law or equity, commenced or prosecuted against one of the United States by Citizens of another State, or by Citizens or Subjects of any Foreign State.

AMENDMENT 12
[RATIFIED JULY 27, 1804]

The Electors shall meet in their respective states and vote by ballot for President and Vice-President, one of whom, at least, shall not be an inhabitant of the same state with themselves; they shall name in their ballots the person voted for as President, and in distinct ballots the person voted for as Vice-President, and they shall make distinct lists of all persons voted for as President, and of all persons voted for as Vice-President, and of the number of votes for each, which lists they shall sign and certify, and transmit sealed to the seat of the government of the United States, directed to the President of the Senate;—The President of the Senate shall, in the presence of the Senate and House of Representatives, open all the certificates and the votes shall then be counted;—The person having the greatest number of votes for President, shall be the President, if such number be a majority of the whole number of Electors appointed; and if no person have such majority, then from the persons having the highest numbers not exceeding three on the list of those voted for as President, the House of Representatives shall choose immediately, by ballot, the President. But in choosing the President, the votes shall be taken by states, the representation from each state having one vote; a quorum for this purpose shall consist of a member or members from two-thirds of the states, and a majority of all the states shall be necessary to a choice. And if the House of Representatives shall not choose a President whenever the right of choice shall devolve upon them, before the fourth day of March next following, then the Vice-President shall act as President, as in the case of the death or other constitutional disability of the President.—The person having the greatest number of votes as Vice-President, shall be the Vice-President, if such number be a majority of the whole number of Electors appointed, and if no person have a majority, then from the two highest numbers on the list, the Senate shall choose the Vice-President; a quorum for the purpose shall consist of two-thirds of the whole number of Senators, and a majority of the whole number shall be necessary to a choice. But no person constitutionally ineligible to the office of President shall be eligible to that of Vice-President of the United States.

AMENDMENT 13
[RATIFIED DECEMBER 6, 1865]

Section 1. Neither slavery nor involuntary servitude, except as a punishment for crime whereof the party shall have been duly convicted, shall exist within the United States, or any place subject to their jurisdiction.

Section 2. Congress shall have power to enforce this article by appropriate legislation.

AMENDMENT 14
[RATIFIED JULY 9, 1868]

Section 1. All persons born or naturalized in the United States, and subject to the jurisdiction thereof, are citizens of the United States and of the State wherein they reside. No State shall make or enforce any law which shall abridge the privileges or immunities of citizens of the United States; nor shall any State deprive any person of life, liberty, or property, without due process of law; nor deny to any person within its jurisdiction the equal protection of the laws.

Section 2. Representatives shall be apportioned among the several States according to their respective numbers, counting the whole number of persons in each State, excluding Indians not taxed. But when the right to vote at any election for the choice of electors for President and Vice President of the United States, Representatives in Congress, the Executive and Judicial officers of a State, or the members of the Legislature thereof, is denied to any of the male inhabitants of such State, being twenty-one years of age, and citizens of the United States, or in any way abridged, except for participation in rebellion, or other crime, the basis of representation therein shall be reduced in the proportion which the number of such male citizens shall bear to the whole number of male citizens twenty-one years of age in such State.

Section 3. No person shall be a Senator or Representaive in Congress, or elector of President and Vice President, or hold any office, civil or military, under the United States, or under any State, who, having previously taken an oath, as a member of Congress, or as an officer of the United States, or as a member of any State legislature, or as an executive or judicial officer of any State, to support the Constitution of the United States, shall have engaged in insurrection or rebellion against the same, or given aid or comfort to the enemies thereof. But Congress may by a vote of two-thirds of each House, remove such disability.

Section 4. The validity of the public debt of the United States, authorized by law, including debts incurred for payment of pensions and bounties for services in suppressing insurrection or rebellion, shall not be questioned. But neither the United States nor any State shall assume or pay any debt or obligation incurred in aid of insurrection or rebellion against the United States, or any claim for the loss or emancipation of any slave; but all such debts, obligations and claims shall be held illegal and void.

Section 5. The Congress shall have power to enforce, by appropriate legislation, the provisions of this article.

AMENDMENT 15
[RATIFIED FEBRUARY 3, 1870]

Section 1. The right of citizens of the United States to vote shall not be denied or abridged by the United States or by any State on account of race, color, or previous condition of servitude.

Section 2. The Congress shall have power to enforce this article by appropriate legislation.

AMENDMENT 16
[RATIFIED FEBRUARY 3, 1913]

The Congress shall have power to lay and collect taxes on incomes, from whatever source derived, without apportionment among the several States, and without regard to any census or enumeration.

AMENDMENT 17
[RATIFIED APRIL 8, 1913]

The Senate of the United States shall be composed of two Senators from each State, elected by the people thereof for six years; and each Senator shall have one vote. The electors in each State shall have the qualifications requisite for electors of the most numerous branch of the State legislatures.

When vacancies happen in the representation of any State in the Senate, the executive authority of such State shall issue writs of election to fill such vacancies: *Provided,* That the legislature of any State may empower the executive thereof to make temporary appointments until the people fill the vacancies by election as the legislature may direct.

This amendment shall not be so construed as to affect the election or term of any Senator chosen before it becomes valid as part of the Constitution.

AMENDMENT 18
[RATIFIED JANUARY 16, 1919]

Section 1. After one year from the ratification of this article the manufacture, sale, or transportation of intoxicating liquors within, the importation thereof into, or the exportation thereof from the United States and all territory subject to the jurisdiction thereof for beverage purposes is hereby prohibited.

Section 2. The Congress and the several States shall have concurrent power to enforce this article by appropriate legislation.

Section 3. This article shall be inoperative unless it shall have been ratified as an amendment to the Constitution by the legislatures of the several States, as provided in the Constitution, within seven years from the date of the submission hereof to the States by the Congress.

AMENDMENT 19
[RATIFIED AUGUST 18, 1920]

The right of citizens of the United States to vote shall not be denied or abridged by the United States or by any State on account of sex.

Congress shall have power to enforce this article by appropriate legislation.

AMENDMENT 20
[RATIFIED JANUARY 23, 1933]

Section 1. The terms of the President and Vice President shall end at noon on the 20th day of January, and the terms of Senators and Representatives at noon on the 3d day of January, of the years in which such terms would have ended if this article had not been ratified; and the terms of their successors shall then begin.

Section 2. The Congress shall assemble at least once in every year, and such meeting shall begin at noon on the 3d day of January, unless they shall by law appoint a different day.

Section 3. If, at the time fixed for the beginning of the term of the President, the President elect shall have died, the Vice President elect shall become President. If a President shall not have been chosen before the time fixed for the beginning of his term, or if the President elect shall have failed to qualify, then the Vice President elect shall act as President until a President shall have qualified; and the Congress may by law provide for the case wherein neither a President elect nor a Vice President elect shall have qualified, declaring who shall then act as President, or the manner in which one who is to act shall be selected, and such person shall act accordingly until a President or Vice President shall have qualified.

Section 4. The Congress may by law provide for the case of the death of any of the persons from whom the House of Representatives may choose a President whenever the right of choice shall have devolved upon them, and for the case of the death of any of the persons from whom the Senate may choose a Vice President whenever the right of choice have devolved upon them.

Section 5. Sections 1 and 2 shall take effect on the 15th day of October following the ratification of this article.

Section 6. This article shall be inoperative unless it shall have been ratified as an amendment to the Constitution by the legislatures of three-fourths of the several States within seven years from the date of its submission.

AMENDMENT 21
[RATIFIED DECEMBER 5, 1933]

Section 1. The eighteenth article of amendment to the Constitution of the United States is hereby repealed.

Section 2. The transportation or importation into any State, Territory, or possession of the United States for delivery or use therein of intoxicating liquors, in violation of the laws thereof, is hereby prohibited.

Section 3. This article shall be inoperative unless it shall have been ratified as an amendment to the Constitution by conventions in the several States, as provided in the Constitution, within seven years from the date of the submission hereof to the States by the Congress.

AMENDMENT 22
[RATIFIED FEBRUARY 27, 1951]

Section 1. No person shall be elected to the office of the President more than twice, and no person who has held the office of President, or acted as President, for more than two years of a term to which some other person was elected President shall be elected to the office of the President more than once. But this Article shall not apply to any person holding the office of President when this Article was proposed by the Congress, and shall not prevent any person who may be holding the office of President, or acting as President, during the term within which this Article becomes operative from holding the office of President or acting as President during the remainder of such term.

Section 2. This article shall be inoperative unless it shall have been ratified as an amendment to the Constitution by the legislatures of three-fourths of the several States within seven years from the date of its submission to the States by the Congress.

AMENDMENT 23
[RATIFIED MARCH 29, 1961]

Section 1. The District constituting the seat of Government of the United States shall appoint in such manner as the Congress may direct:

A number of electors of President and Vice President equal to the whole number of Senators and Representatives in Congress to which the District would be entitled if it were a State, but in no event more than the least populous State; they shall be in addition to those appointed by the States, but they shall be considered, for the purposes of the election of President and Vice President, to be electors appointed by a State; and they shall meet in the District and perform such duties as provided by the twelfth article of amendment.

Section 2. The Congress shall have power to enforce this article by appropriate legislation.

AMENDMENT 24
[RATIFIED JANUARY 23, 1964]

Section 1. The right of citizens of the United States to vote in any primary or other election for President or Vice President, for electors for President or Vice President, or for Senator or Representative in Congress, shall not be denied or abridged by the United States or any State by reason of failure to pay any poll tax or other tax.

Section 2. The Congress shall have power to enforce this article by appropriate legislation.

AMENDMENT 25
[RATIFIED FEBRUARY 10, 1967]

Section 1. In case of the removal of the President from office or of his death or resignation, the Vice President shall become President.

Section 2. Whenever there is a vacancy in the office of the Vice President, the President shall nominate a Vice President who shall take office upon confirmation by a majority vote of both Houses of Congress.

Section 3. Whenever the President transmits to the President pro tempore of the Senate and the Speaker of the House of Representatives his written declaration that he is unable to discharge the powers and duties of his office, and until he transmits to them a written declaration to the contrary, such powers and duties shall be discharged by the Vice President as Acting President.

Section 4. Whenever the Vice President and a majority of either the principal officers of the executive departments or of such other body as Congress may by law provide, transmit to the President pro tempore of the Senate and the Speaker of the House of Representatives their written declaration that the President is unable to discharge the powers and duties of his office, the Vice President shall immediately assume the powers and duties of the office as Acting President.

Thereafter, when the President transmits to the President pro tempore of the Senate and the Speaker of the House of Representatives his written declaration that no inability exists, he shall resume the powers and duties of his office unless the Vice President and a majority of either the principal officers of the executive department or of such other body as Congress may by law provide, transmit within four days to the President pro tempore of the Senate and the Speaker of the House of Representatives their written declaration that the President is unable to discharge the powers and duties of his office. Thereupon Congress shall decide the issue, assembling within forty-eight hours for that purpose if not in session. If the Congress, within twenty-one days after receipt of the latter written declaration, or, if Congress is not in session, within twenty-one days after Congress is required to assemble, determines by two-thirds vote of both Houses that the President is unable to discharge the powers and duties of his office, the Vice President shall continue to discharge the same as Acting President; otherwise, the President shall resume the powers and duties of his office.

AMENDMENT 26
[RATIFIED JUNE 30, 1971]

Section 1. The right of citizens of the United States, who are eighteen years of age or older, to vote shall not be denied or abridged by the United States or by any State on account of age.

Section 2. The Congress shall have power to enforce this article by appropriate legislation.

Index

rate of, 32, 33, 172, 174, 333; Indian, 171–172; median age of, 174; minority, 172; rural, 33–34, 57; urban, 32–34; United States, 31–32

Pornography, 88, 93, 318, 335, 340–341, 353. *See also* Crime, victimless; Obscenity

Postal Service, 130, 295

Post Office and Civil Service Committee, 256, 257

Potter, David M., 29

Powell, Lewis, 86, 132, 318

Powell v. *Texas*, 120

Power, analysis of, 9–13; blocs, 276; concentrated, 268, 286; defined, 9, 328; dispersal of, 195; of elite, 14; and equality, 146; executive, 298–299; extent of, 19–21; federal division of, 64–69; and freedom, 98–99; fusion of, 21; and justice, 124–125; legislative, 267–268; and political parties, 208–209; purpose of, 21–24; resources, 56; structure, 14–15; vacuum, 268; of voting, 231–233

Poverty, *see* Democracy, and wealth

President, appointees of, 21, 108, 117, 122, 130, 132, 142, 179, 216, 242–243, 273, 275, 288, 310, 313–314, 316, 317, 318, 344; "average," 279; cabinet of, 61, 158, 291, 299; as commander-in-chief, 61, 66, 239, 245, 273, 275–276, 287; death of, 204, 205, 278, 282–283, 285; disability of, 284; and the economy, 274, 276, 291–292; election of, 59, 70, 192, 199–200, 215, 217, 280–282, 284; Executive Office of, 288, 291–292, 297; and foreign policy, 195, 275, 349–353; humanity of, 286–287; legislation introduced by, 276–278; pardoning powers of, 277–278; party of, 253, 258, 273; as politician, 273; power of, 68, 124, 272–276, 286–287, 298–299; pressures on, 287; qualifications for, 278–280; staff of, 291; succession to, 282, 284–285; term of, 21, 284–285; veto power of, 67, 195, 263, 273, 277. *See also* Executive branch

Press, Charles, 45

Pressure groups, 61, 153–184 *passim,* 225, 297; contributions of, 217, 265; definition of, 162; influence of, 67, 70, 113, 212; and political parties, 189, 206, 208. *See also* Lobbies and lobbying

Prison and prisoners, 9, 10, 66, 95, 106, 117, 119–123, 124, 181, 290, 305, 310, 330. *See also* Right(s), defendants

Progressive Labor party, 22

Progressive party, 63, 193, 198

Propaganda, 88, 90, 158. 275

Protestants, 35, 47, 84, 138, 166–167, 168, 227, 251, 279, 313, 337; ethic of, 39

Protests, political, 4, 9–10, 56, 94–95, 96, 112, 113, 116, 180, 351; racial, 91, 95, 131, 135, 136–137, 167, 170; student, 174. *See also* Violence

Public Works Committee, 256, 257

Puerto Ricans, 120, 138–139, 168

Punishment, capital, 118, 120; concept of, 119; criminal, 106; cruel and unusual, 119–120, 317; methods of, 103

Racism, 12, 14, 18, 23, 35–36, 37, 38, 40–41, 42, 47, 63, 66, 74, 95, 98, 129–139, 166, 167, 170, 173

Radio, 116, 118, 157–158, 220, 224, 293, 330, 338

Randolph, Edmund, 58

Rayburn, Sam, 253, 349

Regulation of Lobbying Act (1946), 179

Rehnquist, William, 318

Religion, and capitalism, 39; decline of, 4, 11; and democracy, 70–71; freedom of, 62, 71, 81, 82, 86–88, 96; and morality, 120, 335, 353; and politics, 38, 71, 83–88, 251; and prejudice, 35; and racism, 37; and television, 158

Republican party, 13, 155; character of, 23, 192, 194–195, 196, 213, 344; founding of, 197; and gerrymandering, 249; and lobbies, 178; national committees of, 156, 204–205, 208, 222; national conventions of, 199–204, 345; and the press, 157; Protestants in, 168; strength of, 207; and voters, 226–227

Republican Senate Conference, 255

Reuther, Walter, 165

Reynolds v. *Sims,* 141

Richardson, Elliott, 7

Riegle, Donald W., Jr., 240

Right, political, 23–24, 54, 57–58, 113, 175, 207, 278, 295

Right(s), to assemble, 94–95; of children, 146; defendants, 52, 81, 102–125 *passim,* 115–119, 123, 145, 239, 317; homosexual, 146; individual, 75; minority, 68, 72, 83, 87, 98, 137–139, 161, 203, 320; natural, 96, 114; people's, 69–70, 81, 104, 108; to petition, 95, 175; to privacy, 107–113; procedural, 81; student, 91, 103, 173–174, 180, 183; substantive, 81; to unionize, 344, 347; women's, 104, 141–145, 173, 180, 197, 279; workers, 104. *See also* Bill of Rights; Criminal procedures; Due process; Expression, freedom of; Legal counsel, right to; Voting, rights

Robinson v. *California,* 120

Rochin v. *California,* 103

Rockefeller, Nelson, 243, 282, 284, 286, 352

Rockefeller Commission, 286, 352, 353

Rodino, Peter, 243

Roe v. *Wade,* 104

Roosevelt, Franklin D., 34, 68, 193, 285

Roosevelt, Theodore, 193, 198, 279, 285, 313

Roper Organization, 342

Roth v. *U.S.,* 93–94

Ruckelshaus, William, 7

Rules and Administration Committee, 256

Rules Committee, 256, 257, 258, 259, 261, 267

Rumsfeld, Donald, 291

Rural interests, 32–34, 94, 140–141, 165–166, 176, 198, 259, 290, 349. *See also* Farmers; United States, rural

Safe Streets Act, 107

Saxbe, William B., 121

Scaife, Richard Mellon, 216

Scammon, Richard, 159

Schattschneider, E. E., 6, 10, 71

Schneck v. *U.S.,* 89

Science and Astronautics Committee, 257

Secret Service, 290, 298

Securities and Exchange Commission, 293

Segregation, *see* Integration

Segretti, Donald, 219

Select Committee on Intelligence Activities, 352

Senate, committees of, 46, 171, 179, 253–255, 258, 261, 262, 299, 314, 351, 352, 353; confirmation powers of, 21, 67, 179, 242–243, 268, 291, 310, 313, 314; and the Constitution, 58, 60, 62; election to, 63, 70, 213, 217, 222, 251; filibusters in, 261–262, 267; and impeachment, 243–244;